THE ENGLISH

HISTORY 1

The English Novel in History: 1700–1780 provides students with specific contexts for the early novel in response to a new understanding of eighteenth-century Britain. It traces the social and moral representations of the period in extended readings of the major novelists as well as evaluating the importance of lesser-known writers. John Richetti provides:

- readings of a range of writers including Richardson, Fielding, Burney, Sterne, Defoe, Eliza Haywood, Charlotte Lennox and Frances Sheridan
- a consideration of the context of the transformation of Britain in the eighteenth century, from an agrarian to a commercial nation in the first stages of industrialization
- a look at how eighteenth-century novels offered both an outline and a critique of an emerging modern society.

John Richetti is Clara M. Clendenen Professor of English at the University of Pennsylvania. His previous publications include *Popular Fiction before Richardson: Narrative Patterns 1700–1739*, *Defoe's Narratives: Situations and Structures*, and *Philosophical Writing: Locke, Berkeley, Hume*.

THE NOVEL IN HISTORY
Edited by Gillian Beer
Girton College, Cambridge

Informed by recent narrative theory, each volume in this series will provide an authoritative yet lively and energetic account of the English novel in context. Looking at the whole spectrum of fiction, at elite, popular and mass-market genres, the series will consider the ways in which fiction not only reflects, but also helps shape contemporary opinion. Incisive and interdisciplinary, the series as a whole will radically challenge the development model of English literature, and enable each period – from the eighteenth century to the present day – to be assessed on its own terms.

THE ENGLISH NOVEL IN HISTORY
1840–1895
Elizabeth Ermarth

THE ENGLISH NOVEL IN HISTORY
1895–1920
David Trotter

THE ENGLISH NOVEL IN HISTORY
1950–1995
Steven Connor

THE ENGLISH NOVEL IN HISTORY
1700–1780
John Richetti

THE ENGLISH
NOVEL IN HISTORY
1700–1780

John Richetti

London and New York

First published 1999
by Routledge
11 New Fetter Lane, London EC4P 4EE

Simultaneously published in the USA and Canada
by Routledge
29 West 35th Street, New York, NY 10001

Typeset in Baskerville by Routledge
Printed and bound in Great Britain by
Creative Print & Design (Wales), Ebbw Vale

British Library Cataloguing in Publication Data
A catalogue record for this book is available from the British Library

Library of Congress Cataloging in Publication Data
Richetti, John
The English Novel in History, 1700–1780 / John Richetti.
p. cm. (The Novel in History)
Includes bibliographical references and index.
1. English fiction–18th century–History and criticism. 2. Literature and
history–Great Britain–history–18th century. 3. Literature and
society–Great Britain–History–18 century. 4. Historical fiction,
English–History and criticism. 5. Social change in literature.
I. Title. II. Series.
PR858.H5R53 1999   98–8223
823`.509358–dc21   CIP

ISBN 0–415–00950–2 (hbk)
ISBN 0–415–19030–4 (pbk)

FOR DEIRDRE
COME SEMPRE

CONTENTS

ACKNOWLEDGMENTS

This book has been written slowly over a number of years, and during this long haul I have received much aid and assistance. First of all, I am very grateful to Gillian Beer, the editor of this series, for her encouragement and her Job-like patience. The National Endowment for the Humanities provided a fellowship that allowed me to do the initial reading and thinking for the book, and the office of the Dean of the School of Arts and Sciences at the University of Pennsylvania made possible more free time from teaching during which the book was nearly completed. Leonard Sugarman has generously provided financial support for my research over the last ten years, and I owe him a continuing debt of gratitude. I have learned a great deal over these years from my graduate students at Penn, and I especially want to thank Susan Greenfield, George Justice, Kate Levin, Ashley Montague, Sandra Sherman, and Roberta Stack for helping me by their example to think as rigorously as possible about the issues that I treat in this book. Many friends and colleagues have offered advice, essential encouragement, and (most valuable of all) stimulating disagreement on the various issues discussed in this book. For such help and other favors I am grateful to Paula Backscheider, Jerry Beasley, John Bender, David Blewett, Toni Bowers, Barry Dalsant, Leo Damrosch, Bob Folkenflik, J. Paul Hunter, Adam Potkay, David Richter, Michael Seidel, George Starr, James Thompson, and William Warner.

Portions of some of the chapters have appeared previously in earlier versions, and I am happy to acknowledge the following editors and publishers for granting permission to incorporate this material into a larger argument: "Voice and gender in eighteenth-century fiction: Haywood to Burney," *Studies in the Novel* 19 (Fall 1987): 263–272; "The novel and society: the case of Daniel Defoe," in *The Idea of the Novel in the Eighteenth Century*, ed. Robert W. Uphaus (East Lansing, MI: Colleagues Press, 1988); "The old order and the new novel of the mid-

eighteenth century: narrative authority in Fielding and Smollett,"
Eighteenth-Century Fiction 2 (April 1990): 183–196; "Class struggle without
class: novelists and magistrates," *The Eighteenth Century: Theory and
Interpretation* 32 (Autumn 1991): 203–218; "The public sphere and the
eighteenth-century novel: social criticism and narrative enactment,"
Eighteenth-Century Life 16 (November 1992): 114–129; "Ideology and
literary form: Fielding's *Tom Jones*," *The Eighteenth Century: Theory and
Interpretation* 37 (Fall 1996): 205–217; "*Love Letters Between a Nobleman and
His Sister*: Aphra Behn and Amatory Fiction," in *Augustan Subjects: Essays
in Honor of Martin C. Battestin*, ed. Albert J. Rivero (Newark, DE:
University of Delaware Press, 1997).

1

INTRODUCTION

Fiction and society in eighteenth-century Britain

The past recedes very quickly. In old photographs, friends and family look strange, dressed in oddly cut clothing, somehow impenetrable behind the familiar humanity. In their recording of instants that quickly harden into a frozen past, photographs have a distinctive pathos. Reminders of a lost presence, like the figures on Keats' urn, photographs tease us out of thought. But they come powerfully to life when a voice seems to speak for them. The fairly crude eighteenth-century illustrations that accompany some familiar novels – Crusoe in his costume of animal skins or Pamela writing pensively, for example – are memorable only because of their link with narrative voices. These images satisfy a curiosity for external outline, a curiosity provoked by a resonant or tremulous voice that we have heard in these novels.

The strangeness of the past intensifies if we look back before living memory and before photographs, to the documentary remains of the millions who have preceded us. The eighteenth-century British novel is a unique set of documents by which we can try to hear voices that speak something very like our language. We now recognize that the novel adds up in the long run (and retrospectively) to an unprecedented attempt to project a new sort of particularized presence, and to imagine persons speaking about themselves in their singularity, asserting them-selves as unique individuals and thereby breaking with those generalized types and with those communal affiliations that had long served as the primary markers of identity. Such individuals are more than empirical subjects; they are rather what the anthropologist Louis Dumont calls "independent, and autonomous, and thus (essentially) non-social *moral* being[s]" peculiar to modern ideology.[1]

Eighteenth-century strangeness has only recently been fully acknowl-edged. Historians warn us that we have minimized important differences and that the people of only a few centuries ago lived in a world radically distinct from our own. Social historians, especially, have begun the reconstruction of "a world we have lost" which lingered well into the late eighteenth century, and their efforts make that pre-industrial world of the everyday life of ordinary people discontinuous with ours, evoking varieties of eighteenth-century life in the layers below that ruling-class privilege that has come to dominate our images of the period.[2] With those powdered wigs, brocaded clothing, and Palladian villas, there intersected another world of incessant labor and minimal material comforts which had changed little over the generations and in which a traditional culture and customs built up through the centuries survived into the early modern age. In this complicated historical moment, cultural and social hierarchy was far from rigid, and the hegemony of the ruling orders was neither absolute nor framed in our own notions of dominance.

Political and intellectual historians have done their part in this revision by arguing that we have distorted the eighteenth century by a reading backwards from our own values and that in fact institutions such as the aristocracy and the Church retained an authority and unmolested ideological domination that lingered well into the nineteenth century. J.C.D. Clark claims, for example, that Lockean, contractarian Whiggism and secular rationality were in fact marginal, confined to an uninfluential intelligentsia. Current understanding of the period is all wrong, says Clark, because "it misses the religious dimension in which all moved, whether Anglican, Roman Catholic or Dissenter. And it misses those traditional, hierarchical, deferential forms which were neither antiquated, tenuous survivals nor mere veneers or superstructures on a reality which was 'basically' economic, but substantive and prevalent modes of thought and behaviour in a society dominated still by the common people, by the aristocracy, and by the relations between the two."[3] For Clark, the secular eighteenth century has been to some extent a projection backwards from latter-day values. The "realism" that literary criticism has long attributed to the eighteenth-century novel may also need reconsideration, since the reality that these novels seem to mirror (or to dramatize as *real*) is decidedly not like our own and the individuals whom such fiction presents may share less with late twentieth-century persons in the developed Western world than we have been led to believe.

The classic exposition of that realism is Ian Watt's *The Rise of the Novel: Studies in Defoe, Richardson and Fielding* (1957), a synthesis of the consensus that these three novelists represent the consciousness peculiar to an emerging modern world, marking in their fictions "a developing but unplanned aggregate of particular individuals having particular experiences at particular times and at particular places."[4] In place of the traditional understanding whereby such particulars are subordinate to generalized truth, the novel as Watt evokes it is the realization in narrative of that profound epistemological and ontological revolution announced by philosophers like Locke whereby reality is grounded in sense perception and quotidian experience, which is best rendered by the new emphasis in narrative technique and literary value that Watt labels "formal realism": "the premise, or primary convention, that the novel is a full and authentic report of human experience, and therefore under an obligation to satisfy its reader with such details of the story as the individuality of the actors concerned, the particulars of the times and places of their actions, details which are presented through a more largely referential use of language than is common in other literary forms."[5] As Watt describes it, the novel not only locates truth in a newly conceived sociohistorical particularity but effectively narrows that truth to the sensuous particulars of individual experience, which is rendered in a newly accurate referential language that does full justice to the resonantly specific world of historical time.

Realism such as Watt describes may be nothing more than an occasional possibility in eighteenth-century narrative, which lacks a fully established ideological basis for promoting it. What Catherine Belsey calls the "ideology of liberal humanism" underlies realism and "assumes a world of non-contradictory (and therefore fundamentally unalterable) individuals whose unfettered consciousness is the origin of meaning, language and action." "Classic realism," says Belsey, denies ideology by presenting "the subject as fixed and unchangeable, an element in a given system of differences which is human nature and the world of human experience."[6] Belsey must be thinking of nineteenth- and twentieth-century realisms, for these premises (especially what constitutes the "world of human experience") are just what is at issue in many eighteenth-century novels, even those normally considered successfully realistic such as Defoe's and Richardson's. The ideology of individualism, with its fixed and positionless subjects of which Besley speaks, is precisely what much of that fiction examines. Obviously, eighteenth-century narrative does not, in the manner of poststructuralist critics like Belsey, consider the subject an ideological illusion, but this fiction's obsessive theme is nothing less than the contested nature of subjectivity in a world where various possibilities compete for primacy and for simple dominance and where the individual requires support from others, from parents, patrons, friends, lovers, and even from institutions, to continue to exist. The very nature of identity is a recurring philosophical dilemma, and the novel may be said to rehearse that problem at its own level of consciousness and within its particular frame of reference.

Eighteenth-century fiction is an important stage in the fashioning and a key tool for the understanding of this evolving entity, the socially constructed self. Even in the early years of the century, narrative in Britain is increasingly (if implicitly) concerned with the problem of what it means to be an individual, with the value or significance of the particular experience of individuals as they seek to exercise agency, and of course with the related question of what constitutes the best community to support the individual. The novel begins as a heightened, almost obsessive, attention in narratives of various sorts to problems that cluster around issues of self-consciousness and social and moral authority and allegiance. Narratives of all kinds return consistently to that largest of questions: where is the authority that can judge subjectivity? That is, how should domestic and political relationships be constituted? Who rules and who serves and who benefits from the arrangement? Implicit and pervasive, such attention points to a deep, anxious suspicion that life is altering, that things are not now what they once were, that moral standards and individual striving are irrelevant in the face of economic or commercial necessity. Or instead of such fearful nostalgia, much narrative from the eighteenth century voices a progressive, even at times utopian, conviction that things should be different from the way that they have always been and that the new order is full of opportunity for the hard-working and the meritorious. Perhaps such attitudes are perennial, but they have a recurrent centrality in narrative in English since the early eighteenth century.

Of course, such questions are largely implicit and posed, if at all, only in personal or local terms within particular narratives. Generalized social inquiry is a responsibility shouldered self-consciously only in the nineteenth century by certain intellectually ambitious novelists on the European scene. Thanks to Dickens, Eliot, Conrad, Tolstoy, Balzac, Zola, and others, we assume that novelists often provide a unique imaginative truth about the nature of society. Generalizing from what he calls "panoramic" passages in Dickens' later novels, Jonathan Arac describes the novelist as a "commissioned spirit" who surveys society from a commanding height and seeks to render "social motion," to provide thereby "a sense of a coherent social totality, buried but operative, waiting to be diagramed or dramatized in fiction."[7] In one way or another, in the classic nineteenth-century novel, character, author, and reader approach an understanding of sociohistorical necessity and seek to reconcile such necessity with the varieties of individual freedom that seem to be available.

Arac's analysis seems to fit eighteenth-century novels equally well. Social comprehensiveness, or at least a wide range of social representation, is to some extent one of their distinctive features, what separates for most readers, say, *Moll Flanders* or *Tom Jones* from earlier narrative. Yet a commanding overview with its promise of a hidden totality is not quite what the major novels of the period actually provide. What they are about, if looked at closely, is precisely the difficulty of imagining something like the ultimate social and historical coherence that nineteenth-century novelists aspire to reveal. The eighteenth-century novel features an enormous diversity of social representation, and Defoe, Richardson, Fielding, and others present a varied canvas, rather like one of those exuberantly crowded scenes from Hogarth in which the viewer is teased to find a center, in which comic chaos seems a deliberate parody of orderly plenitude. As Ronald Paulson points out, Hogarth's "is an art of multiple gestalts" whereby the initial and immediately graspable scene becomes "a flickering forest in which the viewer's eye then roams about without coming to final rest." Although the intent is to lead the viewer to an ultimate "coherent moral statement of meaning," the risk is that the rococo richness of it all will prevent the unskilled or uninitiated viewer from grasping such coherence.[8]

That same ambiguity operates in the most important eighteenth-century fiction, for in their different ways, novelists pretend to cede authority in the search for a center, deferring to correspondents or fictional narrators to make whatever sense they can of social diversity and a multiplicity of relationships and negotiations for power and pleasure. Such deferral, for example, is part of the function of Fielding's self-depreciating narrative stance in *Joseph Andrews* and *Tom Jones*, and the romantic resolutions of his plots are in this sense a declaration that actuality admits of no clear or self-evident ordering principle. So, too, Richardson's coy invisibility behind his characters' letters and, in *Clarissa* at least, his appeal from the legal complications and socioeconomic entanglements of the plot to the heroine's Christian transfiguration are strategies for avoiding synthesis. Defoe's various narrators, for all their energy and intelligence, concern themselves with local issues of survival and prosperity. Implicitly, it is only the novelist who has any *actual* claim to a comprehensive view of society, but that claim is invariably indirect or ironically deferred.

However, this crucial difference between narratives from the two centuries should not surprise us, since, in a strict sense, "society" as the supervising totality that Arac invokes did not fully exist for the eighteenth century, and society appears in its fiction as a constellation of distinct spheres of influence, a loosely federated collection of interests and smaller social units. As Raymond Williams concludes in *Keywords: A Vocabulary of Culture and Society*, society has come to signify in the most *general* sense possible "the body of institutions and relationships within which a relatively large group of people live" and in the most *abstract* sense "the conditions in which such institutions and relationships are formed." But as Williams shows, those meanings were not prevalent in England until the last third or so of the eighteenth century. Until then the older associations of the word prevailed: from Latin *socius* = companion, and *societas* = companionship and fellowship. Society signified something active and immediate, not an institutionalized totality but a decidedly smaller and specifically connected group of people.[9] As the social theorist, Anthony Giddens, puts it, Britain in the eighteenth century is not yet a modern nation-state but rather what Giddens calls a "class-divided" society in which large spheres "retain their independent character in spite of the rise of the state apparatus."[10] Earlier societies lack the established boundaries of the nation-state, and in them civil society is located more or less in the countryside "in the spheres of agrarian production and local community life."[11] As in earlier tribal societies, life features what Giddens calls a much smaller "time–space distanciation" than our own, one in which there are "relatively few social transactions with others who are physically absent."[12] It is not until the late eighteenth century that Britain ceases to be such a class-divided society, for it is not until the coming of the railroads in the early nineteenth century that the "characteristics of the nation-state replace the city as the administrative center in European nations." As Giddens charts its accelerated development in the eighteenth century, the possibilities for that state and its administrative control clearly emerge as writing becomes more and more "a means of coding information, which can be used to expand the range of administrative control exercised by a state apparatus over both objects and persons," even within the pre-modern state.[13]

John Brewer has argued that England in the eighteenth century developed the most efficiently administered bureaucratic apparatus in Europe, the nation emerging in a period of nearly continuous warfare with France and its allies from 1689 to 1783 as "a fiscal–military state." In order to become the dominant European power by the end of the century, England managed "a radical increase in taxation, the development of public deficit finance (a national debt) on an unprecedented scale, and the growth of a sizable public administration devoted to organizing the fiscal and military activities of the state."[14] Brewer argues that such bureaucratic evolution coexisted with traditional private and political interests. The bonds of patronage and kinship were strong but, compared with other European societies, clientage and graft were moderate and in fact seem to have cooperated and certainly coexisted with increasing departmentalization and institutional loyalty. Various shades of political ideology were, naturally, hostile to this emerging entity, but Brewer's point is that they all gradually reached an accommodation with its salient features: "Placemen were excluded from the commons, but never in their entirety. The peacetime standing army was reduced but not abolished. The issue of public deficit spending became less and less the national debt itself and more and more a question of who should control it (whigs or tories; the Bank or the South Sea Company) and how to avoid its abuse by stock-jobbers."[15]

The eighteenth-century novel thus looks in two directions: it is part of an emerging social formation, connected at the least as a parallel phenomenon to an increasingly efficient ordering of objects and persons through written documents and records, as the organized totality called the nation-state begins to materialize. What the novel also depicts is still decidedly Giddens' class-divided society in which boundaries are uncertain and administrative control loose and irregular, in which life takes place in local units with "high-presence availability" and within a relatively small "time–space distanciation."[16] The novel is part of the process of adapting older social structures to emerging modern conditions. An institution like the family and marriage, for example, is dramatized in many novels as both problem and solution, especially for female characters. Repressive or corrupting, the patriarchal structure that most novels depict reveals in the process of narrative exploration its institutional inadequacy for new forms of self-consciousness, but as such circumstances are transformed by narrative rendering they may also provide insights into personal or local ways of dealing with social change. Such domestic arrangements appear in much fiction as bulwarks against instability and moral corruption in the public world, and they also serve, by analogy that is sometimes explicit, to dramatize in their realignments and power struggles a larger restructuring of social and political authority. Richardson's *Clarissa*, for example, stages a debate about the nature and function of this institution, but the novel's effect may be to make it clear that some sort of alternative or restructured institution suitable to a now newly visible and intensely individual integrity is lacking. Or the intense and melodramatic subjectivity (a fantastic and fatal ignorance of female sexuality and its dangers imposed by cultural circumstances?) of certain heroines of amatory narrative popular in the early years of the century can be regarded as the destructively self-expressive opposite of goal-oriented, regulated and/or repressed, socially self-promoting and accumulative masculine behavior that is more and more the social norm. Such an opposition can exalt excitingly wayward behavior but in effect ratify an emerging rationalized norm of self-interested behavior by thus clearly relegating intensely self-expressive and/or libidinal subjectivity to the special world of fiction.

Paradoxically, then, the novel's individualistic perspective can work to turn readers toward the rationalized bureaucratic norms for personality and identity just beginning to emerge. London's urban scene, to which virtually all British eighteenth-century novels eagerly conduct their characters, encourages individuals, as the historian E.A. Wrigley puts it, to be "treated not as occupying an invariable status position in the community, but in terms of the role associated with the particular transaction that gave rise to the fleeting contact."[17] In eighteenth-century narrative, increasingly, historically specific individuals come into focus with a new clarity and insistence, as the vagueness and looseness of reference of the amatory novellas of Aphra Behn, Delarivière Manley, and Eliza Haywood (and others), for example, yield to the social and psychological specificity of the best novels of the period such as Richardson's *Pamela* and *Clarissa* and Burney's *Evelina* and *Cecilia* in which, as sociologists would say, rational patterns of conduct replace traditional forms and contract seeks to replace custom as the form of interaction.[18] No less intense in their subjectivity than earlier heroines, Richardson's and Burney's figures are pointedly rooted in local sociohistorical circumstances rather than derived from the generalized moral essentialism of literary tradition or the spiritual patterns and types of Christianity, although they certainly appeal for their own sense of self to those patterns. Realism like this is potentially a form of regulation and control, since such persons are increasingly understood in terms of their specific sociohistorical (and especially their economic) determinants instead of some mysterious and extra-historical characterological essence. Indeed, the novel's obsessive rehearsal from mid-century and after of the trials of suffering female paragons, pursued or abused by rogue males, is a powerful critique of the moral nullity and social uselessness of the *rentier*/aristocratic class, for moral heroines in their strivings and sentimental embodiments of virtue act as a corrective and rational critique of these archaic sexual privileges. The moral melodrama of this recurring fictional situation is based upon a particular ideological analysis of society. Novelistic specificity focuses on social relationships that promote self-awareness in characters balanced (or torn) between individualism and communal identity. The effect is to render individuals as (potentially) both socially constructed and individually defined.

But as they appear in eighteenth-century narrative, these newly distinctive individuals and their surrounding social circumstances lack the clear-cut separation between self and a totalized social order that is the troubling by-product of modern bureaucratic arrangements within the nation-state. Some of the protagonists of eighteenth-century narrative are not fairly described in terms of those fictions of selfhood derived from material conditions; rather, such imagined individuals often aspire, thanks to their social and moral privileges as members of a leisure class, to become "characters" in a special sense that the philosopher Alasdair MacIntyre has proposed whereby social role and personality are fused so that character becomes, in his words, the mask worn by the dominant moral philosophy of the time: "A *character* is an object of regard by the members of the culture generally or by some significant segment of them. He furnishes them with a cultural and moral ideal. ... Social type and psychological type are required to coincide. The *character* morally legitimates a mode of social existence."[19] By the 1760s, certainly, varieties of characters have been stabilized in the novel in such formulations as the man of feeling and spontaneous virtue, the redeeming virgin–martyr, the chaste domestic female angel, the irascible benevolist, the amiable humorist, and even on occasion the upright and moral man of business; but in the earlier decades of the century one can say that a wide variety of narratives deploys a range of such types in the process of being formed, including negative embodiments (both serious and comic) like the rake–seducer and the booby squire, or standard female deviations such as the compulsively passionate or just flirtatiously vain virgin or the masculinized and sexually aggressive woman. To that extent, early eighteenth-century narrative is ethically incoherent, since it dramatizes what MacIntyre would call the gap that exists between an individual and his or her social role, a gap that is nonexistent in the *character*, as he defines it.

In an eighteenth-century context, social being exists in manifold forms that are not always susceptible to the generalizing formulas appropriate to the modern nation-state that we now take for granted. For those granted full self-consciousness by property and leisure, moreover, the issue of "character" in MacIntyre's resonant sense was hotly debated. In ruling-class circles, among the landed gentry and the politically self-conscious and active minority, a dilemma presented itself concerning the nature of social identity and political authority. J.G.A. Pocock has outlined this complicated ideological moment which followed the quarter century after the revolution of 1688: "mobile" property, financial instruments, stock certificates, government bonds, and the like, began to be noticed with considerable anxiety by some observers as a rival to land or real property. The ideal for what Pocock has identified as a revived civic humanism was a citizen whose property gave "him independence and autonomy as well as the leisure and liberty to engage in public affairs." His "capacity to bear arms in the public cause was an end of his property and the test of his virtue."[20] This ethos of propertied individualism as the sole basis for "virtue" was strongly challenged by the "financial revolution" of the 1690s. In the new credit economy dominated by investors who owned not property but the paper promises of the government and other entities to pay them interest on their capital, what mattered was not individual virtue but credit, sustained by a volatile network of relationships and interests wherein wealth was produced and power exercised. Pocock's "Machiavellian moment" in the English eighteenth century marks, at one social level anyway, a struggle for social authority between a nostalgic civic humanism and a "territorial–jurisdictional monarchy," between an Aristotelian notion of the autonomy of the citizen–patriot–landowner and the modern realities that made such an individual part of a system of economic and political relationships where autonomy was out of the question.

The early eighteenth century witnessed, in fact, a less rarefied debate than Pocock describes about the nature of society and the role of the individual in relation to what were perceived, if not wholly understood, as radically new circumstances. That debate was conducted, more often than not, in moralizing terms, with many commentators through the century viewing social change as moral decline, as the introduction of an enervating "luxury" that was weakening the moral fibre of the nation.[21] The illuminating exception in that debate was Bernard Mandeville, the Dutch émigré who scandalized many with *The Fable of the Bees: Or, Private Vices, Publick Benefits* (1714–1732), a short allegorical poem to which he added commentaries and responses to his critics. Mandeville offended many by his view that in a modern commercial state individual virtue was irrelevant and that public prosperity depended upon the perpetuation of those consumerist desires that his age conventionally deplored as vice. Mandeville sought

> to expose the Unreasonableness and Folly of those, that desirous of being an opulent and flourishing People, and wonderfully greedy after all the Benefits they can receive as such, are yet always murmuring at and exclaiming against those Vices and Inconveniences, that from the Beginning of the World to this present Day, have been inseparable from all

> Kingdoms and States that ever were fam'd for Strength,
> Riches, and Politeness, at the same time.[22]

Such a society is not simply an association of individuals but "a Body Politick, in which Man either subdued by Superior Force, or by Persuasion drawn from his Savage State, is become a Disciplin'd Creature, that can find his own Ends in Labouring for others, and where under one Head or other Form of Government each Member is render'd Subservient to the Whole, and all of them by cunning Management are made to Act as one" (I, 347).

Mandeville evokes social relations that are obscured in thoughtless day-to-day life by a moral ideology that claims to reconcile virtue with pleasure and privilege. It is not only the vicious and the hypocritical who are guilty, "but the generality of Mankind ... endeavour to hide themselves, their Ugly Nakedness, from each other, and wrapping up the true Motives of their Hearts in the Specious Cloke of Sociableness, and their Concern for the publick Good, they are in hopes of concealing their filthy Appetites and the Deformity of their Desires" (I: 234–235). Society in *The Fable of the Bees* has a hidden coherence whereby the traditional understanding of human nature meshes with the economic realities of a commercial order unprecedented in size and in the scope of its power and organized dominance of the many by the few. One of Mandeville's examples runs this way: "Thieves and Pickpockets ... want to gratify their Senses, have Victuals, Strong Drink, Lewd Women, and to be Idle when they please." The victualler who "entertains them and takes their Money," his "trusty Out-Clerk ... [who] sends him in what Beer he wants," and the "Wealthy Brewer, who leaves all the Mangement to his Servants" – all of these individuals prosper by their blinkered focus on immediate gain (I:87). The wealthy brewer's ignorance is more than a local winking but encompasses a necessary blindness to the whole system: he "keeps his Coach, treats his Friends, and enjoys his Pleasure with Ease and a good Conscience, he gets an Estate, builds Houses, and educates his Children in Plenty, without ever thinking on the Labour which Wretches perform, the Shifts Fools make, and the Tricks Knaves play to come at the Commodity, by the vast Sale of which he amasses his great Riches" (I: 87). Local transactions produce a supervising ruling-class autonomy, in which two incompatible sets of individual narratives constitute in their sustaining interrelation the master narrative that we call society. It is not a question of a controlling and normally invisible network of forces, but rather of a highly visible, if nearly innumerable, series of localized relationships and commercial transactions in which human nature in serving itself articulates the pyramid of narrowing privilege which Mandeville calls society. Modern commercial society is a unique arrangement which exploits more efficiently than ever before in history the selfish essence of human nature to structure its relationships. Mandeville's rendition of modern society is, therefore, inseparable from his narrative instances, from a process in which the perennial struggle for pleasure and power produces in the new and expanded commercial order particular social positions and roles, inseparable for him from success, failure, or intermediate location in that struggle.

Eighteenth-century novels, overall, may be said to depict the "Virtue and Innocence" (I:6) that Mandeville dismisses as utopian even as these same novels also represent the world more or less in his terms as a series of interrelated local transactions in which systematic and amoral coherence is visible (that is to say, the novelists lack Mandeville's sardonic acceptance of an emerging modern commercial order but nonetheless validate his insights about it). Although satire is sometimes the point of this discrepancy, novelists are often enough out to recommend virtue and to say that innocence is possible in spite of the way that society works, or to insist that in the light of such workings virtue is essential. Instead of imagining a tense, mutually excluding, and therefore clear and defining opposition between the self and its social contexts, the novelists present an implicit program for the improvement of social relationships, at least among the inhabitants of the privileged and leisured classes and for those who manage to rise into those ranks. The novelists examine various sorts of intersections and infiltrations between self and its communal surroundings, mutually defining relationships that dramatize an interdependence or even an inseparability between self and society that tends or hopes to nullify the distinction between the two terms. In much eighteenth-century fiction, an awkward adaptation of traditional structures and beliefs is visible, and the novel is well described as various attempts to draw maps of these shifting configurations. Individualistic identity is still dependent upon communal relationships and local traditions and customs. In such arrangements, public and private intertwine, and public life is frequently sustained by private affiliations and alliances which, to modern eyes, look scandalous or corrupt. Fictional characters may be said to move through social spaces with vaguely defined borders, where the domestic and the public overlap, where archaic forms and customs (and their individualized embodiments) jostle against modern forms of emerging rationalized behavior and realigning power structures, where administrative control and definition are still loose or ill defined. Instead of a monolithic and compellingly authoritative social structure, characters in this fiction often encounter a diffuse and diverse collection of individuals only partially defined by the institutional arrangements of which they are a part. Such a society, in Harold Perkin's influential evocation of it, was linked by the quasi-personal relationships summed up in patronage, a "middle term between feudal homage and capitalist cash nexus." As Perkin puts it, eighteenth-century society consisted of "permanent vertical links," a "durable two-way relationship between patrons and clients."[23] But in the narrative versions of such a society, characters often define themselves by elaborate manipulation of or resistance to just these patronage relationships, which appear invariably as tragically inefficient or corruptly self-serving, or sometimes just comically ineffective.

Crowded with fragments of a pressing contemporary actuality that is very much in process, many novels point in vaguely reformist directions at particular institutions such as the court and the aristocracy, the armed forces and the clergy, the game and the debt laws, the inefficient and unjust welfare system for the poor, the justice system in general, and at larger and more generalized social arrangements that touch everyone such as marriage and the family. In that sometimes explicit reformism, eighteenth-century novels may be said to participate in something like the public sphere evoked by Jürgen Habermas. There is an implicit appeal in much of this fiction to the judgments of a universalized rationality such as Habermas says is proper to this sphere, and indeed the novel as a form of intensely privatized reading and reflection is an analogue to the public sphere's rational and unprejudiced exchange of views freed from parochial or sectarian interests.

As Habermas describes it in *The Structural Transformation of the Public Sphere: An Inquiry into a Category of Bourgeois Society* (1962), the public sphere emerges when the dictates of the absolutist state are replaced as the source of authority by those private individuals who, by virtue of their economic power, come together to form a new sort of public. This public opposes and then revises the old way of doing things, Habermas explains, in two distinctive ways. First, it asserts that there is a rationality whereby *veritas non auctoritas facit legem* (truth and not authority is the source of the law), so that the law is conceived of as an embodiment of permanent and universal norms rather than as an imposition by the sovereign for securing order and power; and second, the public sphere insists that such rationality must be determined in public debate and discussion and not within the secret councils of princes. "A political consciousness," as Habermas puts it, "developed in the public sphere of civil society which, in opposition to absolute sovereignty, articulated the concept of and demand for general and abstract laws and which ultimately came to assert itself (i.e., public opinion) as the only legitimate source of this law." This new class of individuals affirmed that only within public debate could the best and truest arguments emerge; only in the open and unclaimed space of rational discussion could the nature of things be free to emerge. In pursuit of nature, bourgeois individuals (owners of property, real or financial) in the public sphere necessarily spoke from a rational, shared universality which rendered them distinct from all pre-existing rules and ranks and affirmed an abstract humanity that granted them, paradoxically, a pure subjectivity.[24]

Except for Richardson, the major male novelists of the mid-century were polemical and political writers first and novelists only as the literary marketplace led them to it. Both Fielding and Smollett, for example, write with the confidence of moral and political essayists, addressing an audience of thoughtful, concerned individuals about social issues, balancing historical specifics and seemingly intractable social problems such as their novels depict against reassuring generality and universality. A potentially utopian version of totality and coherence is available to those who read properly and accept the narrator's authority and the rationality that his narrative embodies. But the crucial problem is that the new novelistic discourse of the mid-eighteenth century is not entirely contained by essayistic assumptions or conventions. Debates and discursive interchange, whether between the reader and the author or represented within the text, are rhetorically and tendentiously pointed. In many ways, Richardson's *Clarissa* is a novel of ideas, with its protagonists articulating opposing notions about personality and social relationships, but we tend as readers to subordinate these exceedingly cogent ideas to the struggle for psychosexual domination which is the novel's theme. As Sterne's *Tristram Shandy* (1760–1767) makes uproariously clear, the effect of novelistic narrative is mainly to enforce the truth of rhetorical self-expressiveness at the expense of objective certainty or even of common sense, and the preposterous theories and obsessions of Sterne's characters articulate the multiple truths of personality as it expresses itself for its own pleasure in tone, gesture, and specific eccentricities. In addition, novelistic narrative is, by its representational aggressiveness, an assertion about the nature and disposition of things rather than the purposeful rational exchange and exploratory communication of the public sphere.

As I see it, novelistic discourse effectively disqualifies its speakers, whether authors or characters, from full membership in the public sphere, and they are unable or unwilling to endorse those assumptions of unified humanity that Habermas says are enforced by participation in it. The rational debate among private citizens who come forth into the public arena to find the most just arrangements and to establish the truth of things is subordinated to the manipulation of ideas and ideologies by individuals for survival or for power or for pleasure, or simply for the self-expressiveness that grants all three. Nonetheless, the public sphere is clearly visible in the eighteenth-century novel, both in its ambitions to achieve a resolving linear narrative that parallels the public sphere's norms of communication and as overtly realized political or moral themes within particular novels. Many eighteenth-century novels can be said to depict what Habermas later called "communicative rationality," which is "not the relation of a solitary subject to something in the objective world that can be represented and manipulated, but the intersubjective relation that speaking or acting subjects take up when they come to an understanding with one another about something."[25]

My argument is that eighteenth-century novels render a bargaining for identity and authority which is at the heart of the profound changes in consciousness taking place in those years. Of course, this fiction is an extremely diverse and, as the century progresses, a shifting set of narrative habits. Among the most significant of those shifts is the appropriation by high-minded and serious moral writers (Richardson especially) of what I call popular "amatory fiction," romantic tales of exciting and often illicit love and passion. In Richardson and his mostly female imitators, such fiction is moralized and localized, purged of erotic effects and rooted more clearly in particular legal and moral circumstances. Such blending of excitement and morality is paralleled in other writers like Defoe, Fielding, and Smollett who domesticate the scabrous European picaresque tradition, adding romance, along with a measure of moral decorum and psychological depth, to energetic social satire. The chapters that follow examine how these various narrative transformations are responses to social change and, to some extent, agents of that change or influences upon it. All such analysis, of course, is haunted by the problematic of representation: non-quixotic readers always realize that books are not life, not exactly a transcription of experience but rather a comment on it, a significant and heightened version of the actual, a fantasy to produce pleasure and perhaps to provide moral and intellectual satisfaction as well. Nowadays, critics and university teachers of literature like to bully readers by insisting that a text is only a text, words on a page and not a mirror of existence. We must not speak, they insist, of characters in novels as if they were like people we know, even if that is precisely what novels, by definition, encourage us to do. But life itself is a text, understood as we live it by means of cultural representations. So to say that these novels do not mirror reality is really to say that in this regard they resemble other means of understanding and perception. Eighteenth-century British novels are part of a debate about the nature of the moral and social world, and it seems to me that their original readers took them in that sense, meant to promote improvement in them and maybe in the world in which they lived by didactic and polemical representations that were understood as such, at least once the book was put down.

Most accounts of the novel in this period are selective according to various standards of narrative quality or thematic continuity. This book will offer, I think, a wider sample of texts than is customary by virtue of my interest in that broadest of themes, social change and social representation. It will include the major novelists, of course, since their dominance is in part owing to their special insightfulness. But I will also treat in some detail works of lesser scope and limited narrative power, partly as foils for the major works but also for the peculiar illuminations offered by their different sorts of narrative failure. Most accounts of this fiction follow its lead in focusing on the individuals whom it renders. I will try to differ from that practice in attempting to see, as steadily as possible, how individuality itself is the issue, how individuals and their social surroundings are in a reciprocal process of re-definition and development that fiction is in a unique position to articulate, if not to understand.

NOTES

1 Louis Dumont, *From Mandeville to Marx: The Genius and Triumph of Economic Ideology* (Chicago, University of Chicago Press, 1977; rpt 1983), p. 8.
2 The work of E.P. Thompson and historians influenced by him seems to me especially relevant to a new understanding of social relationships in the eighteenth century. Thompson's *Whigs and Hunters: The Origins of the Black Act* (New York, Pantheon Books, 1975) and the collection of his essays on eighteenth-century popular culture, *Customs in Common: Studies in Traditional Popular Culture* (New York, The New Press, 1991), as well as the essays by Thompson, Douglas Hay, Peter Linebaugh, John G. Rule, and Cal Winslow in *Albion's Fatal Tree: Crime and Society in Eighteenth-Century England* (New York, Pantheon Books, 1975), and Peter Linebaugh's *The London Hanged: Crime and Civil Society in the Eighteenth Century* (Cambridge, Cambridge University Press, 1992) explore the ways in which a traditional popular or plebeian culture often resisted the economic and political domination of the Whig oligarchy that came to rule the nation in the middle decades of the century. Important descriptions of the lives of the great majority of the ordinary laboring masses can be found in recent revisionist social histories such as Robert W. Malcolmson, *Life and Labour in England 1700–1780* (New York, St Martin's Press, 1981), and Bridget Hill, *Women, Work, and Sexual Politics in Eighteenth-Century England* (Oxford, Basil Blackwell, 1989).

3 J.C.D. Clark, *English Society 1688–1832: Ideology, Social Structure and Political Practice During the Ancien Regime* (Cambridge, Cambridge University Press, 1985), p. 43.

4 Ian Watt, *The Rise of the Novel: Studies in Defoe, Richardson and Fielding* (Berkeley and Los Angeles, University of California Press, 1957), p. 31.

5 Watt, *The Rise of the Novel*, p. 32.

6 Catherine Belsey, *Critical Practice* (London and New York, Routledge, 1980), pp. 67, 90.

7 Jonathan Arac, *Commissioned Spirits: The Shaping of Social Motion in Dickens, Carlyle, Melville, and Hawthorne* (New Brunswick, New Jersey, Rutgers University Press, 1979), pp. 5–6.

8 Ronald Paulson, *Emblem and Expression: Meaning in English Art of the Eighteenth Century* (Cambridge, MA, Harvard University Press, 1975), p. 56.

9 Raymond Williams, *Keywords: A Vocabulary of Culture and Society* (New York, Oxford University Press, 1976), pp. 243–244.

10 Anthony Giddens, *The Nation State and Violence*, Vol. II of *A Contemporary Critique of Historical Materialism*, (Berkeley and Los Angeles, University of California Press, 1985), p. 21.

11 Giddens, *The Nation State and Violence*, pp. 16, 21.

12 Anthony Giddens, *Power, Property and the State* , Vol. I of *A Contemporary Critique of Historical Materialism*, (London, Macmillan, 1981), pp. 144, 145.

13 Giddens, *The Nation State and Violence*, p. 44.

14 John Brewer, *The Sinews of Power: War, Money and the English State, 1688–1783* (New York, Alfred A. Knopf, 1989), p. xvii.

15 Brewer, *The Sinews of Power*, p. 160.

16 Giddens, *Power, Property and the State*, p. 5.

17 E.A. Wrigley, *People, Cities and Wealth: The Transformation of Traditional Society* (Oxford, Basil Blackwell, 1987), p.139.

18 Wrigley paraphrases Max Weber in using these terms to evoke emerging urban behavior. Wrigley, *People, Cities and Wealth*, p. 139.

19 Alasdair MacIntyre, *After Virtue: A Study in Moral Theory* (Notre Dame, IN, University of Notre Dame Press, 1984), p. 29.

20 J.G.A. Pocock, *Virtue, Commerce, and History* (Cambridge, Cambridge University Press, 1985), p.109.

21 The best account of this climate of opinion and its long historical context is John Sekora, *Luxury: The Concept in Western Thought, Eden to Smollett* (Baltimore, Johns Hopkins University Press, 1977).

22 Bernard Mandeville, *The Fable of the Bees: Or, Private Vices, Publick Benefits*, ed. F.B. Kaye, 2 vols (Oxford, Clarendon Press, 1924; rpt 1957), Vol. I: 6–7. All further page references in the text are to this edition.

23 Harold Perkin, *The Origins of Modern English Society* (London, Routledge and Kegan Paul, 1969; Ark pbk edn, 1985), p. 51.

24 Jürgen Habermas, *The Structural Transformation of the Public Sphere: An Inquiry into a Category of Bourgeois Society*, trans. Thomas Burger with the assistance of Frederick Lawrence (Cambridge, MA, MIT Press, 1989; first published 1962), p. 54.

25 Jürgen Habermas, *Theory of Communicative Action, Vol.I: Reason and the Rationalization of Society*, trans. Thomas McCarthy (Boston, Beacon Press, 1984), p. 392.

2

AMATORY FICTION

Behn, Manley, Haywood

I

In 1770 Samuel Johnson observed that the "violence and ill effects" of the "passion of love" had been exaggerated, "for who knows any real sufferings on that head more than from the exorbitancy of any other passion?"[1] But when a lady derided the amatory novels of the day, Johnson protested that "we must not ridicule" a "passion which has caused the change of empires and the loss of worlds – a passion which has inspired heroism and subdued avarice."[2] Even for so rigorous a moralist and literary critic, amatory fiction still had the power to evoke aristocratic themes and heroic achievements. In spite of its extravagance, such fiction could summon up an ethos of honor and duty that continued to resonate powerfully. Challenging that nostalgic aristocratic ethos, increasingly, was the value put upon those bourgeois norms that cut across social orders and ranks, a development that the philosopher Charles Taylor has called the exaltation of "ordinary life," whereby the "life of production and reproduction, of work and the family" took over from the warrior ethic or the life of Platonic contemplation as the highest form of existence.[3] In antiquity, what Taylor identifies as "ordinary life" was "infrastructural," the necessary and sustaining background to a life of heroism or citizenship or contemplation. About the time of the Reformation, says Taylor, for Christianity the significant life occurred in marriage and in one's calling. "The previous 'higher' forms of life were dethroned, as it were. And along with this went frequently an attack, covert or overt, on the elites which had made these forms their province."[4]

Derived from the seventeenth-century French heroic romances and the shorter *nouvelle*, the amatory novella of the late seventeenth and early eighteenth century in England looks at first like nothing more than a simplification and often crudely sensationalized version of the romance tradition's intertwining of heroic action and amatory complexity. But as it develops in the literary marketplace of the early eighteenth century in England, amatory fiction eventually transforms its sources and along with them the ethos of love and honor that supported the tradition of romance which extends from the Middle Ages to Renaissance prose examples such as Sidney's *Arcadia* (1590) to the enormous seventeenth-century French romances of Madeline de Scudéry such as *Artamène, ou le grand Cyrus* (1649–1653) and *Clélie* (1654–1660).

Generally speaking, romance in its classic form transcended ordinary life and, in that very transcendence, stood in a stable relation to mundane existence, the two orders mutually supporting each other. But in English amatory fiction as it emerges at the end of the seventeenth and into the early decades of the eighteenth century, heroic identity and amatory delicacy are largely displaced by a melodramatic or libertine sexuality, and "romance" begins to acquire its modern meaning of amorous (and somewhat unreal or impractical) encountering. Underneath its stylistic extravagance, preposterous actions, and care-lessly formulaic approach to characterization, this new "romance" asserts a continuity between narrative and ordinary life. Quotidian reality is represented as an active impediment to immediate and sponta-neous attraction, and the love plot thus represents a hopelessly futile attempt at a transcendence put into question by what Michael McKeon calls an emerging "naive empiricism" that is deeply skeptical of "romance idealism."[5] "Ordinary life" in Taylor's sense is exalted by its intersections with the intense experience of irregular sexual passion and/or its repression or avoidance. The life of production and repro-duction, of work and family, is the ideal that the heroines of the novella long for but rarely achieve, and their invariably tragic histories of seduction, betrayal, and even death testify to the inevitability of this new ethos of ordinary life but at the same time to a lingering nostalgia for the old values embodied in the romance. For example, in the preface to her collection of love tales entitled *Exilius* (1715) Jane Barker laments the low state of romances and what she calls their "Heroic Love," which has been "rally'd out of Practice, and its Professors laugh'd out of Countenance, while Interest and loose Gallantry have been set up in its Place, and monopolized all its Business and Effects." Little wonder, she continues, that for those who marry for practical or sordid reasons heroic love "appears a Fantom or Chimera; but to those who aim at a happy Marriage, by the Way of Virtue and Honour, need consider but very little, to find that it lyes thro', or borders upon, Heroic Love; so that Romances (which commonly treat of this virtuous Affection) are not to be discarded as wholly Useless."[6] *Exilius*, a collection of inter-twined amatory tales set in ancient Rome, is thus both exotic and domestically relevant, tracing heroic love to its conclusion in a series of happy marriages in which readers can find the best example and encouragement for their own emotional and marital careers.

The love novella sought to depict an interiorized equivalent of that life of public honor peculiar to the elites of antiquity that survived in attenuated forms. Explicitly drawn to glamorous and exotic, or to delib-erately extravagant and even preposterous settings and characters, the amatory novella is at the same time implicitly egalitarian in its represen-tations of a social world where public honor is an empty notion and of an emotional realm (normally assigned to women) in which all its readers are invited to involve themselves. Greatly influenced by the popularity of translations of the anonymous *Lettres Portugaises* (1669), five long letters in which a seduced and abandoned nun evokes her passionate affair with a cavalier, the English amatory novella, as Ros Ballaster has traced its transformations, rendered passion in a disorderly style, a logically inconsistent language that was "ostentatiously 'natural' and implicitly associated with female desire."[7] The heroines of the amatory novella testify in their passionate exaltations and sufferings to the power of a specifically female emotional authenticity and interiority which are validated by their opposition to the empty, merely external signs of corrupt masculine honor. Typically, these heroines speak from a fullness of being that identifies itself in its compelling and often over-whelming articulations as "natural" against a masculine, sexual self-seeking that is structured or licensed by aristocratic privilege and patriarchal custom (often specifically identified as such) and is to that extent dramatized as superficial, inauthentic, and merely "cultural." The amatory novella enables such heroines to emerge from the remote world of courtly romance where women are idealized, decorous, and reticent and to point by their innocence, vulnerability, and intense emotional involvements to an interiority that claims to be universal rather than class specific (although such heroines almost always belong to an aristocratic or at least leisured social stratum). So, too, the seducers of these heroines are often enough dissolute aristocrats for whom amorous conquest is the sole degraded remnant of the heroic ethos of their literary ancestors. Their function as predictable seducers is largely to provoke the interiorized intensities of their victims, and their behavior is, in effect, specific to their order and is implicitly derived from their bored patriarchal privilege. The heroines, in their emotional and sexual intensities, embody a naturalized and universal-ized humanity; their seducers enact the mechanical sexuality granted them by an archaic structure of rank, privilege, and prerogative. However preposterous, the novella's entanglements are provoked against a backdrop of changing material circumstances and social relationships sketched in these broad ideological terms in which a new world of naturalized and universalized feeling opposes an archaic and oppressively patriarchal structure.

Amatory fiction in England would seem to have served precisely as an escapist distraction from mundane existence, and the extravagant intensities that this fiction habitually represents must have been, in practice, the compensatory opposite of an actuality that we can all recognize in which individual passion was necessarily suppressed by domestic necessity and civilized order. The novella's deliberate unreality and its opportunities for readers' romantic or erotic fantasy were probably the two main reasons for its enduring popularity, in the same way that mass-market romance continues to thrive in the late twentieth century. But from the spirited novellas of Aphra Behn in the 1670s to the works of her two most famous successors in the early eighteenth century, Delarivière Manley and Eliza Haywood, there also runs a current of subversive intelligence which offers attentive readers a commentary on sociosexual relationships and which displays a sophisticated self-consciousness about the moral and social relevance of all this fictional extravagance. Feminist criticism has illuminated this aspect of English amatory fiction by finding in the works of the "Fair Triumvirate of Wit" (as a contemporary panegyrist called Behn, Manley and Haywood)[8] a political resistance to masculine constructions of the feminine. For Ros Ballaster these fictions inscribe "a gendered struggle over interpretation" as "a competition between men and women for control of the means of seduction becomes the central theme."[9]

Male seducers (and sometimes female ones) present sexual passion as a liberation, a reproach to the unnatural constraints of society and religion. But even at its most lubricious, as in Behn's and Manley's works, the amatory novel often exposes such libertine rhetoric as a rationalization for exploitative sexuality which is ultimately related to male domination and class privilege. Along with voyeuristic participation in formulaic sexual excitement, the amatory novella can on occasion provide commentary that offers subversive or simply cynical interpretations of the events unfolding. To different degrees, each of these authors conducts a conversation with her readers which tends to bracket the narrative's sensational events and shallow characters, thus marking this material to some extent as conventional and identifying its tangential relevance to real-world issues by making the reader's encounter with the narrative potentially as much an intellectual as an emotional event. Especially in Behn and Manley, the narrative voice suggests an alternative way of reading for more than enjoyable fantasy and that voice distinguishes itself as a moral intelligence from the thoughtless, merely hedonistic characters in the fiction itself. Haywood's writing is largely another story in which the reader is offered intense and uncritical involvement in passion's white-hot excitements and deliciously unbearable tragedies.

In her amatory novellas and most notably in her full-length novel, *Love Letters Between a Nobleman and His Sister* (1684–1687), Aphra Behn makes this double voicing her signature technique. In Behn's fiction amatory intensity is qualified by our shared understanding of the force of literary convention and its liberating distance from the actual, our sense as we read Behn, as Janet Todd remarks, of "the constructed nature of the personalities revealed."[10] The resulting conversation establishes a social relationship between reader and author that counterbalances the novella's histrionic world, in which no one's discourse can be trusted and in which nobody actually speaks to anyone else except for self-serving rhetorical purposes. Whatever the confusions in the story, narrator and reader are secure in their knowledge of certain recurrences in human nature or in leisure-class society in this stylized world. Behn's novellas propose various determinisms, irresistible motions of love, sexual pleasure, worldly power, honor, and so on, and in their articulations presuppose an actual world that is contingent and provisional, where such inevitabilities and patterns do not apply.

The social realm lies not in the sketchy and formulaic representations of the world that the characters inhabit but in these exchanges between the narrator and knowing readers, who understand just how to handle the representations passing in front of them, which provide opportunity, first, for pleasurable fantasy and the contemplation of rhetorical and fictional patterning; and second, for moral, psychological, and even sociohistorical rumination. Behn's only full-scale novel, the three-part (each published separately) *Love Letters Between a Nobleman and His Sister*, marks a crucial advance in complexity: the characters themselves manage to conduct their own analysis of their language and actions and to manipulate both for their profit, pleasure, and advantage. The narrator herself conforms to this pattern, since there is a decided shift in her presence and perspective as this long book unfolds. Part I is entirely epistolary, and Behn herself does not appear *in propria persona* until the second part when she provides a bridge narrative from the exchange of letters in Part I to the further exchanges in Part II. She continues in Part II to comment occasionally on the action, but in due course in Part III she finally steps on stage as a participant–observer as well as a commentator on the events of the narrative as recounted in more letters. More than the mere transcriber of amatory correspondence, Behn's narrator resembles her heroine, Sylvia, who is transformed in the course of events from a swooning victim of involuntary passion into an amoral sexual predator. Sylvia acquires an effective and manipulative rhetorical skill so that she uses amatory language – not just words but erotic self-display in male as well as female clothing – to further her own ends. She also becomes a consummate sexual politician, balancing several lovers at one time. As Ros Ballaster puts it, Sylvia ultimately becomes like her creator, "drawing upon multiple fictional identities and languages in order to secure her control over a lover/reader as sophisticated and cynical as herself." For Ballaster, the identity between author and character is exact and liberating. Both of them are survivors who present readers "with a critique of women's enslavement to a variety of fictions of feminine identity" and offer "an escape route beyond retreat into silence and spurious claims to authenticity."[11]

Based on a contemporary sexual scandal and representing historical personages and prominent political actors like the ill-fated Duke of Monmouth (Charles II's bastard son executed in 1685 for leading a rebellion against his uncle, James II), *Love Letters* began its existence as a *roman à clef* or a scandal chronicle.[12] Reprinted a number of times through the early decades of the eighteenth century along with Behn's shorter fictions,[13] the novel clearly outlived the scandals on which it was based. Just as the world that these characters inhabit could only be taken, even by late seventeenth-century readers, as an opportunity for voyeuristic fantasy of the kind now pandered to by celebrity magazines, so, too, the events of *Love Letters* consist of repetitive patterns and combinations among the lovers. The driving principle in this three-part narrative is, necessarily, repetition with variation, as the characters interact and intertwine like dancers: longing for each other and gradually drawing nearer to anticipated consummation, which is delayed, frustrated, and protracted, and then of course drawing apart and toward others, and so on in a potentially endless fantasy of renewable longings, schemes, betrayals, and anticipated ecstasies. The changes undergone by Philander and Sylvia as they move on to new conquests are as much the result of this drive for new erotic combinations as they are owing to Behn's interest in female psychology and sexual politics.

Nonetheless, there are some remarkable variations in *Love Letters* on its basic narrative rhythm which have implications for amatory fiction's capacity to move away from a self-enclosure in which the reader's needs are paramount and toward a form of representation in which the reader is assumed to want a moral and intellectual perspective on the events and the actors. Part I features unrelenting amatory rhetoric of the most flatulent sort, as the lovers claim to be overwhelmed by their emotions, swept away by volcanic passions. But from the first Philander undermines simple sincerity for even the dullest reader by his deployment of amatory tropes:

> Say, fond love, whither wilt thou lead me? Thou hast brought me from the noisy hurries of the town, to charming solitude; from crowded cabals, where mighty things are resolving, to lonely groves ... where thou hast laid me down to contemplate on Sylvia, to think my tedious hours away in the softest imagination a soul inspir'd by love can conceive, to increase my passion by every thing I behold.[14]

Philander makes a quick transition to an intellectual meditation on the liberating example that such a world sets for "duller man," who is "bound up to rules, fetter'd by the nice decencies of honour" (29). Libertine narcissism turns inevitably to a quasi-theoretical radical statement about social and sexual organization, but of course such theorizing is transparently part of the rhetoric of seduction.

At first, Sylvia describes her passion as the discovery of hitherto unexperienced intensities, and she attempts an apostrophe to nature: "Approach, approach, you sacred Queen of Night, and bring Philander veil'd from all eyes but mine"(30). But she cannot sustain this rhetoric for very long: "thus I would speak a thousand things, but that still, methinks, words do not enough express my soul; to understand that right, there requires looks; there is a rhetoric in looks; in sighs and silent touches that surpasses all ... by this I would insinuate, that the story of the heart cannot be so well told by this way, as by presence and conversation" (31). Sylvia's impatience with purely epistolary dalliance signals that Behn's narrative will eventually move out of this self-enclosed textual world and into the public world of human contact and progressive interaction, of illicit, obsessively hedonistic and acquisitive movement through situations that are always specific and social – elopement from the French countryside where the events begin to Paris and eventually to other parts of Europe such as Cologne and Antwerp. There are a few other touches in Part I of *Love Letters* that undermine amatory vaporizing and push toward action and away from mere rehearsal of amatory tropes: one is Philander's suspect fluency in the language of love, whose most memorable moment is his hilarious account of his *ejaculatio praecox* when he finally meets Sylvia in her boudoir, the entire scene rendered in a broad military allegory of love's progress:

> having overcome all difficulties, all the fatigues and toils of love's long sieges, vanquish'd the mighty phantom of the fair, the giant honour, and routed all the numerous host of women's little reasonings, passed all the bounds of peevish modesty; nay, even all the loose and silken counterscarps that fenced the sacred fort, and nothing stopped my glorious pursuit: then, then, ye gods, just then, by an over-transport, to fall just fainting before the surrendering gates, unable to receive the yielding treasure!
>
> (50–51)

Near-consummation like this drives Part I of *Love Letters*, since actual possession temporarily dissipates erotic energy. Philander's allegory is an extreme instance of the over-elaboration of private moments that defines the amatory novella in general, but in its comic urgency and self-depreciating inventiveness Philander's rendition of his sexual failure points to Behn's impatience with the repetitive self-indulgence built into the genre and her preference for action and movement, as well as for analysis and self-consciousness over excited participation and sympathy.

After several months of their illegal cohabitation, Philander is accused of rape by Sylvia's father and thrown into the Bastille, but he devises a stratagem whereby she marries his friend, Brilliard, "a gentleman, though a cadet" (110) so that their relationship becomes simple adultery (and to that extent nobody's business). Arrested again, this time for high treason for his involvement in Cesario's (Monmouth's) plot to seize the throne, Philander concludes Part I with an account of his escape as he is conducted to certain death in the Bastille: he bribes the messenger into whose hands he was committed, and he writes to Sylvia instructing her to dress in boy's clothes and to meet him in a small cottage by the seashore. As Part II opens, the narrator now speaks in her own voice and tells us how Sylvia (in boy's clothing), accompanied by Brilliard, met Philander and sailed to Holland where they chanced to meet the elegant and courtly Hollander, Octavio, who is taken in ways he cannot quite fathom with the graceful youth accompanying Brilliard and Philander.

Behn opens up the plot so that it requires her supervision to trace rapidly expanding complications and interrelationships that cut across sexual and social lines and encompass an increasingly large cast of characters spread across a widening social scene: Brilliard begins to wonder why, as Sylvia's legal husband, he should not have conjugal rights and "now seeks precedents of usurped dominion, and thinks she is his wife, and has forgot that he is her creature, and Philander's vassal" (117); Octavio begins to suspect that this captivating youth "was not what she seemed, but of that sex whereof she discovered so many softnesses and beauties" (115). Sylvia discovers that she likes the transgressive thrill of her male disguise, as she grows to enjoy the amorous tributes it brings her: "Every day she appeared in the Tour, she failed not to make a conquest on some unguarded heart of the fair sex" (118). Forced to fly to Cologne to avoid prosecution by the French authorities, Philander pursues the beautiful young wife of a Spanish count who befriends him. In due course, he describes his seduction of Calista to Octavio, who is horrified to learn that his friend's new conquest is none other than his sister. Philander's letters to Sylvia, as his affair at Cologne progresses, grow less than ardent, and her worst suspicions are confirmed when Octavio refuses to show her a letter that Philander has written to him about his activities.

Accompanying all these twists and turns are the internal shifts of the characters' dispositions, loyalties, and personalities, as Philander throws himself into his new amour, as Sylvia's infatuation with him is gradually modified by her increasing sense of her own sexual power over other men and by her desire for revenge when she learns of his infidelity, as Octavio grows more and more obsessed with Sylvia and tortured by the conflict between that love and his friendship for Philander, and as Brilliard plots to betray both his rivals and enjoy Sylvia. Eventually, Octavio tells Sylvia of Philander's perfidy, and she agrees to marry him if he will avenge her honor. Besotted with her favors, Octavio is distracted from his political responsibilities as one of the leaders of the United Provinces, "neglecting glory, arms, and power, for the more real joys of life" (285). When Sylvia is ordered to leave the country by the States of Holland, she charms Octavio's misogynistic uncle, Sebastian, who takes her off to his country villa and offers to marry her. Disguised as a page, Octavio arrives and is surprised in bed with Sylvia by his uncle, who is killed accidentally as they struggle. The couple escape to Brussels where, as the result of events too complicated to summarize, Philander and Calista also arrive in due course.

Behn's characters move with her from epistolary self-enclosure to encounters within a thickly rendered social world. That world is defined most of the time by transgressive sex that operates across marital and even heterosexual norms in a European network of leisured aristocrats who recognize each other as potential patrons and clients. There is nothing romantic, in McKeon's sense, about this network,[15] where easy movement across borders provides the possibility of erotic adventure and accompanying financial acquisitions. Necessarily, these are lives crowded with exciting incidents; fullness, variety, and narrative energy, rather than verisimilitude, are their governing principles. Behn's characters soliloquize often but they cannot be called reflective; they take their world of sexual opportunity for granted, and she does not allow them to be troubled in their extraordinary privileges by thinking of those complicated socioeconomic layers that support their hedonistic movements. They dwell, we may say, in an enclave that shields them from knowledge of a supporting totality. But Behn herself is at times moved to understand her characters and to account for their reactions, if not for the privilege that sustains them in their adventures. Although *Love Letters* has no interest in complex plotting and is governed, like her characters' lives, by improvisation, exploitation, and opportunity, Behn's attempts to explain Sylvia's character point to the drive in a novel of this length toward some rudimentary sense of totality. In this regard, Sylvia is the most interesting of the characters, since Behn grants her (and all other women in her position) a natural instability which helps to move the plot along. Behn also wants to understand Sylvia's alterations, and those of the other characters to some extent, within the novel's specifically social constructions of identity, in terms of the circumstances peculiar to this elite. At the beginning of Part III after Octavio and Sylvia are arrested on Brilliard's accusation of treason as they are about to marry, Behn speculates about Sylvia's complicated emotions:

> This suffering with Octavio begot a pity and compassion in the heart of Sylvia, and that grew up to love; for he had all the charms that could inspire, and every hour was adding new fire to her heart, which at last burnt into a flame; such power has mighty obligation on a heart that has any grateful sentiments! and yet, when she was absent a-nights from Octavio, and thought on Philander's passion for Calista, she would rage and rave, and find the effects of wondrous love, and wondrous pride, and be even ready to make vows against Octavio: but those were fits that seldomer seized her now, and every fit was like a departing ague, still weaker than the former, and at the sight of Octavio all would banish.

> (269–270)

A revealing gap marks Behn's analysis of the changes wrought in Sylvia by her evolving situation and the concluding summary of her personality as a "woman." Sylvia is sensitive to external influences, both physical and moral: deeply compromised as an agent, moved almost in a physiological way by her circumstances, she is also impelled to love Octavio by the force of the courtly codes that he embodies, his elegance and grace that confer obligation even as they render service. But the naturalized type of woman that subsumes this particular Sylvia turns Behn away from this delicate analysis of emotional shifts in an older moral and social economy. The resulting personality, however, derives not from nature but from that hedonistic self-seeking common to aristocratic men and women that constitutes the social relations that define the world of *Love Letters*. Thus, when Philander returns and rekindles her desire for him, Sylvia is "a second time undone" (355), and her postcoital rationalizations are necessarily complicated, derived, Behn tells us, from her experience in the world of "men of quality and honour":

> she would not endure to think of losing either: she was for two reasons covetous of both, and swore fidelity to both, protesting each the only man; and she was now contriving in her thoughts, how to play the jilt most artificially; a help-meet, though natural enough to her sex, she had not yet much essayed, and never to this purpose: she knew well she should have need of all her cunning in this affair; for she had to do with men of quality and honour, and too much wit to be grossly imposed upon.
>
> (355–356)

Social experience neutralizes the emotional instability natural to Sylvia the woman, and in fact such experience focuses her desires, allows her to contemplate the contradiction involved in dual possession of Philander and Octavio. This now stable Sylvia is able to treat her emotions as commodified pleasures that can be managed within the network of relationships that matters more than moral values such as love or honor or fidelity. And Sylvia is right to practice emotional *Realpolitik*, since in the morning Philander has had enough of this now dull passion, and Octavio arrives to offer her his estate of over a million in money. But that is hardly the end of things, and in the pages that follow, Sylvia and Philander are lovers again and then grow tired of each other, until finally the long-suffering Octavio decides to enter a monastery. Behn's rendition of a complex, individualized character like Sylvia is eroded by her presentation of social relationships that shape and even determine such a personality. Perhaps Behn's analysis of Sylvia's personality marks her own confusion and ideological inconsistency, caught, as she seems to have been, between a more or less traditional version of yielding female essence and her own worldly Restoration sensibility that understands women, like men, in terms of specific social relationships as they jockey for pleasure and power. Behn offers no moralistic judgments of the rapacious Sylvia, who is last seen (with Brilliard) banished from Flanders after ruining the fortune of a young Spanish nobleman she has seduced: she is "forced to remove for new prey; and daily makes considerable conquests wherever she shews the charmer" (461).

There is one final strand in the weave of Behn's novel: the Cesario (Monmouth) plot in which the young rebel and his allies gather for another try at the Crown. Like Octavio, Cesario is besotted with love for Hermione, his old flame, and distracted by it for a while from the serious business of rebellion. But as Brilliard describes him to Sylvia, Cesario is the sort of hero in love and war of which amatory fiction often dreams but rarely articulates: "he is all the softer sex can wish, and ours admire; he is formed for love and war; and as he is the most amorous and wanton in courts, he is also the most fierce and brave in the field" (415). In the end, Cesario forsakes love for his desperate project, but not without deep and lasting regret, a private passion that colors his public exploits and follows him to the execution block. Behn's romanticized, tragic portrait of Monmouth in these pages competes with her tracing of the final, nasty refinements of Sylvia's amoral individualism, along with Philander's self-serving hedonism and political trimming. The pathos and glory, as Behn saw them, of Monmouth's doomed and ill-advised attempt at the throne propose the possibility of "genuine" romance that the rest of her tale undermines, and her mixture of romantic sentiment and cynical worldliness sets a tone for such fiction that will endure in her two most famous successors, Manley and Haywood. In the larger ideological context of the late seventeenth and early eighteenth century, her portrait in Cesario of archaic sentimental virtue, undone mainly by a modern political world in which unchecked hedonism and corrupt self-seeking are the rule, expresses a resonant oppositional nostalgia that will find expression in Tory polemics in the early years of the eighteenth century and in much of the amatory fiction that is published during the 1720s and 1730s.

II

A popular collection of scandalous anecdotes from the tumultuous years at the beginning of Queen Anne's reign, Delarivière Manley's *The*

New Atalantis (1709), what the French called a *chronique scandaleuse*, is Tory satire, written to vilify the Whig politicians then in power. Returning to earth to see whether things have improved since she left it in disgust with human behavior, the goddess Astrea meets her mother, Lady Virtue (all in rags), who tells her that mankind is as corrupt as ever and that honorable passion has been replaced by self-interest here in the New Atalantis (England):

> I have no sanctuary among the lovers of this age; the youngest virgin and the most ardent youth are contented to quote me only as a name, something fine, that their histories indeed make mention of, a thing long since departed, and which at this day is not to be found among 'em. ... By a diabolical way of argument they prove the body is only necessary to the pleasures of enjoyment; that love resides not in the heart, but in the face. ... Hymen no more officiates at their marriages, the saffron robe hangs neglected in the wardrobe, the genuine torch is long since extinguished, the glare only of a false light appears: Interest is deputed in his room, he presides over the feast, he joins their hands, and brings them to the sacred ceremony of the bed with so much indifferency, that were not consummation a necessary article, the unloving pair could with the utmost indifferency repair to their several chambers.[16]

Such high-minded complaints justify the salacious revelations that fill the two volumes of *The New Atalantis*. Lady Virtue evokes a moral and social universe that explains individual behavior and blames the times and corrupt customs as much as particular sinners.[17] Readers are reminded that these individual stories are contributions to a theory about the condition of society, or at least of the systematic corruption of its upper stratum.

We can be pretty certain that readers of *The New Atalantis* did not turn its steamy and sometimes wickedly funny pages for lessons about civic corruption, and the two goddesses' appalled observations are balanced to some extent by the book's comic relishing of outrageous behavior.[18] That perspective is provided by the worldly Lady Intelligence, who is commanded by the goddesses to guide them around Atalantis and who uncovers, with undisguised gusto, scandal after scandal for the horrified divinities. Lady Intelligence is Manley's mouthpiece, and she sees beneath the glittering surfaces and instructs the goddesses in Atalantis's reigning self-interest. But in spite of this insider's wealth of scandalous details, the book's satire and some of its erotic force depend upon the general truth of a thoroughly corrupt aristocratic sphere. Propping up all the scandalous extravagance of Manley's book, all the proliferating allegorical personages and pseudonymous characters which, as Catherine Gallagher observes, have the effect of "demonstrating not only the fecundity of language but its ability to obscure what it pretends to explore,"[19] is a recurring nostalgia for a social and moral order in which a simpler political virtue and courtly integrity flourished. In its crude political polemic, Manley's *The New Atalantis* contributes to the debate taking place in England from the end of the seventeenth century and through the first half of the eighteenth century. As J.G.A. Pocock has formulated it, the great issue was the nature of political virtue as landed wealth or real property became less important than mobile property – credit and capital in the emerging early modern financial order. Land, as Pocock paraphrases the debate, "tended to make men independent citizens, whereas mobile property tended to make them artificial beings, whose appetites and powers could and must be regulated by a sovereign." In the new economic order, moreover, the sovereign power tended to be exercised not by a monarch who embodied virtue but by an executive branch which could govern tyrannically by bringing society "into personal, political, and economic dependence upon it."[20] Pocock evokes the opposing ideologies of the early eighteenth century: the country ideology, "founded on a presumption of real property and an ethos of the civic life ... perpetually threatened by corruption operating through private appetites and false consciousness"; and the court ideology, "founded upon an acceptance of credit as a measure of economic value and of a psychology of imagination, passion, and interest as the mainsprings of human behavior." For court ideology, says Pocock, men were by nature "factious and interested beings," but all that was required for a viable society was "a strong central executive, which did not itself need to be disciplined by the principles of virtue, but might without suffering harm appeal to the passions and interests of men."[21]

The scandals that *The New Atalantis* exposes match the amoral individualism and unchecked hedonism that Aphra Behn evokes as the glamorous aristocratic norm in her stories, except that Manley's grandees are placed quite deliberately within this ideological opposition that Pocock evokes. Sordidly self-seeking economic and libidinal entities, caricatures of meanness and sexual shallowness, they lack the regulation that a strong and virtuous sovereign might provide. The Whig notables whom Manley pillories are courtiers moved by self-interest and the acquisition of credit and power in the new political order; as Lady Intelligence describes Queen Anne's court to Astrea and

Virtue, it is a place where "avarice, revenge, or favour" are the only motives, for "none serve there but in prospect of making, advancing, or preserving their fortunes" (110). Hypocrisy and self-interest are the rule in public life, just as they are at the heart of the private sexual scandals that Manley delivers. Public and private spheres are continuous, since the treacherous Whig courtiers who prevent Queen Anne from ruling effectively include many of the same seducers who betray and abandon innocent women, like Manley herself whose history, as she provides it, follows the pattern of seduction and betrayal. Tricked by her cousin into a bigamous marriage, Delia (Manley) asks the goddesses in exclamatory style what recourse in such a world was open to her: "What could I? forlorn! distressed! beggared! To whom could I run for refuge, even from want and misery, but to the very traitor that had undone me? I was acquainted with none that would espouse my cause, a helpless, useless load of grief and melancholy! with child! disgrac'd! my own relations, either impotent of power or will to relieve me!" (226). And Lady Intelligence confirms the grieving Delia's contention that in such cases there is no redress, "for the courts of Justice are so corrupt that in the very beginning of a cause we are sure it will be determined on the side, where there is most money or favour, which is seldom or never found upon that of a prosecuting wife" (228).[22]

Behn's manipulation of literary conventions for erotic excitement mitigate satirical judgment of amoral individualism, to say the least. In contrast, Manley's approach to political satire in *The New Atalantis* involves a compound of self-righteousness and prurience in which readers are offered the surefire pleasures of erotic and pathetic representation along with specific scandals that add up to an indictment of those who control the upper reaches of society. Scandalously entertaining presentations of recognizable individuals, her stories belong to the prehistory of the novel, as part of what Lennard Davis has called the novel/news discourse that propels an emerging interest in a new kind of intensely particularized and historicized narrative.[23] Manley's shocking news is that the entertaining moral monsters of amatory fiction have come to life and occupy the halls of power. In place of Behn's overt artifice and erotic patterning, *The New Atalantis* offers a life-like chaos, a teeming panorama of recent history and contemporary, up-to-the-minute dirty politics. Behn's Restoration worldliness offers readers an implicit conversation in which lovers like Philander, Octavio, Caesario, and Sylvia are both entertaining and cautionary, suspended in a universe of unlimited hedonistic opportunity and linked as well (however tenuously and most often negatively) to a high, heroic tradition of love, honor, and political virtue. In *The New Atalantis* Behn's tolerance, amusement, and enthusiasm for love and honor are largely canceled by factional hatred, personal vindictiveness, and Juvenalian indignation. Behn's bantering dialogue with her readers yields most of the time to Manley's declamatory melodrama in which a few Tory heroes and a sad collection of seduced and betrayed women collide with pervasive corruption.

Just after Delia (Manley) finishes her tale, the goddesses find hope in Beaumond, the Tory champion, the Duke of Beaufort, to whom Volume II of *The New Atalantis* is dedicated:

> He that dares be honest; that dares be loyal, when it is so much the manner to be otherwise, when it's scarce more than a name, and that too very nearly forgotten, he who chooses to walk almost alone rather than mingle with the illustrious guilty-herd, rich in that native much becoming pride of well-performing duty, who with a smile of contempt looked down, and despised those inglorious preferments and rewards with which they would have tempted his early, his unwary youth!
>
> (230)

Individuals like Beaumond are the exceptions to the corrupt rule. Such Tory statesmen do not merely belong to an opposing party but are embodiments of a natural aristocracy, disinterested moral exemplars ousted by the representatives of a new, specifically contemporary and distinctively modern species of self-interested individual. Seduced women represent, most of the time, a natural order of equally disinterested virtue, betrayed and exploited by this modern gang. As Delia's story makes emphatically clear, these seducers exercise power within their private enclaves and are beyond the reach of the law, which is corrupt and unresponsive to injustice anyway. For *The New Atalantis*, society is disgracefully fractured and atomized, a collection of aristocratic households where powerful individuals, sometimes women like Manley's *bête noire*, the Queen's favorite, Sarah Churchill, Duchess of Marlborough, but most often men, do just as they please, even as they derive their wealth and power from their machinations in the larger world. At the same time, naturally, like all scandal *The New Atalantis* brings readers wide-eyed fascination with the actions it deplores, and the erotic and sometimes violent scenes enacted in these enclaves gain a prurient attraction from the unchecked power and forbidden energies that their masters embody, just as the helpless innocence that they confront also helps to heighten erotic tension and sado-masochistic excitement.

For a revealing example, consider the narrative in Volume I of the *Duke*, meant to represent Hans Willem Bentinck, 1st Earl of Portland, advisor and rumored homosexual lover of William III (the story is part of Lady Intelligence's retrospective version of the events and personalities surrounding the arrival of William and Mary after the ouster of King James II). The Duke is introduced as a follower of "the wise maxims of Machiavel" (28). He has a "seeming admiration for virtue where ever he found it, but he was a statesman, and held it incompatible (in an age like this) with a man's making his Fortune. Ambition, desire of gain, dissimulation, cunning, all these were notoriously servicable to him" (30). When a friend leaves his daughter, Charlot, in his care, the Duke sees to it that she is educated in the strictest paths of virtue. But one night during an amateur masque in which Charlot enacts the goddess Diana, the Duke is smitten: "He knew not what to resolve upon; he could not prudently marry her, and how to attempt to corrupt her! Those excellent principles that had been early infused into her were all against him; but yet he must love her! He found he could not live without her!" (34) Consulting the works of Machiavelli, the Duke is inspired by a maxim, "*that none but great souls could be completely wicked*" (34). First, he gives Charlot inflammatory reading, "the most dangerous Books of love – Ovid, Petrarch, Tibullus – those moving tragedies that so powerfully expose the force of love and corrupt the mind" (37). To these he adds certain nameless sexological manuals on whose effects Manley dwells with particular prurience, books "dangerous to the community of mankind, abominable for virgins, and destructive to youth; such as explain the mysteries of nature, the congregated pleasures of Venus, the full delights of mutual lovers, and which rather ought to pass the fire than the press" (37). Finally, he surprises her at his villa and presses himself upon her in a near-rape scene suffused with Manley's distinctive eroticism, a compound of fashion-magazine glamour and sadistic violence:

> Charlot no sooner arrived but, the weather being very hot, she ordered a bath to be prepared for her. Soon as she was refreshed with that, she threw her self down upon a bed with only one thin petticoat and a loose nightgown, the bosom of her gown and shift open, her nightclothes tied carelessly together with a cherry-coloured ribbon, which answered well to the yellow and silver stuff of her gown. She lay uncovered in a melancholy careless posture, her head resting upon one of her hands; the other held a handkerchief that she employed to dry those tears that sometimes fell from her eyes. When raising

34

herself a little at a gentle noise she heard from the opening of
a door that answered to the bedside, she was quite astonished
to see enter the amorous Duke. Her first emotions were all joy
but in a minute she recollected her self, thinking he was not
come there for nothing. She was going to rise but he prevented
her by flying to her arms where, as we may call it, he nailed
her down to the bed with kisses. His love and resolution gave
him double vigour; he would not stay a moment to capitulate
[negotiate] with her. Whilst yet her surprise made her doubtful
of his designs, he took advantage of her confusion to accomplish 'em. Neither her prayers, tears, nor strugglings could
prevent him, but in her arms he made himself a full amends
for all those pains he had suffered for her.

(39)

Charlot responds quickly that night, "not at all behind-hand in
ecstasies and guilty transports" (40), and she eventually becomes the
Duke's mistress. Like all such affairs in Manley's universe, this one ends
disastrously, with the surfeited Duke abandoning her before very long in
favor of a worldly countess, Charlot's friend, to whom he proposes in
these terms:

I know you are a woman of the world, fully acquainted with
your own charms and what they can do upon the hearts of
others. You have wit, understand your own interest, therefore if
you have no aversion for my person, 'tis in your power to do
what you please with me. ... I have took time to weigh the
design. All things plead for you – beauty, merit, sense, and
every thing that can render a woman charming. Whilst I
pretend nothing to plead for me, but making it your own
interest to make me happy.

(44)

The word "interest" presupposes what Manley expects her audience to
consider their frightening self-possession and ruthless personal agency.
Heroines like Charlot (and Manley herself in the guise of Delia) are
passively helpless in the face of the managerial self-consciousness of
libertines like the Duke and his Countess. True to the libertine tradition
(invoked, by the way, from the first pages of *The New Atalantis*: "By a
diabolical way of argument they prove the body is only necessary to the
pleasures of enjoyment" [5]), such free spirits are philosophical materi-
alists who understand the psychological and physiological mechanics of

desire, its waxing and inevitable waning: "'Tis not possible," Lady Intelligence comments as the Duke first encounters the desirable Countess, "always to love, or to bear up to the extravagant height of a beginning flame; without new supplies it must decay, at least abate of its first vigour, when not a look, or touch, but are fuel to it" (43). These individuals manage turbulent instincts and urges for their own profit and pleasure; their victims are by definition incapable of such controlling self-interest, since to be virtuous in Manley's melodramatic dramatizations is to defer spontaneously to instinct. Thus early in his seduction of Charlot, the Duke is described as a "master of all mankind [who] could trace 'em through all the meanders of dissimulation and cunning, was not at a loss how to interpret the agitation of a girl who knew no hypocrisy. All was artless, the beautiful product of innocence and nature" (36).

In opposing the libertine personality and its innocent victim, Manley offers a pattern that articulates in the political climate of the time a new and (for many of her contemporaries) a disturbing reality. In their coldly efficient pursuit of interest, the Duke and his Countess belong to this new order; their acquisitive and accumulative self-seeking is placed for scandalous shock value next to the intensely spontaneous and malleable subjectivity of the innocent Charlot, whose lack of agency and passive capitulation in the face of her awakened sexual desire enact, on the crude level of popular scandal, a generalized and repeatable personality type. Female innocents whose impulses are exploited (and indeed in this case provoked and managed) by those with power and knowledge like the Duke are without a position in every sense of the word. Charlot depends upon the Duke for everything, and he manipulates her from his privileged vantage point, which is not simply the result of wealth and status but stems as well from his deep understanding of human nature and of the possibilities of its manipulation in the new world of self-interest. Observing, measuring, and controlling, the Duke is aware of multiple possibilities and complicated relationships (a master of narrative, as it were), but Charlot is an object of psychosexual experimentation who reacts to external stimuli; in her helpless innocence she is a subject without agency and lacking a position relative to others from which she can negotiate or maneuver. In the context of the new political and economic order emerging in the early decades of the century, the Duke and other villains in amatory fiction acquire a sinister ideological resonance as they organize and order persons as objects for their pleasure and utility. More than mere hedonists or sexual athletes, they embody a purposeful rationality and controlled selfhood that is the real scandal in *The New Atalantis* because it announces a new sort of individual for whom behavior is rationalized by pragmatic goals rather than licensed by custom and inhibited by moral tradition. Victims like Charlot, on the other hand, are blank slates ready for the writing, available in their pure and abstracted (female) humanity to be appropriated and organized by the powerful. At its purest and broadest, as in the tale of Charlot, young and innocent women lack secure social location or a sense of role or potential purpose and become instances of a "natural" human (and almost invariably female) base that is subject to construction and appropriation by the historically specific male villain, peculiar to the degenerate modern days that Manley denounces.

To be sure, amatory fiction in the first four decades of the eighteenth century does not always yield this kind of ideologically charged and symmetrical melodrama, and innocence and villainy are not always as broadly or resonantly evoked as they are in *The New Atalantis*. Amatory fiction's customary moral justification, however, never strays very far from the sort of social diagram that Manley draws, and the recurring plots of such fiction depend on a world presented as seriously out of joint, in which a powerfully dominant vice and specifically modern brand of self-interest threaten a "natural," defenseless innocence and in which economic motives thwart irregular or unsanctioned love. The preface to *The Adventures of Lindamira, A Lady of Quality* (1702), for example, claims that the story is "calculated according to the measures of Vertue and Decency" so that it will "expose Vice, and disappoint Vanity ... reward Vertue and crown Constancy with Success." The author appeals to a community of "Vertuous Readers," who "must needs be pleas'd to see the Vertuous and Constant Lindamira carry'd with Success thro' a Sea of Misfortunes, and at last Married to her Wishes." *Lindamira* is a modestly realistic tale in which the heroine is scornful of the amatory rhetoric of one of her lovers: "he was very loquacious, yet he often complained he wanted rhetoric to express his sentiments, which he did in such abominable far-fetched metaphors, with incoherent fragments out of plays, novels, and romances, that I thought he had been really distracted."[24] Lindamira loves the impecunious Cleomidon, and she is so concerned for his material welfare that she insists that he obey the wishes of his uncle, Alcander, whose estate will come to him if he marries the rich but undesirable Cleodora. All ends well in due course when Cleodora dies in childbirth and Lindamira and Cleomidon marry, rich, happy, and fulfilled. Comically good humored, *Lindamira* anticipates mid-century domestic narrative, as does the work of Mary Davys, two of whose comic novels, *The Reform'd Coquet* (1724) and *The Accomplish'd Rake; or Modern Fine Gentleman* (1727), have reminded some modern critics of Fielding. Amoranda, her "reform'd coquet," is a rich orphan and good-natured flirt who is saved from the machinations of several unscrupulous lovers by an old guardian appointed by her uncle. Formator is revealed at last to be the disguised young Lord Alanthus, who saves Amoranda from a vicious rapist and sweeps her off her feet.[25] With a little melodrama and a heroine quickly brought to her virtuous senses by a brave and wise hero, Davys's *Reform'd Coquet* and her other novels offer a moderate, mostly comic realism.

But during the 1720s and 1730s the most successful purveyors of amatory fiction offered other thrills, and in the eyes of some contemporary commentators Eliza Haywood had inherited the mantle of Behn and Manley. She provided an emotional intensity quite distinct from the eroticized political scandal associated with Behn and Manley. Haywood's fiction shifts from the exposure of moral imbalance in the upper reaches of society and the spectacle of suffering innocence to the exaltation of female passion, which is almost invariably provoked by restrictive social circumstances in a social sphere in which men and women have (literally) nothing to do but desire one another in unsanctioned or illicit ways. But there is very little protest against those circumstances or even examination of the facts of leisured existence. Fiction like this aims to please, and the nature of that pleasure is more democratic in its implications than the erotic and political pleasures that Behn and Manley, in their distinct ways, provide. Here the narrative focus is obsessively on the articulation of passion itself, most of the time a volcanic and ineffable female emotionality, which sweeps all prudence and caution before it and dwarfs its causes in social or familial or economic relationships.

III

Beginning with the best-selling *Love in Excess* (1719), Eliza Haywood played just about every variation possible on the formulae of amatory narrative through the 1920s and 1930s, as she and her publishers sought to market her as the queen of fictional passion, the Barbara Cartland or Danielle Steele of her day. Here is part of a testimonial poem ("By an unknown Hand") prefixed to *Love in Excess* that is typical of such advertising:

A Stranger Muse, an Unbeliever too,
That Womens Souls such Strength of Vigour knew!

Nor less an Atheist to Love's Power declar'd,
Till you a Champion for the Sex appear'd!
A Convert now, to both, I feel that Fire
Your Words alone can paint! Your Looks inspire!

...

No more of Phoebus rising vainly boast,
Ye tawny Sons of a luxurious Coast!
While our bless'd Isle is with such Rays replete,
Britain shall glow with more than Eastern Heat!

On Haywood's title pages, in her various prefaces to her novels, and in commentary within the novels themselves during the years that follow, she conducts several different projects: some of her novels (usually labeled "secret histories") contain specific reference to contemporary scenes and locales, and indeed she produced two imitations of the Manley pattern in *Memoirs of a Certain Island* (1725), and *The Secret History of the Court of Caramania* (1727), which are stocked with contemporary gossip, including the 1722 financial scandal, the South Sea Bubble.[26] But most of her works ("novels") feature exotic characters and settings, often French, Spanish, and Italian; and pervading all of them is the claim of the dedicatory poem that Haywood's novels will render an intense and irresistibly infectious sexual passion. Characteristically, Haywood insists that she is delivering emotional truths with insights peculiar to her sex. In the dedication to *The Fatal Secret* (1724), she complains that as a woman she is "depriv'd of those Advantages of Education which the other Sex enjoy," and that she can write only about love, "that which Nature is not negligent to teach us." She draws inspiration not from her experience nor her knowledge of books nor her native wit, since the female novelist as such needs "no general Conversation, no Application."[27] In this dedication to the Whig politician William Yonge (1724), she explains that to write about love "a shady grove and purling stream are all things that's [sic] necessary to give us an idea of the tender passion." Disparagement like this of mere amatory fiction and the accompanying outline of female limitation are conventional enough.[28] And yet it seems all wrong, this obviously shrewd Grub Street veteran explaining her work as innocent dreaming, real and moving precisely because it comes unbidden, unmediated by culture, provoked by nature. Obviously fluent herself and producing fiction at an astonishing rate in these years, Haywood aligns herself with her heroines who, at their most distressful moments, are in the throes of emotions that cannot be expressed. Like those suffering heroines, Haywood defines herself as a woman writer not by her mastery of literary language (and all that involves, such as learning and experience of the world) but by her spontaneous, uncultivated ability to imagine passion and its effects.

In the world of her novels and in the narrative persona that she sometimes develops, Haywood makes intelligence and verbal ability completely subordinate to rendering the absolute limits of female experience in an emotional sublimity quite beyond words. In this fictional universe, a measure of education and a superior understanding are, if anything, intensifiers of this specifically defining female suffering. That seems the lesson to be drawn from the fate of the learned and beautiful Emanuella in Haywood's *The Rash Resolve* (1724). Daughter of the governor of Puerto Rico, she is orphaned at 15 and placed in the hands of a treacherous guardian, Don Pedro, who demands that she marry his son, Don Marco. Pursued by the guardian yet aided by the smitten but humane son, she flees to Spain and defends herself with great eloquence before the king against accusations of theft brought by Don Pedro.

> Wonder not, royal Sir! said she, that conscious of my perfect innocence, and of a soul too nice to bear such rude suspicions, as this monstrous legend may perhaps create, should lodge a moment in the breasts of any here; I not await the dull formalities of law, nor ask advice from learned counsel drawn, but here presume to make my own defence, unaided but by truth – Permit me then, great King! to unfold a story must make my vile accuser's heart grow cold within him, tho' warm'd with all the fires from Hell.[29]

But the king is unconvinced and Emanuella escapes not because of anything persuasive in her pleading but through the shocking public suicide of Don Marco, who sick with hopeless love for her throws himself on his sword in front of the court. His father, Don Pedro, snaps here and admits his guilt. Woman's language, at least in the lurid universe of such fiction, is irrelevant in the face of melodramatic situations and events unpredictably engineered by cunning male masters. In the long run, Emanuella's learning makes her predicament even worse and renders her ultimate misery even more exquisite. Having escaped from Don Pedro, she meets and loves Count Emilius. After granting him the "last favor," she is betrayed by her serving maid, who convinces

Emanuella that the Count has abandoned her and is about to marry someone else. She enters a convent only to discover that she is pregnant. Haywood pulls out all the stops of her style as Emanuella leaves the convent:

> She found she was now destin'd to go through all that can be conceived of shame – of misery – of horror – in fine, she found herself with child! – with child without a husband! with child by a man who she had heard from all hands was going to be married to another! – and what was yet worse, by a man whom she accounted the vilest, and most perfidious of his sex! – What words – nay what imagination can paint out her distress as it deserves! – She was infinitely more wretched than any other woman would have been in the like circumstances, by the addition of a superior understanding – and the greatness of her spirit, and that fortitude which had so well enabled her to bear all other misfortunes, serv'd her but to encrease the misery of her condition.
>
> (84–85)

Over and over again, Haywood's narrators dramatize the inadequacy of their writing in the face of female experience at its most intense, extreme, and therefore inarticulate. Haywood's novellas build repeatedly to these evocations of specifically female disaster that defies adequate description, indeed that can illustrate the irrelevance of language for depicting female suffering. Characters like Emanuella are not allowed to express themselves but signify their heroism by a silent intensity evoked as unutterably sublime by Haywood's tumbling and turbulent melodramatic style. In these recurring circumstances, Haywood's voice is entirely and deliberately formulaic, a breathless rush of erotic/pathetic clichés that is in a real sense unreadable. Such prose is designed to be scanned hastily, not to be pondered closely or logically as language and thought but to evoke by its conventional formulas familiar and thrilling scenes. Like Italian arias for Anglophone opera lovers, Haywood's voice is more like expressive noise than language. To some extent, the especially hectic quality of Haywood's style at those central or climactic moments signals her audience to imagine a blocked erotic intensity that can only be evoked rather than named or even clearly identified by a more controlled, moderated, or focused writing.

Something like that kind of controlled speaking does appear in these novels in the discourse of some of the characters. Speech, or at least the purposeful and effective use of the resources of language, is marked in fiction like this as inauthentic, a sign of masculine self-seeking, even when it appears in women. But such language is also powerful in these books, irresistible in the persuasive arguments of seducers, the subversive moral casuistry that so often leads Haywood's heroines astray. As such, speech is marked as masculine, a sign of fraudulent and manipulative self-invention rather than authentic self-expression. Pulp fiction like Haywood's identifies the heights of emotional inexpressibility as the defining, essentially female moment, not just for the women that it represents but for the female narrator herself as the originating and certifying imaginative experience behind her writing.

The appeal for Haywood's audience of such a devaluation of language is clear enough: this fiction offers a pure opportunity for compelling amatory reverie devoid of distracting moral complexity or social knowledge or particularized reference. In place of Behn's and Manley's distinct forms of implicit dialogue between author and reader, Haywood employs an almost purely declamatory manner that bypasses anything like thoughtful or critical distance from the process of representation and its conventions in order to concentrate on rendering something like actual passion and real distress. Literary language, along with the aesthetic, moral, and representational issues it raises, is exchanged in Haywood's amatory fiction for a purely functional expressive rendition of passionate distress. As the raffish poet Richard Savage (who may have been Haywood's lover for a time and moved in the same Grub Street milieu) proclaimed in a tribute prefixed to *The Rash Resolve*, Haywood "gives Form, and touches into Life/ The Passions imag'd in their bleeding Strife." Eliza possesses "a strong, a glorious, a luxurious Fire,/ Which warms cold Wisdom into wild Desire!" Haywood's fiction thus presumes a solitary writer imagining isolated individuals experiencing emotions that are ineffable but communicable, excitingly infectious for the equally isolated reader who, in Savage's rendering, finds judgment overwhelmed by these evocations of wild desire.

With some significant exceptions, the majority of Haywood's amatory fictions are heavily formulaic in order to provide this heavy breathing, and I cannot imagine that readers bothered very much to keep them apart. Their repetitiveness is the essence of their appeal, and with a few interesting variations whereby men and women change places as heroes and villains, they offer each and every time the affecting distress of frustrated and absolutely compulsive passion. Haywood established her particular version of the formula in her first, longest, and most popular amatory novel, the three-part *Love in Excess* (1719), and her pronouncements about passion there can be taken as the rule that she followed in the rest of this phase of her career.[30] The

beautiful Melliora has been raised in solitary innocence, "intirely unacquainted with the Gayeties of a Court, or the Conversation of the Beau
Monde." As her father lies on his deathbed, he makes her the ward of
his friend, the young and handsome (and married) Count D'Elmont.
Their attraction for each other is instantaneous:

> he was not an Object to be safely gaz'd at, and in spight of the
> Grief she was in, she found something in his Form which dissi-
> pated it; a kind of painful Pleasure, a mixture of Surprize, and
> Joy, and doubt ran thro' her in an instant; her Father's Words
> suggested to her Imagination, that she was in a possibility of
> calling the charming Person that stood before her, by a Name
> more tender than that of Guardian, and all the Actions,
> Looks, and Address of D'Elmont serv'd but to confirm her in
> that Belief. For now it was that this insensible [i.e. D'Elmont]
> began to feel the power of Beauty, and that Heart which had
> so long been Impregnable surrender'd in a Moment, the first
> sight of Melliora gave him a Discomposure he had never felt
> before, he sympathiz'd in all her Sorrows, and was ready to
> joyn his Tears with hers, but when her Eyes met his, the God
> of Love seem'd there to have united all his Lightnings for one
> effectual Blaze, their Admiration of each others Perfections
> was mutual, and tho' he had got the start in Love, as being
> touch'd with that Almighty Dart, before her Affliction had
> given her Leave to regard him, yet the softness of her Soul,
> made up for all that little loss of time, and it was hard to say
> whose Passion was the strongest.[31]

These love-at-first-sight passages are the key event in Haywood's novels,
an electrified version of the more gradual, transactional attachments
that lovers experience in Behn's and Manley's fiction. Seduction
become largely irrelevant or unnecessary in Haywood's imaginative
universe, and in place of the manipulative discourse that lovers
exchange as one of them at least jockeys for advantage, we have often
enough a wordless encounter in which lovers are jolted by a current of
high-voltage attraction and simultaneous vibration. Such encounters
challenge rationalized notions of personality and moral agency,
presuming a depth of absolutely compelling sexual desire and a unique
authenticity as a sort of emotional personal sublime in which every
reader is invited to participate vicariously and uncritically. In the
context of amatory fiction as defined in the early eighteenth century by
Behn and Manley and by a host of anonymous productions in a similar

vein, Haywood's representation of instant and irresistible passion is a transformation of the erotic utility of this tradition, a refusal of the pornographic or playful contract of amatory fictions or of their intellectual and often subversive explorations of the shifting varieties of human self-interest and definition. Instead, Haywood's fictions for the most part give us singular and obsessed characters; her novels exalt the passive suffering of love's power as an erotic whirlwind that transforms the stricken (usually female) individual's loss of agency into a powerful and noble identity, a higher and exalted state of consciousness. Since most (but by no means all) of those who are possessed by love in the Haywoodian sense are women, it can be assumed that female readers took comfort in such a paradoxical scheme in which passivity equals power or at the least moral superiority. As defined at the beginning of Part III of *Love in Excess*, true love is pure self-expression that is indifferent to any and all external circumstances. Defiantly unreal and absolutely unconcerned with probability or normal experience, the following extraordinary definition of love locates value in emotional extravagance and obsession and is a refusal of everyday necessity and the regulated selfhood that it requires:

> But how strangely do they deceive themselves, who fancy that they are Lovers, yet on every little Turn of Fortune, or Change of Circumstance, are agitated, with any Vehemence, by Cares of a far different Nature? Love is too jealous, too arbitrary a Monarch to suffer any other Passion to equalize himself in that Heart where he has fix'd his Throne. When once enter'd, he becomes the whole Business of our Lives, we Think – we Dream of nothing else, nor have a Wish not inspir'd by him: those who have the Power to apply themselves so seriously to any other Consideration as to forget him, tho' but for a Moment, are but Lovers in Conceit, and have entertain'd Desire but as an agreeable Amusement, which when attended with any Inconveniences, they may without much difficulty shake off. Such a sort of Passion may be properly enough call'd Liking, but falls widely short of Love. Love, is what we can neither resist, expel, nor even alleviate, if we should never so vigorously attempt it; and tho' some have boasted, Thus far will I yield and no farther, they have been convinc'd of the vanity of forming such Resolutions by the Impossibility of keeping them. Liking is a flashy Flame, which is to be kept alive only by ease and delight. Love needs not this fewel to maintain its Fire, it survives in Absence, and Disappointments,

it endures, unchill'd, the wintry Blasts of cold Indifference and Neglect, and continues its Blaze, even in a storm of Hatred and Ingratitude, and Reason, Pride, or a just sensibility of conscious Worth, in vain Oppose it. Liking, plays gayly round, feeds on the Sweets in gross, but is wholly insensible of the Thorns which guard the inner, and more refin'd Delicacies of Desire, and can consequently give neither Pain, nor Pleasure in any superlative degree. Love creates intollerable Torments! unspeakable Joys! raises us to the highest Heaven of Happiness, or sinks us to the lowest Hell of Misery.

(III, 4–5)

In practice, Haywood's presentation of love is more varied than this manifesto indicates, but the ideal of resistance to the normal and the ordinary (mere "liking") is the key to her fiction, which presents a burning intensity and inexhaustible variety as the implicit corrections to a static norm, and which invokes the compulsions of an irresistible fate ("what we can neither resist, expel, nor even alleviate") as the only transcendence available in the deeply pragmatic, the wholly secular world, as it happens, that is the background to her fictional universe. Even in those few novellas where Haywood descends to familiar settings and more or less plausible (if always melodramatic and sensational) events, this same psychosexual fullness persists and doubtless points to a boredom and emptiness in leisured readers' lives.

A revealing instance of fullness and variety is the three-part novel entitled *Idalia: or, The Unfortunate Mistress* (1723).[32] In its opening pages, *Idalia* pretends to be a cautionary tale, warning readers about the dangers of excessive "Spirit" in a young girl, whether such by nature or spoiled by doting parents so that she is "unable to endure Controul, disdainful of Advice, obstinate and peremptory in following her own Will to what Extremes soever it led her."[33] But the heroine's headstrong quality is only the trigger for a long and elaborate series of events in which Idalia is harried and hounded from pillar to post, the victim first and foremost of her irresistible beauty ("Imagination cannot form a Face more exquisitely lovely; such Majesty, such Sweetness. ... The least and most careless Motion of her Head or Hand, was sufficient to captivate a Heart." [2]).

Here is a brief précis of the action. When Florez, a youth of inferior status, makes advances, Idalia encourages him and her father banishes him from the house. But Florez's patron, Don Ferdinand – although we are in Venice everyone has vaguely Spanish names! – takes his place at an assignation and Idalia is undone. But with her father in pursuit the lovers fly to the house of Don Henriquez, who takes her to Padua and is (of course) smitten in spite of his engagement to Laura. Henriquez refuses to surrender Idalia to his friend, and he and Ferdinand kill each other in a duel. News of the event is brought to Idalia by Henriquez's brother, Don Myrtano, who instantly declares his own love which she returns but holds out this time for marriage. An anonymous letter informs her that Myrtano is married, and Idalia leaves for Verona, hoping to enter a convent. On the road her guide threatens to kill her but quickly relents and takes her to a rural retreat and agrees to inform her father in Venice of her whereabouts. Alarmed, however, by the guide's passionate admiration for her, Idalia escapes on foot and goes to Ancona, taking ship there for Naples. She is about to be raped by the ship's captain when a Barbary pirate overwhelms the crew, and she finds herself the privileged captive of Abdomar and his bride, the Princess Bellraiza, who recount their own story of unsanctioned love which has driven them to piracy. When the pirate ship is suddenly wrecked and all aboard seem to perish, Idalia is preserved, "reserv'd to know much more and greater Ills than yet she had endur'd" (106). Saved by a coastal dweller, she sells the diamonds that she luckily took with her and sets off for Rome dressed in man's clothing, but on the way robbers beat her and leave her for dead. Found by Antonia who falls in love with this youth, Idalia is nursed back to health only to discover to her horror that Antonia is married to Myrtano, who recognizes her and becomes her lover. After Antonia tries to poison everyone, the Pope intervenes and orders the lovers never to see each other again. Idalia sees Florez in the street and arranges an assignation with him so that she can avenge herself on this source of all her troubles. But her invitation has been taken to Myrtano, and Idalia stabs him to death. When she realizes her mistake, she plunges the dagger into her own heart.

Unrelentingly inventive in its sequence of calamities for Idalia, the novel overbalances this tide of onrushing incidents with regular outbursts of emotional and erotic intensity, operatic moments of crisis, surging and swelling rehearsals of the formulas of sex and pathos. In fact, the incidents that I have summarized are quickly sketched and lightly told, and most of the space in the text is devoted to renderings of these high-pitched elaborations of extremity. Such unbalanced alternation is inevitable, since the novel's disasters are contrived to elicit its moments of operatic intensities. But the narrative rhythm also points to a crude version of what the later and more sophisticated amatory fiction from mid-century on will seek to evoke as the paradoxical but enabling relationship between an oppressive external social world and the compensatory and potentially liberating subjectivity it provokes, if not for the people on the page then for those perusing it. Idalia herself projects an interesting incoherence, at once an opportunity for cautionary lessons about the dangers of female vanity and an eloquent enunciator of high heroic female virtue. As Haywood herself remarks at one point, incoherence and inconsistency are Idalia's strengths as a character; she needs them to survive for as long as she does. The reader's pleasure, after all, comes first, and Haywood is profoundly opportunistic and even improvisatory as a narrator in her presentation of character. Thus, as Idalia thinks about her ravisher, Ferdinand, and waits for the eager Henriquez to return to her, she weighs the two suitors and concludes that marriage to Henriquez will repair her reputation. Haywood apologizes for her heroine's shallowness:

> I doubt not but the Reader will be pretty much surpris'd to find she could so easily be brought from one Extreme to another; and that she, who but a few Days before, was all Despair and Rage, was already grown so temperate and calm: But there was a happy Instability in this Lady's Nature, which prevented her from regretting any Thing for a long Time together; and it was this Disposition which carry'd her thro a Sea of innumerable Troubles, each of which would have been sufficient to have overwhelm'd another Woman.
>
> (35–36)

In Haywood's revision of the amatory novel, instability of character licenses variety of incident and intensity of episode, and the mercurial Idalia (an extreme case, to be sure) acquires precisely in her inconsistency the ego strength to survive and experience a typical moment of stress like this when she realizes that Antonia's husband is her own Don Myrtano:

> how in an Instant, was all the Sedateness she had assum'd change'd into Confusion, Shame, Horror, Distraction, when the Moment they enter'd the Room she saw the Husband of Antonia was no other than Myrtano! What Words can represent, what Heart can conceive what hers endured at this so unexpected, so shocking a View! A Thousand Furies all at once possess'd her, chill Fear and burning Rage, wild Jealousy and mad Despair, and Thought-disjointing Amazement, with all the black Ideas they could raise, crow[d]ed into her Soul. – Of all the surprising Accidents of her unhappy Life, nothing is

more to be wondered at, than that she survived this dreadful Moment, or at least did not by some Extravagance discover both her Sex, and the Cause of her Distraction: But though her Eyes shot perfect Fires, and seem'd to start from forth their glowing Orbs, – her Lips trembled, her Hair stood an [sic] End as though some Spectre had met her Sight, and every Limb was shook with inward Agonies, yet she neither spoke nor acted any Thing which could give the Standers-by the liberty of guessing from what Cause the Alteration they beheld had sprung.

(118–119)

Such moments are more theatrical and rhetorical than properly novelistic, as Idalia's emotions are enacted on her face and person as well as in her soul. But thanks to her male disguise, the "Standers-by" cannot read those signs, and Haywood, improbably enough, claims that she remains a private and reserved figure even as for the book's readers she is a thrillingly dramatic public spectacle.

This might be said of all of Haywood's beleaguered heroines, whose sufferings exist within this public and private divide where readers are privy to interior intensities and hidden shames in the bedrooms of the leisured rich. And readers are more like privileged onlookers, not in dialogue with the narrator but accepting her invitation to observe and to feel with the heroine. Thus the voyeuristic thrill is an exclusive view of what is otherwise secret and hidden. The effect is not scandalous exposure of a corrupt social order as in Manley but rather the effacement of the public realm and the restriction of amatory narrative to private, personal, and secret transactions that turn their back, as it were, on the tradition of romance and have nothing at all to do with an aristocratic intertwining of honor, military glory, and amatory fulfillment. Haywood's novellas discard the lingering resonances of romance, and nostalgia and ironic disparagement of the present such as Behn and Manley exploit are exchanged for the focused immediacy of sex and suffering. In her way, then, and in spite of the superficial exoticism of her stories, Haywood in her many novellas promotes the present, the here and the now with a new immediacy.

Notes

1 *Boswell's Life of Johnson*, ed. George Birkbeck Hill and L.F. Powell, 6 vols (Oxford, Clarendon Press, 1964), Vol. II, p. 122.

2 Hester Lynch Piozzi, *Anecdotes of the late Samuel Johnson, LL.D, during the last Twenty Years of his Life*, in *Johnsonian Miscellanies* (New York, Barnes and Noble, 1966; first published 1897), Vol. I, p. 290.

3 Charles Taylor, *Sources of the Self: The Making of the Modern Identity* (Cambridge, MA, Harvard University Press, 1989), p. 23.

4 Taylor, *Sources of the Self*, pp. 13–14.

5 Michael McKeon, *The Origins of the English Novel: 1600–1740* (Baltimore, Johns Hopkins University Press, 1987), p. 21. McKeon insists on "the persistence of romance, both within the novel and concurrently with its rise" (p. 3). What he means by romance is an anti-individualist, communal, and supernaturally informed view of reality. And of course the amatory novella specifically rejects all three of those views.

6 Jane Barker, *Exilius* (London, 1715), Preface. Cited in John Richetti, *Popular Fiction Before Richardson: Narrative Patterns 1700–1739* (Oxford, Clarendon Press, 1969), pp. 231–232.

7 Ros Ballaster, *Seductive Forms: Women's Amatory Fiction from 1684 to 1740* (Oxford, Clarendon Press, 1992), pp.62–63.

8 From a verse "tribute" prefixed to the third edition of Eliza Haywood's collected *Secret Histories, Novels, and Poems* (1732). For a discussion of this poem and of Haywood's work, see Richetti, *Popular Fiction Before Richardson*, pp. 180–183.

9 Ballaster, *Seductive Forms*, p. 40. See also Janet Todd, *The Sign of Angellica: Women, Writing and Fiction, 1660–1800* (New York, Columbia University Press, 1989).

10 Todd, *The Sign of Angellica*, p .83.

11 Ballaster, *Seductive Forms*, pp.110, 113.

12 In 1682, Lady Henrietta Berkeley had eloped with her brother-in-law, Forde, Lord Grey of Werke, who was accused of rape and found guilty by a jury. But the Attorney General dropped the charges soon after. Grey escaped with Lady Henrietta to the Continent, and he was subsequently involved in the Duke of Monmouth's rebellion against James II.

13 See Robert A. Day, *Told in Letters: Epistolary Fiction Before Richardson* (Ann Arbor, MI, University of Michigan Press, 1966), p. 78.

14 Aphra Behn, *Love Letters Between a Nobleman and His Sister*, introduction by Maureen Duffy (Harmondsworth, Penguin/Virago, 1987), p. 28. All further page references in the text are to this edition.

15 See above, note 5.

16 Delarivière Manley, *The New Atalantis*, ed. Rosalind Ballaster (London and New York, Penguin Books, 1991), pp. 5–6. All further page references in the text are to this edition.

17 Scholars have noted that Manley's overheated gossip had a basis in fact. As Patricia Köster puts it, Manley may have felt that "literary truth is more important than historical accuracy," but she "is often quite as accurate as the typical party-biased historian of her own time." Köster finds that Manley is "being faithful to contemporary rumors and presenting pictures of the great as others saw them." *The Novels of Mary Delarivière Manley*, 2 vols, ed. Patricia Köster (Gainesville, FL, Scholars' Facsimiles and Reprints, 1971), Vol. I, p. xxi.

18 In *Nobody's Story: The Vanishing Acts of Women Writers in the Marketplace, 1670–1820* (Berkeley and Los Angeles, University of California Press,

1994), Catherine Gallagher sees Manley as flaunting "the inflationary unreality of her libels" and creating "a narrative persona who admittedly relished scandal" (136).

19 Gallagher, *Nobody's Story*, p.123.

20 J.G.A. Pocock, *Virtue, Commerce, and History* (Cambridge, Cambridge University Press, 1985), pp. 68, 66.

21 J.G.A. Pocock, *The Machiavellian Moment: Florentine Political Thought and the Atlantic Republican Tradition* (Princeton, Princeton University Press, 1975), pp. 486, 487.

22 Manley returned to her autobiography in the fictionalized *Adventures of Rivella* (1714) and tells in more detail there how she was seduced into a bigamous marriage by her cousin, John Manley. But Patricia Köster doubts that she was simply an innocent victim in this affair. *The Novels of Mary Delarivière Manley*, Vol. I, pp. vii–viii.

23 See Lennard Davis, *Factual Fictions: The Origins of the English Novel* (New York, Columbia University Press, 1983).

24 Delarivière Manley, *The Adventures of Lindamira, A Lady of Quality*, ed. Benjamin Boyce (Minneapolis, MN, University of Minnesota Press, 1949), pp. 3, 12.

25 See the reprint in *Popular Fiction by Women: 1660–1730*, ed. Paula R. Backscheider and John J. Richetti (Oxford, Clarendon Press, 1996), pp. 251–252.

26 For a discussion of *Memoirs of a Certain Island*, see Richetti, *Popular Fiction Before Richardson*, pp. 154–167.

27 Eliza Haywood, *The Fatal Secret*, in *Masquerade Novels of Eliza Haywood*, ed. Mary Anne Schofield (Delmar, NY, Scholars' Facsimiles and Reprints, 1986), n.p. Little is known or certain about Eliza Haywood's life, but she was for thirty years (from 1719 to 1749) one of the most prolific and successful producers of fiction on the London literary scene, credited with the authorship of over eighty works, including plays, essays, translations from the French, and over sixty narratives. For a summary of her career and the texts of two of her novellas, *The British Recluse* (1722) and *Fantomina* (1725), see *Popular Fiction by Women: 1660–1730*, pp. 153–154.

28 Sir William Yonge (d. 1755) was a prominent Whig politician and crony of Sir Robert Walpole.

29 Eliza Haywood, *The Rash Resolve: Or, The Untimely Discovery*, introduction by Josephine Grieder (New York, Garland Publishing, 1973), a reprint of the 1724 London edn, p. 33. All further page references in the text are to this edition.

30 With the success of Richardson's and Fielding's novels in the 1740s, Haywood altered her style and narrative methods, producing a number of novels in the new extended moral manner: *The Fortunate Foundlings* (1744), *The History of Miss Betsy Thoughtless* (1751), and *The History of Jemmy and Jenny Jessamy* (1753). See Chapter 6.

31 *Love in Excess* was an exceedingly popular work, reaching a "seventh edition" in the third edition of Haywood's collected *Secret Histories, Novels and Poems*. This quotation is from Part II, pp. 4–5. All further page references in the text are to this edition.

32 Defoe's *Roxana: The Fortunate Mistress* (1724) may well be his counter-state-
   ment to Haywood's hapless heroine, since Roxana is precisely the
   managerial opposite of Idalia's passivity.
33 Eliza Haywood, *Idalia: Or, The Unfortunate Mistress. A Novel In Three Parts*
   (London, 1725; the Third Edition), p. 2. All further page references in the
   text are to this edition.

3

DEFOE

Mapping social totality

Defoe's *The Great Law of Subordination consider'd; Or, The Insolence and Unsufferable Behaviour of Servants in England duly enquir'd into* (1724) offers this description of the state of society:

> the miserable Circumstance of this Country is now such, that, in short, if it goes on, the Poor will be Rulers over the Rich, and the Servants be Governours of their Masters; the *Plebeii* have almost mobb'd the *Patricii*; and as the Commons, in another Case, may be said to be gotten above the Lords, so the Cannaille of this Nation impose Laws upon their Superiors, and begin not only to be troublesome, but in time may be dangerous; in a *word*, Order is inverted, Subordination ceases, and the World seems to stand with the Bottom upward.
>
> (17)[1]

Defoe's narrator, Andrew Moreton, is a naturalized English citizen, a Frenchman explaining to a friend back home the history of England's social problems. The trouble began in the Civil War when Charles's citizen army lacked proper discipline and continued during the Restoration when the custom of drinking healths spread from the upper classes to common folk. The frequent Parliamentary elections since then have been marked by bribery and corruption, and "all those Treatings attended with Excessive Drinking, increased to such a Degree, that in a few Years the Habit of Drunkenness, and the Drinking of Healths … spread by the Example of the Gentlemen to the Tennants, to the common People in the Corporations, to the Servants, and in short, to the whole Body of the People" (61). This behavior is tied to the corrupt customs of their masters, as well as to the "glut of Trade" that enables them to "work but two or three Days in the Week, or till they get Money enough to keep them the rest of the Week, and all the other part of their Time they lie in the Alehouse to spend it" (82). Drinking, swearing, fighting, and whoring, Defoe's common people are both coherent and irrational. Instead of obeying those principles of diligence and frugality that should come naturally, they undermine prosperity by working only enough "to support them in their extravagant Follies and Wickedness, prompt their Vices, and fill them with Pride and Insolence, both against God and Man" (90).

Pawns of history as well as victims of inevitable human weakness, the poor seem to lack any possibility of that individualized self-consciousness that the narrator necessarily claims for himself. Andrew Moreton is crucially disengaged, able not only to understand social relationships but agile enough to move through them, reporting first-hand and from within on their instabilities. Like Defoe's other narrators, he marks shifting social borders and testifies to their permeability by his free movements even as he remarks on the inability of others to achieve a similar freedom. In disguise, he has observed the subversive counter-culture of servants:

> mingl'd in among the Mob of such Fellows as those, who we call Footmen; I have convers'd with them over a Mug of Porter, as they call their Alehouse Beer and Ale; and there how have I heard them boast over their Master's Kindness to them, and how they cou'd do any-thing they pleas'd? that they valued not their Masters a Shilling, and that they durst not be Angry with them; that if they did quarrel, d___ 'em they wou'd be gone, and their Master cou'd not do without 'em.
>
> (261)

Moreton claims that this grousing points to extensive resistance to traditional order, a subversive plebeian culture: "*In a word*, while the Gentlemen in the Parliament House are making Laws to preserve the Game, their own Servants are the greatest *Poachers* in the Country; and under Pretence of killing the Game for their Masters, they make a Property of the Sport, and supply the Hucksters and Carriers with all kinds of Fowls, which the Law forbids them to touch" (274). Such undermining is pervasive, extending to plowmen, carters, husbandmen on the land, and including secret "combinations" of weavers, pump-makers, coachmen, and watermen in London. Moreton's polemic is elastic, and the poor who "govern" in England includes, we may say, anyone who only seems to lack authority. Clearly, what he has in mind is not the spontaneous popular disorder of the eighteenth-century mob but rather a self-consciously dissident and oppositional entity, a modality of resistance to order. Instead of the helpless and feckless masses, Moreton here evokes a dangerously focused counterculture, precisely reversing the effects of laws enacted in Parliament, controlling where they seem to be subservient, cunning and self-possessed as a unit in their oppositional solidarity. Although both aspects of the lower orders disturb Defoe, their conspiracy is truly dangerous, since in his rendering it may be said to replace individual striving with corporate consciousness. Incapable of enlightened selfhood and its profitable moral–economic strategies, able only to respond as a generalized mass to economic and historical forces, the governed become a threatening collective acquiring in mass action the purpose and effect that they lack as individuals.

As a political journalist and an aggressive expositor to the public of what we now call economics, Defoe took from the beginning of his career an explicitly totalizing view of society in order to promote practical measures to make it more efficient and, to some extent, more rational. *An Essay on Projects* (1697), his first published book, is concerned with schemes for national improvement, as the subtitle puts it, with "the means by which the subjects in general may be eased and enriched." Defoe consistently displays in his economic and political journalism an ambition to comprehend something like the whole of society. But his vision was in fact necessarily partial. As the historian Peter Earle points out, Defoe "wrote voluminously on the sections of society which he knew best or whose problems interested him but he never really tried to analyse society as a whole."[2] But Defoe does have recurring moments of totalizing socioeconomic and political vision. His imagination was stirred by what he saw as the grand spectacle of "trade," a socioeconomic sublimity visible in the market system's combination of finely calibrated efficiency and all-encompassing variety. Defoe's *A Tour Thro' the Whole Island of Great Britain* (1724–1726) is punctuated by wonder at the inexhaustible plenitude of modern economic life, with its quantities beyond individual comprehension: the million and a half turkeys driven to London from Suffolk each year, the uncountable number of mackerel caught off the Dorsetshire coast, the hundreds of thousands of sheep sold at the Weyhill fair in Wiltshire, the corn markets at London ("the whole world cannot equal the quantity bought and sold here"), and the seemingly endless lines of ships in the river from London Bridge to Blackwall: "The thing is a kind of infinite, and the parts to be separated from one another in such a description, are so many, that it is hard to know where to begin."[3] Defoe's renderings of this totality naturally involve an observer who comprehends it by preserving a certain distance. Such an overview seems available only to the contemplative outsider, or at least would seem to require the spectatorial posture of the eighteenth-century essayist, a matter in Addison's famous formulation in the *Spectator* of considering the world as a theater, observing the world without having anything to do with it. But in the *Tour* and his other economic journalism, Defoe speaks as a participant, involved in the vast system he evokes, delivering an insider's first-hand experience as the sustaining precondition for his moments of contemplative wonder.

Defoe's perspective on socioeconomic totality thus includes the possibility of meaningful action within it. Within this grand socioeconomic panorama stands the heroic individual whose actions help to produce that totality, pre-eminently the tradesman, who is in the process of transforming English society and reinvigorating the ruling class. "How are the antient families worn out by time and family misfortunes," he wrote in 1725, "and the estates possess'd by a new race of tradesmen grown up into families of gentry and establish'd by the immense wealth gain'd, as I may say, behind the counter; that is, in the shop, the warehouse and the compting-house? How are the sons of tradesmen rank'd among the prime of the gentry?"[4] And even when the tradesman is defeated, his unfailing energies can bring him to the top again. "No condition," Defoe insists, "is so low or so despicable in a tradesman, but he may with diligence and application recover it." A force of nature, the tradesman "rolls about the world like a snowball, always gathering more, always increasing, till he comes to a magnitude sufficient to exist of himself, and then he boldly shews himself in the same orbit, in which he first shin'd."[5] Defoe's own experience bears out only part of this evocation of the heroic merchant. Bankrupt twice for substantial sums, he continued to struggle financially all his life and, in his transformation into a journalist and covert political agent and propagandist for opposing factions, exemplified the difficult, specifically social relationships that he renders in his fiction. The comprehensive vision of society that Defoe offers in his economic journalism inevitably breaks down in his life and in his fiction, giving way to the experience of particular and personal patron–client relationships in which society appears not as a grand and all-embracing totality but is experienced necessarily from within as a set of pressing local problems. Defoe was in his lifetime a servant of various aristocratic masters, a client begging for grace and favor much of the time.[6] In practice rather than from the enthusiastic generalizing heights of theory, Defoe's vantage point on social experience is internal, partial and pragmatic, an insider's perspective, sometimes subversive and manipulative, sometimes deeply and confusingly implicated.

55

Pseudo-autobiographies such as Defoe produced in the 1720s were clearly designed to appeal in their immediacy to a wider audience than perhaps more overtly fictional and generalizing third-person narratives would have reached. Yet as they appear in Defoe's fictions, social relationships are not mastered in the long run by retrospective knowledge. Defoe's autobiographers tend to negate the potentially totalizing force of society by rendering it from the point of view of their defensive participation within it as a series of discrete and essentially discontinuous moments. Defoe's narratives offer rough paradigms for the practice of fiction through most of the century: they both celebrate and deplore an aggressive self-seeking, dramatizing a social context for individual action that inhibits and thereby provokes it. His narratives ratify myths of individual agency and action, and some of them also record something like the fear of sociohistorical necessity and lower-class intransigence that his polemical writing so copiously displays. The curiously monological quality of Defoe's narratives is thereby a function of that same anxiety, as his garrulous autobiographers in effect silence other possible voices and deny the oppositional dialect of the lower orders in recording only their own distinctively singular idiolects, self-generated and unique, developed not within the determining or at least limiting contexts of social interaction but by the literary institutions and conventions that cooperate to shape Defoe's narrative mimicry of socially marginal individuals. Literature and literary tradition, even the diluted picaresque and spiritual autobiography out of which Defoe fashions his narratives, are institutions that work to defuse the potentially disturbing individuality of his narrators. Moll Flanders is a lower-class exception who proves the social rule, and it is the spotlight of literary convention as Defoe refocuses it that isolates her from a surrounding obscurity and muteness and allows her to articulate a voice and therefore a consciousness wholly exceptional. The documentary surface of Defoe's case histories ratifies as genuine these exceptional individuals, whose extraordinary status both transcends and verifies those ordinary circumstances from which they spring. The documentary force of these narratives is, to a large extent, an effect of the detached freedom of the narrative voice, which also at the same time insists on its location within specific social experience, its derivation from the circumstances it simultaneously documents and transcends.

On the one hand, as Ian Watt says, novels like Defoe's depend upon the value that society places on each and every individual so that daily life at its most trivial acquires serious significance.[7] On the other hand, Defoe's novels argue powerfully for the inherent insignificance and merely private nature of individual actors, whose claim to our attention is their miraculous survival in the face of an external world that is, normally, inescapably determining. His narrators exist as responses (sometimes inventive ones, to be sure) to the stimuli of material circumstances. Intensely present individuals, they are at the same time recurring testimony to a larger, repressive reality that produces them and constantly threatens to reabsorb them as simply part of the faceless masses all around them.

Of all Defoe's characters, Colonel Jack has the most varied career. The book's title page sketches crudely the broad historical sweep of his career: *The History and Remarkable Life of The Truly Honourable Col. Jacque commonly call'd Col. Jack, who was born a gentleman, put 'prentice to a pickpocket, was six and twenty years a thief, and then kidnapp'd to Virginia. Came back a merchant, married four wives ... went into the wars, behav'd bravely, got preferment, was made Colonel of a regiment, came over, and fled with the Chevalier, and is now abroad compleating a life of wonders, and resolves to dye a General* (1722). This wide-eyed summary is in fact untrue in its simple exuberance to the book's complex evocation of experience. Defoe renders Jack's early days as a street urchin and teenage hoodlum with rare psychological sensitivity. Told by the old woman who raises him that he is the bastard son of a gentleman, Jack recalls his sense of his special destiny, manifest especially in two characteristics: intellectual curiosity and moral sensitivity. "I was always upon the Inquiry, asking Questions of things done in Publick as well as in Private," he remembers, and thus became "a kind of an Historian," illiterate but able to "give a tollerable Account of what had been done, and of what was then a doing in the World."[8] Jack has a "strange kind of uninstructed Conscience" (55) that makes him, at least as he remembers it, less than a full participant in his criminal subculture. He has an awareness at once moral and economic, a reverence for the mysterious documents of the mercantile world that intertwines with his reluctance to hurt others. So he cannot bring himself to destroy the "Bills and Papers" of the merchants whose pockets they pick: "things that would do them a great deal of hurt, and do me no good; and I was so Tormented about it, that I could not rest Night or Day, while I made the People easie, from whom the things were taken" (55). Taken before a Justice, his "Heart was full of Terror and Guilt" (77); hearing that his comrade, Will, is in Newgate, Jack's "very Joints trembl'd" and his "Head run upon nothing but *Newgate*, and the Gallows, and being Hang'd; which I said I deserv'd, if it were for nothing but taking that two and twenty Shillings from the poor old Nurse" (75). Placed at the margins of society, Jack validates society's efficient centrality by the intensity of his defensive interior life, by the energy and variety of his attempts to avoid its power, and in the end by his internalization and recapitulation of its organizing principles. Paradoxically, Jack acquires a complex selfhood (as opposed to a merely sociological identity as street urchin or the literary role of picaro-adventurer) by articulating a relationship with the comprehensive social structure exemplified in the terrifying penal system. In so doing Jack testifies to the effectiveness of that system as a deterrent to crime, although the total lack of self-consciousness in his comrades illustrates just the opposite effect of that system.

As a young criminal, Jack experiences the British model of power and social control and that model is recapitulated in Jack's own experience, made a part of his own ultimate reformation as an indentured servant in Maryland, where he is next an overseer and then a plantation slave master. Jack understands that the unsystematic and *ad hoc* suppression of the black slaves is inefficient; merely particularized and reactive, such management lacks the calculated purpose and long-range effectiveness of the policy that Jack devises.

> But I began to see at the same time, that this Brutal temper of the *Negroes* was not rightly manag'd; that they did not take the best course with them, to make them sensible, either of Mercy, or Punishment; and it was Evident to me, that even the worst of those tempers might be brought to a Compliance, without the Lash, or at least without so much of it, as they generally Inflicted.
>
> (128–129)

Jack the managerial innovator is an overseer who develops a mode of punishment for his master's slaves whereby simple brutality is replaced by psychological manipulation: Jack's threats to recalcitrant slaves of terrible punishment are tempered by the possibility of mercy from above, from the "Great Master" Jack serves.

Such terrorizing resembles in its workings the brutal strategy behind the penal code that Jack has experienced. Jack expresses in America what he may be said to have internalized as an untutored and terrified street urchin, an appreciation of the ways in which institutions regulate their members. In Maryland, Jack becomes the perfect exporter of social forms, for he successfully institutionalizes the controlling threat of punishment that has shaped his life. Defoe's brilliant insight in the sequence that stretches from Jack's urchin days to plantation overseer is that psychological development, such as we might identify it, takes place within ideology and indeed as a response to ideology. Jack experiences the tangled relationships between an untutored sense of self and the fearful positioning in a network of patronage relationships that provides opportunities for expression and establishment. To be sure, there is much more to *Colonel Jack* than this transition from marginalized thief to colonial manager, and Jack's subsequent career as Jacobite adventurer and illegal trader in the Spanish Caribbean complicates his personality considerably, and in the somewhat forced variety that makes Jack a soldier in European wars and a much-married man, his career also dissipates the implicit coherence I have outlined. Or perhaps Defoe's audience, as he envisioned it, wanted more than the psychosocial coherence that we treasure in novelistic character.

Moll Flanders (1722) is more unified in its rendering of an implicit social coherence. Like Jack, she derives her identity from an avoidance of the inevitability of her circumstances. Looking back and evoking her distinctive subjectivity, Moll renders her introspective self-consciousness as a means of separation from actuality. From her early days at Colchester, Moll resembles Jack in her self-defining apartness, but she is more quickly absorbed as an upper servant and mistress and then as a wife into the middle-class family that adopts her. Moll acquires a greater ease than Jack and learns rather quickly the tricks of self-preservation and plausible self-invention, defining herself as someone who learns quickly to analyze social possibility in generalized terms and to situate herself accordingly. Moll surveys the sexual field after her second husband leaves her: "They, I observe insult us mightily, with telling us of the Number of Women; that the Wars and the Sea, and Trade, and other Incidents have carried the Men so much away, that there is no Proportion between the Numbers of the Sexes; and therefore the Women have the Disadvantage; but I am far from Granting that the Number of the Women is so great, or the Number of the Men so small."[9] The problem, says Moll, lies rather in the limited number of men "fit for a Woman to venture upon." Moll thus begins her career with a cynical sense of the fluidity or indeed the irrelevance of society's categories.

As a female con artist and pickpocket–shoplifter, Moll's *modus operandi* is social impersonation. However, Moll makes crucial errors of social judgment: not only does her (second) tradesman husband prove feckless, but the Irish gentleman she marries later turns out to be a fortune-hunter and the Virginia planter she marries is none other than her brother. Of course, this last is hardly an error of judgment; Moll seems trapped by an inscrutable, unavoidable pattern of enclosing coincidence. Right next to her exuberant chronicle of self-improvisation within the unpredictable, linear sequentiality of her life is a circular pattern of fatality and necessity, exemplified by her inadvertent return to her biological family in Virginia, just when she thought she was getting as far away as possible from her origins. So, too, her career as the most successful thief of her day (the "greatest Artist of my time" (214)) leads inevitably back to her Newgate origins. Yet Moll hardly prepares us for that development. In narrating the relationships that make up her varied life, she ruthlessly renders them in economic terms and shows how she managed them by shrewd sexual liaisons and opportunistic crime. The book has its stabilizing center in just that economic analysis, which reduces and particularizes, tracking (in a proto-cinematic sense) from crowded social possibility and generality to focus on individual motives and solutions within that larger and constantly shifting scene. The force of the individualized narrative perspective is such that the camera looks outward from itself, as it were, at an external scene that appears increasingly fragmentary and foreign next to the emerging wholeness and familiarity of the protagonist.

Moll locates herself within a system of causes, variously social, economic, psychological, and even providential, that point to something like a controlling totality. But the parts do not quite add up to that whole, since these moments of destiny are at one and the same time opportunities for escape and expansion in which experience promotes a more liberating mode whereby necessity becomes redefined as imperfectly confining and serves to release hitherto unexplored resources in the self. Yet Defoe dramatizes a coherence larger than the sum of Moll's individual transactions, and that underlying unity is present in part through the pattern of coincidences that appears as the narrative unfolds. So there is in the narrative a final turn to the screw that evokes something like a social totality. *Moll Flanders* rehearses the contradiction that the free, intensely unique individual is somehow the result of an exactly rendered and accumulating necessity, a social totality partly obscured by the energy and inconsistency of Moll's autobiographical retrospection. Consider Moll's seduction by the elder brother in the family at Colchester. Innocent and inexperienced, she is surprised by the desires he arouses in her but even more flustered by the discovery of the eroticized force of more money than she has ever seen. Young Moll, interloper in the upper middle-class house in Colchester, speaks instinctively in these scenes with her body as the elder brother fires her blood with ardent kisses and declarations: "my heart spoke as plain as a voice, that I liked it; nay, whenever he said, I am in Love with you, my Blushes plainly reply'd, 'would you were, Sir'" (22). After her lover tumbles her on the bed, he gives her five guineas: "I was more confounded with the money than I was before with the love, and began to be so elevated that I scarce knew the ground I stood on" (23–24). Moll can only look back and wonder at her own inability then to "think," for she "thought of nothing, but the fine Words, and the Gold" (25). The elder brother's person *and* his gold ("I spent whole hours in looking upon it; I told the Guineas over and over a thousand times a Day"(26)) intertwine sexual and social necessity, so that in Moll's rendering sexual and social movement are reciprocally engulfing, one cooperating with the other. Moll, of course, rushes by these implications, translating this unifying cooperation of socioeconomic and sexual desire into a missed and misunderstood opportunity. But she understands as she looks back that she and her seducer were both in their own way unaware of the other's true position, unable to read accurately the motives that Moll retrospectively sees as given so obviously by a supervising network of socioeconomic relationships: "Nothing was ever so stupid on both Sides, had I acted as became me, and resisted as Vertue and Honour requir'd, this Gentleman had either Desisted his Attacks, finding no room to expect the Accomplishment of his Design, or had made fair, and honourable Proposals of Marriage; in which Case, whoever had blam'd him, no Body could have blam'd me"(25–26).

Such moments are usually admired for their psychological acuity; the heroine speaks of her innocent youth in just the way we would expect from a cynical old veteran of the sexual wars. One can also say that such moments extend the psychological by giving it a social context and by endowing old Moll with a retrospective wisdom that encompasses social as well as personal knowledge. Moll recounts both her immersion in complex circumstances and her acquired sense of how to manage a tactical apartness from them. In her formal capacity as narrator, Moll is forced to balance her character's instinctive tactical awareness against an inescapable fate that she knows looms constantly and is only delayed rather than avoided by such maneuvers. Indeed, by their variety and inventiveness these moves point to a supervising totality, a fate merely postponed. Retrospective narration like hers produces a knowledge of experience by treating it as both freely chosen or at least freely adaptive behavior and fatefully circumscribed and fully determined.

Such contradiction is richly enacted in the climax of the narrative in Newgate. In her rendering, the prison is exactly what she has hitherto evaded: the massive, inexorable force of psychosocial determinants. Newgate implicitly resolves the paradox of Moll's free but fated movement, forcing her to change her conception of her career from clever improvisation to inevitable fate: "It seem'd to me that I was hurried on by an inevitable and unseen Fate to this Day of Misery ... that I was come to the last hour of my life and of my wickedness together. These things pour'd themselves in upon my Thoughts, in a confus'd manner, and left me overwhelm'd with Melancholy and Despair" (274). Moll's recourse to intensely figurative language is unique here. For once, the scene controls her discourse and resists the mapping of contours that has been her signature, as in the rendering of the London streets, for example, in her days as a thief. Defoe's peculiar strength as a narrator fits Moll's personality: he renders the relationships of persons and objects rather than their integrity and depth as individual substances. For Defoe the political analyst, personal identity is equivalent to position and relationship. But all this changes, at least temporarily, in Newgate, where shifting surfaces yield to stasis and the experience of depth. Moll renders the prison in graphic terms: "the hellish Noise, the Roaring, Swearing and Clamour, the Stench and Nastiness, and all the dreadful croud of Afflicting things that I saw there" (274). Newgate's effects on Moll provoke the novel's single most metaphorical passage:

> Like the Waters in the Caveties, and Hollows of Mountains, which petrifies and turns into Stone whatever they are suffer'd to drop upon; so the continual Conversing with such a crew of Hell-Hounds as I was with had the same common Operation upon me, as upon other People, I degenerated into Stone; I turn'd first Stupid and Senseless, then Brutish and thoughtless, and at last raving Mad as any of them were; and in short, I became as naturally pleas'd and easie with the Place, as if indeed I had been Born there.
>
> (278)

At least for the moment, Moll is completely absorbed by environment, the hitherto self-defining distance between herself and her social relationships canceled by a natural (that is, a social) force. If we think back to Moll's sexual initiation by the elder brother at Colchester, there is an inevitability in this equation of the force of a social institution like Newgate and the transforming power of nature. In the earlier scene, socioeconomic determinants (summed up in the thrilling guineas) are absorbed by the natural, compulsive inevitability of sexual desire. Invoking the natural as an ultimate explanatory frame of reference is an ideological strategy for neutralizing the threatening, alienated objectivity of social institutions by shifting their origins to a universalized interiority. But Newgate can hardly be rendered as just an intense interior experience. Moll insists that she is literally transformed by the place. She becomes just like her brutish fellow prisoners, "a meer *Newgate-Bird*, as Wicked and as Outragious as any of them," but she also becomes someone else, "no more the same thing that I had been, than if I had never been otherwise than what I was now" (279). Newgate as a concrete instance of social totality effectively replaces Moll, and that obliteration leads in due course to a newly distinct self, defined now by *opposition* rather than marginalized or subversive participation.

Paradoxically, Moll becomes pure object here but also at last an even more powerful and coherently self-conscious subject. Up to now, we may say, what Moll's narrative patches together is a fitful local necessity, the intermittent difficulties of survival and the varied obstacles to prosperity. Both as locale and as narrative climax, Newgate offers a pre-existent and self-sufficient system that functions independently and to whose laws she must inevitably conform. But she evades the prison's monumental necessity by slowly turning it into a means of narrative coherence, transforming it from the embodiment of social inevitability for born thieves like her to a locale where her personality acquires a desperate coherence and sharp self-definition in opposition to the now visible determining force of state regulation. In place of the scattered, improvised resistance to a diffuse and inefficient social necessity, Newgate forces her by its totalizing transformation to muster a countervailing transformation.

Moll begins to recover when she sees her Lancashire husband, now a famous highwayman captured at last. As she observes him enter the prison, her sense of her ultimate responsibility for his fate restores her abhorrence of Newgate and something like her old identity. She is restored within an appropriated version of totality, as she constructs a coherence modeled on the fateful ordering that Newgate enforces. She sees Jemy and suddenly perceives a coherent network of guilt and responsibility in her past. Within the totalizing precincts of Newgate, where scattered self-inventiveness has been forced to give way to external social determination, Moll is moved to discover a new and coherent approach to self-understanding. Newgate's confinement brings the experience of the inescapable connection between social circumstances and personality and points implicitly as the resolution of Moll's career to a larger and indeed comprehensive social inevitability.

Moll's repentance, the "freedom of discourse" to which the minister leads her, enables her for the first time in her life to tell her story, indeed to have a coherent story to tell. "In a word, I gave him an abridgement of this whole History; I gave him the Picture of my Conduct for 50 Years in Miniature" (288). Having experienced Newgate, having in fact become indistinguishable from it, Moll can now experience a subjectivity conscious of its relationship to the necessity that Newgate embodies. She is, as she herself says, restored to thinking: "My Temper was touch'd before, the harden'd, wretch'd boldness of Spirit which I had acquir'd in the Prison abated, and conscious Guilt began to flow in upon my Mind. In short, I began to think, and to think is one real advance from Hell to Heaven. All that Hellish, harden'd state and temper of soul ... is but a deprivation of Thought; he that is restored to his Power of thinking, is restored to himself" (281).

But what possible restoration does Moll have in mind? Moll's redeemed state is, in effect, a new identity, defined and crystallized within Newgate's complex of determining relationships. Moll constructs a moralized individuality that is dialectically related to the impersonality that she has so profoundly experienced. In response to Newgate's alienated objectivity and impersonal subordination of individuals to the pattern of judicial retribution, Moll discovers in her past a personal connection with other subjects like Jemy and replaces secular conviction and impersonal punishment with personal guilt and responsibility as she shifts the defining acts of her narrative from the violation of external statutes to private offenses against God and particular men. In the Newgate episode of *Moll Flanders*, Defoe coherently dramatizes as nowhere else in his fiction, I think, a sense of a determining social totality and something of a solution to the problem that it poses for self-understanding. Moll's new mode of self-apprehension accomplishes what is logically impossible but historically both necessary and inevitable in the emergence of the novel; it constructs a free subject wholly implicated in a determining objectivity but deriving its freedom from an intense apprehension of that surrounding objective world. Next to the improbably resilient Moll who enters the prison, this character has a self-conscious psychological density and coherence that are produced or at least provoked by the experience of social totality. This sequence in *Moll Flanders* thus predicts the main direction that the novel will take in the nineteenth century. As society is increasingly experienced as mysteriously all-encompassing in its determinations, novelistic representation will seek to imagine a compensating richness of subjectivity whereby individuals can extract a version of freedom precisely from the novel's rendering of a nearly suffocating social and historical necessity. Inevitably, such freedom will take place in various sorts of richly imagined guilty subjectivities (like Moll's) that operate as antidotes to a world that seems to lack such meaning.

As some critics have argued, however, the only necessity Defoe believed in was the ultimately resolving force of divine Providence, and the controlling generic expectation for contemporary readers of his fiction was to a large extent defined by spiritual autobiography.[10] But in his voluminous political journalism, Defoe sought to teach his readers about secular history and what England could do to control it. For him, obviously, these two forms of necessity were not separate but complementary ways of understanding destiny, although the providential in his historical and political writing is something of an imponderable last instance rather than an active and visible force. His fictionalized narrators, Crusoe for one, do argue strenuously for "particular" providences, but they thus highlight the difficulty of understanding such operations. In two of his novels, as I see it, Defoe dramatizes an implicit subordination of simplifying providential explanation to the complications wrought by secular energies and material circumstances. Considered together, *Robinson Crusoe* (1719) and *Roxana* (1724), Defoe's first and last fictions, represent diametrically opposing attempts to solve the unique dilemma posed by his intensely individualized renderings of character. Both books record the exuberance of masterful social movement as well as the deep anxiety that accompanies the acquisition of such power. Superficially, the source of that anxiety for both of these figures is their violation of traditional notions that subordinate the individual to a divinely instituted moral order. In practice, however, each of them may be said to exemplify the Mandevillean pattern whereby individual and selfish action (vice) produces social benefits – an increase in the production of goods and services, a contribution to the accumulation and circulation of wealth that constitutes an economically healthy society (as Defoe would have defined it).

In their different ways, Crusoe and Roxana grasp the nettle of necessity and pluck the flower of freedom. But their accompanying guilt and anxiety are also an index of Defoe's grasp of a situation where individual desire and its satisfaction dramatize the paradox of social being. Such self-consciousness exists in those relationships to others and to institutions that produce the economic entity that Mandeville describes, so that the intense guilt that Crusoe and Roxana project is a means of substituting authentic immediacy for the radically mediated existence provided within social being. The novel, as it emerges in the early eighteenth century, potentially promises unmediated existence of an unprecedented fullness, but in these two narratives such being is constructed and realized precisely in its interactions with social process. Identity is narrated as if it were a matter of local adaptation to shifting circumstances even as it is understood by the characters as a matter of conformity to general moral principles that exist independently of those circumstances. Psycho-moral turbulence such as these novels place at their centers is, thus, an assertion of immediacy and coherence, of individuals somehow longing for a being that is not constituted within social relationships even as they station themselves inside those relationships and demonstrate, paradoxically, that self and society are nothing less than inextricable.

In the transition from his first to his last novel, Defoe stages a version of the debate about the proper subject for serious fiction that was taking place within English narrative in the first half of the eighteenth century: a rivalry for the attention of sober readers between the novel of external and inevitably masculine exotic adventure and the novel of domestic happenings, of courtship and (often) of turbulent female inte-riority. In *Dreams of Adventure, Deeds of Empire*, Martin Green describes a "moral revolution" that "redirected spiritual intensity toward home life, marriage, and sex; away from older objects of devotion, like the litur-gical life of the church, and the cults of the aristomilitary caste."[11] Green sees this revolution as the work of the "merchant caste" that in the eighteenth century appropriated literature and culture. His thesis highlights the lingering controversy about the novel's proper subject matter. The adventure novel is relegated by the early nineteenth century to the nursery, as simplified and expurgated versions of *Robinson Crusoe* and *Gulliver's Travels* become children's classics. That transformation, in the case of Defoe's tale, testifies to its rendition of an apparently no longer acceptable (dismissed as implausible) freedom and individualized power, as well as to its essentially metaphoric and mythic rendering of social relationships.

And yet Green's thesis oversimplifies, since the tale of adventure in the early eighteenth century features a good deal of self-examination and interiority for its protagonists. *Robinson Crusoe* itself is obviously not a pure adventure story, since the external and exotic locale is radically domesticated and in due course subordinated to Crusoe's interior struggle for self-understanding and self-justification. *Roxana* is quite another matter, for there I think Defoe himself clearly recognized in the confusion of the novel's last part that he had gone too far in imagining social relationships uncomfortably close to their home truth, without metaphor or myth. Roxana's field of action is the exactly rendered socioeconomic battlegrounds of England and Europe, not the exotic, far-flung locales of Crusoe's adventures. In negating the special, fright-eningly subversive (and matter-of-fact) consciousness of his heroine by placing her self-serving energies within an exceedingly frank psycho-sexual case history, Defoe anticipates with special force the development of the domestic novel in which the interior life and the affections and alliances that it generates become the realm of meaningful human action and change.

Robinson Crusoe also has an interior life. He embodies a culturally resonant resourcefulness as he is forced into elaborate feats of survival, domesticating his island and reconciling himself to its dreadful solitude. Rejecting at the beginning of his story the traditional submission to circumstances urged on him by his old father and launching out onto the boundless seas of economic individualism, Crusoe eventually re-establishes patron–client relations on his island and draws boundaries such as he had earlier denied. But psychological survival in absolute solitude is as difficult as physical maintenance in a wilderness, and the narrative is a memorably shrewd balance of two kinds of self-definition. In rendering that balance of inner and outer, *Robinson Crusoe* is an alle-gory of modern individualism that sketches its achievements and its accompanying deep anxieties. Although the story no doubt had that dimension for many a contemporary reader who saw it through the filters of spiritual autobiography that Crusoe himself repeatedly inserts, what is at stake is a more immediate process whereby Crusoe projects an intensified version of social relationships and the individual identity that they sustain or cancel. Extended fictions like *Robinson Crusoe* satisfy their implicit audience by performing experiments in how sociability might work in rarefied but plausible situations.

Crusoe's enforced solitude on the island inspires both a fear of society and a profound longing for the company of others. His coher-ence as an individual is worked out in this double relationship to society (in the older sense of the company of others), and he may be said to enact on his island both a longing for communal integration and a productively fearful competitive separation from others that defines the paradoxical location of the newly visible bourgeois individual. *Robinson Crusoe* seems, at first glance, to promote a simple, heroic version of that individualism in Crusoe the domesticator of the wilderness and founder of what eventually becomes a settlement in which cannibals, Spaniards, and English mutineers are absorbed by his reconciling colonialist authority.[12] But the book gives as much space and much more impor-tance to Crusoe's inner turmoil, to the psychological effects of a longing for human contact and a terror of unknown others against whom the building of fortified shelter and mastering of the environment are defensive reactions. The realm of sociohistorical relationships, the material and concrete world, is radically contingent and even at times downright threatening, rather like Moll's Newgate in its resistance to human control and understanding. Crusoe's narrative is a record in large measure of the resistance of that realm to comprehension and organization. He places its randomness and unpredictability next to divine pattern, such as he claims to have discovered so painfully in his isolation, where various intuitions, what Crusoe often calls "secret hints and notices of danger," enable him to make his way through the mine fields of this external world.[13] In other words, his ultimately coherent spiritual autobiography is produced in fruitful opposition to that intractably incoherent sphere of experience; providential pattern imposes itself miraculously and cryptically on the randomness of the natural world that Crusoe experiences and struggles to master, although such hidden divine ordering is revealed only to the trained and tested retrospection of the autobiographer.

Crusoe experiences the difficult transition from solitude to society very slowly, even if the discovery of the single footprint is a sudden revelation for him of the problem of society in all its ambiguity. One day, as Crusoe remembers it, he "was exceedingly surprized with the print of a man's naked foot on the shore, which was very plain to be seen in the sand. I stood like one thunder-struck, or as if I had seen an apparition" (162). Bewildered and terrified, Crusoe flees: "looking behind me at every two or three steps, mistaking every bush and tree, and fancying every stump at a distance to be a man; nor is it possible to describe how many various shapes affrighted imagination represented things to me in, how many wild ideas were found every moment in my fancy, and what strange unaccountable whimsies came into my thoughts by the way" (162). Crusoe is especially struck by the irony of the situation: longing for human company, so "that to have seen one of my own species would have seemed to me a raising from death to life," he is now "ready to sink into the ground at but the shadow or silent appearance of a man's having set his foot in the island" (164). Fear aside, the lesson that Crusoe underlines as he recalls this key incident is the disturbing fragility of his hard-won internal stability: "How strange a chequer work of providence is the life of man! and by what secret differing springs are the affections hurry'd about as differing circumstances present!" (164). Despite his faith in an overseeing providential order, Crusoe's interior life now appears to him as mysterious and chaotic as its external provocations, and the narrative turns quite clearly here into his attempt to stabilize both the external world and his moral–psychological responses to it. There is an accompanying shift in the tempo of the narrative after the discovery of the footprint, as Crusoe moves from patient natural observation and the trial and error of animal husbandry and crop management to a more intense focus on multiple possibilities generated by his own delusions and hallucinations. After solving the mystery of the footprint when he observes the remains of a cannibal feast, Crusoe examines his own fears and revulsions and eventually articulates as his final response to those feelings a sophisticated anthropological and historical relativism that causes him to reject his own plans to obliterate the cannibals as they sit down to their odious feasting.

Simple prudence and religious common sense join with this intellectual examination to produce a temporary serenity.

But extreme moral revulsion cancels moderate rationality the next time he observes a group of cannibals, and Crusoe is "so filled with indignation at the sight" that he falls into "the murthering humor" and is tormented by rage and fear. At last, Crusoe comes to a resolution of this potentially interminable alternation of his moods by crossing the bridge from self-examination that seeks to construct stability to tactical analysis and an alert readiness to contingency. Prompted by a dream in which he captures a man whom the cannibals were about to eat, Crusoe decides to place himself in readiness for that possibility, "to put my self upon the watch, to see them when they came on shore, and leave the rest to the event, taking such measures as the opportunity should present, let be what would be" (203).

The entire sequence, far more complicated and agonized than my summary, marks Crusoe's surrender to a *modus operandi* that has been implicit in his reactions up to now. His surrender to the "event" resembles, I think, a situation that the anthropologist Pierre Bourdieu has described. Crusoe withdraws from his attempt to understand his situation theoretically and depends instead upon what Bourdieu calls "practice," his term for the specific and situational activities within a society that cannot be adequately theorized about within that society. As introspective participant and retrospective narrator of his own actions, Crusoe is both social agent and anthropologist observer, and his explanation of his actions, like those of agents that Bourdieu observed in his fieldwork in Algeria, is a "quasi-theoretical reflection" on his practice and conceals from Crusoe the true nature of his practical mastery, "that it is *learned ignorance* (*docta ignorantia*), a mode of practical knowledge not comprising knowledge of its own principles."[14] What Crusoe wants is theoretically impossible but practically necessary; in his social relationships to the cannibals, he wants to reconcile moral indignation, rational toleration, and practical mastery for self-advantage. The individualistic will to survive that Crusoe exemplifies so memorably requires an adherence to its instinctive practical imperatives, which exist in the context of an early eighteenth-century uncertainty about the theoretical structures that should govern or regulate behavior but tend to operate as after-the-fact and ill-fitting rationalizations. To borrow more of Bourdieu's terms, such structures are like the geometrical space imagined by a map, whereas the trajectory of individuals in much eighteenth-century fiction follows what he evokes as "the network of beaten tracks, of paths made ever more practicable by constant use." The map, says Bourdieu, is "a totality present in simultaneity," but the practice of the native culture is fluid and improvisational, not a map but actual terrain.[15] The divergence between moral and religious theory and secular practice in all of Defoe's novels becomes, by these lights, not simply an index of his realism but of his instinctive grasp of the social process that Bourdieu describes whereby agents are both producers and reproducers of social meaning. "It is because subjects do not, strictly speaking, know what they are doing that what they do has more meaning than they know."[16] Crusoe's subsequent career as a more and more powerful and efficient master not just of his environment but of other individuals, both non-European and European, testifies to his success at leaving behind paralyzing theoretical hesitations. He is liberated by instinctive practice into assuming an agency that grows more and more confident because Crusoe becomes more and more an unhesitating tactician, openly manipulating for practical advantage the moral and social structures that had been theoretical impediments to action. That process can be seen in the final sequence of the island episode when Crusoe defeats the English mutineers who suddenly materialize on the island and seems in the process totally transformed from the irresolute observer of the cannibals.

After acquiring his man Friday in an encounter with the cannibals that matches his earlier dream, Crusoe virtually exterminates a larger party of them as they prepare to consume two victims, a Spaniard and an older native, who turns out to be Friday's father. Crusoe jokes that his island is now peopled and that he looks like a king: "I was absolute lord and lawgiver; they all owed their lives to me, and were ready to lay down their lives, if there had been occasion of it, for me" (241). He makes it clear in the conversations with the Spaniard that he understands the negotiated reciprocities that govern social relationships. His power is a lever for obtaining their cooperation in a mutually beneficial enterprise. Learning from the Spaniard of sixteen of his countrymen and some Portuguese living with the cannibals, Crusoe carefully offers him a plan for escape: "I told him with freedom, I feared mostly their treachery and ill usage of me, if I put my life in their hands; for that gratitude was no inherent virtue in the nature of man; nor did men always square their dealings by the obligations they had received, so much as they did by the advantages they expected" (243). From simple antagonism with those savage strangers, the cannibals, Crusoe progresses to complex relationships with members of rival nation-states, fellow Europeans whose psychology is familiar and predictable, dangerous but manageable. With the Spaniards and, a few pages later, with the English captain who has been marooned on the island by mutineers, Crusoe devises contracts, appealing in both cases to the necessities of their circumstances and promising help in return for equal consideration. The shift in the narrative is clearly marked, a continuation of the focus on action and instinctive agency from that crucial moment when Crusoe managed to forego irresolute and theoretical introspection as he contemplated his relation to the cannibals.

In these closing sequences, *Robinson Crusoe* becomes a real adventure story in that it features a hero freed from paralyzing introspection and capable of strategic movements and tactical manipulations. From an obsessive *isolatio*, Crusoe is abruptly transformed into a patron surrounded by clients; from a pattern of radical individualism he turns into an organizing center of specifically social relationships involving dozens of other people in a communal enterprise. Surrounded by others and involved in their fates to promote his own, Crusoe also makes a crucial transition in self-presentation: from the intimate introspections that he shares only with the reader he passes to a mode of being in the world that is rhetorical and calculated for its effect on others. Thus, when the three victims of the English mutiny are set on the island Crusoe and Friday observe them, and Crusoe resolves to discover himself to them, remarking as he does so on the formidable figure he presents. As he calls to them, in Spanish, "'What are ye, gentlemen?'" they start up at the noise, "but were ten times more confounded when they saw me, and the uncouth figure that I made" (252). In the sequence that follows, Crusoe exploits external appearances, including various theatrical aspects of his own physical bearing and voice to assure the Captain that he can help him and to trick the mutineers into submission. In telling his remarkable story to the Captain, he reconceives it for the moment from confused spiritual autobiography into a means of assurance for this new social alliance. When the Captain wonders if the mutineers will be too powerful for them, Crusoe replies with the confidence of his first smile:

> I smiled at him, and told him that men in our circumstances were past the operation of fear: that seeing almost every condition that could be, was better than that which we were supposed to be in, we ought to expect that the consequence, whether death or life, would be sure to be a deliverance. I asked him what he thought of the circumstances of my life, and whether a deliverance were not worth venturing for. 'And where, sir,' said I, 'is your belief of my being preserved here on purpose to save your life, which elevated you a little while ago? ... depend upon it, every man of them that comes a-shore are our own, and shall die or live as they behave to us.'

As I spoke this with a raised voice and chearful countenance,
I found it greatly encouraged him; so we set vigorously to our
business.

(258)

That business is a complicated series of feints and stratagems. The
English mutineers are overpowered by guile and false representations,
as Crusoe maneuvers his inferior force to give the impression of over-
whelming power. Pretending to be the governor of the island with a
large garrison at his command, Crusoe in effect reproduces the providential pattern (with its psychological effects) that he has experienced on
the island, as he delivers worthy individuals from dangers, rewarding
and punishing like a mysterious and remote force and also forgiving and
setting terms for repentance, leaving some of the subdued rebels on the
island in his place. He enacts on the social and public level a moral
order that he has experienced and internalized as a purely private individual. Crusoe's narrative of these events is as precise and detailed as a
manual of military tactics, for by now he has neither leisure nor need
for justification and its hesitations. Crusoe's stratagems may just articulate in their inspired, rapid-fire improvisation the profoundly pragmatic
base of eighteenth-century English political and moral ideology.[17]
Although it proves short-lived and, without his supervising authority,
splinters to pieces, as Crusoe learns when he returns to the island in *The
Farther Adventures of Robinson Crusoe*, the community thus projected by the
novel grows out of the efforts of a strong central figure who manipulates the symbols of authority to rule effectively, rather like Defoe's great
hero, King William III.[18]

So *Robinson Crusoe* reconciles lonely and tortured individualism with
confident communal movement and social integration. In fact, that individualism for which Robinson Crusoe has become an embodiment is
crucial preparation for his emergence as the leader of a community that
subdues in the mutineers precisely the aggression that he feared most
when he landed on the island and began anxiously to erect his fortifications. In *Robinson Crusoe* such dangers and fears are finally swept away in a
triumphant integration of self and society in this concluding episode, as
theoretical considerations like the nature of authority and the source of
law are subordinated to the force of social relations forged in the precise
moment when survival is the issue and the stakes are life and death. In
Defoe's novels that follow in the early 1720s, survival is also always the
issue, although the arena for the struggle is not the delimited space of
Crusoe's island but the amorphous immensity of modern urban society,
which poses different and much more difficult problems.

That sense of society as simultaneously a threat and an opportunity comes to a head in Defoe's deeply problematical last novel, *Roxana*. The heroine's troubles begin as her feckless husband literally disappears one day when the financial affairs of his neglected brewery grow desperate.

> It must be a little surprizing to the Reader to tell him at once, that after this, I never saw my Husband more; but to go farther, I not only never saw him more, but I never heard from him, or of him, neither of any or either of his two Servants, or of the Horses, either what became of them, where, or which Way they went, or what they did, or intended to do, no more than if the Ground had open'd and swallow'd them all up, and no-body had known it; except as hereafter.[19]

Roxana calls this disappearance extraordinary, but her narrative thereafter takes for granted an encircling social ocean where local identities can dissolve and into which individuals can disappear without a trace and assume other guises in a metropolitan sphere beyond individual comprehension. Moreover, the opening scenes of the novel reinforce our sense of social dysfunction by presenting a case in which there is no system of support for a family unit suddenly splintered. Traditional communal props collapse, as Roxana's relatives heartlessly turn a deaf ear to her plight, and of course for the upper commercial sector to which she belongs there is no adequate institutional recourse in such a case. As Roxana contemplates a future for her children in the hands of the dreaded parish welfare system, she is horrified: "I was at first, sadly afflicted at the Thoughts of parting with my Children, and especially at that terrible thing, their being taken into the Parish-keeping; and then a hundred terrible things came into my Thoughts; *viz.* of Parish-Children being Starv'd at Nurse; of their being ruin'd, let grow crooked, lam'd, and the like, for want of being taken care of; and this sunk my very Heart within me" (52). But Roxana quickly depends, in the course of the calamitous events that inaugurate her narrative, on this same lack of official or institutional regulation in order to make her way out of destitution. Her dreadful opening dilemma is grounded in social circumstances that offer opportunities for their amelioration. In her case, survival requires not only a ready wit and a cool hand but a social terrain in which the individual can move quickly away from the constraints of local identity into anonymity in a metropolitan context, free to assume other guises and to traverse social boundaries and even national borders that are lightly policed and easily penetrated.

Roxana quickly learns from her resourceful maid, Amy, to maintain a supervisory distance and dominion over others, rather like Crusoe on his island knowing its contours and observing invaders from hidden and secure vantage points. Roxana a few years later discovers her brewer-husband serving in the French army in Paris and manages with Amy's help to conceal her whereabouts. Like so much of *Roxana*, this sequence features a detailed account of Roxana and Amy's strategies of conceal-ment and manipulation of others. Amy lies about her mistress to the brewer-husband who, they discover, has in his turn lied to Amy about his prospects for becoming an officer when he asks her for money to buy a commission. Finding him seriously wanting in character, Roxana is "satisfied that he was the same worthless Thing he had ever been" (130) and resolves to "withdraw my Hand from him, that had been my first Destroyer, and reserve the Assistance that I intended to have given him, for another more desirable Opportunity" (131). She hires a spy to watch him and thereby to prevent their meeting, ordering the spy to keep a journal for her to read of her husband's movements. This journal, she tells us, reveals that he "was a meer motionless Animal, of no Consequence in the World; that he seem'd to be one, who, tho' he was indeed alive, had no manner of Business in Life, but to stay to be call'd out of it"(132). By her vigilance and the authoritative distance it provides, Roxana ensures that the dangerous randomness of the world she travels through is controlled and made to serve her ends, which are opportunistic but never unfocused. Her contempt for her "Fool" husband identifies her own specially constructed identity in the world, distinct from his aimless picaresque drifting in her hawk-eyed exploita-tion of that same world's opportunities. Like him, she depends upon an urban transnational scene in which identity is not fixed and in which an indifferently regulated social arena facilitates movement, expansion, impersonation, and acquisition.

Roxana develops alongside this rendition of social movement in her narrative, however, an intense, steadily mounting retrospective remorse. Such remorse operates as yet another distancing device, although one that Defoe clearly loses full control of as the narrative progresses. In her individualizing torment, Roxana stands even further apart from social relationships in which she is only functionally involved. But such secret guilt seems at first glance in this context also a retraction of her story's subversive insight that selfhood is radically contingent, improvised in the context of fluid social relations. Guilt is the only constant feature that Roxana acknowledges, and that mounting feeling claims to be an essential and unvarying personal core in a field of social flux. This schizoid inconsistency is the novel's defining emphasis, and it begins in earnest when Roxana finds herself suddenly alone in Paris, where she has gone with the first of her lovers, the landlord–jeweler who has come to her rescue after her husband decamps. When he is suddenly murdered by robbers, her situation as she renders it is desperate and complicated: "I was in a strange Country; and tho' I had a pretty many Acquaintances, had but very few Friends that I could consult on this Occasion" (89). But even as she grieves and sees visions of the murdered man, she improvises expertly for self protection and financial advantage:

> I had him Buried as decently as the Place would permit a Protestant Stranger to be Buried, and made some of the Scruples and Difficulties on that Account, easie, by the help of Money to a certain Person, who went impudently to the Curate of the Parish St. *Sulpitius*, in *Paris*, and told him, that the Gentleman that was kill'd, was a Catholick; that the Thieves had taken from him a Cross of Gold, set with Diamonds, worth 6000 Livres; that his Widow was a Catholick, and had sent by him 60 Crowns to the Church of —, for Masses to be said for the Repose of his Soul; Upon all which, *tho' not one Word of it was true*, he was Buried with all the Ceremonies of the *Roman* Church.
>
> (89)

Bribery, an assumed identity, a falsified crime report, the expert manipulation of local customs, the secret accumulation of valuables not quite legally acquired – Roxana's *modus operandi* involves rapid mastery of a complicated network of particular social relationships. She has few "friends," that is, she lacks a local base of traditional patronage links in this community, but in the Parisian metropolitan context money will do the work for those who know how to distribute it and establish an effective strategy for getting on in place of a traditional network of relatives, friends, or patrons.

After this bold initial foray, Roxana will commence her sensational career as mistress and courtesan, and she will also develop her extensive opinions on sexual politics and high finance – related topics in her experience. Her fiercely intelligent, stirring proto-feminism shocks the Dutch merchant who later proposes to her: "I thought a Woman was a free Agent, as well as a Man, and was born free, and cou'd she manage herself suitably, might enjoy that Liberty to as much Purpose as the Men do; that the Laws of Matrimony were indeed otherwise, and Mankind at this time, acted upon other Principles; and those such, that a Woman gave herself entirely away from herself, in Marriage" (187).

Living in style in London a few months later and attracting lovers by
her wealth and beauty, she says much the same thing to her financial
advisor, Sir Robert Clayton, who brings her an offer of marriage from a
rich merchant: "I knew no State of Matrimony, but what was, at best, a
State of Inferiority, if not of Bondage ... it was my Misfortune to be a
Woman, but I was resolv'd it shou'd not be made worse by the Sex; and
seeing Liberty seemed to be the Men's Property, I wou'd be a *Man-
Woman*, for as I was born free, I wou'd die so" (211–212). Even as she
rehearses this feminist independence, however, Roxana provides arguments against it that her experience has brought home. More
important, she also offers an analysis of where those sentiments came
from, derived not from a generalized rational vantage point but from
the particular psychological and social circumstances of a woman in her
position. Her fiery speeches, she explains, were the result of vanity and
ambition:

> I was rich, beautiful, and agreeable, and not yet old; I had
> known something of the Influence I had had upon the Fancies
> of Men, even of the highest Rank; I never forgot that the
> Prince de – had said with an Extasie, that I was the finest
> Woman in *France*; I knew I cou'd make a figure at *London*, and
> how well I cou'd grace that Figure; I was not at a Loss how to
> behave, and having already been ador'd by Princes, I thought
> of nothing less than of being Mistress to the King himself.
>
> (201)

To be sure, it is impossible to know just where the truth lies in such a
case history, and the effect of Defoe's narrative is to render truth as situational rather than absolute, despite the heroine's after-the-fact
moralizing. Roxana begins her story as a desperate, resourceless woman
who is forced into the arms of her first lover, her jeweler–landlord, after
her husband deserts her. As that seduction proceeds, Roxana offers
various and contradictory explanations. "I did," she insists, "what my
own Conscience convinc'd me at the very Time I did it, was horribly
unlawful, scandalous, and abominable" (73). Such blame is mitigated
on the same page by circumstances ("But Poverty was my Snare") and
by natural inclination ("Besides this, I was young, handsome ... vain,
and that not a little"). But just after that, Roxana protests that desire
played no part in her capitulation to the landlord: "my Spirits were far
from being high; my Blood had no Fire in it, to kindle the Flame of
Desire" (75). What she insists upon in this sequence and throughout is
the recurrence of her moral consciousness and her more or less steady

resistance to the easy rationalizations of her partner: "In this I was a double Offender, whatever he was; for I was resolv'd to commit the Crime, knowing and owning it to be a Crime; he, if it was true as he said, was fully perswaded it was Lawful" (75).To the end of the story, Roxana will claim that her guilt sets her apart from her thoughtless sexual partners. Even in the middle of feasting and merry-making with her landlord and Amy, "I was quite of another Side, nay, and my Judgment was right, but my Circumstances were my Temptation; the Terrors behind me ... and the dreadful Argument of wanting Bread, and being run into the horrible Distresses I was in before, master'd all my Resolution, and I gave myself up, as above" (78).

Roxana is entirely correct to make such complicated assessments of how blame is mitigated by circumstances. But as a character in her own narrative she claims a singular guilt and clarity of moral vision which accompanies action and places herself at the same time on a higher plane where such mitigation seems irrelevant and blame is accepted as a sign of dreadful authenticity and unsparing self-consciousness lacking in those around her. Roxana consistently exposes the inadequacy of the self-justifying responses of Amy and her various lovers and insists on her absolute guilt and personal responsibility – this in a fictional universe where particular circumstances operate to qualify such absolutes. Roxana works directly against the grain of the novel's exculpatory texture, looking in effect for an authenticity beyond the social status that she both achieves and rejects.

As royal mistress, aristocratic courtesan, bourgeois wife, and Amazonian feminist ideologue, Roxana enacts various roles for the profit of a self carefully presented as quite separate from any of them. Her career as mistress and courtesan is founded on elaborate false pretenses and on her extra-legal, extra-institutional manipulations, which have the effect of making public life merely an expressive medium for the private self rather than a forum where identity is achieved or articulated in some straightforward fashion. The self exists through its relationships to a carefully delineated public world where it negotiates for its power and pleasure, and in Roxana's case that public world becomes increasingly irrelevant and insignificant next to her remarkable talent for manipulating it to her advantage *and* to her intense sense of remorse for doing so. The resulting subjectivity is in effect incommunicable except in the silent reading world of her narrative. The narrative in its extended articulations of a selfhood beyond public revelation tends to negate the entire category of the public sphere in Jürgen Habermas's sense; indeed, it also renders relationships between private and public experience as oppositional rather than productively open. Roxana's story can only be whispered to herself, told in effect to no one, a monologue rather than the progressive dialogue of the public sphere.

Near the end of her story, Roxana longs for what the novel cannot provide – a confidante and a comforter:

> as I had no Comforter, so I had no Counsellor; it was well, *as I often thought*, that I was not a *Roman-Catholick*; for what a piece of Work shou'd I have made, to have gone to a Priest with such a History as I had to tell him? and what Pennance wou'd any *Father-Confessor* have oblig'd me to perform? especially if he had been honest and true to his Office.
>
> (310–311)

Roxana's interiority, in other words, is beyond institutional frameworks; no official discourse can encompass it, and she stands outside the consolations of any brand of Christianity. Like Defoe's other novels, *Roxana* persistently revises and subverts the link that Habermas says existed between what he calls the intimate and the public spheres. In the private or intimate sphere, individuals develop the identity that they bring to the public sphere, where everyone shares in an abstract humanity that encompasses and is defined by each person's individually validated identity. The Enlightenment ideal of rational communication between human beings that sustains the public sphere is, at least implicitly, undermined by two features of Defoe's narratives that are especially visible in his last one: first, the abstract humanity that Habermas associates with the public sphere is relativized, in fact, by the deeply historical and pragmatic particularism that is so familiar and obsessive a feature of Defoe's narratives; second, Roxana's autobiographical mode seeks to create an incommunicable or ineffable subjectivity, projects a private person speaking wholly within the secularized confessional of the novel and never on a public podium where her personal history could resonate and find precedents and social meaning or relevance, where it could accommodate itself to a recognizable public mode of action. Roxana's rapacious appetite for wealth and power leads her to manipulate public action for her own profit, just as her resulting tortured subjectivity is, she insists, entirely of her own making and places her even further from the public sphere.

Roxana undermines the essence of public participation from within by practicing a subversive revision of those transitional social relationships that helped to stabilize early eighteenth-century English political and institutional life. As an astonishingly successful courtesan, Roxana enacts a powerful parody or perversion of patron–client relationships. In place of the mutuality and reciprocity that should drive those relationships, an expensive mistress like Roxana delivers her body to those who can afford it. She serves these buyers by displaying her body in enticing postures and glamorous costumes as an object of inexhaustible delight but crucially reserving herself, claiming a sexual indifference and even a deep-seated loathing for the desire that she excites in men and for the men themselves. What she gives her patrons is the temporary satisfaction of a commodity rather than the service and loyalty over time that clients are supposed to render.

The guilt-obsessed personality that Roxana develops in her narrative would seem to be a compensating antithesis to this resourceful entity that exploits distinctively loose early modern social relations. Some critics consider her agonized reflections as Defoe's warning about the moral decadence of early Georgian England, but others just as plausibly discount the chorus of guilty reflections as conventional moralizing and see in Roxana an embodiment of economic energies that Defoe was eager to promote.[20] Like all of Defoe's narratives, *Roxana* is not a clear or wholly coherent narrative statement, and the debate among the critics cannot be finally resolved. The revealing contradictions that the book displays arise to some extent out of its mixture of narrative formats. Both criminal memoir and spiritual autobiography, it is also a scandal novel and indirect satiric attack upon courtly decadence. The effect of this mixture is never simple since Roxana, for all her unbalancing remorse, seems a familiar character in Defoe's rogues' gallery, delighting in the techniques of survival and capital accumulation and asking readers to admire them. Is it possible that Defoe expects readers to see that Roxana is lying about her state of mind during the events that she narrates? Even if we say that all this remorse is well after the fact, the evocation of herself as a tortured sinner that accompanies Roxana's partially expansive narrative may just be the ultimate manifestation of Defoe's effort to imagine a selfhood that stands productively apart from social and institutional structures, manipulating them for personal fulfillment and simultaneously exploiting that public realm for the dramatization of a private and penitential authenticity defined as such in its scornful relation to its public antithesis. In other words, remorse may serve as the final underlining of his character's singularity, the only authentically interior quality remaining in a world of pure surfaces.

But does Roxana's resourceful individuality effectively cancel the notion of social totality? Does Defoe represent the world as anything other than a scattered series of opportunities for a resourceful self within a shifting ocean of social relations? Roxana, of course, is not interested in the question, but the last and most unresolved sequence in the book brings readers back to the issue of a supervising if not wholly coherent totality. In the end, Roxana suffers her final agonies of guilt and insecurity as she tries to evade the efforts of one of her former servants to prove that she is one of Roxana's abandoned children. In one of those coincidences that the book features which depend for their effect upon the assumption of normal randomness, it turns out that Susan, Roxana's daughter, had indeed been one of the maids at the London house where she scored her greatest triumphs and earned her sobriquet as a famous courtesan – Roxana. Having evaded public life and communal responsibility, having improvised a series of immensely profitable disguises, Roxana is now threatened by a lingering residue of private life at its most elemental and by a fateful pattern that cancels her sense of agency and the randomness on which it thrives. Building from coincidence, Susan's attempt to reclaim her mother imposes a sort of maternal essence as the agent of what looks like destiny, although it may only be ironic accident. Roxana's response is a flurry of further disguises, this time more radical than her professional anonymity as mistress–courtesan. At Amy's suggestion, she lodges with a Quaker woman and dresses like a Quaker herself. Her last days as she fades out of sight find her married to her wealthy Dutch merchant but still pursued by the persistent Susan and tormented by "Apparitions of Devils and Monsters; falling into Gulphs, and off from steep and high Precipices" (310). At last, Susan disappears and Roxana has reason to believe that she has been murdered by Amy.

But in spite of all this terror that one aspect of her past will be revealed, Roxana keeps us up to date on another part of it, her expanding finances, now greater than ever as she combines her fortune with that of her new Dutch husband, a wealthy merchant. All along, naturally, she has accumulated a financial base that grows and grows as she makes shrewd investments and watches her capital swell as she is able to let the interest multiply. The climax of such triumphant accumulation comes when Roxana becomes for three years a royal mistress, totally supported as such and able to take the advice of the financier, Sir Robert Clayton, to leave her interest alone. The sums she mentions are worth contemplating in something like their early eighteenth-century magnitude: some £14,000 in interest has been added to her original capital, and thanks to presents from her admirers she has another £5,000 "in Money, which I kept at-home; besides abundance of Plate, and Jewels, which I had either given me, or had bought to set myself out for Publick Days. In a word, I had now five and thirty Thousand

Pounds Estate; and as I found Ways to live without wasting either Principal or Interest, I laid-up 2000 £ every Year, at least, out of the meer Interest, adding it to the Principal; and thus I went on" (224). By the time she marries her Dutch merchant, their combined estate is nearly, she tell us, a hundred thousand pounds. Multiply at least by forty (or even as high as sixty) to arrive at a low approximation of modern purchasing power. Roxana's wealth is astonishing.

These accountings in Defoe's novels have always puzzled and even offended modern critics, but coming as this final one does just at the moment when Roxana's improvised selfhood begins to unravel, it has a clear significance. Anchored in the accumulated and exactly rendered past of compounding interest, Roxana's financial history is the only stable history the novel allows. The stability of financial markets has all along been the assumed base of Roxana's improvisations; her escalating value as a sexual commodity has depended upon her continuing recourse to such a base, and these enumerations of wealth accumulated remind us of that silent steadiness of multiplying and compounded interest and the economic relationships that lie behind it. Eventually, as Susan makes her life miserable, Roxana declares herself alienated from all this staggering wealth and what it can buy, apart from it all by virtue of her lacerating remorse. Her ultimate stunt as a unique individual is to gain the whole world and then to declare it meaningless, but of course its meaning lies precisely in the freedom that it grants to its possessors to declare their independence from it. For readers who have rather less than the whole world and long for a bit more, that superficial alienation of stupendous wealth is a breathtaking if unbelievable act of egoism and privilege. Only those who have this kind of wealth have the time and leisure to contemplate its worthlessness. Defoe's Roxana is from one point of view a soul in torment and a dire warning to those who think they can depend on their own daring to prosper. But from an equally compelling point of view she is his attempt to imagine a radical individualist who cannot be contained by any totality.

NOTES

1 The page references in the text are to the 1724 London edition.

2 Peter Earle, *The World of Defoe* (London, Weidenfeld and Nicolson, 1976), p. 165.

3 Defoe, *A Tour Thro' the Whole Island of Great Britain*, Everyman's Library Edition, introductions by G.D.H. Cole and D.C. Browning, 2 vols (London, J.M. Dent, 1962), Vol. I, pp. 345, 347.

4 Daniel Defoe, *The Complete English Tradesman: Directing him in the several Parts and Progressions of Trade*, 2 vols (first published 1725–1727; 3rd edn, 1732), Vol. I, p. 308.

5 *The Complete English Tradesman*, Vol. II, pp. 182, 185.

6 The definitive account of these relationships can now be found in brilliantly specific detail in Paula R. Backscheider's biography, *Daniel Defoe* (London and Baltimore, Johns Hopkins University Press, 1989), pp. 139–345.

7 Ian Watt, *The Rise of the Novel: Studies in Defoe, Richardson and Fielding*, (Berkeley and Los Angeles, University of California Press, 1957), p. 60.

8 Daniel Defoe, *Colonel Jack*, ed. Samuel Holt Monk (London, Oxford University Press, 1965), p. 11. All further page references in the text are to this edition.

9 Daniel Defoe, *Moll Flanders*, ed. G.A. Starr (London, Oxford University Press, 1971), p. 74. All further references in the text are to this edition. Starr notes that in *The Great Law of Subordination Consider'd* (1724) Defoe makes the point about the depletion of males that Moll questions here, but that in *Applebee's Journal* for April 10, 1725, he suggests that those numbers are matched by the emigration of women to the plantations in America.

10 Modern understanding on this dimension of Defoe's narratives was established by two landmark studies: George A. Starr, *Defoe and Spiritual Autobiography* (Princeton, Princeton University Press, 1965), and J. Paul Hunter, *The Reluctant Pilgrim: Defoe's Emblematic Method and Quest for Form in "Robinson Crusoe"* (Baltimore, Johns Hopkins University Press, 1966).

11 Martin Green, *Dreams of Adventure, Deeds of Empire* (New York, Basic Books, 1979), p. 63.

12 For an extended analysis of this process, see my *Defoe's Narratives: Situations and Structures* (Oxford, Clarendon Press, 1975), pp. 58–62.

13 Daniel Defoe, *Robinson Crusoe*, ed. Angus Ross (London, Penguin, 1987), p. 249. All further page references in the text are to this edition.

14 Pierre Bourdieu, *Outline of a Theory of Practice*, trans. Richard Nice (Cambridge, Cambridge University Press, 1977), p.19.

15 Bourdieu, *Outline of a Theory of Practice*, p. 38.

16 Bourdieu, *Outline of a Theory of Practice*, p.79.

17 In *The Canonisation of Daniel Defoe* (New Haven and London, Yale University Press, 1988), P.N. Furbank and W.R. Owens identify improvisation as central to Defoe's view of the world: "Defoe's 'projecting' spirit, his Whiggism, his contempt for the past and for tradition: all these could be predisposing factors to such an improvisatory notion of literary form, in which ends are not embryonically contained in beginnings" (p.130).

18 Manuel Schonhorn's *Defoe's Politics: Parliament, Power, Kingship, and Robinson Crusoe* (Cambridge, Cambridge University Press, 1991) develops a convincing view of Defoe's politics that emphasizes his admiration for a strong and decisive sovereign like William.

19 Daniel Defoe, *Roxana: The Fortunate Mistress*, ed. David Blewett (Harmondsworth, Penguin, 1982), pp. 44–45. All further page references in the text are to this edition.

20 David Blewett's *Defoe's Art of Fiction* (Toronto, University of Toronto Press, 1979) is the most cogent and extensive explanation of *Roxana* as a cautionary moral tale. See also Maximillian Novak, *Realism, Myth, and History in Defoe's Fiction* (Lincoln, NE, University of Nebraska Press, 1983),

pp. 13–17 for a discussion of Defoe's ambivalence toward the Restoration, a period that repelled and fascinated him. Bram Dijkistra's *Defoe and Economics* (London, Macmillan, 1987) is the most extreme exponent of the view that the novel is a "didactic entertainment" that dramatizes Defoe's economic opinions (p. 80).

4

FROM PASSION TO SUFFERING

Richardson and the transformation of amatory fiction

I

In its density of social scene and sweep of historical reference radically absent in its amatory predecessors, Samuel Richardson's *Pamela* (1740) is a true original. That much is obvious but crucial, since amatory fiction (even at its most intelligent and expansive) treats such circumstances as invariable, essentially inert materials, a mere backdrop rather than part and parcel of the representational project.[1] As we have seen, the social realm in amatory fiction (when it appears) is a function of the plot rather than an object of representation; sociohistorical conditions exist to license pleasure and to institute danger for the chosen and privileged few, the Philanders and Sylvias, the Charlots and Idalias.

Such conservatism is on view in Eliza Haywood's *Fantomina: Or, Love in a Maze. Being a Secret History of an Amour Between Two Persons of Condition* (1725), which William B. Warner has identified provocatively as an example of just the kind of popular, racy narrative that Richardson (and Fielding) sought to discredit (and to appropriate) as they established the main tradition of what Warner calls "moral fiction" in English.[2] Haywood's heroine has everything she needs: "A Young Lady of distinguished Birth, Beauty, Wit, and Spirit happened to be in a Box one Night at the Playhouse."[3] Observing how men flock to the prostitutes there, she resolves upon a "Frolic," to dress "herself as near as she could in the Fashion of those Women who make sale of their Favours, and set herself in the Way of being accosted as such a one"(227). Approached in her disguise by "the accomplished Beauplaisir," a man she has met in proper society, Fantomina is herself fatally attracted. From Fantomina, woman of the town, she transforms herself when he leaves for Bath into a serving maid from the country, and a month later into the Widow Bloomer. Her final metamorphosis to retain the mercurial Beauplaisir is as the mysterious Incognita, who receives his caresses wearing a mask in a carefully darkened room. At last "Fantomina" discovers that she is pregnant, and with the return of her mother all is revealed. When Beauplaisir declines to offer marriage, the lady is dispatched to a French convent.[4]

With this unconventional heroine bent on her own frankly sexual pleasure, *Fantomina* looks back to Aphra Behn, although in its brisk brevity Haywood's novella lacks space to develop her predecessor's subversive proto-feminism. Fantomina's masquerade is inventive self-expressiveness, but very quickly her sexual play serves mainly to reveal the strength of inner compulsions and irresistible attraction. Intending a mere "Frolic," Fantomina evades his urgent proposals and escapes undetected, but soon "All the Charms of *Beauplaisir* came fresh into her Mind; she languished, she almost died for another Opportunity of conversing with him" (229). Her subsequent disguises and aggressive enjoyment of her lover, in which he becomes in effect a sex object, are her clever improvisations but they are still directed by her "wild and incoherent" desires. It is only Beauplaisir "whose Solicitations could give her Pleasure, and had she seen the whole Species despairing, dying for her sake, it might, perhaps, have been a Satisfaction to her Pride, but none to her more tender Inclination" (234). Fantomina's disguises entail skillful alteration of her dress and even her accent. As Celia, a servant maid at Bath, she employs "a broad Country Dialect, a rude unpolished Air, which she, having been bred in these Parts, knew very well how to imitate" (234). But her body in these amorous encounters is, inevitably, invariable, an undisguisable collection of luscious female parts that she can arrange for Beauplaisir's consumption: he "devoured her Lips, her Breasts with greedy Kisses, held to his burning Bosom her half-yielding, half-reluctant Body, nor suffered her to get loose till he had ravaged all and glutted each rapacious Sense with the Sweet Beauties of the pretty *Celia*" (235). Beauplaisir may be fooled by Fantomina's "Power of putting on almost what Face she pleased" (238), but the identical body in each case leads him to satiety, "to the same Degree of Tastelessness" (240).

Fantomina works her magic within the conventional psychology and physiology of male sexuality, and her manipulations also enforce the balancing stereotypes of essential female needs:

> Had he been faithful to me, (*said she, to herself,*) either as *Fantomina,* or *Celia,* or the Widow *Bloomer,* the most violent Passion, if it does not change its Object, in Time will wither:

Possession naturally abates the Vigour of Desire, and I should
have had, at best, but a cold, insipid, husband-like Lover in my
Arms; but by these Arts of passing on him as a new Mistress
whenever the Ardour, which alone makes Love a Blessing,
begins to diminish, for the former one, I have him always
raving, wild, impatient, longing, dying.

(243)

Fantomina explores how a woman might value control as much as
actual sexual pleasure (for the novella suggests that control is inseparable from sexuality), but Haywood operates within the artificial space
of the masquerade where social privilege (economic self-sufficiency and
leisured idleness) is a given, where (in a crucially detailed aspect of the
tale) dress seems at first glance an accessory for play and pleasure rather
than an indicator of social station. In fact Fantomina's status as a fine
lady is not devalued by her impersonations of others lower on the social
scale; rather, her sexual play across ranks and economic situations ratifies their rigidity and even their permanence. Like the contemporary
vogue for large public masquerades, this disguising requires confidence
in the existing order, since such garb produces a controlled and temporary chaos built on a surrounding and unquestioned stability and
privilege.[5] As a rendition of such social and sexual privilege, *Fantomina* is
an engaging, witty exercise, rather like a graphically explicit stage
comedy of manners, but it has obvious limitations. Readers' range of
responses to it might look like this: delight in role reversal and in the
heroine's smart and witty analysis of male sexuality; voyeuristic interest
in the amoral hedonism of the privileged classes; mild arousal over its
intense evocations of sexual abandon,; a touch of regret or even anger
at the heroine's sad ending behind French convent walls. Moral and
social judgment of a sort is an inevitable part of the intellectual pleasure of all narrative, and if we use the philosopher Alasdair McIntyre's
analysis of how such judgment works we can say, first, that readers are
invited by Haywood to place Fantomina's intentions "in causal and
temporal order with reference to their role in [her] history." But,
second, as McIntyre says, we need for coherent moral judgment to
place those intentions of the agent "with reference to their role in the
history of the setting or settings to which they belong."[6] What *Fantomina*
(and the amatory tradition in general) lacks or sees no need to try to
supply is precisely what *Pamela* provides – a sense of the protagonist's
role in the history of the settings (the specifically rendered sociohistorical world) of which she and others are a part. In its witty symmetries
and role reversals, in its brevity and sketchiness, but most of all in its

ahistorical gender essentialism, *Fantomina* encounters the sociohistorical realm in the spirit of the masquerade that is its main conceit. The only history that Haywood (and the popular amatory tradition) acknowledges is the recurrent history of passion as embodied in particular and often enough varied but completely interchangeable stock characters.

One might argue that these whims are in fact the inevitable result of upper-class idleness, that Fantomina's and Beauplaisir's intrigue is the predictable pattern of empty lives, and that the tale is to that extent an accurate rendition (without being a detailed representation) and satirical judgment of their class. Richardson's originality in *Pamela* is precisely to stage at length the defining moments in the life of an individual who resists this kind of sociohistorical inevitability and these essentialist gender categories, and who claims uniqueness (via an earnest rejection of hedonistic triviality) in her self-conscious articulation and enactment of moral and social roles. The conventional word for his achievement is realism, but that is a misleading and static label. What marks *Pamela* as something new is exactly its refusal of the objective "realities" of social rank and distinct gender identities and its highlighting of the negotiations whereby those "realities" can be achieved or established by a particular personality. What *Pamela* offers its readers is not just a *representation* of a world but an *expression* of an individual within it, so that the dynamic and transactional essence of experience within the social as much as the psychosexual realm is to some extent enacted on the page. In *Pamela* (and *a fortiori* in *Clarissa*) the social and the individual spheres interact and interpenetrate, and each area of experience is dramatized as in some important sense a construction, an entity with an evolving or at least a shifting history in which the social and the personal animate one another.

Like Fantomina, Pamela is self-conscious about dress, and clothing is one of the recurrent concerns of her narrative's early pages. Mr B gives Pamela some of his late mother's clothing, including what women's magazines would now call "intimate apparel" – underwear: "My master has been very kind since my last; for he has given me a suit of my late lady's clothes, and half a dozen of her shifts, and six fine handkerchiefs, and three of her cambric aprons, and four Holland ones. The clothes are fine silk, and too rich and too good for me, to be sure."[7] In *Fantomina*, clothing and social rank have exact equivalence, and in the make-believe world of the novella life for the privileged few can become a masquerade, with members of the highest ranks putting costume on or off at will, although actual impersonation like Fantomina's is a fantastic and interesting exaggeration of that privilege. But in *Pamela* clothing is not fancy dress; it commits the wearer to a social position. In an age before the advent of cheap, mass-produced clothing, when wearing apparel as a labor-intensive product was in fact among the most costly of consumer goods, when clothing thus signified social status more dramatically than in later times, dress in its complex details is understood in Richardson's novel as a finely calibrated system of social signifying and economic display. At a masquerade, identity resides precisely in the playful distance between the assumed hidden reality and the mask and costume, but in *Pamela* identity is enacted in that moment of choosing what to wear and in presenting to the world an external appearance meant to signify the interior reality. Mr B attempts to dress Pamela in the intimate garments of a rich man's mistress, a sort of livery whereby the sexual ownership of a lower-class woman is announced to the world (such dressing across class lines is also a masquerade with deep erotic implications whereby a man enjoys the disparity between the upper-class costume and the degraded sexual status of the wearer) Pamela's resistance is not simply a matter of refusing to wear this livery of sexual service in the name of honest poverty and plainness. As a privileged "upper servant" who served as a sort of companion to her late mistress, as the child of literate but down-wardly mobile and economically demoted parents (they had once "lived creditably" and "brought up a great family," but by "doing beyond their abilities for two unhappy brothers, who are both dead" (475), they lost everything, and her father is now a day laborer), Pamela is a complex figure far removed, obviously, from the back-breaking realities of domestic service in the early eighteenth century. She is by education and experience a dispossessed but finely tuned member of the middle ranks. She has observed life around her from the margins and can to that extent be negatively self-conscious about her station. Her writing operates as a recurrent affirmation of a personal authenticity which is asserted not absolutely but negotiated as tactical defense and response within the amatory clichés of inter-class seduction that are the substance of her story.[8]

Pamela's fashion-magazine self-consciousness about the fine points of her clothing is both "dramatic" and "self-expressive." Teenaged vanity of a sort to which the adult reader may well feel superior is dramatically rendered by such passages, but Pamela's shrewdly effective self-expressiveness is simultaneously at work, shifting the narrative perspective from the reader's knowing superiority to Pamela's tenacious purposefulness and self-assertion. Such consistently doubled signifi-cance, although not everywhere equally present in the narrative, is the essence of Richardson's originality whereby necessity and freedom are rendered with a new force as concurrent, interpenetrating forces in the life of an individual. Unlike other amatory heroines, Pamela cannot simply be categorized as part of the taxonomy of female behavior; her intelligence enables her to confront her own psychosexual stirrings and to redirect them in productive ways. And putting on clothing, it turns out, is the perfect trope for such complex behavior, since wearing apparel arrives for all of us in a modern consumer society full of pre-existing meanings and becomes, in the act of dressing, with all of its personalized alterations, individualized variations, and choices of accessories, an externalization of how a new and intensely self-conscious personality like Pamela can present herself. As *Pamela* renders it, getting dressed is the moment of free choice within the available possibilities, although a controlled understanding of the range of those sartorial options is clearly not what everyone can manage.

Determined to leave Mr B's service to avoid his sexual importunities, Pamela writes to her parents to describe her change of appearance for her trip:

> And so, when I had dined, up stairs I went, and locked myself into my little room. There I tricked myself up as well as I could in my new garb, and put on my round-eared ordinary cap; but with a green knot, however, and my home-spun gown and petticoat and plain leather shoes; but yet they are what they call Spanish leather. A plain muslin tucker I put on, and my black silk necklace, instead of the French necklace my lady gave me; and put the earrings out of my ears, and when I was quite equipped, I took my straw hat in my hand, with its two green strings, and looked about me in the glass, as proud as anything.
>
> (87–88)

Pamela's self-approving gaze complements her satirical and critical view of the upper-class ladies (Mr B's neighbors and friends) who, in her previous letter, have observed her improbable beauty with ribald amusement as they imagine seduction scenarios. Pamela's self-satisfaction over her clothes is part vanity and part expressive moral agency. What she calls in her next paragraph "the pleasure of descending with ease, innocence, and resignation!" is naked self-determination, a metamorphosis that (as Mrs Jervis, the housekeeper, says) transforms Pamela for the moment from an attractive servant into an independent young woman, a "pretty neat damsel," as Mr B describes the person he sees talking to the housekeeper. When Mrs Jervis insists that Pamela disabuse Mr B, he is quick to make a game of her new appearance, kissing her and addressing her as Pamela's sister: "'O sir,' said I, as much surprized as vexed, 'I am Pamela. Indeed I am Pamela, *her own self!*'" (89). Pamela clings sweetly to a core authenticity such as her actions in this scene and her behavior in the rest of the novel revise and complicate virtually out of existence. Over and over again, she inhabits and appropriates available roles, and her sense of self as readers perceive it lies in those transactions with antagonists like Mr B and then his sister, Lady Davers, who assume incorrectly that she can be boxed into the corner of a stable lower-class identity.

Along with its unprecedented popularity, *Pamela* provoked in some of its first readers the same sorts of class-bound suspicions about her motives. Fielding's *Shamela* and the *Anti-Pamela: or, Feign'd Innocence Detected* (both published in 1741, the latter attributed to Eliza Haywood) treat the heroine as simply a designing hypocrite.[9] Fielding's parody and Haywood's picaresque revision upset the delicate balance that Richardson is at pains to establish, for they propose the author as the ultimate judge and creator of a character for whom biology and social rank equal destiny. Haywood's Fantomina is bound to enact the compulsive patterns of the female personality, just as Shamela and Syrena in *Anti-Pamela*, comically and viciously respectively, play out the characterological inevitabilities of scheming lower-class wenches. For all her naiveté and insufferable priggishness, Pamela constructs herself out of the materials that come her way, and Richardson imagines (as no one else before him) an individual improvising a selfhood that is not entirely or essentially constrained by the boundaries of rank and social status (instinctively or self-consciously – either explanation is too simple or definitive to fit the novel) to meet the shifting demands of her experience. What Richardson later called "writing to the moment," the present-time immediacy (much ridiculed by Fielding in *Shamela*) created by Pamela's letters written in the first half of the novel in near-constant crisis, highlights the essentially improvisatory or *ad hoc* nature of this self-construction. And at times, naturally, Pamela is awkward and obvious, but these ungainly and embarrassing performances thereby express personality even more strongly than polished artifice or deliberate and convincing pretense ever could.

The single most embarrassing and at the same time most strongly expressive of such performances is Pamela's division of her clothing into three separate bundles as she prepares to leave Mr B's London house: one bundle contains the clothing given to her by her late mistress, the second the items proffered by Mr B, and the third consists of her own clothes, which she has acquired through her own effort and expense. Writing to her parents, she repeats the speech she made over her own bundle to Mrs Jervis:

> 'Now comes poor Pamela's bundle, and a little one it is, to the others. First, here is a callico night-gown, that I used to wear o' mornings. It will be rather too good for me when I get home; but I must have something. Then there is a quilted calimanco coat, and my straw hat with green strings; and a piece of Scots cloth, which will make two shirts and two shifts, the same I have on, for my poor father and mother. And here are four other shifts; and here are two pair of shoes; I have taken the lace off, which I will burn, and this, with an old silver buckle or two, will fetch me some little matter at a pinch. ... Here are two cotton handkerchiefs and two pair of stockings, which I bought of the pedlar'; (I write the very words I said) 'and here too are my new-bought knit mittens: and this is my new flannel coat, the fellow to that I have on. And in this parcel pinned together are several pieces of printed callico, remnants of silks, and such-like, that, if good luck should happen, and I should get work, would serve for robings and facings, and such-like uses. And here too are a pair of pockets, and two pair of gloves. Bless me!' said I, 'I did not think I had so many good things!'
>
> $(110–111)^{10}$

Pamela hugs her little bundle and treats it as the outward sign of her innocence, but it is also in her rendering a record of her resourceful accessorizing and sartorial improvising. The bundle is transformed by her performance from a collection of pretty bargains, tokens of her clever assertiveness even on a modest budget, into rags that will reproach dishonest riches and pomp at the hour of her death. So Pamela moves from girlish memories of shopping bargains to morbid moralizing on the vanity of worldly coverings, and the naive awkwardness of such an incongruity gives her soliloquy its force:

> 'But,' said I, 'come to my arms, my dear *third* parcel, the companion of my poverty, and the witness of my honesty; and may I never have, as I shall never deserve, the least rag that is contained in thee, when I forfeit a title to that innocence which I hope will ever be the pride of my life! and then I am sure it will be my highest comfort at my death, when all the riches and pomp in the world will be more contemptible than the

vilest rags that can be worn by beggars!' And so I hugged my *third* bundle.

(111)

Mrs Jervis, B's housekeeper, quickly points out that this humble posturing constitutes dangerous arrogance, "the highest affront that can be offered" (112). But Pamela's instincts are sound, since all the while B has been watching this scene, moved Mrs Jervis reports nearly to tears two or three times. Reducing B to sentimental moral spectator is nothing less than Pamela's great accomplishment, and his ultimate transformation from inept seducer/rapist to adoring husband is effected by the deeper apprehension of her performance as sentimental heroine when he reads Pamela's letters. Pamela's impressive powers of composition and representation remind B (and other readers) that this is not merely a scene of private seduction and that these amorous interiors are connected to the wider and encompassing social world. Pamela's innocence, in her staging of it, is based on the affecting melodrama of the vast social disparity between herself and her powerful antagonist.

Pamela's interiority is functionally subordinate to the external social and political drama that she insistently keeps in front of us and her would-be seducer. Compared to the heroines of the amatory tradition, Pamela is emphatically a public rather than private figure, for next to their inexpressibly powerful emotions and ineffable passions (evoked by a whole range of metaphors of depth and volatility and by a rhetoric of inexpressibility) she is a master (a few tactically appropriate fainting spells aside) of dramatic control and rhetorical articulation in which the hectic present moment is consistently recast into a hypothetical future for maximum effect on readers and on spectators. Pamela's journal re-examines the immediate past and tries to link what has just happened to what may with proper management happen in the future. Naturally, Richardson wants readers to see Pamela as a terrified teenager, the victim of an attempted rape (however botched by the hopeless Mr B), kidnapped and held in the country against her will, driven to the verge of suicide, and we are not meant to see her resistance as calculated or her protestations of virtue and innocence as nothing but performances. Here, for example, is Pamela at one of her lowest points. She has jumped from her window at B's Lincolnshire house, and after throwing some of her clothes in the pond to make it look as if she has drowned herself, she attempts to clamber over the estate's wall. But the bricks give way, and she falls back, stunned and bruised. Now she considers throwing herself in the pond and ending it all; here is part of her rendition of her inner dialogue for her parents as she contemplates suicide,

92

imagines its pleasant aftermath, and then rehearses the Christian arguments against it:

> And then, thought I (and O that thought was surely of the
> devil's instigation; for it was very soothing and powerful with
> me) these wicked wretches who now have no remorse, no pity
> on me, will then be moved to lament their misdoings; and
> when they see the dead corpse of the miserable Pamela
> dragged out to these dewy banks, and lying breathless at their
> feet, they will find that remorse to soften their obdurate hearts,
> which, now, has no place in them! And my master, my angry
> master, will then forget his resentments, and say 'Alas!' and it
> may be, wring his hands. 'This is the unhappy Pamela! whom I
> have so causelessly persecuted and destroyed! Now do I see she
> preferred her honesty to her life, She, poor girl! was no
> hypocrite, no deceiver; but really was the innocent creature she
> pretended to be!'
>
> ...
>
> I was once rising, so indulgent was I to this sad way of
> thinking, to throw myself in: but again my bruises made me
> slow; and I thought, What art thou about to do, wretched
> Pamela? How knowest thou, though the prospect be all dark to
> thy short-sighted eye, what God may do for thee, even when all
> human means fail? God Almighty would not lay me under
> these sore afflictions, if he had not given me strength to
> grapple with them, if I will exert it as I ought; and who knows,
> but that the very presence I so much dread, of my angry and
> designing master, (for he has had me in his power before, and
> yet I have escaped) may be better for me, than these perse-
> cuting emissaries of his, who, for his money, are true to their
> wicked trust, and are hardened by that, and a long habit of
> wickedness, against compunction of heart? God *can* touch his
> heart in an instant: and if this should *not* be done, I can *then*
> but put an end to my life by some other means, if I am so
> resolved.
>
> (211–212)

Pamela renders her abortive escape as full of confused emotions that
come crowding upon her: imagining suicide provides a vision of satisfying closure and moral justification. But reflection aided by particular
circumstances ("my bruises made me slow") brings both Christian

caution and socioeconomic considerations to bear: B may be moved as his creatures, paid professionals and dependent menials, cannot be. Calculation of an intelligent and pragmatic sort shares the stage in Pamela's journal with a whirlwind of emotions. In choosing the journal and letter format in which Pamela dominates the discourse and the means of representation, Richardson provides her with an intelligence and will that subordinates that experience of compulsion to a control that we know from the first page can manage matters very well indeed. Pamela triumphs by externalizing her plight, by textualizing it. For all of her psychosexual transparency, that vulnerability to interpretive readings that translate her innocence into a knowing self-seeking, Pamela represents a rejection of the sexualized "individualism" of heroines in the amatory tradition, but also a modification of the heroically subversive individualism generated by the criminal/picaresque tradition exemplified in Defoe's narratives. Pamela enacts her special kind of lower-class identity to protect and promote herself, just as she varies it to assert her virtue and honesty, claiming at once a social location and a moral individuality that is her own. Pamela's deeply pragmatic selfhood is papered over with girlish innocence and naiveté to counteract her independence. But the wrapping is pretty thin, for like Clarissa, her formidable successor, Pamela has plenty of wit and intelligence; she is able to hold her own in dialogue and argument with Mr B as he finds that intimidation will not do the job.

Isolated as she is at B's Lincolnshire estate, bullied by the monstrous Colbrand and grotesque Mrs Jewkes, threatened with rape, Pamela continues (necessarily, given the format of the narrative) to write and to attempt to enlist the aid of others, such as the ineffectual Parson Williams. B summons her to his presence after Mrs Jewkes has seized some of her voluminous "papers," her journal (which we have been reading) of everything that has happened to her since her forced removal to B's country estate. In Pamela's precise accounting, as she records in her latest journal addressed to her parents, Jewkes has confiscated her account of part of the last ten days of her "distress," some of the rest having been smuggled (through Parson Williams) to the Andrews, and the remaining and most recent record sewed up in her petticoats. Pamela's and B's exchanges after he has read what Jewkes has confiscated begin the process of his conversion, as B half playfully assumes the role of judge: " 'Now, Pamela, you come upon your trial.' 'I hope, sir,' said I, 'that I have a *just* judge.' 'Ay,' returned he, 'and you may hope for a *merciful* one too, or else I know not what will become of you' " (266–267). Menacing as this remark is, B's seduction/rape scenario has been pretty much neutralized by now, transformed by

Pamela's resistance into what he himself now characterizes as a "pretty novel" (268). Although in a last gasp of sexual bravado B threatens to strip Pamela to find the remaining journals, even that gesture is desexualized by its textual object. In an amazingly coherent (and slightly ludicrous) sequence, B's desires are channeled obsessively toward Pamela's writing, as he longs for nothing more than to read her version of the events that he, after all, has precipitated, succumbing in that desire to her version of them, converted from violent seducer to sentimental lover by the moral force and pathetic recastings of her narrative. As they walk together by the pond where Pamela staged her own drowning and actually contemplated suicide, B is moved as he reads at the very spots described in the journal: "'O my dear girl! you have touched me sensibly with your mournful tale, and your reflections upon it. I should truly have been very miserable had that happened which might have happened'"(276).

There is one small quarrel, however, as Pamela – shrewd to the end – resists B's less than definitive expression of affection and tentative honest intentions ("'If my mind hold, and I can see these former papers of yours, and that these in my pocket give me no cause to alter my opinion, I will endeavour to defy the world, and the world's censures'" (276)), and she asks simply to go back to her parents. But as she sits next morning in an inn, ready to finish her journey back home, a message arrives from B who, after reading over her journals, is now truly converted and sick, he says, "'with vexation that I should part thus with the delight of my soul, as I now find you are, and must be, in spite of the pride of my heart'" (286). Pamela's journals, the record of her greatest distress and resistance to B's most malevolent plots, such as a planned sham marriage, are what B reads and re-reads in the pages that follow, in the fortnight preceding the wedding. *Pamela* doubles back on itself, as it were, and becomes the triumph of the heroine's writing as it reprocesses the materials of amatory plot into her resistant subjectivity, with its personalized revisions and reversals of that plot's simplicities.

B's conversion and his marriage to Pamela are complete just a bit more than half way through the book, for the post-nuptial conquest of Mr B's gentry world is an essential part of Richardson's revision of the amatory pattern. Lacking the sexual titillation and melodrama of the first half of the book, this part of the novel opens up the confined artifice of the amatory conflict and takes Richardson's heroine beyond the bedroom and into the drawing room where the gentry into which she has married are charmed and gladly yield to superior talents, compelled by the force of Pamela's beauty and self-presentation to admit that their ranks have been not so much penetrated by an interloper as morally reinvigorated by energy from below. B's neighbors in Bedfordshire, on one occasion early in the novel, gather to see his "servant-maid, who is the greatest beauty in the county" (82). Pamela here gives as good as she gets, as she remarks on four ladies in this dinner party, taking what she calls "freedoms with my betters" (84). These pages take the reader out of the closeness of the seduction plot, with its small and directed cast of characters and into the spacious houses and gardens of the country gentry, of visits, dinners, teas, and conversations. The isolated Pamela is now the center of a coherent social group, her singular personality providing a center for reaffirmation of the landed gentry's way of life. Indeed, Pamela herself recedes somewhat, necessarily becoming a recorder of the scene around her.

B invites his Lincolnshire friends and neighbors to dine with him to see his Pamela before their marriage. "'Be then dressed just as you are,'" he urges Pamela, "'for since they know your condition, and I have told them the story of your present dress, and how you came by it, one of the young ladies begs it as a favour, that they may see you in it: and the rather as I have boasted, that you owe nothing to dress, but make a much better figure with your own native stock of loveliness, than the greatest ladies they have seen, arrayed in the most splendid attire, and adorned with jewels'" (308–309). In her dress (which is decidedly not costume), Pamela has seized the high moral ground and occupies the natural realm, opposed in its "native stock of loveliness" to the gaudy artifice of the "greatest ladies." Such naturalizing of what the novel demonstrably presents as the highest artifice is what troubled cynical readers like Fielding. Of course, there is a good deal of condescending curiosity in the neighbors' visit. Pamela is on exhibit, a rarity of a servant who in her exceptionalism proves the rule of difference and division among the social orders. And all the while Pamela's discourse is for a modern reader fairly offensive in its exaltation of B and in its self-abasing humility, as she declares over and over again that she is unworthy of her master's goodness to her. For most modern readers (and for that matter for some eighteenth-century ones) Pamela's protestations are deeply embarrassing, and yet within the narrative they have the effect of keeping social realities in full view, of emphasizing two related and crucial facts – that B inhabits a realm of wealth, power, and privilege beyond the wildest dreams of the daughter of a day-laborer and that Pamela (weak and utterly powerless as she is) has extracted by her extraordinary virtue and beauty this amazing condescension. Flattery and self-abasement become in this special context reminders of Pamela's dominance.

But even for Richardson such rehearsals of virtue rewarded are not quite enough to sustain narrative interest, so he introduces Mr B's sister, Lady Davers, who turns up with her nephew, the rakish Jacky, to confront this upstart Pamela while B is away, comforting a dying friend. With the wedding not yet made public, Pamela finds herself accosted without ceremony or delicacy as B's mistress, browbeaten, frightened, and soon reduced to tears. Lady Davers is far more impressive than her brother, and the long scene in which Pamela bears up under Jacky's pert insolence and the Lady's wittily frank abuse comes as a great relief after Pamela's cloying endearments with the besotted B. Pamela's ultimate triumph, inevitable after all from the scene's beginning, is to provoke Lady Davers by her quiet but tenacious resistance to rising heights of incredulity and indignation. In the social scale Lady Davers, thanks to her marriage, is a notch up from the country gentry, and the presence of the stage rake, Jacky, as well as his aunt's theatricalized hauteur make this a new challenge for Pamela. Here at last Pamela encounters at its highest pitch the true style and scorn of the ranks that she is invading, as her classless and self-authenticating eloquence rises and then subsides into fear and flight against the totally unsentimentalized discourse of the aristocracy, as Richardson encourages readers to imagine it.

Richardson is shrewd enough to retain differences and distance between his heroine and her sister-in-law, and part of Pamela's appeal is her preservation of an innocence and simplicity that continue to mark her as a special kind of servant maid even as she is exalted as Mrs B. As Lady Davers puts it after her conversion: "'There is such a sweet simplicity in thy story, as thou tellest it; such an honest artlessness in thy mind, and such an amiable humility in thy deportment, that I believe I shall be forced to love thee, whether I will or not'" (475). What holds this post-nuptial part of *Pamela* together, then, is the re-enactment of the heroine's curious (and quite preposterous) immunity to her new social status, improbably innocent and unspoiled in the face of her triumph, inexhaustibly interesting because her personality and her inspiring example embody both the possibility of social change and its absolute rarity. In one sense, Pamela is simply the exception who proves the invariability of the rules of rank and degree, but on the other hand she holds out the subversive promise to readers of understanding such arrangements as external and arbitrary, subject to correction and adaptation by an intelligence and moral consciousness defined as internal and essential to the individual. In Pamela's case this integrity from the beginning defines itself (illogically, of course) as an essence created by her deprived history and offered with powerful naiveté as the alternative to an artifice expressed in the external adornments of the rich, which seek to express privilege but in the face of Pamela's personal history signify nothing except their arbitrariness. Here is the most overt statement of that opposition, part of Pamela's detailed response to one of the articles of B's proposal that she become his mistress:

> Your rings, sir, your solitaire, your necklace, your ear-rings, and your buckles, will better befit some lady of degree, to whom you may give a lawful claim to them than me. To lose the best jewel, my virtue, would be poorly recompensed by the jewels you propose to give me. What should I think, when I looked upon my finger, or saw, in the glass, those diamonds on my neck, and in my ears, but that they were the price of my honesty; and that I *wore* those jewels outwardly, because I had none inwardly? When I come to be proud and vain of gaudy apparel, and outside finery, then (which I hope will never be) may I rest my principal good in such trifles, and despise for them the more solid ornaments of a good fame and a chastity inviolate.
>
> (229)[11]

Pamela has its limits, obviously, as a novel with insights into the ideological world of the mid-eighteenth century, for it elides and even denies the power of those sociohistorical factors it outlines. Even if Richardson does not want readers to doubt her sincerity, virtue works for Pamela and reaps more than its own reward. The innocent heroine claims a disinterested moral essence and integrity that her instinctively pragmatic behavior repositions as a means toward social advancement. Lucky as well as beautiful, Pamela is not meant to be plausible; her virtuous resistance to enormous temptation marks her as a romantic heroine, though not of the disreputable and extravagant popular kind. Disdaining what he always referred to in his correspondence as "the pomp and parade of romance-writing, and dismissing the improbable and marvellous, with which novels generally abound," Richardson sought in *Pamela* to "introduce a new species of writing."[12] But his first novel, as many readers have sensed, retained deep elements of amatory fantasy and traditional romance: Mr B is the lustful knight and Pamela the innocent country maiden of the pastourelle. But in this case the romance turns into a folk tale in which, thanks to the maiden's instinctive shrewdness and her skill as a self-fashioner of sentimental fiction, wedded bliss replaces rape. *Pamela* is a special modern sort of heterosexual romance-novel in which the man is transformed by female example and virtuous resistance from an aggressive patriarch bent on his pleasure and power into a nurturing lover, still strong and powerful but now devoted to the needs of his beloved, sensitive, caring, partly feminized in crucial ways. That essentially "female" wish-fulfillment plot is still the staple of mass-market romance in the English-speaking world, and Richardson is the somewhat unlikely initiator of that enduringly popular species of narrative.[13]

II

Clarissa, Or, The History of a Young Lady: Comprehending the Most Important Concerns of Private Life (1747–1748) is a massive rejection of romance, a transformation of the clichés of the amatory pattern into a monumental novel without parallel in English or in European fiction. Such praise would surely have offended the pious Richardson who set out quite deliberately to write what he described to a friend as a "Religious Novel," designed (as he said in a preface to the novel's third and revised edition) "to investigate the highest and most important doctrines not only of morality, but of Christianity, by shewing them thrown into action in the conduct of the *worthy* characters; while the *unworthy*, who set those doctrines as defiance, are condignly, and, as may be said, consequentially, punished."[14] But in frustrating readers who expected what he called in the preface a "light novel, or transitory romance," Richardson began with nothing less than the classic amatory formula: the incomparably beautiful and immensely wealthy Clarissa Harlowe, much sought after by various suitors, is pressed by her family to marry the rich but repulsive Solmes and to reject the advances of the handsome and dashing Robert Lovelace, an aristocratic rake who tricks her into running away with him and ultimately rapes her. Unlike the hard-pressed producers of commercial amatory fiction, Richardson had the luxury to please himself and as a successful printer–businessman he had earned for himself the creative leisure to complicate the amatory formula and turn fiction away from mere entertainment and toward his ambitious didactic and religious purpose. To test his heroine properly, Richardson imagined a representation of a segment of the mid-eighteenth-century social–historical world without fictional precedent in its range, depth, and intensity. He ventriloquized a large cast of distinct characters, mainly across the upper strata of eighteenth-century social degrees – the landowning gentry, the upper, commercial middle classes, and the aristocracy – but also included their servants and a varied cast of clients and shady retainers from various social backgrounds, from the criminal underworld and *demi-monde* to the lower middle classes. And of course in Clarissa and Lovelace themselves he rendered characters unique in English amatory narrative in psychological depth, sociohistorical and moral complexity, and rhetorical virtuosity. From the opening pages, Richardson's most remarkable innovation is to immerse this large cast of characters in a minutely rendered, densely articulated world of social and economic circumstances.

The book's length is an aspect of the complexity of the social relations it seeks to evoke. Richardson articulates a network of connections encompassing the Harlowes and the Lovelace clan, a tangled web of alliances, inheritances, obligations, courtships, rivalries – all of these actions and accidents remembered, analyzed, and almost endlessly rehearsed. These networks form an enveloping past within which the characters conduct their present activities. Amatory fiction, strictly speaking, recognizes no past; it dwells in an electrified present and broods on a delicious, rapturous, or most often a tragic future. Narrators and characters focus, and Pamela is no exception, on the unfolding event, whose roots in the past are of no real consequence, since the present as it leaps into bounding immediacy has no important connection with what preceded it. This quality of amatory fiction is supplemented in this regard by a "presentism" that highlights and isolates erotic and pathetic moments, and indeed even *Pamela*'s immediacy is in the service of such essentially "pure" or mindless intensities as it exploits at least until the wedding of the principals the sexual suspense of imminent violence and rape. But Pamela's somewhat compromised spontaneity is impossible for the excruciatingly self-conscious Clarissa, who for most of the novel is "all mind," as Lovelace's fellow rake, Belford, reverently observes after his first meeting with her.[15] This complex past that suffuses *Clarissa* from its opening pages renders the present as it emerges paralyzingly contingent and provisional, subject always in the heroine's obsessive contemplation of her narrowing options to revisions and adjustments mandated by her developing grasp of the history of her family and those connected to it, to say nothing of the reader's own immersion in an expanding complexity, uncertainty, and pervasive moral ambiguity. At first glance, this situation looks paradoxical, since the letters are fresh accounts of an immediate present, sometimes literal transcriptions of conversations as they have just occurred between the characters. But the epistolary format muddies and relativizes the present it claims to deliver, as it offers conflicting and partial accounts of the moment that is passing. The past (that is to say, the past before the book opened, the biographical and historical past that contains the characters and may be said to have produced them) is really the only relatively clear point of reference as the characters contemplate their future in a confusing and increasingly uncertain present.[16]

Well before the lamentable events leading to the impasse at the center of the novel, Clarissa and her best female friend and chief correspondent, the feisty Anna Howe, have considered the looming destiny of the Harlowe clan: "You are all too rich to be happy, child. For must not each of you by the constitutions of your family marry to be *still* richer? People who know in what their *main* excellence consists are not to be blamed (are they?) for cultivating and improving what they think most valuable?" (68). As she resists her family's plan to marry her to the odious Solmes and desperately offers to negotiate an alternative fate, Clarissa confirms Anna's analysis many times, identifying herself as a specifically novelistic intelligence in the sense that she understands profoundly two related and contradictory issues: her place in the history of her family as it grows in wealth and power, and the necessity of her own resistance as a separate and special individual to that dynastic drive:

> I should have been very little better for the *conversation-visits* which the good Dr Lewin used to honour me with, and for the principles *wrought*, as I may say, into my earliest mind by my pious Mrs Norton, founded on her reverend father's experience as well as on her own, if I could not thus retrospect and argue in such a strange situation as we are in. *Strange*, I may well call it; for don't you see, my dear, that we seem all to be *impelled*, as it were, by a perverse fate which none of us are able to resist? – and yet all arising (with a strong appearance of self-punishment) from ourselves? – Do not my parents see the hopeful children, from whom they expected a perpetuity of worldly happiness to their branching family, now grown up to answer the *till* now distant hope, setting their angry faces against each other, pulling up by the roots, as I may say, that hope which was ready to be carried into a probable certainty?
>
> Your partial love will be ready to acquit me of capital and intentional faults – but oh, my dear! my calamities have humbled me enough to make me turn my gaudy eye inward; to make me look into myself! – And what have I discovered there? – Why, my dear friend, more *secret* pride and vanity than I could have thought had lain in my unexamined heart.
>
> (333)

The subversive thoughtfulness of such remarks is striking; Clarissa's meditations on the intertwinings of individual freedom and its enveloping "fate" or necessity represent a complicating shift from the largely self-expressive and spontaneous discourse of characters like Pamela and Mr B. Clarissa and Anna Howe, Lovelace and Belford (complementary pairs of friends) seek above all to understand them-selves and others in relation to their past experiences, and their characters are constituted most of the time precisely in that irrepressible analytical consciousness of social and personal necessity. Anna is more positive and assertive than Clarissa, and Belford is at first merely an onlooker, although in the end he becomes an active analyst and debater with his former rakish soul-mate. Lovelace, of course, offers most often a jeering parody of thoughtful self-examination, but even his extrava-gant self-dramatizations as imperious lover and consummate plotter are intended as autobiographical inventions or assertions and to that extent belong to the same class of utterances as Clarissa's self-effacing rumina-tions: both characters are defined by a process of constant introspection, personal discovery, and even of self-construction and performative self-display. In these meditations and assertions, we may say, Richardson's characters assume the traditional prerogatives of readers and critics, constituting themselves as characters not so much by their actions but precisely in their own attempts as they communicate their thoughts to others to understand themselves. Their writing is extended to us and to their correspondents as cognitively and morally meaningful as well as rhetorically self-expressive. Action and event, when they do occur in *Clarissa*, are notoriously brief (the rape itself elided as too horrible to represent, although its circumstances are given in detail), and the novel focuses on its main characters' extended, repeated, and indeed obsessive contemplation of that tangle of circum-stances, personal and social, that has produced those actions and events. As richly individualized and complex persons, they define themselves as such by these examinations, those ponderings of the central paradox that the novel as a genre uncovers and that Clarissa herself articulates so clearly: can it be, she asks, that "we are all *impelled*, as it were, by a perverse fate which none of us are able to resist? – and yet all arising (with a strong appearance of self-punishment) from ourselves?" As Anna considers the eloped Clarissa's circumstances, she sees a "strange fatality! As if it were designed to show the vanity of all human prudence" (577). And yet for all of the characters' brooding on fate and destiny, *Clarissa* is an affirmation or at least an exploration of human agency and efficacy, which are rendered as theoretically elusive and strenuous but practically attainable in particular and local transactions and interactions. In *Clarissa*, intellectual force and moral will (both for good and ill) are shown to operate and to effect individual purposes, and the novel's enormous canvas is necessary precisely to dramatize the densely situational and historically specific moments in which individual will can manage to operate successfully. For all its melodramatic sensationalism and indirect prurience, *Clarissa* is a deeply serious, highly intellectual inquiry into the possibility of human freedom and authentic communication in an atmosphere charged with various forms of dehumanizing social and psychological necessity and manipulation.

In this light, Clarissa and Anna (neither yet 20) are precociously serious intellectuals, and the first few hundred pages of the novel presuppose a long-running dialogue between these friends about the Harlowe family, its problems and shortcomings, but also a more generalized discussion of moral and social relations as they impinge upon two fiercely intelligent young ladies of leisure who resist conventional views of the institution of marriage (with all that entails) among females of their rank and affluence. Their ongoing seminar on personal and general topics is part of a wider interest in ideas and issues that *Clarissa* presents as basic to leisure-class existence at these exalted levels. And their correspondence is only one instance of such interests, since the correspondence between Lovelace and Belford is, in its ironic mode, just such another ongoing seminar on various social and political issues. Indeed, while conducting his quickly withdrawn suitorship of Arabella Harlowe, Lovelace ingratiates himself at Harlowe Place by his intellectual parts and worldly experience. Clarissa's Uncle Hervey is thinking of sending a young man entrusted to him on the Grand Tour, and it is proposed that the elegant Robert Lovelace should provide an account of courts and countries so that the family can plan the young man's itinerary (and also, it is implied, expand its own understanding). His writing commended by Papa Harlowe, who has traveled in his youth, as displaying a "person of reading, judgement, and taste," Lovelace is invited to "write down a description of the courts and countries he had visited, and what was most worthy of curiosity in them" (47). Lovelace stipulates that he will address his commentary on the Grand Tour to Clarissa, and he exploits this opportunity to initiate their correspondence. Although the return home from Scotland of James Harlowe, Clarissa's brother, will turn the family against Lovelace and set in motion the turbulent events that follow, the novel opens in a much calmer mood, with a polite salon, as it were, where Lovelace is more than simply a scion of an aristocratic family. He recommends himself by his intellectual abilities, his rhetorical powers, and his grasp of the sociohistorical world and its moral lessons that this leisure class is uniquely privileged to contemplate.

Lovelace and the Harlowes, in their distinct ways, violate that moral responsibility and intellectual privilege, revealing by their libidinal and acquisitive actions in subsequent events the shallowness of their commitments to this intellectual public sphere. Very quickl,y the polite salon invoked as the novel's opening scene gives way to a protracted and violent struggle for financial, material, and sexual dominance, and the exchange and discussion of ideas among these leisured and affluent classes is replaced by violence and threats of violence quite outside any central or controlling social order. Indeed, the level of lawless and extra-institutional violence in *Clarissa*, both actual and threatened, is extensive: Clarissa is imprisoned and menaced with a forced marriage by her family, and they in turn fear that Lovelace will try to kidnap her. Like Lovelace during the "elopement"/abduction of Clarissa, the Harlowe uncles travel armed and with armed servants; the Harlowes are said to be planning a counter-abduction of Clarissa, and Anna Howe enlists a female dealer in contraband (Mrs Townsend and her rough sailor brothers) to rescue Clarissa. To manipulate Clarissa and lull her into complacency, Lovelace employs elaborate deceits featuring impersonation, fraud, and forgery, and of course her long imprisonment in the Sinclair brothel is the ultimate lawless act of violence, nothing less than a kidnapping as well as a rape.

All this illegal or extra-legal violence (along with the two duels that Lovelace fights) presupposes a very loosely regulated social order where the elaborate legal and financial arrangements surrounding marriage among the wealthy that preoccupy many of the characters are accompanied by behavior more appropriate, one would think, for gangsters or warring primitive clans than members of the eighteenth-century landed gentry. The contest is nothing less than a struggle between rival gangs or private armies, and command and control in each case are local and particular, with no central or supervising institutional authority in sight. These are opposing households, tribal antagonists only nominally or partially within a supervising municipal or national legal order, and the situation reflects the realities of mid-eighteenth-century law enforcement, which was loose, irregular, local, based on custom as much as statute, far from efficient or bureaucratically centralized.[17] As many critics have emphasized, *Clarissa* is built on broadly defined social antagonisms – the conflict between the fabulously rich Harlowes, those pillars of the upper commercial bourgeoisie who, by accumulating landed estates, have entered the gentry and seek to barge into the aristocracy, and Lovelace, that pampered and privileged representative of the ruling nobility.[18] Lovelace gives special offense to young James, the hope of the family's social rise, by his embodiment of a *droit de seigneur* that is achieved partly by his financial independence but largely by his confident possession of the archaic privileges and prerogatives traditional to a young man of his rank (at least in Richardson's dramatization of an extreme case). Lovelace's intellectual and physical superiority to James Harlowe flows from those privileges, and his reputation as a rake is simply their most glaring effect.

And yet in spite of all the bluster and bravado on both sides, threats of violence (with the awful exception of Clarissa's rape) are just that – feints, charades, stratagems, and half-baked plots. The "implacable" (Lovelace's favorite term for them) Harlowes are a clumsy lot in their unbending demands, and the inability of the Harlowe brothers (father and two uncles) to understand the vindictive and envious resentment of Clarissa's two siblings distorts and dooms their enterprise. And even that slick plotter, Lovelace, is compromised by his posturing vanity and finds himself forced to improvise somewhat frantically, however effectively, in the face of the unexpected, as Clarissa overawes him and resists and evades and even for a while escapes his clutches. Failure and fatal misprision rule this world, in other words, and Richardson's novel dramatizes administrative incompetence and political ineptitude as much as moral blindness and economic rapacity. The book's epistolary format promotes a reader's sense of such failure, as the partial and frequently misinformed correspondents add to the confusion.

In this context of failure, Clarissa herself is a wonderfully improbable character, offering against her adversaries' naked assertions of power and their blundering mistakes in administering it her irrepressible intelligence and moral will, along with a persuasive and serene eloquence both of word and physical presence that all her adversaries respect and indeed fear. And yet Richardson refuses to make his heroine a victim. From the first, we may say, Clarissa denies these treacherous depths and seeks, by her mastery of logical and historical analysis and above all by her employment of rhetorical and persuasive power, to assert a meaningful superficiality, that is, to be exactly what she appears to be, to signify and embody freedom, virtue, and integrity. In its tremendous elaborations of scenes and its repetitive, exhaustive articulations of distinct voices within those scenes, Richardson's novel implicitly values scope, breadth, and comprehensiveness, and ultimately disparages mere depth as unstable and destructive. Although Clarissa is physically penetrated, she preserves an intellectual and moral invincibility that baffles Lovelace, and, as Anna Howe says much earlier, she is capable of penetrating his misleadingly attractive surface: "But were he deep, and ever so deep, you would soon penetrate him, if they would leave you to yourself"(75).[19]

The contest between Clarissa and Lovelace at the heart of the book can be described as a struggle to occupy the calm and stable surfaces of being, an essentially social and political location in which one can claim to be exactly what one appears to be to others, and at the same time refuse to be defined by a turbulent interiority where unruly desires and impulses operate beyond full control of the will. Lovelace's most effective early stratagems do confuse Clarissa and provoke not just fear but unacknowledged emotions that bear out, in part, the accusations of her enemies and critics. For example, when Clarissa is tricked into running away when Lovelace fools her into thinking that her enraged relations are just the other side of the garden door, her rendition of the moment evokes thoughtless and unpremeditated action and the spontaneous fears of a nightmare featuring an enraged family and a father too terrible to behold:

> Now behind me, now before me, now on this side, now on that, turned I my affrighted face in the same moment; expecting a furious brother here, armed servants there, an enraged sister screaming and a father armed with terror in his countenance, more dreadful than even the drawn sword which I saw or those I apprehended. I ran as fast as he, yet knew not that I ran; my fears at the same time that they took all power of thinking from me adding wings to my feet: my fears, which probably would not have suffered me to know what course to take, had I not had him to urge and draw me after him.
>
> (380)

Clarissa follows this description (to Anna Howe) of her elopement with an elaborate inculpatory analysis, translating these revealing spontaneities into which she has been betrayed into *her* slow-motion rendition of her own moral failure and of course into her particular responsibility: "As to this last rashness; now that it is too late, I plainly see how I ought to have conducted myself. ... I should not have been solicitous whether he had got my letter or not. ... And so, to save him an *apprehended* rashness, I have rushed into a *real* one myself" (381). To some extent, Clarissa is deluded, and her moral responsibility (and control) is not quite what she thinks it is, since Lovelace has laid a trap which she could hardly avoid. This is just the beginning of a long series of Lovelace's schemes whereby Clarissa's moral agency will be deeply compromised, shifted away from the sequence of meaningful suffering that she imagines she is enduring toward a sinister and deeply fraudulent charade meant to end in seduction and a devastating, degrading fate (perhaps as one of the whores at Sinclair's).

For all their crazy inventiveness, Lovelace's plots are compromised by Clarissa's resistance and suspicion, but there is one interesting exception when Lovelace, in typical fashion, mixes fact and fiction when he brings on real if temporary illness by taking a dose of ipecacuanha (a dried herb used as an expectorant and emetic) and, with some chicken blood, feigning a burst vessel. Clarissa's reaction is revealing, and all that Lovelace could wish for, as she blames herself and wonders about her feelings for him: "How lately did I think I hated him! – But hatred and anger, I see, are but temporary passions with me. ... I wish he had not been ill in my sight. I was too much affected – Everybody alarming me with his danger – The poor man, from such high health so *suddenly* taken! – And so unprepared!" (678–679). Surprised by her emotions – "I shall have cause to regret this surprise; which has taught me more than I knew of myself" (679) – Clarissa now admits as much as she ever does to the possibility of her own passions and to the necessity of subduing them by rational vigilance: "I hope my reason will gather strength enough from his imperfections (for Mr Lovelace, my dear, is not a wise man in all his ways) to enable me to keep my passions under – What can we do more than govern ourselves by the temporary lights lent us?" (679).

For Clarissa self-management is a contest between reason and the "passions," but for Lovelace the conflict is between opposing passions: active sexual voracity and passive sentimental abasement. He is mainly troubled by his susceptibility to Clarissa's blend of beauty and virtue, and he finds in himself over and over again an attraction and a quality of desire quite new to him. Such feelings get in the way of his grand project, a psychosexual experiment grounded in an essentialist view of women familiar to the readers of amatory fiction:[20]

> As to my CLARISSA, I own that I hardly think there ever was such an angel of a woman. ... Who will be afraid of a trial for this divine lady? – Thou knowest that I have more than once, twice or thrice been tempted to make this trial upon young ladies of name and character: but never yet found one of them to hold me out for a month; nor so long as could puzzle my invention. I have concluded against the whole sex upon it. And now, if I have found a virtue that cannot be corrupted, I will swear that there is not one such in the whole sex. Is not then the whole sex concerned that this trial should be made? – and who is it that knows her, that would not stake upon her head the honour of the whole? – Let her who would refuse it, come forth and desire to stand in her place.
>
> (429)

Let me begin then, as opportunity presents – I will – and watch her every step to find one sliding one; her every moment to find the moment critical. And the rather, as she spares not me but takes every advantage that offers to puzzle and plague me; nor expects, nor thinks me to be a good man. If she be a *woman*, and *love* me, I shall surely catch her tripping: for love was ever a traitor to its harbourer: and Love *within*, and I *without*, she'll be *more* than woman, as the poet say, or I *less* than man, if I succeed not.

(431)

The significance that Lovelace attaches to this trial whereby Clarissa represents "the whole sex" is appropriately and even comically grandiose but also especially revealing in its linking of uncontrollable interiority with a demeaning female generality. Seen in this light, Clarissa struggles to preserve not just her chastity but her individuality and integrity, which are defined in Lovelace's scenario as her doomed attempt to refuse the comic or tragic patterns of female behavior as he has experienced it. Cunning plotter and incipient comic dramatist that he is, Lovelace confronts in Clarissa's resistance a far more complex situation than those in a Haywood novella. He knows that she is not to be tempted with the usual traps, that the customary plot of seduction or the lucky accidents of love will not in this case be sufficient. He shows in the following analysis of the difficulties before him a profound understanding of Clarissa as an individual formed by circumstances rather than a female character who will respond to the devices of romance.

But with what can I tempt her? – RICHES she was born to, and despises, knowing what they are. JEWELS and ornaments, to a mind so much a jewel, and so richly set, her worthy consciousness will not let her value. LOVE, if she be susceptible of love, it seems to be so much under the direction of prudence, that one unguarded moment, I fear, cannot be reasonably hoped for: and so much VIGILANCE ... LOVE OF VIRTUE seems to be *principle*, native, or if *not* native, so deeply rooted that its fibres have struck into her heart, and, as she grew up, so blended and twisted themselves with the strings of life that I doubt there is no separating of the one, without cutting the others asunder.

(657)

To face this complicated entity, an interwoven fabric of principle and feeling in his insightful metaphor of Clarissa's moral and psychological habits, Lovelace marshals plausible and superficial falsity. All his impersonations and inventions involve the creation of audaciously altered identities: the bloated brothel keeper and her whores become the respectable Widow Sinclair and her servants, and the Irish forger and smuggler Patrick MacDonald is transformed into the worthy neighbor of Uncle Harlowe, the frugal retired officer and devoted father of his own daughters, Captain Tomlinson. Such are Clarissa's powers of creating sympathy and pathos, however, that as Tomlinson is introduced to her as potential mediator with her family, the scene for Lovelace turns from its fraudulence to become disturbingly authentic. He tells the imposter Tomlinson that he will be reconciled to the Harlowe clan and will disclaim any future share of their estates: "enough rewarded, were she not to bring a shilling in dowry, in a lady who has a merit superior to all the goods of fortune. True as the Gospel, Belford! Why had not this scene a real foundation?" (694). As Clarissa's eyes sparkle with gratitude, she is moved to a rare failure of speech ("Oh Mr Lovelace, said she – you have infinitely – and there she stopped –"); Lovelace finds himself "puzzled by my own devices ... drawn five or six ways at once" (694). Clarissa thanks Lovelace, weeping at the thought of reconciliation with her family:

> Then drying her eyes with her handkerchief, after a few moments pausing, on a sudden, as if recollecting that she had been led by her joy to an expression of it, which she had not intended I should see, she retired to her chamber with precipitation – leaving me almost as unable to stand it as herself.
>
> In short, I was – I want words to say how I was – My nose had been made to tingle before; my eyes have before been made to glisten by this soul-moving beauty; but so *very* much affected, I never was – for, trying to check my sensibility, it was too strong for me, and I even sobbed – Yes, by my soul, I *audibly* sobbed, and was forced to turn from her before she had well finished her affecting speech.
>
> (695)

Fraud and duplicity are rammed down Lovelace's throat by Clarissa's expressive powers, by the intensity of a feeling dramatized by her physical presence. The truth of Clarissa's being, read in her eyes and gestures and matched by her simple eloquence ("You see me already, said she, another creature. You know not, Mr Lovelace, how near my heart, this hoped for reconciliation is"), extracts, indeed forcibly compels, Lovelace's involuntary emotions and transforms his heartless machinations into authentic and "audible" eruptions from somewhere inside himself. Like all such moments, this is a temporary state for the mercurial Lovelace, but taken all together and culminating in Clarissa's extended death sequence they illustrate the nature of the struggle between these antagonists and its eventual outcome. In a reversal of the amatory pattern, Lovelace's turbulent interiority is provoked by Clarissa's moral and physical presence, a presence that Lovelace is increasingly compelled to read as an inviolable emanation of an integral self whose beautiful surface manifestations are indistinguishable from the radiant interior that they express.

Clarissa's intellect is disordered immediately after the rape, and its main effect seems at first a disruption of her powers of composition and coherent expression. The torn drafts and fragments she writes then (retrieved for Lovelace by Dorcas) are intensely expressive, but she discards them because they describe an interior – mind and soul – no longer radiant and consonant with her beautiful exterior but anguished, confused, unable to imagine a narrative or an argument, lacking in transitions and a clear grasp of consequences and sequences. Here is part of her letter to Lovelace, radically lacking her signature coherence and mouthing the old accusations of her enemies:

> Mr Lovelace, now that I remember what I took pen in hand to say, let me hurry off my thoughts, lest I lose them again – Here I am sensible – And yet I am hardly sensible neither – But I know that my head is not as it should be, for all that – Therefore let me propose one thing to you: it is for *your* good – not *mine*: and this is it:
>
> I must needs be both a trouble and an expense to you. And here my uncle Harlowe, when he knows how I am, will never wish any man to have me: no, not even *you*, who have been the occasion of it – Barbarous and ungrateful! – A less complicated villainy cost a Tarquin – but I forget what I would say again –
>
> Then this is it: I never shall be myself again: I have been a very wicked creature – a vain, proud, poor creature – full of secret pride – which I carried off under an humble guise, and deceived everybody – My sister says so – and now I am punished – so let me be carried out of this house, and out of your sight; and let me be put into that Bedlam privately, which once I saw: but it was a sad sight to me then!
>
> (895)

In spite of this disorientation, Clarissa's recovery is rapid; she attempts an escape a few days later and that night confronts Lovelace in person, with what he calls "an air and action that I never saw equalled" (899). "Air" and "action" are dramatic and oratorical terms of art, for the Clarissa who addresses the cowed and inarticulate Lovelace in this scene is both in manner and in the substance of her speech more than a ruined maid. She appeals to her rights as a political subject, and her interrogation of Lovelace admits of no reply:

> Let me therefore know whether I am to be controlled in the future disposal of myself? Whether, in a country of liberty as *this*, where the sovereign of it must not be guilty of *your* wickedness; and where *you* neither durst have attempted it, had I one friend or relation to look upon me, I am to be kept here a prisoner, to sustain fresh injuries? Whether, in a word, you intend to hinder me from going whither my destiny shall lead me?
>
> (901)

In the few days that follow, Lovelace offers "instant marriage" (942) but Clarissa demands that she be set free: "Why, Mr Lovelace, must I be determined by your motions? – Think you that I will voluntarily give a sanction to the imprisonment of my person?" (942).

Lovelace attempts to negate Clarissa's legalistic and prosecutorial definitions of her situation by staging in characteristically manic fashion a fake trial of his own: a note that Clarissa has written promising Dorcas a reward to help her escape is produced and a noisy farce of a trial is held to lure Clarissa from her locked room for a second violent sexual assault. But the elaborately staged judicial parody is instantly silenced by Clarissa's entrance as "she seemed to tread air, and to be all soul"(949). Her behavior here marks the high point of her post-rape eloquence, and it achieves a new level of blank-verse majesty and denunciatory formality, reducing to awed silence not just Lovelace but the grotesque jury of whores who attend him:

> Oh thou contemptible and abandoned Lovelace, thinkest thou that I see not through this poor villainous plot of thine, and of these thy wicked accomplices?
>
> Thou woman, looking at the mother, once my terror! always my dislike! but now my detestation! shouldst once more (for thine perhaps was the preparation) have provided for me intoxicating potions, to rob me of my senses –

And then, *turning to me*, Thou wretch, mightest more securely have depended upon such a low contrivance as this! –

And ye, vile women, who perhaps have been the ruin, body and soul, of hundreds of innocents (you show me *how*, in full assembly), know that I am not married – ruined as I am by your helps, I bless God, I am *not* married to this miscreant – And I have friends that will demand my honour at your hands! – And to whose authority I will apply; for none has this man over me. Look to it then, what further insults you offer me, or incite him to offer me, I am a person, though thus vilely betrayed, of rank and fortune. I never will be his; and to your utter ruin will find friends to pursue you: and now I have this full proof of your detestable wickedness, and have heard your base incitements, will have no mercy upon you! –

...

But she turned to me: Stop where thou art, Oh vilest and most abandoned of men! – Stop where thou art! – Nor, with that determined face, offer to touch me, if thou wouldst not that I should be a corpse at thy feet!

To my astonishment, she held forth a penknife in her hand, the point to her own bosom, grasping resolutely the whole handle, so that there was no offering to take it from her.

I offer not mischief to anybody but myself. You, sir, and ye women, are safe from every violence of mine. The LAW shall be all my resource: the LAW, and she spoke the word with emphasis, that to such people carries natural terror with it, and now struck a panic into them.

(949, 950)

This "penknife scene," as critics call it, is Clarissa's definitive recasting of the terms and actors of Lovelace's seduction plot. By all the moral and rhetorical force she can muster, she enforces a generalized significance for her story that rejects Lovelace's comedy of female essentialism: "Innocence so triumphant: villainy so debased" (951) is Lovelace's summary. The tremendously emphatic "LAW" she invokes terrifies the whores, but this is not English justice, not man's but God's law. Thrillingly melodramatic as it surely is, the scene is in its way ultimately tactical, Clarissa's final revision of a negotiating position that she has attempted to sustain since her initial dilemma at Harlowe Place. Browbeaten and threatened by her family, tricked and violated by Lovelace, Clarissa turns to this melodrama and then to morbid transcendence to expose the bankruptcy of the moral and legal order upon which her actions from the beginning have relied. The Harlowes and Lovelace have refused good faith negotiation, debased the coin of rational exchange, and subverted by force and violence the meeting of minds in the public sphere that Clarissa has proposed. She rejects marriage to her rapist, rules out public prosecution for her wrongs, and now refuses to consider emigration to America because each of those seemingly sensible courses has been negated as a possibility by her opponents, whose actions taken together have redefined and degraded the realm of discourse and action and pushed her into a corner where desperate symbolism is her only option if she is to triumph or dominate.

Fully a third of *Clarissa* occurs after her escape from the Sinclair brothel and much of that space (as long as most novels) is taken up with Clarissa's slow dying and its complicated aftermath, including not just general mourning by all concerned but a series of Clarissa's posthumous letters to Lovelace and the Harlowes and her will, written during her last days on earth. Although Richardson does not choose to assign any particular physiological cause to Clarissa's illness, her decline sets in dramatically after the Sinclair women discover her whereabouts and have her arrested for debt. As Belford (now her devoted historian) evokes for Lovelace the bailiff's house where he finds her, a crucial scenic shift takes place. We have been living, as it were, in Lovelace's various fake locations and plots, full of imposters and lies, dependent upon the lines of power that he exercises, his will carried out by servants and disreputable clients. Those spaces have also featured Clarissa's beautiful but lonely resistances, the noble attitudes of heroic virginity and the eloquent protests of wronged innocence. But as Belford renders Clarissa's sordid room (the single most detailed descriptive passage in the book, indeed one of the very few in it), readers are transported to the material realities and truths papered over by Lovelace's plots.[21] We encounter with a shock the naturalistic obverse of romance, a degraded and deeply ordinary world that has been lurking behind Lovelace's London stage set:

> A horrid hole of a house, in an alley they call a court; stairs wretchedly narrow, even to the first-floor rooms: and into a den they led me, with broken walls which had been papered, as I saw by a multitude of tacks, and some torn bits held on by the rusty heads. ... The floor indeed was clean, but the ceiling was smoked with variety of figures, and initials of names, that

had been the woeful employment of wretches who had no other way to amuse themselves.

(1064)

Modern readers of *Clarissa* (and other eighteenth-century novels) are often surprised by their thinness of descriptive detail, their emphasis on plotting relationships and their interest in emotional and intellectual complications rather than in rendering the concrete sights and textures of the material world in which they are set. For all of its particularized settings, from the Harlowe estates to the roads, streets, suburbs, and neighborhoods of London (as well as their interiors and furnishings), *Clarissa* depends upon our supplying (as readers no longer can) the physical appearances of such places. Men and women in thought and action is where mature attention is directed, so when Belford offers this proto-Dickensian *mise-en-scène* the breakdown of order and significance is precisely the issue. Clarissa is swallowed up by the degraded specific physicality of a world over which she has hitherto presided, and she is inserted into a scene in which things and their small histories over-whelm the tragic pageant and heroic generalized meanings of virtue betrayed. Situated among these shabby furnishings and tokens of past despair, Clarissa herself is an object, diminished but still remarkable and heart-breakingly lovely in Belford's hushed rendition:

> She was kneeling in a corner of the room, near the dismal window, against the table, on an old bolster (as it seemed to be) of the cane couch, half-covered with her handkerchief; her back to the door; which was only shut to (no need of fasten-ings!); her arms crossed upon the table, the fore-finger of her right hand in her Bible. She had perhaps been reading in it, and could read no longer. Paper, pens, ink, lay by her book on the table. Her dress was white damask, exceeding neat; but her stays seemed not tight-laced. ... Her headdress was a little discomposed; her charming hair, in natural ringlets, as you have heretofore described it, but a little tangled, as if not lately kembed, irregularly shading one side of the loveliest neck in the world; as her disordered, rumpled handkerchief did the other. Her face (Oh how altered from what I had seen it! yet lovely in spite of all her griefs and sufferings!) was reclined, when we entered, upon her crossed arms; but so as not more than one side of it to be hid.
>
> When I surveyed the room around, and the kneeling lady, sunk with majesty too in her white, flowing robes (for she had

not on a hoop), spreading the dark, though not dirty, floor, and
illuminating that horrid corner; her linen beyond imagination
white, considering that she had not been undressed ever since
she had been here; I thought my concern would have choked
me.

(1065)

Although she will continue as she weakens unto death to write as much
as ever, Clarissa from here begins to assume an icon-like stability, an
object of wonder to the small (but socially comprehensive) group who
tend to her final needs and worship at her shrine: Belford, her cousin,
Colonel Morden, the Smiths (to whose house she is returned from the
bailiff's), the Widow Lovick (her fellow lodger there), and the doctor
and the apothecary who attend her in her illness. With Lovelace
keeping his distance, Belford reports on the lady, and Clarissa is more
often than not in these pages a character in his narrative, assuming an
increasingly objective status as others observe her rather than a
constructor of her own personality or identity. Clarissa's writings begin
to turn away from narrative and the hopeful investigations and negotiations of the secular novelistic mode with which she began. Biblical
paraphrase, religious meditation, moral homilies framed as contrite
corrections of past errors and misunderstandings, a series of letters to
be delivered after her death to the principals in the story, and her metic-
ulously detailed will – Clarissa's deathbed writings partake of the new
objectivity that she is acquiring as she turns away from self to the
community of grief and moral affirmation that her death will create.
There is an allegory of literary genres lurking just under the surface of
the story, as Clarissa's transfiguration marks her final repudiation of the
amatory tradition in both its comic and tragic forms. Her disappearance into a ghostly voice speaking from beyond the grave is a definitive
rejection of the novelistic interrogations of possibility with which she
began so hopefully. Her old subjectivity in pieces after the rape, her
reputation as unsullied paragon (in her eyes) destroyed, Clarissa in her
extraordinary extended death scene not only rebuilds a new, etherealized selfhood but in the process restores a community around her, a
group united in mourning and in the case of Lovelace and the
Harlowes in desperate lamentation. Lovelace's destruction of Clarissa,
one might argue, has worked by severing her from the social network
and family history within which she achieved and might well have
maintained her singular personality. With their betrayal of trust and
credit, their substitution of impersonation and improvisation for identity and history, his plots have created through bribery and violence a

communal anti-world where all coherence breaks down and where the reciprocal and interpenetrating interactions of self and society that Clarissa needs to be herself are not possible. But now and to the end of the novel Clarissa is nothing less than the organizing center of the characters' lives, and she becomes, in her slow and majestic dying as well as in the post-mortem phase of the narrative, an object of wonder. She thus restores authenticity and objectivity to social relations and renews that network of trust and reciprocity that Lovelace and her family have destroyed. Moreover, in leaving behind an elaborate will and sending Lovelace and her family those moral homilies from the grave, this etherealized shade restores the currency of the material world that supports that social network as she leaves careful directions for the disposition of her estate: just the right bequests for mourning rings; the correct sums according to rank to servants and to humble friends ("To the worthy Mrs Lovick...and to Mrs Smith...I bequeath all my linen, and all my unsold laces; to be divided equally between them, as they shall agree; or, in case of disagreement, the same to be sold, and the money arising to be equally shared by them" (1417)); her philanthropies to the deserving poor to be continued at the appropriate levels; her library to her cousin, Dolly Hervey; her locket with a miniature of Anna Howe to her worthy suitor, the good Mr Hickman; and so it goes for many pages. The will, in short, is a move back to human relations and the material objects that cement and signify them. Clarissa is a great soul who is mindful, even from beyond the grave, of the social network of recognitions and reciprocities in which she will continue to have her special sort of being.

Clarissa's transfiguration tips the balance against Lovelace, whose shallow triumphs have always been compromised by her dignity and resolute principles. But as he wrote portions of the novel and showed them to a circle of friends and admirers, Richardson was alarmed by the positive reactions that some had to this witty and charming rake. As he wrote to Lady Bradshaigh in 1748, he thought he "had made him too wicked, too Intriguing, too revengeful, (and that in his very first Letters) for him to obtain the Favour and good Wishes of any worthy Heart of *either* Sex."[22] Responding to the sympathy that Lovelace provoked in many of his first readers, Richardson "threw into his Character some deeper Shades," and by the third 1751 edition of the novel he had made substantial alterations designed to blacken Lovelace even further.[23] What Richardson could not revise away, of course, was the mythic resonance of his character, the perfect "aristocratic" antithesis of his "bourgeois" heroine who embodies, as Richardson imagines him, an ethos of socially licensed privilege that seems to have fascinated and frightened eighteenth-century readers for whom the rake figure suggested a protracted juvenile criminality and a dashing freedom from normal moral constraints. The mid-eighteenth-century British state could exert very little physical force to protect its citizens, and social order seems to have been maintained by the force of ideology, custom, and tradition. As a number of historians have observed, the ruling oligarchy, in the words of E.P. Thompson, maintained its hegemony largely through a theatricalization of power in its appearance and bearing: "the elaboration of wig and powder, ornamented clothing and canes, and even the rehearsed patrician gestures and the hauteur of bearing and expression, all were designed to exhibit authority to the plebs and to exact from them deference."[24] Lovelace, in his command of those gestures of power, is both an embodiment of that hegemony and a shameless exploiter of the extra-legal privileges that it confers upon him. In the moral and social economy projected by *Clarissa* in which an individual earns his or her status by original moral action in the face of a surrounding fatality, Lovelace is an archaic and dangerously nostalgic figure who must be repudiated and turned from an aristocratic exemplar into a psychological subject. Richardson tries to accomplish that throughout the novel by exposing Lovelace to Clarissa's steadfast adherence to self-imposed moral regulation; her lonely, beleaguered virtue is sustained against the crowded field of Lovelace's gang, his private army of fellow rakes, servants, and other co-conspirators drawn from the ranks of a rootless urban criminal class. Through her passion play of holy dying Clarissa raises her own cult or community as a counter-force to that gang, and her personal transfiguration is also a social transformation.

NOTES

1 In *A Natural Passion: A Study of the Novels of Samuel Richardson* (Oxford, Clarendon Press, 1974), p. 24, Margaret Anne Doody traces Pamela's divergence from "a minor tradition established by the writers of love-stories told in the feminine voice."

2 William B. Warner, "The elevation of the novel in England: hegemony and literary history," *ELH* (1992), vol. 59, pp. 586–587.

3 The 1725 London edition is reprinted in *Popular Fiction by Women: 1660–1730*, ed. Paula R. Backscheider and J. Richetti (Oxford, Clarendon Press, 1996), p. 227. All further page references in the text are to this edition.

4 The abbess of this monastery is the "particular Friend" of Fantomina's mother, and it may just be that Haywood intends readers to see this as a temporary banishment rather than an actual taking of the veil and

monastic vows. See Paula Backscheider's note in *Popular Fiction by Women 1660–1730*, p. 248.

5 In *Masquerade and Civilization: The Carnivalesque in Eighteenth-century Culture and Fiction* (Stanford, CA, Stanford University Press, 1986), p. 6, Terry Castle argues that the eighteenth-century masquerade "projected an anti-nature, a world upside-down, an intoxicating reversal of ordinary sexual, social, and metaphysical hierarchies. The cardinal ideological distinctions underlying eighteenth-century cultural life, including the fundamental divisions of sex and class, were broached."

6 Alasdair McIntyre, *After Virtue: A Study in Moral Theory* (Notre Dame, IN, University of Notre Dame Press, 1984), p. 208.

7 Samuel Richardson, *Pamela*, ed. Peter Sabor, with an introduction by Margaret Anne Doody (Harmondsworth, Penguin, 1980), pp. 49–50. All further page references to *Pamela* in the text are to this edition, which is based on an 1801 edition prepared by Richardson's daughters which incorporated all the fairly numerous revisions that he had made in an interleaved copy of *Pamela*. In this edition, Richardson made Pamela much more genteel than she is in the first edition of 1740. Shifts: women's undergarments; handkerchiefs: women's neckwear, worn folded and draped over the shoulders and knotted over the breasts; Cambric aprons, and four Holland ones: aprons were a decorative overgarment to female dress; cambric is fine French linen, Holland is Dutch linen for everyday use.

8 Margaret Anne Doody sees *Pamela* as anti-pastoral and the heroine as an authentic servant: "there is no hint in this vivid little person of high birth below stairs. She is a respectable servant- girl." But she also sees her, misleadingly and romantically I think, as "a downright rebel" who "seeks personal and spiritual" freedom and becomes "a revolutionary heroine." Doody, *A Natural Passion*, pp. 43, 60. Such remarks miss the complexity of the heroine's social positioning.

9 But Tom Keymer claims that *Shamela* is not an "attack on plebeian adventurism" but is a continuation of Fielding's satire "on the dubious ethos of Walpole's enterprise culture: Shamela is presented as the very type of the corrupt and pharisaical entrepreneur." Tom Keymer, *Richardson's "Clarissa" and the Eighteenth-century Reader* (Cambridge, Cambridge University Press, 1992), p. 25. On the controversy excited by the novel and its parodies, see Bernard Kreissman, *Pamela-Shamela: A Study of the Critiques, Parodies and Adaptation of Richardson's Pamela* (Lincoln, NE, University of Nebraska Studies, 1960).

10 Sabor (*Pamela*, ed. Sabor) glosses these two terms. *Callimanco*: glossy woollen material from Flanders; *burn*: burnish, polish; Pamela plans to polish the silver braid on the shoes and sell it with some old silver buckles.

11 Sabor (*Pamela*, ed. Sabor) notes that the last sentence represents one of Richardson's additions, added to the 1801 edition that his Penguin reprints. Sabor observes that this sentence is Richardson's response to critics who were troubled by what seemed to be her excessive interest in clothes.

12 *Selected Letters of Samuel Richardson*, ed. John Carroll (Oxford, Clarendon Press, 1964), To Aaron Hill, 1741, p. 41.

13 See the influential and revealing study of twentieth-century American popular romances by Janice Radway, *Reading the Romance: Women, Patriarchy,*

and Popular Literature (Chapel Hill, North Carolina, University of North Carolina Press, 1984).

14 *Selected Letters*, To Lady Bradshaigh, 26 October 1748, p.92. *The Clarissa Project, Clarissa, The Third Edition, 1751*, 8 vols (New York, AMS Press, 1990), Vol. I, viii–ix.

15 Samuel Richardson, *Clarissa; or The History of a Young Lady*, ed. Angus Ross (Harmondsworth, Penguin, 1985), p. 555. All page references in brackets in the text are to this edition, which reprints the first edition of the novel.

16 Tom Keymer's *Richardson's "Clarissa" and the Eighteenth-century Reader* is a brilliant historicizing (and modifying) of the claims made by two earlier deconstructionist readings of *Clarissa* by Terry Castle and William B. Warner. Keymer finds in *Clarissa* a deliberate and complex didactic project in which Richardson (rather like Milton in *Paradise Lost*) tests and traps his reader by making "reading not simple but problematic; and his expectation is that the reader's activity in addressing the resulting difficulties will itself be a source of instruction" (p. 68). For Keymer, there is more at stake than the "slippage between world and word" or "the deformations that arise from the rhetorical or performative tendencies of first-person discourse" that deconstructionist critics pursue. In Clarissa's flight from her "father's house," in her self-serving moral superiority and blindness, Keymer finds a complexity that, for eighteenth-century moral and political ideology, renders her a misleading paragon and to some extent justifies her implacable and stupidly brutal family. He concludes, powerfully, that *Clarissa* is "an adversarial collection of subjective visions, each vying to establish its own pre-eminence and challenging the assumptions of its rivals" (231). My own view is that Keymer is more systematically intelligent than Richardson and that the didactic project is not as seamlessly effective or as ideologically coherent as he claims.

17 J. M. Beattie's *Crime and the Courts in England 1660–1800* (Princeton, Princeton University Press, 1986), p. 29, emphasizes how rudimentary the law enforcement system was in the period. Social control (even in the London parishes) was a matter of the force of moral and communal custom and the traditional authority of "parents, gentry, and magistrates" rather than of police force and judicial prosecution.

18 The classic statement of the sociohistorical theme in *Clarissa* is Christopher Hill's 1955 essay, "Clarissa Harlowe and her times," reprinted in *Samuel Richardson: A Collection of Critical Essays*, ed. John Carroll (Englewood Cliffs, NJ, Prentice Hall, 1969), pp. 102–103, 105. Hill describes the historical coherence of the Harlowes' plot to marry Clarissa to Solmes, and he notes that the economic and political realities of the early eighteenth century in Britain left the landed class "in possession of its power but deprived of power to check the development of capitalism." The Harlowes, Hill points out, hope to consolidate their commercially derived wealth and ally themselves to the landed gentry and nobility, but Grandfather Harlowe's will has interrupted that grand design by leaving his estate to Clarissa. So the proposed marriage to Solmes (who agrees that, if they have no surviving children, his estates and Clarissa's will revert to the Harlowes) is a strategy to keep her estates in the family, and "the grandfather's will from the start sets personal affection in conflict with family ambition."

19 Keymer in *Richardson's "Clarissa" and the Eighteenth-century Reader* makes much of Clarissa's subtle flaws and, like many commentators, dwells on Dr Johnson's remark that "there is always something which she prefers to truth" (*Anecdotes of the late Samuel Johnson, LL.D. during the last Twenty Years of His Life, by Hesther Lynch Piozzi*, in George Birkbeck Hill (ed.) *Johnsonian Miscellanies* (New York, Barnes and Noble, 1966; originally published 1897), Vol. I, p. 297). His amazing contention is that her "basic strategy" is "to claim exemption from the duty to obey on rigorously casuistical grounds" (130). "Her letters," he insists, "seem determined not by 'reality' but by the self-image she prefers to project, and they are based on a model of daughterly exemplariness that is increasingly at odds with her actual state" (135). And yet if Clarissa is not to be trusted and valued, who in the book is?

20 Margaret Anne Doody explains that *Clarissa* was Richardson's adaptation of the "conventions of the 'inflaming Novels' and 'idle Romances' which he condemns," and Lovelace a deepening of the charming "rake-hero" of the popular novel of seduction, as practiced, pre-eminently, by Eliza Haywood (*A Natural Passion*, pp. 128, 140–147). James Grantham Turner's essay, "Lovelace and the paradoxes of libertinism," places him in a tradition of "libertine sexuality" and brilliantly explores the contradictions that Lovelace (and the tradition) enacts where his "intense assertion of individual rebellion and individual libido turns out to be quite conformist, since it aims to prove an existing theory, on the established (if scandalous) ideology of female submission and female arousal" (*Samuel Richardson: Tercentenary Essays*, ed. Margaret Anne Doody and Peter Sabor, Cambridge, Cambridge University Press, 1989, p. 72).

21 As Tom Keymer, otherwise concerned to stress *Clarissa*'s dramatizing of uncertainty and indeterminacy, notes, Belford's descriptions at the end possess a "rigorous circumstantial realism" that in "their radical attention to the physical" are unique in the novel. To be sure, Keymer disparages (with Lovelace) Belford's narrative as simply "a new form of unreliability, as inadequate as its predecessors in establishing a viewpoint from which all the complications of the history may be sorted and understood" (*Richardson's "Clarissa" and the Eighteenth-century Reader*, pp. 241–242).

22 *Selected Letters*, ed. Carroll, 15 December 1748, p.113.

23 *Selected Letters*, ed. Carroll, p. 113. Richardson revised his novel almost continuously in response to readers' reactions. He was especially troubled by those who wanted the novel to have a happy ending in which a reformed Lovelace married Clarissa, so he went out of his way to make Lovelace a less attractive character. The 1751 third edition contains his final revisions, and in that edition he marked new passages with "bullets" in the margins. *Clarissa. Or, The History of a Young Lady*, *The Clarissa Project*, Vols 1–8, is a facsimile reprinting of the 1751 third edition, with an introduction by Florian Stuber and a bibliographic note by O. M. Brack (New York, AMS Press, 1990).

24 E.P. Thompson, *Customs in Common: Studies in Traditional Popular Culture* (New York, The New Press, 1991), p. 45.

5

FIELDING

System and satire

I

Since all happy families are perhaps boringly alike, amatory fiction requires domestic strife. Passion breeds isolation and turns individuals upon themselves; the plot's recurring motion is the dramatic unraveling of those bonds and loyalties that should sustain domestic relationships. Sexual desire separates individuals from a social self defined by obligations and reciprocities, a self that should be rooted in institutions, in custom and tradition, expressed not in exalted passion but in those visible, external, concrete property relationships that for eighteenth-century British society signify identity and status. And much amatory fiction, even Richardson's, also effectively isolates readers, who are offered vicarious involvement with suffering individuals and are encouraged first and foremost to exercise sympathy and enjoy participation before judging or considering critically.

Although they express deep unhappiness with many aspects of society, Fielding's novels are affirmations of community and defenders of a neglected sense of connection and tradition. Each encourages a form of dialogue and exchange between the narrator and a knowing reader, and often enough the narrator appeals to a shared understanding with his reader about the continuities of literary tradition and its moral and social implications. Each of Fielding's three novels to some extent relies upon an audience aware of the problems surrounding the moral and aesthetic shortcomings of modern narrative. And those problems are defined in the novels, both explicitly and implicitly, as how to affirm community and continuity in the face of their erosion by this rival narrative impulse that is not only shapelessly maladroit but overvalues an isolated and aberrant individuality. In pursuit of the striking particular case, popular narrative, as seen from Fielding's perspective, misrepresents the larger, overseeing social world with which morally useful and aesthetically pleasing narrative should concern itself.

In distinct but related ways, amatory fiction and its transfiguration in Richardson's novels render the individual person as essentially mysterious, a receding dark cavern of contradictory, unpredictable impulses and desires. Those emotions that amatory fiction, no matter how sophisticated or piously didactic, renders as mysterious, Fielding's narratives classify and contextualize by means of continuous reference to communal and historical relationships. Fielding's narrative program aims to demystify the individual, to apply moral analysis and to make satiric judgments that classify persons in terms of their actions and circumstances, their practical relationships, reciprocal obligations to others, and most of all their longings for the actualities of riches, power, pleasure, or, in the noblest instances, their desire for virtuous happiness. In place of the interminable analytic sessions, as we may call them, of amatory fiction, Fielding articulates in his novels a finite external system that presents a social and moral cross-section of humanity who are striving to define their place (more often to improve their position) in an institutional order. Within that system, both knowledge and action (moral agency, in short) are possible, if complicated and hindered by pervasive knavery, and the subject matter of narrative is more extensive than the compulsions of individual psychology which, as Fielding presents it, at least in his first two novels, is essentially settled and stable. The unfinished and the unpredictable in Fielding's narratives is the political and historical realm, where recurrent human types adapt in distinct ways to their particular circumstances, where individuals are contesting for pleasure, power, and happiness, and where the production of narrative itself is an aspect of such competition. Like his fictional characters, Fielding is an active and political presence, plotting, cajoling, seeking favor and patronage from readers, flattering his friends, attacking his enemies, identifying his activities as a writer as a contest for superiority with other writers.

Fielding was drawn to fiction by circumstances, partly of his own making, that forced him to abandon his career as England's leading comic playwright in the 1730s.[1] His scorn for rival narratives is in part a continuation of the satirical spirit of his plays and of his polemical political journalism during the preceding decade. Deprived of the major source of his livelihood and (apparently) provoked to write *Shamela* by his amused contempt for *Pamela*, Fielding turned in his first two novels, *Joseph Andrews* (1742) and *Tom Jones* (1749), to a style energized and to some extent organized by his rejection of the Richardsonian novel and its amatory predecessors. The origins of his

new brand of fiction lie in Fielding's distinctive social and cultural position and in the attitudes that he developed during his later career as a
reforming magistrate and social pamphleteer. Descended from patrician
stock, educated at Eton and then at Leiden in Holland, the young
Fielding found himself without patrimony and dependent upon his
talents as a writer to make a living and to attract rich or powerful
patrons. Culturally privileged but economically deprived, Fielding in all
his writing but especially in his novels nonetheless resists the role of
mere literary producer for hire in the emerging commercial order in the
1740s and 1750s. Early in his career as a moral essayist, Fielding looked
back to writers in the political and cultural opposition in the age of
Queen Anne and George I. Styling himself "Scriblerus Secundus," he
evoked Pope, Swift, Arbuthnot, and Gay as his models, and indeed as a
dramatist he continued their assault on the corruption of the Walpole
government. Years later when he came to write fiction, Fielding was by
habit and disposition still a satirical and political polemicist, and his
targets are equally what he sees as the prevailing low standards of
popular narrative and its larger context, the moral and political state of
things. Fielding's fiction is rooted in his ideas about the proper nature of
narrative, and those ideas are in turn part of encompassing notions
about literature, morality, politics, and society.

Fielding's main predecessors, Defoe and Richardson, had produced
fictions in which characters speak for themselves and authors are in
some sense coyly absent, leaving readers then and now to wonder who
speaks for them, or indeed if they have a proper voice and position.
Fielding's narrator is nothing if not discursive and argumentative; he
seeks to suppress individuation in his characters in order to insist much
of the time on their generalized moral and social meaning and to give
primacy in his text to the play of thought and satiric laughter in the
dialogue that he conducts with his implied audience. In all three of his
novels, Fielding attempts to reshape popular narrative by weaving some
of its strands into a new fabric – the most obvious are amatory fiction
and picaresque adventure – and by his satiric thoughtfulness to make
fiction meaningful by redirecting it from the vicarious experience of the
particular. Fielding takes the expressively realistic shapelessness of
popular fiction (the deliberate randomness of picaresque adventure
fiction and the opportunistic intensities of the amatory formula) and
subjects the events of his plot to artificial arrangement and literary
structuring that have several circular implications. The romance pattern
in *Joseph Andrews* and *Tom Jones* and the epic model in *Amelia* serve as
stable counterpoints to each narrative's sprawling contemporary
specifics and messy historical particulars: recurrence and repetition are

dramatized as primary in human affairs, and the universal is in theory able to replace the particular as the standard of meaningfulness. The burden of the narrator's conversation with his readers is precisely the necessity for reprocessing contemporary realities into these much more aesthetically pleasing and morally symmetrical patterns and repetitions, since the scandal of contemporary life, as Fielding's novels approach it, is the absence or at least the continued erosion of traditional order and the rarity of virtuous action. The narrator's optimistic drift is that modern disorder is really a form of comic recurrence; what else can you expect from human nature? he asks, and warns readers in *Joseph Andrews* not to mistake his characters for particular individuals whom they are bound to resemble:

> I declare here once for all, I describe not Men, but Manners; not an Individual, but a Species. Perhaps it will be answered, Are not the Characters then taken from Life? To which I answer in the Affirmative; nay, I believe I might aver, that I have writ little more than I have seen. The Lawyer is not only alive, but hath been so these 4000 Years, and I hope God will indulge his Life as many yet to come. He hath not indeed confined himself to one Profession, one Religion, or one Country; but when the first mean selfish Creature appeared on the human stage, who made Self the Centre of the whole Creation; would give himself no Pain, incur no Danger, advance no Money to assist, or preserve his Fellow-Creatures; then was our Lawyer born; and whilst such a Person as I have described, exists on Earth, so long shall he remain upon it.[2]

Fielding imagines with some grandiosity that the Lawyer's moral deformity will bring private shame to "thousands in their Closets" as they mark in their mirrors their resemblance to him. Readers who proceed from here through Fielding's novels will see in many instances that eighteenth-century lawyers and the mid-century legal code and its enforcement are matters of grave concern for him. Lawyers figure in Fielding's narratives as crucially particularized and specifically historicized entities, and he is often at pains to make his readers see the scandalous contemporaneity of such characters as they operate within the special brutalities and corruptions of the mid-eighteenth-century legal system. Published in the year that Walpole fell from power, *Joseph Andrews* is an attack on the abuses in contemporary English society, and indeed the list of Fielding's satiric targets is comprehensive: the law, the aristocracy and landed gentry, ecclesiastical preferment, and various professions, including lawyers, clergymen, and doctors. In one very clear sense, the satire is traditional and to that extent merely literary, part of the Cervantic manner which Fielding advertises on his title page. Particular reference and local or topical resonance are balanced, and yet they are hardly negated by these comic recurrences and repetitions of literary tradition, which are compromised by the joking and self-deprecation with which Fielding delivers them. Fielding's problem, in this balancing act, between satiric generality and contemporary specificity, is to prevent the moral complacency built into rehearsals of comic recurrence, to preserve indignation and ironic scorn in the social here and now by marking at times the difference between these modern instances and their literary antecedents without giving up the pleasures of recognition or succumbing to the vulgar particularity and illusionistic immediacy of the Richardsonian novel. Narrative representation is inevitably a form of controlling and stabilizing reality, but Fielding's universalizing is undercut and made tensely interesting, I will argue in the pages that follow, by its interactions with recalcitrant contemporary materials. Romance and epic patterns laid over the mid-eighteenth-century social scene produce a jarring effect whereby Fielding's arch literary shapings and structurings are factitiously funny, signifying profound disgust with modern life in their divergence from it as well as offering attentive readers temporary comic compensation and the satisfactions of moral and intellectual superiority.

Consider in this regard the history of Lady Booby in *Joseph Andrews*. Hers is an oft-told tale. Like Potiphar's wife or Phèdre or any number of amorous middle-aged women in literature, she lusts after a younger man. But Joseph is her footman and the immediate joke is the hilarious reversal of the Pamela story. Even as Fielding laughs at Joseph's priggish refusal of her favors, he uses the occasion to contribute to what we might call the book's satiric system and to give this comic scene an edge of protest at the abuse of power in high places. The lady asks Joseph why he should retain his virtue when she as his social superior has condescended to compromise her own with him:

> 'Madam,' said Joseph, 'I can't see why her having no Virtue should be a Reason against my having any. Or why, because I am a Man, or because I am poor, my Virtue must be subservient to her Pleasures.' 'I am out of patience,' cries the Lady: 'Did ever mortal hear of a Man's Virtue! Did ever the greatest, or the gravest Men pretend to any of this Kind! Will Magistrates who punish Lewdness, or Parsons, who preach

against it, make any scruple of committing it? And can a Boy,
a Stripling, have the Confidence to talk of his Virtue?'

(I, viii, 41)

Lady Booby is quite at home in a world of purely nominal ethical
action, where in fact the enforcement of virtue is really a means for the
great and the grave she invokes to control those below them. Her obsession with Joseph soon enough turns nasty and becomes much more
overtly a question of her assertion of class privilege and power than of
mere sexuality. For all of Fielding's ridicule of the Pamela story and his
contempt for the self-satisfaction of merely technical virginity, Joseph's
defense echoes a serious aspect of his sister's resistance in its questioning
of sexual servitude, for he is being subjected to what we would nowadays call sexual harassment. Racked by her lingering passion for Joseph
and fiercely jealous of his innocent Fanny, Lady Booby exemplifies in
her specific abuses of power the corruptions attendant upon property
and economic privilege that are Fielding's recurrent targets.
Significantly, she is the only character in *Joseph Andrews* who possesses
something like that turbulent interiority and psychosexual confusion
(without any of the mystery, of course) that, for amatory fiction, are
signs of an authenticity beyond social and historical circumstances but
in Lady Booby are precisely the identifying tokens of her rank and privilege. So Fielding's exploration of her psychosexual intensities treats
them with a comic scorn based on a contempt for them as nothing
more than the self-indulgent, leisure-class luxury of introspective sexual
fantasy that the virtuous, lower-class characters obviously lack time or
opportunity to indulge. Lady Booby's passions are so powerfully
consuming and self-destructive that only "Pride" can rescue her, and
her resolution of her tortured longings is like those desires themselves
rooted in the imperious prerogatives of wealth:

> Her Passion at length grew so violent that it forced her on
> seeking Relief, and now she thought of recalling him: But
> Pride forbad that, Pride which soon drove all softer Passions
> from her Soul, and represented to her the Meanness of him
> she was fond of. That Thought soon began to obscure his
> Beauties; Contempt succeeded next, and then Disdain, which
> presently introduced her Hatred of the Creature who had
> given her so much Uneasiness. ... Revenge came now to her
> Assistance; and she considered her Dismission of him stript,
> and with a Character, without the utmost Pleasure. She rioted
> in the several kinds of Misery, which her Imagination

suggested to her, might be his Fate; and with a Smile composed of Anger, Mirth, and Scorn, viewed him in the Rags in which her Fancy had drest him.

(IV, I, 279)

Lady Booby's pleasure in the pain and social humiliation of others is the class-bound egoism that Fielding's novels are out to castigate (and of course Lady Booby will be frustrated in her desires for revenge) and to replace with a form of generous ridicule and tolerant contempt. And yet "Anger, Mirth, and Scorn" describe in a way the very satisfactions that Fielding also hopes to provide for his readers as they survey the gallery of knaves, rogues, and viciously self-absorbed hustlers across the broad range of eighteenth-century life that *Joseph Andrews* offers. These strong and morally deforming reactions are tempered and softened by Fielding's comic universalizing and literary structuring, which mollify hatred and turn his narrative toward sentimental and nostalgic resolutions, which are always of course qualified by their comically arbitrary and artificial highlighting as literary (and outrageously improbable or wonderfully preposterous) effects.

If Lady Booby receives Fielding's harshest treatment as an embodiment of the class-specific self-indulgence licensed by amatory fiction, Parson Abraham Adams is the book's true hero, a learned innocent, sweetly naive in a world of pseudo-sophistication and ruthless self-seeking. Where Lady Booby derives from the amatory fiction that Fielding loves to deride, Adams marches out of the picaresque, Cervantic mode which he proposes to imitate. Her volatile emotions and confused and circular psychosexual movements are parallel and inferior to Adams' (and Joseph's and Fanny's) literal and purposeful travel through the English countryside and through the twists and turns and happy accidents of what turns out to be a romance plot. Joseph's struggle to get home after his dismissal by Lady Booby, along with Fanny's quest for him and Parson Adams' lucky discovery of his injured former pupil, is the subject of the plot, and it provides occasion for the social panorama which is Fielding's broadening of the narrow *mis-en-scène* of Richardson's *Pamela*.

And in this parodic substitution Fielding presents Adams and Joseph as exemplary replacements for modern individuals such as Pamela and Colley Cibber, who have the gall to offer themselves for readers' emulation:

It is a trite but true Observation, that Examples work more forcibly on the Mind than Precepts: And if this be just in what is odious and blameable, it is more strongly so in what is amiable and praise-worthy. Here Emulation most effectually operates upon us, and inspires our Imitation in an irresistible manner. A good Man therefore is a standing Lesson to all his Acquaintance, and of far greater use in that narrow Circle than a good Book.

(I, i, 17)

Fielding's opening joke is to take seriously the preposterous claim that degraded modern books like Cibber's *Apology* and Richardson's *Pamela* make that their characters' exemplary lives can serve as powerful examples that supersede general moral instruction, and behind his joke is the more serious worry that modern narrative has appropriated and trivialized the truism that particular examples are more effective than generalized moral truth. *Joseph Andrews* is emphatically a book, a parody of what Fielding considers bad books and an imitation of a great one, *Don Quixote*. And Parson Adams, especially, is a bookish character who lives very happily much of the time in a world of classical learning and literature which for him is clearly superior to the actual world of which he is virtually ignorant. As he maintains in an argument with an innkeeper who has been a sailor, traveling in books is "the only way of traveling by which any Knowledge is to be acquired" (II, xvii, 182). And as he says to Joseph a bit earlier, "'Knowledge of Men is only to be learnt from Books, Plato and Seneca for that; and those are Authors, I am afraid Child, you never read'" (II, xvi, 176). But unlike his bookish predecessor, Don Quixote, Adams understands in practice at least the difference between life and books, and his journey through the English countryside dramatizes his capacity for spontaneous moral action, for good works and generous sentiments that mark him as an embodiment of the activist Christian ethic that Fielding admired. But where does Adams' behavior leave Fielding and his readers, who are committed to the value of moral generality and resistant to the modern overvaluing of the particular and the exemplary force of individual personality such as novels are uniquely equipped to evoke? Something like a solution is implicit in Fielding's construction of this particular very bookish book and this sort of enthusiastically literary central character: *Joseph Andrews* never lets readers forget its status as parody, an attack on *Pamela* and by extension on the amatory formula, and by the same token neither Parson Adams nor any of the other good characters in the book is proposed as an object of moral imitation. Rather, they represent in their idealized eccentricity opportunities for exploring moral and social issues, for raising contemporary problems and controversies precisely without the powerful distractions of highly individualized and psychologized characters who transform ideas into vehicles for a voracious self-expressiveness. Ideas and comic personalities remain usefully separate in Fielding's narrative economy.

So Adams' foolishly absolute insistence on the superiority of books to actual experience is dramatized as comically inadequate on more than one occasion. His claim in the debate with the innkeeper that books have taught him "'that Nature generally imprints such a Portraiture of the Mind in the Countenance, that a skilful Physiognomist will rarely be deceived'" (II, xvii, 182) is manifestly untrue, since he has been deceived in the previous scene by the local squire, who has offered him a hospitality and even ecclesiastical preferment that he has no intention of ever providing. And yet Adams' foolish trust is in some larger sense justified, for in the controlling mode of comic moralism that defines the discourse of *Joseph Andrews* the nature of particular characters can be safely predicted and placed in Fielding's system of moral and psychological recurrence and repetition. But in all three of Fielding's novels what prevails until their romantic happy endings (for some of the characters) is a natural (that is to say, an *unnatural*, a social and political) unintelligibility whereby persons and appearances can never be trusted. Fielding extracts or sublimes his airy comic resolutions from the solid material of contemporary eighteenth-century life, and the resolutions of comic fiction such as his presuppose the intractability and moral ambiguity of actual experience. Ingenuous and transparently honest, Adams, Joseph, and Fanny are pure and deliberately improbable exceptions to the norms of behavior that the book represents across a range of social ranks: selfish calculation and manipulation for advantage, financial gain, pleasure, and power add up to a familiar scene for twentieth-century readers of ruthless, possessive individualism in a world that is political in an elemental sense.

Just after the conversation with the sailor turned innkeeper, Book III begins with Joseph, Fanny, and Adams finding shelter with Mr Wilson who has seen, as we will discover, too much of the world in his time to trust to appearances: "The Master of the House, notwithstanding the Simplicity which discovered itself in *Adams*, knew too much of the World to give a hasty Belief to Professions. He was not yet quite certain that *Adams* had any more of the Clergyman in him than his Cassock" (III, ii, 196). He therefore tests him by quizzing him about Pope's translation of Homer, which Adams has never heard of, although he has "heard great Commendations of that Poet." This raises suspicions until Adams begins to declaim Homeric Greek and Mr Wilson "now doubted whether he had not a Bishop in his House" (III, ii, 199). Unlike the other two interpolated narratives in *Joseph Andrews*, Wilson's story is no comic romance but rather a grimly realistic Hogarthian progress of a young man succumbing to the moral degeneration of London life and then climbing his way back to virtuous happiness through marriage to a devoted woman. But the world proves too much for them, and Wilson describes his disillusion with his trade as a wine merchant: "I had sufficiently seen, that the Pleasures of the World are chiefly Folly, and the Business of it mostly Knavery; and both, nothing better than Vanity: The Men of Pleasure tearing one another to pieces, from the Emulation of spending Money, and the Men of Business from Envy in getting it" (III, iii, 224). Wilson and his wife and children have retreated to a modest country retirement in the face of this universal knavery, where, except for the kidnapping of their eldest son by gypsies, they have been happy.

Parson Adams tries to supply a romantic ending as he wonders at the end of Wilson's story if his lost son might not be "'some Great Man, or Duke, and may one day or other revisit you in that Capacity'" (III, iv, 225). Wilson's initial suspicion of these travelers, his search for the reality behind the appearances, marks him as an inhabitant of another kind of fictional universe with more complex moral and social demarcations than the narrative proper. Consider Wilson's comment:

> there is a Malignity in the Nature of Man, which when not weeded out, or at least covered by a good Education and Politeness, delights in making another uneasy or dissatisfied with himself. This abundantly appears in all Assemblies, except those which are filled by People of Fashion, and especially among the younger People of both Sexes, whose Birth and Fortunes place them just without the polite Circles; I mean the lower Class of the Gentry, and the higher of the mercantile World, who are in reality the worst bred part of Mankind.
>
> (III, iii, 217–218)

How is a reader, especially nowadays, to react to such an extraordinarily precise analysis of behavior and social class? Nothing of the sort can be deduced from the actions of all the other characters in *Joseph Andrews*, who are all too broadly conceived to deal in the small snobberies of making "another uneasy or dissatisfied with himself" and are for the most part intent on enriching themselves with money, pleasure, or power of a cruder and funnier sort. Wilson's discourse is exact and serious, based on observation and experience in a world more subtle than the comic uproars of Fielding's novel. Wilson's comments are useful because they illuminate by their uniqueness the nature of discourse and the status of ideas as they are transformed by Fielding's comic fiction, whose perspective on contemporary manners and morals is oblique, bent and filtered by literary convention and by his own ideological ambivalence.

The oblique vision that the narrative features can be seen in an incident, full in one sense of serious issues, from the last chapters of Book I of *Joseph Andrews*, where the battered Joseph (left for dead by robbers) is dropped by the coachman at the Dragon Inn, where he is relieved by the landlord, Mr Tow-wouse, and visited by the local surgeon and by the neighborhood clergyman, Parson Barnabas. Instrumental in this timely succor is Betty the chambermaid, who reassures the fiercely uncharitable Mrs Tow-wouse that she is bound to be paid for her trouble by the wounded man, whose fine white skin and soft hands declare that he must be a gentleman. Like the postilion who gave up his great coat to the naked Joseph rather "'than suffer a Fellow-Creature to lie in so miserable a Condition'" (I, xii, 53), Betty is part of the novel's satiric design, setting off by her simplicity and generosity the complicated selfishness of the bourgeois characters all around her. In due course, she is at the center of a riotous scene precipitated by an irrepressibly amorous disposition that is inseparable from her redeeming simplicity and generosity.

As Joseph recuperates, various travelers arrive and the inn turns into a gathering of a cross-section of middle-class and professional types, including Parson Adams and Barnabas, the surgeon, an exciseman, a bookseller, and two of the local hunting gentry. Out of the banter and babble of these characters there emerges a debate (continued throughout the novel and constituting its serious theme) on various legal, economic, moral, and theological issues. Parson Adams tries to persuade the innkeeper, Mr Tow-wouse, to accept one of his manuscript volumes of sermons as security for a loan to pay the reckoning that he and Joseph owe when a coach arrives:

> There alighted from the Coach a young Fellow, and a Brace of Pointers, after which another young Fellow leapt from the Box, and shook the former by the hand, and both together with the Dogs were instantly conducted by Mr *Tow-wouse* into an Apartment; whither as they passed, they entertained themselves with the following facetious Dialogue.
>
> 'You are a pretty Fellow for a Coachman, Jack!' says he from the Coach, 'you had almost overturned us just now.' 'Pox take you,' says the Coachman, 'if I had only broke your neck,

it would have been saving somebody else the trouble: but I should have been sorry for the Pointers.' 'Why, you Son of a B__ ,' answered the other, 'if no body could shoot better than you, the Pointers would be of no use.' 'D__n me,' says the Coachman, 'I will shoot with you, five Guineas a shot.' 'You be hang'd,' says the other, 'for five Guineas you shall shoot at my A__.'

(I, xvi, 74)

There is much more in this vein, as we pass into the inn where this hunting gentry join Parson Adams, an exciseman, the doctor who is treating Joseph, and Parson Barnabas in "a general Conversation" (75). Several days pass as Joseph recovers from his wounds, and one evening the London bookseller arrives. Hoping to persuade him to buy his sermons, Adams offers to read two or three samples, but the bookseller protests that there is no market for such wares: "'for my part, the Copy that sells best, will be always the best Copy in my Opinion; I am no Enemy to Sermons but because they don't sell: for I would as soon print one of *Whitfield's*, as any Farce whatever'" (I, xvii, 80–81). Mention of this radical religious reformer leads to a spirited discussion of the worldliness of the Church, culminating a few pages later in a theological dispute, a rehashing of the Bangorian controversy in which Adams defends Bishop Hoadly's *A Plain Account of the Nature and End of the Sacrament*, scandalizing Parson Barnabas, who declares that "'he expected to hear the Alcoran, the *Leviathan*, or *Woolston* commended, if he staid a few Minutes longer'" (84).[3] As Adams prepares to answer Barnabas, "a most hideous Uproar began in the Inn. Mrs *Tow-wouse*, Mr *Tow-wouse*, and *Betty* (the chambermaid), all lifting up their Voices together: but Mrs *Tow-wouse's* voice, like a Bass Viol in a Concert, was clearly and distinctly distinguished among the rest, and was heard to articulate the following Sounds" (84). Mrs Tow-wouse has caught Betty and her husband *in flagrante* and her speech is outrage and abuse directed at her husband and at Betty, who answers in kind. In these pages, from the arrival of the coach with its idiotic hunting gentry to the sexual squabbles of publicans and their servants, ordinary speech is no more than noise, a babble of predictable comic formulas rather than meaningful utterance. One would not expect anything else in a comic novel of the road, but this comic noise infects and indeed cancels the serious theological debate under way, although the debate is not really serious since Parson Barnabas is an ignoramus and Adams' generous paraphrase of his position is totally misunderstood by his adversary's comic obtuseness and ignorance.

Mikhail Bakhtin has defined the novel as "a diversity of social speech types (sometimes even diversity of languages) and a diversity of individual voices, artistically organized." Novels replace, he says, the unitary and static literary language of other forms with the "social dialects, characteristic group behaviour, professional jargons, generic language, languages of generations and age groups, tendentious languages, languages of the authorities, of various circles and of passing fashions," and it is this "internal stratification" of language's historical existence in its "heteroglossia" that marks for him the uniqueness of the novel. As Bakhtin points out, "comic style (of the English sort)" not only stratifies common language but is based on "the possibilities available for isolating from these strata, to one degree or another, one's own intentions, without ever completely merging with them."[4] Fielding's fiction seems to resist the liberating principle that Bakhtin proposes as the secret of the novel's achievement, that "it is precisely the diversity of speech, and not the unity of a normative shared language, that is the ground of style."[5] Stratification, rather, appears at high comic moments like these as a racket (in both senses of the word – a cacophony of noise and also a fraud), an exploitation, distortion, and deliberate fragmentation of what should be a common and coherent language by ignorant professionals and foolish knaves out to serve and enrich themselves. The narrator separates himself and his audience from these linguistic strata and implicitly appeals, if only by ironic disparagement of the dialects and professional jargons that he presents, to a cognitively meaningful and stable discourse, the language of reasonable men of the world. In this scene, he draws back from this battle and babble of voices to explain in a separate and concluding chapter for Book I how Betty's history has made this comic scene inevitable:

> Betty, who was the Occasion of all this Hurry, had some good Qualities. She had Good-nature, Generosity and Compassion, but unfortunately her Constitution was composed of those warm Ingredients, which, though the Purity of Courts or Nunneries might have happily controuled them, were by no means able to endure the ticklish Situation of a Chamber-maid at an Inn, who is daily liable to the Solicitations of Lovers of all Complexions, to the dangerous Addresses of fine Gentlemen of the Army, who sometimes are obliged to reside with them a whole Year together, and above all are exposed to the Caresses of Footmen, Stage-Coachmen, and Drawers; all of whom employ the whole Artillery of kissing, flattering,

bribing, and every other Weapon which is to be found in the whole Armoury of Love, against them.

Betty, who was but one and twenty, had now lived three Years in this dangerous Situation, during which she had escaped pretty well. An Ensign of Foot was the first Person who made any Impression on her Heart; he did indeed raise a Flame in her, which required the Care of a Surgeon to cool.

While she burnt for him, several others burnt for her. Officers of the Army, young Gentlemen travelling the Western Circuit, inoffensive Squires, and some of graver Character were set afire by her Charms.

(II, xviii, 86)

Since then, the narrator explains, her heart has been won by John the Hostler, and she has been pretty faithful to him, only allowing Tom Whipwell the Stage-coachman "and now and then a handsome young Traveller to share her Favours" (87). Like Lady Booby, Betty has thrown herself at Joseph only to confront his unwavering chastity. She actually considers suicide after this refusal, the narrator assures us, but the possibilities of self-destruction are so varied that she is bewildered. Into this unfocused resolution there rushes domestic duty, or so she says: "In this Perturbation of Spirit, it accidentally occurred to her Memory, that her Master's Bed was not made, she therefore went directly to his Room" (88).

Betty's body is nothing less than an intersection for the movements and key institutions of the emerging nation-state, its armed forces, its legal system, its mobile ruling gentry, those large historical developments which *Joseph Andrews* ignores but obliquely represents and takes for granted as the context of action. She is indeed a minor character and a comic servant girl, but in these comic precincts at the Dragon Inn she stabilizes such movements and de-historicizes those institutions in the predictable and reciprocal sexual/social relationships of which she forms the center and the efficient cause. She enacts in her amours a debased modern pastoral, a parody of high life in courts and nunneries where her warmth would simply bring her less grief. Her sexual history contains and thereby trivializes modern socioeconomic determinants subordinating them to the perennial and therefore "natural" comedy of exploitative sexual reciprocity so fully visible in her relationships.

This over-elaborate intersection of social particulars and moral–psychological generality points, I think, to Fielding's uneasiness with his own comic strategies. Why single out Betty for this treatment among all the participants in the uproar at the inn? As comic servant and lower-class parody of the romance heroine, subject to her own warm disposition and the entire range of social/sexual pressures, Betty may be the only member of the crowd at the inn whose story can be safely elaborated in comic fiction. As a woman of the working classes and a lower servant, she has no possibility of joining the potentially dangerous, socially disruptive crowd constituted by the varieties of *petit-bourgeois* and professional self-seeking on view at the Dragon and at all those other public gathering places in Fielding's fiction. In their different ways, the clergymen, the surgeon, the exciseman, the bookseller, the publican and his wife, even the booby squires, contain in their social specificity and particularized functions an obstreperous (noisily defiant is exactly what they are) individuality and potential resistance to the control represented by comic recurrence and moral universalizing. Fielding wants us to read Betty's history as wholly expressed by comic recurrence and sexual reciprocity, including the trading of venereal infections. Whatever *ressentiment* she might be imagined to have as an exploited servant girl is subordinated to the energies of a classless and perennial female sexual competition. The dissident expressiveness that voices in fiction can project, in ways that Bakhtin has made clear, are contained by histories like Betty's, since her energy as servant and lower-class female is comically subsumed by class and biology. Betty's sexual history allows both social comprehensiveness and moral–psychological inevitability. In its bringing together of the social and the sexual, her history permits the narrator to sustain a knowing distance by dissolving social diversity and the disruptive energies that it suggests into comically sexual reciprocities. It is worth noting, sadly, that she is turned away at the insistence of the enraged Mrs Tow-wouse, and we can only guess what her fate would have been in the unforgiving world adjacent to the comic romance in which she plays a brief part.

II

In *Tom Jones* Fielding broadens his canvas and makes more serious claims than in his first novel for the independent significance of what he calls his "new Province of Writing," which is now much more than a parody of a particular ludicrous contemporary narrative like *Pamela*.[6] Halfway through *Tom Jones* in the introductory essay to Book IX, he contemplates at some length the cultural and aesthetic disaster of modern popular narrative: the success of some recent authors "will probably serve as an Encouragement to many others to undertake the like. Thus a swarm of foolish Novels and monstrous Romances will be produced" (IX, I, 487). Novels, he explains, are especially apt to attract incompetent writers, since to produce them "nothing is necessary but Paper, Pens and Ink, with the manual Capacity of using them" (489). So Fielding enumerates the qualifications that he thinks essential for "this Order of Historians" (490), and these are "Genius" (a natural gift that has two parts, "Invention and Judgment"), "Learning" ("a competent Knowledge of History and of the Belles Lettres"), and "another Sort of Knowledge beyond the Power of Learning to bestow, and this is to be had by Conversation," that is to say, by experience in the social world of men and manners, "with all Ranks and Degrees or Men"(490–494). *Tom Jones* is an elaborate and seductively complex literary artifact, its plot and its range of characters marvels of construction and design.[7] But in its artifice, the result of literary talent supplemented by formal learning (and class and gender privilege, let it be said), the plot collides to some extent with Fielding's third requirement for a modern novelist: extensive worldly experience that certifies narration as correct and comprehensive representation. Constructed out of the interrelationships of a large cast of characters as they scheme and contrive to acquire property, pleasure, and power, and, like *Joseph Andrews*, based upon a rehearsal of the pattern of comic romance overlaid on the Cervantic and picaresque model of the road narrative, *Tom Jones* is a complex entity which does indeed provide a full rendering of life across a wide range of society, from servants, rural proletarians and publicans through clergymen, intellectuals, bureaucrats, soldiers, and business and professional men to the landed gentry and the aristocracy. Such fullness of representation immerses readers in a communal reality and provides knowledge of an interlocking social system.

And yet in spite of his artistic control, Fielding the narrator remains a curiously evasive rhetorical entity, working against the lamentable moral drift and degraded cultural functions of the new mode of narrative in which he finds himself writing and which he proposes to reform by this example. *Tom Jones'* elaborate structuring is a defensive bulwark against the vulgar simplicities of popular narrative and also a replacement for the alternative complexities of the social and historical world which Fielding, as the good classicist that he was, promises to represent in general and meaningful terms that will preserve that complexity but bring order and stability to it. Fielding finds himself in the awkward position of offering an ambitious revision of popular narrative tradition without discarding the central pleasures of such fiction – to re-present contemporary actuality for the reader's pleasure and curiosity and to submit to the tyranny of the literary marketplace. The entire project is thereby wreathed in ironies that are often reflexive and self-depreciating, directed at his own difficult enterprise and cautioning readers to keep in mind the special balance of comedy and serious social and moral meaning that they must remember to add to the vulgar pleasures of a modern "history" or what we would call realistic fiction.

In the very first chapter he offers an extended and facetious comparison between his book and a "public Ordinary" or eating house which sets the tone for the rest of the novel. Each book, he tells us, will feature a bill of fare or menu describing the dishes to follow, which the reader may peruse and decide whether he wants to buy and eat. An author hopes to please a hungry but fickle public, and what matters is not the food itself so much as its effective preparation. Writing is like cookery, a matter of dressing or preparing the foodstuffs of human nature:

> the Excellence of the mental Entertainment consists less in the Subject, than in the Author's Skill in well dressing it up. How pleased therefore will the Reader be to find, that we have, in the following Work, adhered closely to one of the highest Principles of the best Cook which the present age, or perhaps that of *Heliogabalus*, hath produced.
>
> ... we shall represent Human Nature at first to the keen Appetite of our Reader, in that more plain and simple Manner in which it is found in the Country, and shall hereafter hash and ragoo it with all the high *French* and *Italian* Seasoning of Affectation and Vice which Courts and Cities afford. By these Means, we doubt not but our Reader may be rendered desirous to read on for ever.
>
> (I, i, 33–34)

But good reading is not quite like such eating, and moral discrimination such as Fielding's novel encourages in his readers has exactly the opposite trajectory from decadent gourmandizing. In offering his customer-readers a preliminary bill of fare and promising to please them so that they will pay for the privilege, Fielding is parodying or echoing the language of the marketplace, evoking vulgar readers/consumers who long for the voyeuristic excitements of represented vice and whose insatiable curiosity will keep them reading past all moderation as they seek to satisfy an artificially extended appetite for narrative, such as that catered to by his rivals in the novel market, the purveyors of amatory and sensational fiction.

Bakhtin in his essay "Discourse in the novel" says that we should think of the novelistic work "as a rejoinder in a given dialogue, whose style is determined by its interrelationship with other rejoinders in the same dialogue."[8] Such a style, in Bakhtin's phrase, is "dialogized," and he notes that the most obvious instances of this stylistic category – "the polemical style, the parodic, the ironic – are usually classified (erroneously and misleadingly) as rhetorical and not as poetic phenomena."[9] In this paragraph from the opening of *Tom Jones* Fielding is in dialogue with a classic satiric strain of argument and feeling about consumption and cookery, and in fact the moment is rhetorical but the ultimate resonance within the novel might be called poetic, as the consumption of food ultimately becomes synonymous with a self-absorption that is innocent in all those inns where travelers like Tom and Partridge arrive but that also encompasses at its most sinister Blifil's voracious longing for Sophia and other forms of selfish possession and consumption. Consumption, both literal and metaphorical, is a central activity in the novel that follows, where characters have large appetites for food, sex, and of course most of all for money and power. But novel readers' appetites resemble at their worst the voracious instincts of his worst characters who, like Blifil or Lady Bellaston, seek to consume and possess the goods and persons they encounter.

In this opening essay of his novel, Fielding is invoking a tradition going back to Plato's *Gorgias* (which attacks rhetoric for resembling cookery in its transformatory deceitfulness; making bad food taste good or changing the taste of food is like the Sophistical trick of making the worse appear the better cause). But his attack on gourmandizing is more immediately accessible in classical satiric (as well as John Bullish) suspicion of the art of cookery as a disguise of essence and as a sign of moral unsoundness. Fielding's ideal reader knows that the Emperor Heliogabalus was synonymous with gluttony, and he may well wonder at first if this book is really going to model itself on the deeply suspect practice of *haute cuisine*. The exact resolution of the joke is not obvious in this opening, and Fielding's ironies both echo and refuse the hucksterish idiom of the new consumerism that partially impels readers to buy long and expensive novels like *Tom Jones*. In moments like these, we may say, Fielding takes a chance with his own authority as narrator and surrenders by virtue of the force of the novelistic moment something of the stability and finality of the essayistic mode of his introductory chapters; and we find his discourse in Bakhtin's sense "subject to the same temporally valorized measurements, for the 'depicting' authorial language now lies on the same plane as the 'depicted' language of the hero, and may enter into dialogic relations and hybrid combinations with it (indeed, it cannot help but enter into such relations)." For Bakhtin, the novelist's voice becomes like the discourses in the temporal world that he represents. Fielding is negotiating his relationship to this contemporary institution of narrative in the literary marketplace; his speech is positional and self-expressive in its disingenuous ironies as he admits his complicity in the current economic moment but also expresses his own distaste for it.

This crucial opening chapter conveys the following implicit irony: as the purveyor of human nature "dressed," Fielding is pretending to cater to a depraved modern taste for scandal, lubricity, gossip, and vice. This description of his work is transparently false, of course, and Fielding's opening statement that what matters is not the subject but the author/cook's skill in dressing is shown in the events and his own running commentary on those events that follow as decidedly not true. A good deal of Fielding's effort moves in the other direction: as a satirist his aim is in part to undress, to present underneath the sauces or clothing or speech the raw and the naked, the self-seeking "design," as he calls it, of many of the characters. But faithful, overall, to ideological complexity, the novel also offers readers a far less absolute state of things in which individuals (and the narrator himself) are situated in those two divergent realms that I have been evoking: the patterns and symmetries of comic romance and universalized moralism, and the ongoing history of a large variety of changing institutions of mid-eighteenth-century England like the new novel and the literary marketplace, the country house ideal, patron–client relationships, the game laws, the justice system, and the marriage market, to name the most obvious areas explored by the novel. To render truthfully eighteenth-century English humanity, Fielding will present it "dressed" in the situational clothing of the historical moment, but as a moralizing satirist he balances against that depiction another order of uniform and universal, "naked" human recurrence.

In *Tom Jones*, in the act of being that new kind of writer, the serious novelist, Fielding exemplifies "political" behavior, as he negotiates with moral and literary tradition, with his divided responsibility to represent the unique features of the historical moment as well as the satirical generality that gives them coherence. Social relations as *Tom Jones* renders them have this same divided and deeply political quality, and the book's generalized system is the sum of individual motives and designs. All the characters have a plot or design (a frequent term), and even the good characters like Tom, Allworthy, and Sophia behave at times so that their motives are not perfectly transparent. Blifil is the most perfectly political individual in the novel, since the crucial secrets he harbors are completely hidden and drive the plot. Paradoxically, the narrator is himself most like Blifil, since his strategies involve disguising (with transparent irony, to be sure) his moral motives and, of course, withholding crucial information from us so that we will keep reading. A striking instance of this similarity is young Blifil's manipulations after Tom's drunken celebration of Allworthy's recovery from sickness. Thwackum, the narrator informs us, had wanted to tell Allworthy that very day of his young ward's drunken behavior, of their catching him fornicating in the woods that same day with Molly Seagrim, and the fistfight that followed between Tom and his two enemies, but Blifil had prevailed on him to wait. When Western bursts in and announces to Allworthy some days later that his "Daughter hath fallen in Love with your Bastard" (VI, x, 305), Blifil recounts the story of Tom's excesses:

> In reality, *Blifil* had taken some Pains to prevail with the Parson, and to prevent the Discovery at that Time; for which he had many Reasons. He knew that the Minds of Men are apt to be softened and relaxed from their usual Severity by Sickness. Besides, he imagined that if the Story was told when the Fact was so recent, and the Physician about the House, who might have unravelled the real Truth, he should never be able to give it the malicious Turn which he intended. Again, he resolved to hoard up this Business, till the Indiscretion of *Jones* should afford some additional Complaints, for he thought the joint Weight of many Facts falling upon him together, would be the most likely to crush him; and he watched therefore some such Opportunity as that, with which Fortune had now kindly presented him. Lastly, by prevailing with *Thwackum* to conceal the Matter for a Time, he knew he should confirm an Opinion of his Friendship to *Jones*, which he had greatly laboured to establish in Mr *Allworthy*.
>
> (VI, x, 308–309)

More than a smooth hypocrite, Blifil is the arch villain of the book precisely by virtue of his functional and political use of language whereby words are purely pragmatic or instrumental, a means of acquiring and managing power. Like an orator, or a politician, or even like a novelist, he is a master of timing and trimming, of achieving effects by watching changing circumstances and seizing opportunities, of pleasing and agreeing with both his tutors, of persuading Allworthy that he is Tom's friend even while he effectively destroys his reputation.

Through his good characters – Tom, Allworthy, Sophia, Mrs Miller – the narrator holds out the possibility of uncompromised virtue in spite of the novel's proof that political self-interest is universal. Much of the time, we may say, this reality is simultaneously affirmed and denied by means of the comic plot, which treats such a situation as the main source of its humor but also makes the point that, adjacent to the novel's literary abstraction of the world, self-interest is deep and silent and essentially unobservable. Here is the narrator making that point about Thwackum. As he comes to know the tutor, "upon longer Acquaintance" and "more intimate Conversation, this worthy Man saw Infirmities ... which he could have wished him to have been without." Allworthy balances what he sees against Thwackum's good qualities as he and others understand them:

> For the Reader is greatly mistaken, if he conceives that
> *Thwackum* appeared to Mr *Allworthy* in the same Light as he
> doth to him in this History; and he is as much deceived, if he
> imagines, that the most intimate Acquaintance which he
> himself could have had with that Divine, would have informed
> him of those Things which we, from our Inspiration, are
> enabled to open and discover. Of Readers who from such
> Conceits as these, condemn the Wisdom or Penetration of Mr.
> *Allworthy*, I shall not scruple to say, that they make a very bad
> and ungrateful Use of that Knowledge which we have commu-
> nicated to them.
>
> (III, v, 135)

Within the universalizing frame of *Tom Jones*, very obviously and effec-tively, Thwackum and his opposite number Square are defined, contained, and even neutralized by their comic balancing, but the narrator reminds us that the controlling knowledge of moral order he grants us has an ironic relation to another level of potential representa-tion in which such transparent symmetry does not obtain, in which identity and virtue such as the Rev. Mr Thwackum possesses are earned in the give and take of relationships within a larger world that includes not simply his patron Mr Allworthy but all those unnamed others within that arena that Fielding invokes wherein Thwackum "had a great Reputation for Learning, Religion and Sobriety of Manners" (III, v, 135). On the one hand, Fielding's comic panorama is reductively satisfying in its simplicities and symmetries, but on the other hand he reminds readers of the ironic distance between that pattern and an alternative realm far larger and more sprawling than his canvas where truth is negotiated, identity situational and provisional, and personality opaque and uncertain. That reminder, and the complicated interplay between fact and fiction that it invites in his reader, mark *Tom Jones* at moments like this as ideological: dramatizing and encouraging a complex understanding of comic art and life and their relationship to one another.

This relationship between Allworthy and Thwackum, patron and client, is itself deeply ideological in its relevance to changing eighteenth-century institutions and values, and the success or failure of relationships like it is nothing less than the novel's main subject. Fielding invites us in the opening books of *Tom Jones* to consider Paradise Hall and its inhabitants in the light of two kinds of context which, the philosopher Alasdair MacIntyre reminds us, accompany moral judgments: "We place the agent's intentions ... in causal and temporal order with reference to their role in his or her history; and we also place them with reference to their role in the history of the setting or settings to which they belong."[10] Thwackum, Square, the odious elder Blifil brothers, and even the duplicitous Brigid Allworthy and Mr Summer (Tom's father, seen only in retrospect from the final revelations) are all being evaluated in this dual context in the early books of *Tom Jones*, and their various schemes take place not only in the pattern of their lives but within the larger cultural and moral history of the decline of the country house ideal and the possibility of mutual and honestly productive relationships between a patron and his client such as that between Fielding and his patrons, Ralph Allen and George Lyttleton, with which the novel begins. The entire plot of the novel rests not just on the personal histories of these characters but on their exploitation and negotiation within the ideology surrounding the country house and the patron–client system as such arrangements are replaced by newer forms of economic individualism. There are similar ideological and historical resonances surrounding, say, the characters in *Clarissa* but one would be hard pressed indeed to find anything like that resonance in, say, Haywood's *Idalia*, where the characters have a deliberately self-enclosed emotional and sexual quality which cuts off any reader's interest in any history other than the personal. Fielding's narrative's assumptions and artificialities are subject to examination and ideological qualification by readers and in one remarkable instance by Tom Jones himself. A philosophical dialogue takes place between Tom and the Man of the Hill, whose career has allowed him to survey precisely those "mores hominum multorum" that the book's title page promises. To the Man of the Hill's disparagement of man as the only work in God's creation that does the deity any dishonor, Tom responds:

> 'You will pardon me,' cries *Jones*, 'but I have always imagined, that there is in this very Work you mention, as great Variety as in all the rest; for besides the Difference of Inclination,

Customs and Climates have, I am told, introduced the utmost Diversity into Human Nature.' 'Very little indeed,' answered the other; 'those who travel in order to acquaint themselves with the different Manners of Men, might spare themselves much Pains, by going to a Carnival at *Venice*; for there they will see at once all which they can discover in the several Courts of *Europe*. The same Hypocrisy, the same Fraud; in short, the same Follies and Vices dressed in different Habits. In *Spain*, these are equipped with much Gravity; and in *Italy*, with vast Splendor. In France, a Knave is dressed like a Fop; and in the Northern Countries, like a Sloven. But Human Nature is every where the same, every where the Object of Detestation and Avoidance.'

(VII, xv, 482)

The Man of the Hill's attitudes are plausible but unacceptably extreme within the book's satiric universalism. The Man of the Hill's story contextualizes his attitudes and makes them to a large extent the result of his own unfortunate experiences, renders them primarily self-expressive rather than generally valid. Tom himself realizes this weakness in the reasoning. In the give and take of their dialogue, Tom accuses his interlocutor of generalizing about mankind "'from the worst and basest among them; whereas indeed, as an excellent Writer observes, nothing should be esteemed as characteristical of a Species, but what is to be found among the best and most perfect Individuals of that Species"' (VIII, xv, 485). As Battestin's note informs us, the excellent writer Tom cites is Cicero in the *Tusculan Disputations* (presumably read under Thwackum's tutorship), and Tom's positive philosophy resembles the ethics of Shaftesbury (imbibed from Square?) and the Latitudinarian divines. But the intellectual source of these ideas (if not their biographical basis for Tom) is less important in the context of the dialogue and the novel that contains it than their function: they are no less expressive of Tom's particular personality and history than the Man of the Hill's satire is for his.

Tom Jones has two lessons: within the comic fiction that the narrator constructs, order and symmetry prevail, and on that level this dialogue and others in the book address matters of fact or concern questions that possess a degree of cognitive stability; but the characters' discourse also points to that world (represented by implication and hypothetically, the anti-world of the comic narrative, the potential actuality known only by its differences from the structured and artificial order) in which Thwackum has earned his reputation for piety and learning and in which Tom would have probably been hanged or pressed into the navy. That is a public world in which subjects compete for status and power and in which personal worth and even virtue exist only in an ideological context, as individuals are shown being socially and rhetorically constructed out of the available materials. Although Tom and the Man of the Hill are responsible and well-informed individuals, their dialogue cannot be totally separated in its implications for self-expression and ideological negotiation from other more obviously self-expressive and comically non-cognitive interchanges and verbal exchanges such as those between Thwackum and Square, or Squire Western and his sister, Di Western. One of the exchanges between the Squire and his sister as they pursue Sophia to London will serve to illustrate how those comic conversations can also work in the opposite direction, moving from comic self-expressiveness to supporting the novel's thematic coherence.

Having lost the scent of his runaway Sophia in Book XV of *Tom Jones*, Squire Western sits brooding, his affliction doubled by the blame heaped on him by his sister. But Sophia is betrayed by a letter from her cousin, Harriet Fitzpatrick, who reveals that the runaway is harbored in London by Lady Bellaston. Throwing his pipe in the fire and "huzza[ing] for Joy," the squire proposes to reclaim his daughter, armed with his legal rights:

> I have not been in the Country so long without having some Knowledge of Warrants and the Law of the Land. I know I may take my own wherever I can find it. Shew me my own Daughter, and if I don't know how to come at her, I'll suffer you to call me Fool as long as I live. There be Justices of Peace in *London*, as well as in other Places.
>
> (XV, vi, 805)

His sister replies that Lady Bellaston is beyond such law: "Do you really imagine, Brother, that the House of a Woman of Figure is to be attacked by Warrants and brutal Justices of the Peace?" What she counsels is properly ritualized social negotiation, conducted according to unwritten protocols of propriety and deference:

> As soon as you arrive in Town, and have got yourself into a decent Dress (for indeed, Brother, you have none at present fit to appear in) you must send your Compliments to Lady *Bellaston*, and desire Leave to wait on her. When you are admitted to her Presence, as you certainly will be, and have told her your Story, and have made proper use of my Name,

(for I think you just know one another only by Sight, though you are Relations) I am confident she will withdraw her Protection from my Niece, who hath certainly imposed upon her. This is the only Method. – Justices of Peace indeed! do you imagine any such Event can arrive to a Woman of Figure in a civilized Nation?

(805)

Aunt Western understands aristocratic power and invokes a network of patrons and clients, friends in a special eighteenth-century sense, whose relationships take precedence in practice over the legal structure which her brother trusts. Country magistrate and fierce enforcer of the game laws, the Squire has heard "his Lordship say at 'Size, that no one is above the Law. But this of yours," he protests to his sister, "is Hannover Law, I suppose" (806). Neither of the Westerns speaks the whole truth, for the social order as Fielding represents it is regulated by a variety of norms, some legal and statutory, some traditional and customary, but all in a broad sense political rather than ideological, that is to say, open to negotiation within a context of distributed power relations. All varieties of law in *Tom Jones* are represented as, in practice, subordinate to their manipulation by individual policy for an invariable and thereby comic self-interest. Fielding himself helped to systematize and regularize the loose traditional order that he satirizes, and in the year that the novel was published he was commissioned as a magistrate. In that capacity he was to play a key role in reforming and strengthening the machinery of law enforcement in London. But in *Tom Jones* at least he carries out quite another project whereby these competing varieties of enforcement and regulation that he depicts are contained by a narrative structure that makes their conflicting claims part of his comic mechanism. In *Tom Jones*, political behavior is not only simplified by comic symmetries but neutralized by a powerfully implicit ideology that silently transcends politics.

Squire Western complains earlier in the novel that his sister has filled Sophia's head with "a Pack of Court Notions," and "made a Whig of the Girl; and how should her Father, or any body else, expect any Obedience from her?" (VII, iii, 336). Opposed to these court notions, the squire calls himself a "true Englishman, and not of your Hannover Breed, that have eat up the Nation" (336). Mrs Western also links the domestic and political and calls her brother "one of those wise Men ... whose nonsensical Principles have undone the Nation; by weakening the Hands of our Government at home, and by discouraging our Friends, and encouraging our Enemies abroad" (337). Both Westerns translate their domestic crisis into national political terms; such obsessive unifying of separate realms marks them as comic characters. In these very funny exchanges, the language of politics is on the same level as the language of the chase that the squire employs to fit every occasion, notably the domestic crisis that sends him in pursuit of his foxy daughter. But there are other moments when these translations make a good deal of sense. In Book VI, for example, Aunt Western instructs Sophia in the way of the "polite World," advising her that marriage to Blifil would be understood as a political act: the case there is that "Love (so the good Lady said) is at present entirely laughed at, and … Women consider Matrimony, as Men do Offices of public Trust, only as the Means of making their Fortunes, and of advancing themselves in the World" (xii, 316).

In Aunt Western's parody of court values, the political and domestic worlds are parallel, with politics as the dominant order by which domesticity is understood and regulated. In his comic fashioning, Fielding separates these realms, but everything in his narrative brings them together, as indeed his comic architectonics ultimately resolves everything into a presiding comic wholeness. In fact, Aunt Western's neat equation is different only in degree from the narrator's explicit comparisons between domestic and political events, just as the narrator consistently uses more sophisticated versions of the squire's hunting metaphors to satirize various aspects of the social order.[11] His comparisons, though, run the other way and make the domestic primary, or claim to diminish the political by showing that it is only an inflated version of the lowest sort of domestic relations. "Here we cannot help observing, that as there is so much of Policy in the lowest Life, great Men often overvalue themselves on those Refinements in Imposture, in which they are frequently excelled by some of the lowest of the Human Species" (XII, ix, 653). Low life is on the same political level as high life, and what moralists take to be class-specific behavior in the upper ranks is simply human and natural.

As a narrator who slyly imitates providential thoroughness and inscrutability, Fielding in *Tom Jones* promotes the reader's sense of an analogous balance of an old story and new materials. Assimilating classical epic by parodic inflections, Fielding stabilizes the formless materials of modern life and forces potentially wayward readers toward his brand of comic recurrence. To that extent, his version of the novel modifies Bakhtin's requirements for the genre: the comic recurrences look to an inescapable past rather than to that realm of pure experience, knowledge and practice that marks the novel for Bakhtin as "the genre of becoming."[12] In their reliability, Fielding's repetitions evoke a world where God is in his heaven because the narrator is a surrogate Providence. The narrator's authority is supported, like the Hanoverian monarchy, by the narrative equivalent of the distribution of favors or patronage in return for the recognition of a sovereignty granted by Providence and indeed embodied in the sovereign.

Like any parody, this rendering of the power that he has over his readers depends upon a canonical text whose power and stability license the joke: "I am, indeed, set over them for their own Good only, and was created for their Use, and not they for mine. Nor do I doubt, while I make their Interest the great Rule of my Writings, they will unanimously concur in supporting my Dignity, and in rendering me all the Honour I shall deserve or desire" (II, I, 78). This narrator flatters and rewards his readers, who are complicit with his simultaneous presentation of a contingent historical scene where self-interest and corruption are rife and of a universalized moral–psychological corrective to that actuality. The more the narrator explores the so-called accidents that make up this history, the firmer the reassuring inevitability becomes. The result, as Theodor Adorno and Max Horkheimer put it in their rendition of the dialectic of Enlightenment, is to explain "every event as repetition."[13] That is to say, as we look closely at the relationship between reader and narrator in *Tom Jones* we see an unspoken agreement, a perfect understanding between them in which nothing explicit need be said because everything is always already understood. The reader posited by *Tom Jones* knows exactly what is happening; he understands completely the universalist and uniformitarian psychology behind the book's sustaining network of ironies, the transparency of the narrator's disingenuous claim that he is forced to reveal what he in fact has made up, that the little "accidents" that he chooses to reveal out of the multitude of possibilities (for example, Sophia's fall from her horse and her loss of the £100 note on which the plot turns) are crucial in the scheme of things and understood as part of the pleasure of reading a comically suspenseful plot, a predetermined whole from which much has been left out that will always be revealed in due course.

The ideal reader of *Tom Jones* understands that the narrator speaks in a political mode; the issue of truthful communication is secondary, subordinated to the organizing purposes of narrative, to a narrative personality who sustains an order analogous to the political one. Michael McKeon calls this "an instrumental belief in institutions whose authority may be fictional – social deference, custom, the law."[14] This is Fielding's way out of what McKeon sees as a profound ideological crisis to which the novel responds whereby social and moral categories are perceived as radically unstable. As his fiction develops, however, Fielding moves away from this instrumentality of belief by internalizing institutions "as an authorial capacity," thereby reclaiming "specifically literary fiction as a mode of telling the truth." In other words, narrative authority in *Tom Jones*, in its commanding articulation of an evident fiction, in McKeon's formulation, negates the negation of fiction "by ostentatiously enacting, even announcing, its impotence to tell an imme- diate truth."[15] What matters, as most readers of *Tom Jones* have long recognized, is the narrator's authority and the deferred truthful whole- ness that it always promises to deliver.

In his introductory chapters the narrator expounds certain ideas about literature, morality and life in general, but that discourse is essen- tially oratorical, not so much arguing as affirming notions identified as self-evident. Fielding marks these essays as part of his narrative identity, what separates him from lumpish chroniclers and the ignorant authors of "the Romances and Novels with which the World abounds" (IX, I, 488). Like so much else in the novel, these essays are primarily tactical rather than substantive discourse; they both legislate new narrative rules and manifest the authority of the legislator. Of course, in spite of his self-dramatization, the narrator for all his volubility never tells his story. He remains a narrative persona, a source of continuous and intensely supervising commentary, so that events in *Tom Jones* are inseparable from his manner of delivering and contextualizing them. But in the last third of the novel, the London books, the narrator claims that he is abridging that commentary because events have grown so tangled that a purer kind of narration is necessary. And as he opens the final book, he declares that there will be "no Room for any of those ludicrous Observations which I have elsewhere made, and which may sometimes, perhaps, have prevented thee from taking a Nap. … All will be plain Narrative only; and, indeed, when thou hast perused the many great Events which this Book will produce, thou wilt think the Number of Pages contained in it, scarce sufficient to tell the Story" (XVIII, I, 913). Plain narrative turns out to be the missing narratives, correct and complete at last, that various characters are now forced by circum- stances to tell. Lawyer Dowling, Mrs Waters, Mrs Miller, and Partridge resolve matters by telling all and thereby exposing Blifil's plot to suppress the truth that Tom is no ordinary bastard but the son of Brigid Allworthy and Mr Summer. The most interesting of these confessions for my purposes is the one that is least relevant to the unraveling of the plot – Partridge's summary of his life after losing favor at Paradise Hall as the supposed father of baby Tom.

Tediously circumstantial and digressive, lacking direct relevance, undisciplined and unfocused, his story is the familiar silly discourse given to servants in *Tom Jones* (and in other fiction), a rival and to some extent subversive alternative to the efficient meaningfulness of the novel proper.[16] Fielding has, inevitably, invented it all, but in this particular speech of Partridge's he indulges in a bravura narrative gesture, placing against his controlling authority and his weaving together of many separate plot strands something like its lumpish opposite. Here is the center of Partridge's tale. After his shrewish wife dies, he leaves the neighborhood and goes to Salisbury and enters the service of a lawyer:

'Here I kept a Pig; and one Day, as ill Fortune would have it, this Pig broke out, and did a Trespass I think they call it, in a Garden belonging to one of my Neighbors, who was a proud, revengeful Man, and employed a Lawyer, one – one – I can't think of his Name; but he sent for a Writ against me, and had me to Size. When I came there, Lord have Mercy upon me – to hear what the Counsellors said. There was one that told my Lord a Parcel of the confoundedest Lies about me; he said, that I used to drive my Hogs into other Folks Gardens, and a great deal more; and at last he said, He hoped I had at last brought my Hogs to a fair Market. To be sure, one wou'd have thought, that instead of being Owner only of one poor, little Pig, I had been the greatest Hog-Merchant in *England*. Well –' 'Pray,' said *Allworthy*, 'do not be so particular, I have heard nothing of your Son yet.' 'O it was a great many Years,' answered *Partridge*, 'before I saw my Son, as you are pleased to call him. – I went over to *Ireland* after this, and taught School at *Cork* (for that one Suit ruined me again, and I lay seven Years in *Winchester* Goal.)' – 'Well,' said *Allworthy*, 'pass that over till your Return to *England*.' – 'Then, Sir,' said he, 'it was about half a Year ago that I landed at *Bristol*, where I stayed some Time, and not finding it do there, and hearing of a Place between that and *Gloucester*, where the Barber was just dead, I went thither, and there I had been about two Months, when Mr *Jones* came thither.'

(XVIII, vi, 937–938)

Partridge's meandering reminiscences appear at the very moment when Fielding's plot symmetries are approaching completion, and one result of his story is to display a comically intractable alternative to the magical conjunctions and dispensations from circumstances that the plot is about to arrange. Partridge's seven years in "*Winchester* Goal" records a matter-of-fact accounting of a grim actuality, and it makes Tom's brief if melodramatic stay in prison in the Gatehouse after the duel with Fitzpatrick look like a lark. Against the shapings and inevitabilities of Fielding's comic system, the truly accidental (that is, socioeconomically coherent) materials of ordinary life lack all significance for a narrative like *Tom Jones*, even if they point, in the story of Partridge's pig and his "proud, vengeful" neighbor whose suit ruins him, to the same capriciously inefficient legal system that the narrator exploits for comic effect. No one is really hurt by the law in *Tom Jones* proper, but in Partridge's tale its results are painfully long lasting and yet circumscribed by the comic convention of servants' garrulity. Partridge's comic testimony here points, both as an undisciplined and largely excluded voice and as a record of intractable experience, to a deliberately unassimilated contemporaneity (to echo Bakhtin), social historical material rigorously excluded by Fielding's comic authority, a realm where his comic system will not work and his patronage does not care to reach.[17]

Amelia (1751) is Fielding's exploration of that contemporary territory. Its realism may derive from his increased involvement after 1749 as a reforming London magistrate with the actualities of urban social disorder and the heartless operations of modern justice. The opening chapters in Newgate Prison have an almost hallucinatory quality in which the universalizing comic control of the first two novels is only fitfully at work.[18] These chapters are noteworthy for their rapid movement from the grotesque injustices of Justice Thrasher's night court, where the action begins, to the squalor of Newgate Prison, to which the hero, Billy Booth, is committed by the Justice for his part in a street brawl (where in fact Booth has tried to rescue someone from assailants). The first scene is reminiscent of the controlled comedy of the earlier novels as the narrator lectures us in his bantering manner on the corruption of the justice system as embodied in Justice Thrasher: "who, if he was ignorant of the Law of *England*, was yet well versed in the Laws of Nature. He perfectly well understood that fundamental Principle so strongly laid down in the Institutes of the learned *Rochefoucault*; by which the Duty of Self-love is so strongly enforced, and every Man is taught to consider himself as the Centre of Gravity, and to attract all things thither. To speak the Truth plainly, the Justice was never indifferent in a Cause, but when he could get nothing on either Side."[19] La Rochefoucauld's cynical *Maxims* evokes the universalism of the earlier novels, and Justice Thrasher's ignorance and predictable greed mark him as a type of the comically corrupt judge.

Newgate is another matter, since it features characters and situations that resist in their particularity most of the satisfactions of comic universalizing. Packed with a sordid, threatening, and pathetic variety of inhabitants, resonating with a clamorous din of curses, groans, and desperate merriment, the prison is a Hogarthian panorama full of contemporary references but lacking an organizing principle and a clear narrative function, a breakdown of the comic order found in Fielding's first two novels. The scene is a disconnected series rather than a meaningful plenitude, and it is to some extent a gratuitous representation if we think in terms of the novel's plot. And indeed most of the people in this prison tableau are not part of the subsequent events of this long novel but provide an atmosphere, set an initial tone of confusion and contradiction, of aimless disaster and hopelessness that is never fully dissipated in the rest of the book. Such atmosphere is a new formal aspect of Fielding's fiction, as the thematic transparency and sharp comic outlines of the two earlier novels give way to a complicated and even confusing sequence of events that defy easy or even coherent resolution.[20]

Booth is accosted by various prisoners when he enters the jail, with the first group demanding money to buy drink and stripping him of his coat. Another who asks him to buy her a dram of gin is the most striking of the several prostitutes in the prison, the one-eyed, noseless, obese "Blear-Eyed Moll," and she carries grotesquerie so far past any conceivable humorous effect that she serves as a reproof in her particular and accurate embodiment of contemporary ugliness to the falsity of stage conventions: "I wish certain Actresses on the Stage, when they are to perform Characters of no amiable Cast, would study to dress themselves with the Propriety, with which *Blear-Eyed Moll* was now arrayed. For the sake of our squeamish Reader, we shall not descend to Particulars. Let it suffice to say, nothing more ragged, or more dirty, was ever emptied out of the Round-house at *St. Giles's*" (I, iii, 28). In the next chapter Booth and one Robinson, a gambler who has preceded him in Newgate, move on and survey some of the other inhabitants and consider stories that lack even the corrective realism of Blear-Eyed Moll:

> they beheld a Man prostrate on the Ground, whose heavy Groans, and frantic Actions, plainly indicated the highest Disorder of Mind. This Person was, it seems, committed for a small Felony; and his Wife, who then lay-in, upon hearing the News, had thrown herself from a Window two Pair of Stairs high, by which means he had, in all Probability, lost both her and his Child.

A very pretty Girl then advanced towards them, whose Beauty Mr *Booth* could not help admiring the Moment he saw her; declaring, at the same time, he thought she had great Innocence in her Countenance. *Robinson* said she was committed thither as an idle and disorderly Person, and a common Street-walker. As she past by Mr *Booth*, she damn'd his Eyes, and discharged a Volley of Words, every one of which was too indecent to be repeated.

...

 This was immediately followed by another Bustle. *Blear-Eyed Moll*, and several of her Companions, having got Possession of a Man who was committed for certain odious unmanlike Practices, not fit to be named, were giving him various Kinds of Discipline, and would probably have put an End to him, had he not been rescued out of their Hands by Authority.
 When this Bustle was a little allayed, Mr *Booth* took Notice of a young Woman in Rags sitting on the Ground, and supporting the Head of an old Man in her Lap, who appeared to be giving up the Ghost. These, Mr *Robinson* informed him, were Father and Daughter; that the latter was committed for stealing a Loaf, in order to support the former, and the former for receiving it knowing it to be stolen.

(I, iv, 32–34)

All of these instances point to contemporary circumstances that Fielding deplored in all his writing such as the prevalence of vice and the unpitying severity and inflexibility of the penal code, but as he narrates them here they also have a tabloid newspaper sensationalism that derives from their random and gratuitous quality as much as from the moral or social scandals that they illustrate. In their randomness and disconnection they offer the ultimate scandal of a formless disorder, of disasters all the more cruel for being arbitrary, of the erosion of moral agency or responsibility, of a system where no one seems to be in charge, of a world apparently deserted by Providence.

 At the same time, Fielding challenges his reader by placing individual moral agency in the foreground, arguing that Fortune may not be to blame in most cases for the misfortunes of men, since "natural means account for the success of Knaves, the Calamities of Fools" (I, i, 16). Life, the narrator continues, is an art, "and the great Incidents in it are no more to be considered as mere Accidents, than the several

Members of a fine Statue, or a noble Poem" (17). The events of these opening chapters would seem to question the validity of such elegant formulations about life as a moral work of art and to support something closer to the opposing opinions of Booth and Robinson. Free-thinkers both, they contemplate this Newgate misery with varieties of fatalism, as Booth responds to his new companion's contention that "all Things happen by an inevitable Fatality; and a Man can no more resist the Impulse of Fate, than a Wheel-barrow can the Force of its Driver" (I, iii, 29–30) with his own theory "that every Man acted merely from the Force of that Passion which was uppermost in his Mind, and could do no otherwise" (32). In fact, the events of the novel dramatize neither fatalism nor heroic moral agency, and Booth's and Robinson's theories explain character and events no better than the narrator's. In the books that follow this tour of the prison, Booth tells his own long story of romance, financial difficulties, and professional frustrations to Miss Mathews, an old acquaintance who offers her own tale of Haywoodian passion, betrayal, and murderous revenge that has landed her in Newgate. Neither of these stories bears out Booth's theory of person-ality, since they feature an impenetrable mix of circumstances, accidents, good and bad luck, as well as a measure of misguided or short-sighted personal agency in Booth's and erotic obsession and betrayal in Miss Mathews'. These stories are serious, more disciplined cousins of Partridge's meandering tale, but they lack moral symmetry and comic resonance, as they mix the commonplace and the romantic in ways that set the tone for the rest of the novel.

An odd mixture of degraded romance and social realism, *Amelia* is from the start a deeply anti-theoretical and anti-systematic novel, offering no answers to the social and moral problems that it contem-plates as it turns on the real-life disasters of a feckless, hopelessly indebted half-pay officer who has no resources or connections with which to advance in his profession, along with a wife and three children to support. Fielding renders circumstances at their most depressingly prosaic and intimately domestic, and his originality (as well as his failure) lies in the attempt to present society as something less than a coherent system, for good or ill, and to treat human agency as real but exceedingly limited by moral weakness as well as by social pathology and systemic malfunction, to say nothing of bad luck. The occasional tedium of *Amelia* flows very precisely from its realistic ambition to render these overseeing forces, from Fielding's refusal of the comic universalizing of his earlier novels and his avoidance of the psycholog-ical narrowness and emotional fatalism of the amatory tradition. All of the events in *Amelia* are exactly derived from some of the same particular social issues that had exercised Fielding before, only here they are at the exact center of the plot, a recalcitrant, complicated bulk in the face of which moral or social theorizing has little explanatory force or resolving power: the corrupt injustice of the penal code and the debt laws, along with the malfeasance of the officers of those laws, the lack of equity in the clerical and military systems of preferment, and the abuse of its privileges by a decadent aristocracy. To be sure, there are occasional bursts of indignation from the narrator, as he contemplates his own representation of what he knows to be the prevailing abuses of power and patronage. For example, he recounts how Booth is persuaded to offer a bribe of £50 to a Great Man at the War Office to help him acquire a commission and he hopes that some of his readers will be moved to protest: "A worthy Family, the Wife and Children of a Man who had lost his Blood abroad in the Service of his Country, parting with their little all, and exposed to Cold and Hunger, to pamper such a Fellow as this" (XI, v, 477).

Fielding does attempt, half-heartedly one might say, to bring classical and romance motifs to bear on some of the novel's ugly materials and to suggest a measure of literary and moral recurrence. Booth's amorous encounter in a Newgate cell with Miss Mathews, for example, echoes a number of famous illicit dalliances – Antony and Cleopatra, Mars and Venus, and (especially) Dido and Aeneas. And Booth's narrative to Miss Mathews of elopement, marriage, and then mustering to Gibraltar includes several folk-tale and romance motifs: he hides in a hamper of wine to meet Amelia, he forgets a love token she gives him as he rides off to war and sends his servant back for it (out of Ariosto, as Battestin's note points out (III, iii, 106)). But Fielding is oddly reserved as a narrator in this novel, and he makes little capital out of these elements. He gives over that responsibility for long stretches of the novel to the characters themselves: Miss Mathews tells her story to Booth, he reciprocates with his own long account of his life, and various other figures deliver their own stories as they enter the narrative. Although there are flashes of the old narrative bravura, Fielding allows his characters to dominate in every sense, not only telling their stories but acting without much explanatory commentary from the narrator.

One of these stories is especially revealing, partly because it is an anticipatory parallel to one crucial aspect of Amelia's own troubles and partly because in its disconcerting jumble of romance, sexual melodrama, domestic and financial struggle, and social criticism it matches the Booths' story and thereby highlights the essential interchangeability of all such personal histories. That is to say, the Booths' moving but essentially commonplace plight – deserving military merit and brave service go unrewarded and long-suffering female virtue is assailed on several sides by would-be seducers and betrayers – repeats other stories told by lesser characters like this Mrs Bennet, and there is no particular comfort or symmetry in such recurrences but only a joyless and ultimately numbing sameness – which novelists in the following few decades will attempt to rehabilitate by means of an unabashed sentimentalism foreign to Fielding's sensibility.

Mrs Ellison, the Booths' jolly landlady, invites Mrs Bennet to join them for cards. A 25-year-old clerical widow in "very indifferent Circumstances" (IV, ix, 192), her hard life has left her with only traces of her former beauty, but Amelia senses a kindred spirit in her grave and reserved manner. In due course, she tells Amelia her story to warn her of the dangers she faces in her intimacy with this treacherous Mrs Ellison and the complaisant Lord who is her relation. After the death of her beloved mother, Mrs Bennet begins, her wicked young stepmother turned her clergyman father against her, leaving her penniless after his death. She married a poor curate, and their life was hard and unpromising. Mrs Bennet's story has one extraordinary climactic scene when her life acquires a wildly melodramatic cast. She and her late husband were lodgers, she reports, in this same house where the Booths now reside, where Mrs Ellison introduced her to one of her other guests, a noble Lord to whom she has lately introduced Amelia under strikingly similar circumstances, the peer promising to obtain preferment for her husband and showing a tender interest in her children. One fatal evening when Mrs Bennet's husband was away to solicit at the Lord's recommendation a clerical office from a Bishop, she was persuaded to attend a masquerade with Mrs Ellison and the Lord, by whom she was charmed. But upon their return home, he drugged and raped her: "Here, Madam, I must draw a Curtain over the Residue of that fatal Night. Let it suffice, that it involved me in the most dreadful Ruin; a Ruin, to which I can truly say, I never consented; and of which I was scarce conscious, when the villanous Man avowed it to my Face in the Morning" (VII, vii, 295). But worse follows, as a short time later her husband confronts her with shocking evidence of her adultery. The scene is without precedent in Fielding's fiction, and indeed there is nothing nearly so desperate and frantic, so brutally shocking and embarrassing in the main narrative. It is worth quoting at length:

'He entered the Room, with a Face as white as a Sheet, his Lips trembling, and his Eyes red as Coals of Fire, and starting as it were from his Head. – "*Molly*," cries he, throwing himself into his Chair, "are you well?" – "Good Heavens," says I, "what's the Matter? – Indeed, I can't say I am well." "No!" says he, – starting from his Chair, "false Monster, you have betrayed me, destroyed me, you have ruined your Husband." Then looking like a Fury he snatched off a large Book from the Table, and with the Malice of a Madman, threw it at my Head, and knocked me down backwards. He then caught me up in his Arms, and kissed me with most extravagant Tenderness; then looking me stedfast in the Face for several Moments, the Tears gushed in a Torrent from his Eyes, and with his utmost Violence he threw me again on the Floor – Kicked me, stamped upon me. I believe, indeed, his Intent was to kill me, and I believe he thought he had accomplished it.

'I lay on the Ground for some Minutes I believe, deprived of my Senses. When I recovered myself, I found my Husband lying by my Side on his Face, and the Blood running from him. It seems when he thought he had dispatched me, he ran his Head with all his Force against a Chest of Drawers which stood in the Room, and gave himself a dreadful Wound in his Head.

'I can truly say, I felt not the least Resentment for the Usage I had received; I thought I deserved it all; tho' indeed I little guessed what he had suffered from me. I now used the most earnest Entreaties to him to compose himself; and endeavoured with my feeble Arms to raise him from the Ground. At length, he broke from me, and springing from the Ground flung himself into a Chair, when looking wildly at me, he cried, – "Go from me, *Molly*. I beseech you leave me, I would not kill you." He then discovered to me – O Mrs *Booth*, can you not guess it? – I was indeed polluted by the Villain – I had infected my Husband – O Heaven! why do I live to relate any thing so horrid – I will not, I cannot yet survive it. I cannot forgive myself. Heaven cannot forgive me. –'

(VII, viii, 299)

Mrs Bennet offers this lurid scene of domestic despair and near insanity without comment from the narrator, who reminds us of his presence only to remark on her confusion when Sergeant Atkinson, Amelia's faithful lower-class childhood friend and devoted supporter of the Booth family, enters and nearly betrays their secret (he and Mrs Bennet have been recently married). Fielding's reticence is worth noticing, since the scene and indeed the appalling situation (especially in its embarrassing, nearly comic prosaic details: the book Mr Bennet hurls at his wife, the chest of drawers against which he dashes his head) would destabilize the dignity and decorum of any romantic or literary plot, even one as attenuated as *Amelia*'s. In Mrs Bennet's story, actions have inescapable, irremediable consequences that drive innocents like Mr Bennet weirdly mad; in this world undiscriminating degeneration of character and motive spreads through several classes and poisons all those relationships and institutions that Fielding's novels in general seek to rehabilitate or ridicule back to health. This lustful Lord and his pimp, Mrs Ellison, exploit and defile the patron–client bonds and the rewards that patient merit hopes to obtain from them. In this regard these villains are hardly singular or unusual. Betrayal for sexual pleasure is the thread that runs through the various stories that make up *Amelia*. Booth's infidelity with Miss Mathews is distinct in its spontaneity and in his remorse afterwards, since just about everyone else we meet is self-consciously bent without shame or scruple upon conspiracy and betrayal to serve their own pleasure. It is an interesting if partial confirmation of the narrator's opening theory of moral agency that those who control their lives in *Amelia* are precisely those characters who have the economic privilege and power to do so for malevolent and destructive ends. All that can defend readers from the subversive proposition that (im)moral agency is a class privilege is the sentimental force of the heroine's unwavering goodness and patience in the face of crushing adversity and of course the ultimate restoration of the Booths to their proper status as property owners by the last arbitrary turn of the plot.

At the beginning of Book VIII, Booth is suddenly arrested by a bailiff because of an action brought by their supporter and moral advisor, the clergyman Dr Harrison, for an unpaid debt of £500. Amelia and her children are plunged into new wretchedness by this the latest of their many misfortunes. Mrs Ellison promises to save the day if Amelia will come to the masquerade with her, where the lascivious Lord plans to complete his plan for her seduction. But Mrs Atkinson, past victim of the identical ruse, overhears these plans and warns Amelia, sending Mrs Ellison away furious and prompting this summary from the narrator of the superiority of virtue even in affliction to vice:

> Indeed, how much the Superiority of Misery is on the Side of Wickedness, may appear to every Reader who will compare the present Situation of *Amelia*, with that of Mrs *Ellison*. Fortune had attack'd the former with almost the highest Degree of her Malice. She was involved in a Scene of most exquisite Distress; and her Husband, her principal Comfort, torn violently from her Arms; yet her Sorrow, however

exquisite, was all soft and tender; nor was she without many Consolations. Her Case, however hard, was not absolutely desperate; for scarce any Condition of Fortune can be so. Art and Industry, Chance and Friends have often relieved the most distrest Circumstances, and converted them into Opulence. In all these she had Hopes on this Side the Grave, and perfect Virtue and Innocence gave her the strongest Assurances on the other. Whereas in the Bosom of Mrs *Ellison* all was Storm and Tempest; Anger, Revenge, Fear, and Pride, like so many raging Furies, possessed her Mind, and tortured her with Disappointment and Shame. Loss of Reputation, which is generally irreparable, was to be her Lot; Loss of Friends is of this the certain Consequence; all on this Side the Grave appeared dreary and comfortless; and endless Misery on the other, closed the gloomy Prospect.

(VIII, iii, 319–320)

The hopes of self-satisfied virtue and moral superiority are partly statistical; art and industry, or chance and friends do sometimes come to the rescue. And if they do not, virtue is its own reward and brings the serenity of mind that the vicious (at least those who fail in their plots like Mrs Ellison) lack. So Fielding addresses the "worthy Reader" to assure us that "Innocence, is always within thy own Power; and tho' Fortune may make thee often unhappy, she can never make thee completely and irreparably miserable without thy own Consent" (320). Although *Amelia* is not a philosophical tract and it is not quite fair to search for consistency in the narrator's commentary, such a conventional position is a retreat from his opening remarks about the irrelevance of fortune and the possibility of creative moral agency. Where the reader might have expected a tale of successful if difficult effort to achieve happiness, Fielding's novel finds action and agency to be, in the world of the mid-eighteenth century, purely or at least largely private and internal matters. The community and communication that he values and redeems in his comic novels simply do not work in this world, and the narrator chooses not to represent things otherwise.

Piling on calamities and even more feckless behavior by Billy so that disaster follows disaster for the hapless Booths, Fielding's plot extricates them only with a last-minute coincidence and a set of accidents ("Chance and Friends" and not "Art and Industry") that look like the book's final rejection of the mode of romance as well as of any representation of "art and industry." Booth is arrested yet again for a debt of £50 to an old military friend, who is in fact a perfidious pimp for

Colonel James (another old military friend who lusts after Amelia and is jealous of Booth's affair with Miss Mathews). So it would appear that villainy is inexhaustible and complex, pervasive, inescapable, hard to summarize adequately in any description of the book.

Coming to rescue Billy once again, Dr Harrison is asked by the bailiff to attend on his deathbed a man wounded resisting arrest, who turns out to be the gambler, Robinson, from the opening Newgate chapters. Robinson has seen Amelia at a pawnbroker's (where she has pawned her clothes) and remembered his part in the fraud perpetrated by the lawyer, Murphy (glimpsed in the Newgate scene when he comes to arrange Miss Mathews' release), and Amelia's sister (a female Blifil, as it were) to change her mother's will and to deprive her sister of the estate which had actually been left to her. After so much relentless bad luck and remorseless villainy, this lucky rescue hardly fits the description that Dr Harrison gives it: "Providence hath done you the Justice at last, which it will one Day or other render to all Men" (XII, vii, 522). The universal justice that Harrison speaks of is not of this world. If anything, Fielding goes out of his way to mark the ending as a lucky accident or fortunate coincidence, as inexplicable as the disconnected scenes of misery in Newgate with which the novel began. Despite Harrison's intelligent and robust piety, social and moral realism of the kind that *Amelia* features is disturbingly and thoroughly secular in this regard, and the novel's happy ending feels like a stroke of just that good fortune that the narrator warned us about at the beginning. It is good news for the Booths, but they are clearly the happy exception to the dismal rule revealed by *Amelia*.

NOTES

1 Stung by repeated satirical attacks on him in anti-government plays, Walpole on June 21, 1737 had Parliament enact The Licensing Act, which limited the number of theaters to those that already had licenses from the government, thereby closing all unlicensed ones, including Fielding's Little Theatre in the Haymarket. The Act required that all new plays and revisions of old ones be approved by the Lord Chamberlain, a government functionary. Fielding was out of business in the theater.

2 Henry Fielding, *Joseph Andrews*, ed. Martin C. Battestin (*The Wesleyan Edition of the Works of Henry Fielding*, Middletown, CT, Wesleyan University Press, 1967), III, i, 189. All further references in the text in brackets are to this edition.

3 Thomas Hobbes' *Leviathan* (1651) was widely denounced for its pessimistic view of human nature and its subordination of the Church to the state. Thomas Woolston (1670–1733) was a notorious free-thinker who was

convicted of blasphemy and imprisoned for his *Discourses on the Miracles of our Saviour* (1727–1729).

4 M.M. Bakhtin, *The Dialogic Imagination: Four Essays*, ed. Michael Holquist, trans. Caryl Emerson and Michael Holquist (Austin, TX, University of Texas Press, 1981), p. 308.

5 Bakhtin, *The Dialogic Imagination*, p. 308.

6 Henry Fielding, *The History of Tom Jones: A Foundling*, ed. Martin C. Battestin (Middletown, CT, Wesleyan University Press, 1975), II, i, 77. All further page references in brackets in the text are to this edition.

7 "What a master of composition Fielding was! Upon my word, I think the *Oedipus Tyrannus*, the *Alchemist*, and *Tom Jones* the three most perfect plots ever planned." *Table Talk*, July 5, 1834, *Complete Works of Samuel Taylor Coleridge*, ed. W.G.T. Shedd (New York, Harper and Brothers, 1856), VI, p. 521.

8 Bakhtin, *The Dialogic Imagination*, p. 274.

9 Bakhtin, *The Dialogic Imagination*, p. 274.

10 Alasdair McIntyre, *After Virtue: A Study in Moral Theory* (Notre Dame, IN, University of Notre Dame Press, 1984), p. 208.

11 In Book XVII (iv, 887), metaphors of hunting and consumption come together in a suggestive fashion, as the narrator considers Sophia's position as a rich heiress in London, like a "plump Doe" escaped from the forest and pursued by everyone, "hunted from Park to Play, from Court to Assembly, from Assembly to her own Chamber, and rarely escapes a single Season from the Jaws of some Devourer or other."

12 Bakhtin, *The Dialogic Imagination*, pp. 15, 22.

13 Max Horkheimer and Theodor Adorno, *The Dialectic of Enlightenment*, trans. John Cumming (New York, Herder and Herder, 1972), p. 12. I owe this reference to Adam Potkay.

14 Michael McKeon, *The Origins of the English Novel: 1600–1740* (Baltimore, Johns Hopkins University Press, 1987), p. 392.

15 McKeon, *The Origins of the English Novel 1600–1740*, p. 393.

16 See Bruce Robbins, *The Servant's Hand: English Fiction from Below* (New York, Columbia University Press, 1986).

17 "Comic style (of the English sort) is based, therefore, on the stratification of common language and on the possibilities available for isolating from these strata, to one degree or another, one's own intentions, without ever completely merging with them. *It is precisely the diversity of speech, and not the unity of a normative shared language, that is the ground of style.*" Bakhtin, *The Dialogic Imagination*, p. 308. In *Tom Jones*, at least, Fielding tries to contain by comic patterning this diversity of speech and to uphold his version of a "normative shared language."

18 Robert Alter calls *Amelia* Fielding's "problem novel," for there is in it "a disconcerting sense that the tone of the writing is not always fully under the writer's control." As he says a bit later, Amelia is "an embryonic novel of social protest." *Fielding and the Nature of the Novel* (Cambridge, MA, Harvard University Press, 1968), pp. 142, 148.

19 *Amelia*, ed. Martin C. Battestin (Middletown, CT, Wesleyan University Press, 1983), I, ii, p. 21. All further page references in brackets in the text are to this edition.

20 Claude Rawson offers the most powerful evocation of the situation in
Amelia when he points to these opening scenes as displaying a "bare factu-
ality" that Fielding refuses to explain: "If fact defies explanation, its
outrageousness is highlighted in such a way that the betrayed expectation
remains as a helpless norm, the absence of gloss itself a gloss." Rawson sees
Amelia in this regard as potentially a novelistic advance as "the brutal forces
of an absurd universe meet the Augustan rage for order face to face." *Henry
Fielding and the Augustan Ideal Under Stress* (London, Routledge and Kegan
Paul, 1972), p. 83. So, too, J. Paul Hunter in his judicious discussion calls
Amelia "Fielding's most prophetic work," as it refuses "to provide a modal
frame that insulates the comic resolution of events from their tragic possi-
bilities." *Occasional Form: Henry Fielding and the Chains of Circumstances*
(Baltimore and London, Johns Hopkins University Press, 1975), pp. 193,
207.

6

SMOLLETT

Resentment, knowledge, and action

In *English Literature in History 1730–80: An Equal, Wide Survey*, John Barrell finds writers "concerned to represent the diversity of English society more fully" than ever before.[1] That ambition brings an increasing sense of the impossibility of achieving a comprehensive view of society, now widely perceived as increasingly, bewilderingly complex and diverse. In the face of what Barrell labels a "crisis in social knowledge," the periodical essay, the georgic poem, and the "picaresque or comic epic novel" seek to elaborate a possibility of comprehensive understanding.[2] The main problem is where to place an observer so that he (and, especially in the eighteenth-century novel, *she*) transcends an encompassing social structure in which individuals are defined by their partial and necessarily self-interested economic and political roles. As the economic structure of society becomes more apparent and what the eighteenth century called the landed interest is revealed as one among several competing factions, even the myth of the gentleman spectator, disinterested by virtue of the leisure guaranteed by his estate, begins to fade. One solution, says Barrell, is worked out in Smollett's novels, and he quotes the definition of a novel in the dedication to *Ferdinand Count Fathom* (1753):

> A Novel is a large diffused picture, comprehending the characters of life, disposed in different groups, and exhibited in various attitudes, for the purpose of an uniform plan, and general occurrence, to which every individual figure is subservient. But this plan cannot be executed with propriety, probability or success, without a principal personage to attract the attention, unite the incidents, unwind the clue of the labyrinth and at last close the scene by virtue of his own importance.[3]

Barrell points out that the novel's hero, the "principal personage," adds a crucial historical dimension to the frozen motion of Smollett's crowded picture. By virtue of his sampling a wide variety of its specific possibilities without ever limiting himself to any particular one, the hero is enabled to write the novel, that is, to become a gentleman autobiographer and achieve both participation and contemplative perspective. As Barrell observes, such a gentleman is palpably a fiction, possible only in fiction.[4] But such a solution and such a fictional narrator are conspicuous by their absence or, more often, by their dramatized difficulty or rarity, in the work of several of the other major eighteenth-century novelists. Indeed Smollett himself in his last novel, *Humphry Clinker* (1771), makes the difficulty of comprehensive understanding and effective moral action in society his explicit theme. In a rare moment of reflection on his methods and aims, Smollett anticipates a perennial problem for his readers, as he claims that beneath the vivid diversity and particularity of his novel there is actually a pattern forming to which the individual episodes contribute. Smollett's insistence here on the static metaphors of visual representation to evoke his local effects indicates clearly that he is well aware not just of the diffuseness of his narratives but most especially of the mobility and kinetic particularity they seem to feature in place of stability of representation and thematic meaning.

After the episodic particularity and improvisational inclusiveness of his first two novels, which most readers have always agreed are infinitely superior to *Ferdinand Count Fathom* and its successor, *Launcelot Greaves* (1760–1761) precisely for those energetic qualities, Smollett's anxiety about coherence in his fiction is an odd and nervous denial of his characteristic talent. Smollett's novels are read (when they are read) as compellingly vivid and decidedly episodic rather than praised for their coherence and complexity. G.S. Rousseau admits that Smollett is "imperfect in almost every conceivable stylistic aspect," but he finds in Smollett an eloquently expressive and unifying rage and malice, a raw, crude, and powerful force that exceeds in its ferocious vigor even the considerable violence to be found in satire and in the picaresque. Smollett's novels taken cumulatively possess a rhetorical unity; they project what Rousseau memorably calls a desire for violent "perpetual revenge" on the inhabitants of a social scene that is evoked as so corrupt that conventional literary categories are inadequate.[5] So Smollett's claim to have a plan is dismissed, for his value as a novelist resides in intensely local effects that communicate a uniquely disturbing Smollettian outrage.[6] At stake is whether Smollett needs a different kind of attention and analysis than he customarily receives, whether his novels – curiously absent from landmark studies of the eighteenth-century novel from Watt to McKeon and Bender – deserve a more important place in our understanding of the eighteenth-century novel.

The dedication to *Ferdinand Count Fathom* projects Smollett's deeply irascible dissatisfaction with the customary purpose of such a preface. Instead of hoping to flatter a patron, Smollett dedicates the novel to an alter ego – Dr ***** – and his description of the methodical coherence of his narrative is part of a defense against anticipated attacks from "the prejudice, misapprehension and temerity of malice, ignorance and presumption." Smollett goes on, after describing his plan, to explain that he has deliberately chosen his "principal character from the purlieus of treachery and fraud" to serve as a "beacon for the benefit of the unexperienced and unwary," who may thereby "learn to avoid the manifold snares with which they are continually surrounded in the paths of life" (5). Like the novelist who anticipates and defends himself against "malice, ignorance and presumption," the innocent reader of *Ferdinand Count Fathom* will learn to expect trouble and look out for danger after finishing Smollett's book. But will such nervous vigilance after the book is put down be balanced by the memory of the satisfying underlying coherence of Smollett's plan, that comprehensive exhibition of social and moral plenitude purged of disorganized or random particularity by its focus on "a principal personage" whose life history unites all this diversity? The answer to that is obviously no. Does the unity that Smollett promises have anything to do with the moral effect that he also claims to provide? Actually, I think the answer in this case is yes, since Smollett's novels convey something like totality in their dramatization of suspicion and hostility as the defining, the absolutely dependable characteristics of social experience. In Smollett's two previous novels, the central character provides a nominal unity, but the structure thus achieved is in one sense superficial, especially given Smollett's lack of aptitude for complex characterization. In the special case of *Fathom*, that central figure who is essential to the plan will not just provide a unifying narrative focus but make a major contribution by his thoroughgoing villainy to the coherence of a represented social order where virtue has no secure place, the same social order that has driven Smollett to dedicate his third novel to himself, a "censorious age" where the warmth and praise of dedication are always ascribed "to interested views and sordid adulation" (3). Smollett offers his auto-dedication as simultaneously a tribute to his own literary powers of insight and synthesis and a defiance of the world that will always disparage and deny them. But his novel derives its powerful coherence, its claims to aptness and plausibility, by its revelation of the recurrence of just that moral and aesthetic blindness that Smollett attacks in his dedication.

Like all of Smollett's novels, *Ferdinand Count Fathom* is both scandalized and deeply satisfied by the predictable villainy that the world offers. Smollett's vaunted novelistic plan, if we take it seriously and extend it to his other fictions, depends for the unity it extracts from diversity upon an obsessive organizing theme of injured and unrewarded merit in a world dominated by what seems to be an almost institutionally established corrupt self-interest. His choice of a Jonathan Wilde-like central character for his third novel is an inevitable move from the self-indulgent, morally compromised heroes of his first two and indicates just how crucial such an understanding of unrewarded merit is for that "propriety, probability and success" which, he says, is his aim. The success, for most of the novel anyway, of the odious Fathom underlines the moral incongruity that enrages Smollett and his heroes elsewhere.

Fathom himself at one significant low point in his fortunes looks back on his disgraceful life and thinks that he sees it whole, projecting a morally incongruous alternative to his career of self-seeking and betrayal and seeing now an emerging general pattern of retribution canceling his improvisations of self-seeking villainy. He discovers that the woman he has recently married for her fortune is suing him for bigamy and that several creditors are fast closing in on him: "his resources were all dried up, his invention failed, and his reflection began to take a new turn." Smollett allows Fathom to soliloquize in fatuously self-dramatizing fashion, his remorse coming very late indeed:

> To what purpose (said he to himself) have I deserted the paths of integrity and truth, and exhausted a fruitful imagination, in contriving schemes to betray my fellow-creatures; if, instead of acquiring a splendid fortune, which was my aim, I have suffered such a series of mortifications, and at last brought myself to the brink of inevitable destruction? By a virtuous exertion of those talents I inherit from nature and education, I might, long before this time, have rendered myself independent, and, perhaps, conspicuous in life ... I should have paid the debt of gratitude to my benefactors, and made their hearts sing with joy for the happy effects of their benevolence; I should have been a bulwark to my friends, a shelter to my neighbours in distress; I should have run the race of honour, seen my fame diffused like a sweet-smelling odour, and felt the ineffable pleasure of doing good: whereas I am, after a vicissitude of disappointments, dangers and fatigues, reduced to

> misery and shame, aggravated by a conscience loaded with treachery and guilt. ... Shall the author of these crimes pass with impunity? Shall he hope to prosper in the midst of such enormous guilt? It were an imputation upon providence to suppose it – Ah, no! I begin to feel myself overtaken by the eternal justice of heaven! I totter on the edge of wretchedness and woe, without one friendly hand to save me from the terrible abyss.
>
> (274–275)

The narrator is skeptical, indeed cynical, telling us that such reflections are produced not by the "misery of his fellow creatures" but by "the sensation of his own calamities." This reformation, like so many others, says Smollett, is "generated from unsuccessful vice," and if an avenue of escape from these evils through deceit had presented itself "he would not, in all probability, have scrupled to practise it upon his own father, had a convenient opportunity occurred" (275). Fathom's moralizing retrospection is provoked by the particular turn in his fortunes, and it has the status for the novel's satiric economy of particular "sensation" rather than of general or reasoned moral understanding, a protective reflex or mechanical response to calamity that has the same moral and intellectual weight as his life of improvisatory deceit. Such imposition of pattern, such prediction of justice and providential symmetry, is nothing but Fathom's specific psychological defense against the accumulated failures of his villainy.

But what, exactly, distinguishes Smollett's rendition of this recurrent self-seeking and downright villainy from the ahistorical resolutions of the Augustan moral essay or the uniformitarianism of satiric tradition? How does Smollett's disgust with contemporary society achieve anything more than these sorts of rhetorical coherence? Fathom, after all, is an easy target, a dependable and shallow villain. My argument is that the special malice and fury that G.S. Rousseau acutely sees as obsessively recurrent is a *ressentiment* in the resonant sense afforded by that French noun that transforms Smollett's vivid fragments of anger and spleen into a coherent representation of an emerging early modern social totality. Specifically, Smollett seems obsessed by the absolute lack of what J.G.A. Pocock has reminded us was traditionally associated with civic virtue, "the moral quality which only propertied independence could confer, and which became almost indistinguishable from property itself." [7] In the 1765 *Continuation of the Complete History of England*, Smollett sprinkles through the historical narrative outbursts of indignation: "The tide of luxury still flowed with an impetuous current, bearing down all the mounds of temperance and decorum; while fraud and profligacy struck out new channels, through which they eluded the restriction of the law, and all the vigilance of civil policy. New arts of deception were invented, in order to ensnare and ruin the unwary; and some infamous practices, in the way of commerce, were countenanced by persons of rank and importance in the commonwealth."[8] Smollett's novels depict in their relentless, savagely unforgiving energy, perhaps more forcefully than any other eighteenth-century rendering, the unstoppable trajectories of mobile property which makes men, in Pocock's terms, artificial beings guided only by a demented and utterly unfixed and free-flowing self-interest. One might argue that the kinetic quality of Smollett's narratives, his appetite for every conceivable variety of grotesque self-seeking, is in the largest possible sense his reaction to this situation. But there is no one particular textual locus to illustrate such an assertion, and most critics have dismissed Smollett's treatment of social forces as schematic and generalized, conveying in Michael Rosenblum's words "little of the novelist's interest in the infinite degrees of dependence and independence in society."[9] That is true enough if we simply consider the texts and what they represent, although there is in Smollett a good deal of furious attention paid to the failure and corruption of eighteenth-century patronage relationships in their uneasy transition with emerging bureaucratic forms and regulations.

However, if instead of looking at any particular moment in the texts we examine our own difficulties as we read Smollett in finding in his novels' structural coherence or moral complexity or social realism, then we reproduce in our suspicions the conditions that lead him to write his defensive dedication to *Ferdinand Count Fathom*, and in a sense we attribute to him the distorting and self-serving delight in vivid particularity and personalized satiric attack that he both denies and perpetuates as the locus of interest in his novels. There is, then, a central adversarial relationship between Smollett as misunderstood or undervalued author and hostile readers or critics who correctly understand his novels as expressions of the very same self-seeking that he claims to attack and on which he grounds his plan. In failing to achieve structure and coherence, the three early Smollett novels move away from the generalized moral and satiric universalism which is their superficial justification and enact in their disturbing encounters with particular readers the social and political conditions that they do not directly represent.

Smollett the author presents himself as an example *par excellence* of injured merit, of virtue and ability passed over, and paradoxically it is just this aggrieved stance, both actual and anticipated, that allows him to grasp and project a vision of the social order that claims, in however simplified or exaggerated a manner, some sort of implicit comprehensiveness. As an author denied the *bona fides* essential to his profession, he, more than anyone, understands that the institutionalized self-seeking and mutual suspicions that govern all personal relations in the new commercial order and credit economy are the comic and frightening unifying features of what otherwise looks hopelessly diverse. Lacking Fielding's confident affiliations to English literary and juridical institutions, Smollett from the outset of his career turns his inchoate *ressentiment* into his defining novelistic stance, first imbuing his narrative persona with it, in due course embracing it himself as a public personality, and finally dramatizing it as an inadequate posture for social and moral understanding in his last novel. But from the first his virtues lay, I submit, in his limitations, in his readiness to articulate irreducible diversity rather than to impose unifying form and structure. His vivid fragments constitute a new and valuable sense that totality is too large and diverse for literary rendering and to that extent those fragments point to that totality.

Smollett's characterization of his technique in the preface to *Ferdinand Count Fathom* might well be seen as an embarrassed modification of the aggressive claims made in the preface to his first novel, *Roderick Random* (1748), where he promised not to tire the attention of the reader "with a bare Catalogue of characters," but to divert his audience with a "variety of invention" that offered them "the vicissitudes of life … in their particular circumstances."[10] The paragraph in *Fathom* also seems to be a distinct retreat from the slap at Fielding near the end of *Peregrine Pickle* (1751).

I might here, in imitation of some celebrated writers, furnish out a page or two, with the reflections he [Peregrine is in debtors' prison] made upon the instability of human affairs, the treachery of the world, and the temerity of youth; and endeavour to decoy the reader into a smile, by some quaint observation of my own, touching the sagacious moralizer: but, besides that I look upon this practice as an impertinent anticipation of the peruser's thoughts, I have too much matter of importance upon my hands, to give the reader the least reason to believe that I am driven to such paultry shifts, in order to eke out the volume. Suffice it then, to say, our adventurer passed a very uneasy night, not only from the thorny suggestions of his mind, but likewise from the anguish of his couch, as well as from the natural inhabitants thereof, which did not tamely suffer his intrusion.[11]

Peregrine's extraction from debtors' prison, like the career that brought him there, will be minutely circumstantial, bursting with rowdy incidents and crowded with irrepressible organic life, like those "natural inhabitants" of his couch. That variety of scene and range of experience is the "matter of importance" that drives out the "paultry shifts" of Fielding's moral–psychological commentary. In the context of mid-century and in the wake of Fielding's presence as a dominating model, Smollett's refusal of elaborate and systematic commentary and his preference for driving, richly particularized, relatively uncluttered narrative is significant. As a rather less well connected author and failed playwright, an angry and disaffected (Scottish) provincial and an actual participant in institutional, extra-literary life (like his first hero, Roderick Random, he had been a surgeon's mate in the navy), Smollett in these early years of his career did not have Fielding's intense political and literary involvements, and his distance from the inside of political life may in part explain why *Peregrine Pickle* and its predecessor, *Roderick Random*, lack anything that resembles Fielding's comic system and his literary, moral, and social theorizing. But Smollett's relative transparency allows a fullness and intensity of representation too often undervalued by modern criticism.

In that variety both novels defy summary. Both feature protagonists whose function is to render as wide a range of experience as possible. Like Smollett, these are Scottish provincials: Roderick, the seemingly orphaned grandson of a rich landlord whose son has married a woman of a lower social class without his permission; Peregrine, the son of a failed and feckless merchant and a mother who loathes him. Roderick's mother dies shortly after he is born and his disconsolate father disappears, leaving his son to the tender mercies of his grandfather. Where Roderick is cast out by this miserly grandfather and has to seek his fortune in the world, Peregrine, thanks to the benevolence of his godfather, Commodore Hawser Trunnion, goes to Oxford and leads a dissipated life. Roderick and Peregrine, it is worth noting, leave England for a good deal of their histories and, in doing so, encounter what might be called an emerging European world order, Peregrine taking the Grand Tour to France and Belgium and Roderick serving in the English navy and in the Picardy regiment of the French army (he is at the battle of Dettingen), as well as making his fortune (and finding his father) at the very end of the book in a slaving voyage from the east African coast to Argentina. Their relationships, moreover, are thickly social, institutional in a specific and entangling mode; and the social world they inhabit is felt in the narrative as separate and threatening, to some extent unresolved and unprocessed, effectively corrupt and controlling rather than fully managed as a comic analogue for the domestic and personal as it is in Fielding's first two novels. To put it another way, Smollett's protagonists encounter individuals identified by bureaucratic and political affiliations for which the tradition of comic and moral fiction offers no immediate or exact precedents: Roderick, for example, confronts the naval licensing board as he seeks to be certified as naval surgeon; Peregrine runs for Parliament and is the victim of political/financial manipulations that land him in Fleet Prison. Tom Jones, by contrast, is only quite by accident a gentleman volunteer in the army, and personal preoccupations (his pursuit of Sophia) prevent him from participating in the historic battle of Culloden and the defeat of Prince Charles. In *Tom Jones*, the main characters are abstracted from such areas of historical and potentially troublesome experience to be more or less appropriated by comic pattern and plot. The sociohistorical is a backdrop from whose involvements characters are snatched by the benevolent hand of a narrative system with its own aesthetic and didactic purposes.

Smollett's real originality follows from this representational fullness and attention to intractable historical materials, and yet such originality also seems a deviation from the responsibilities that representation entails. His most remarkable moments, derived by Ronald Paulson from a tradition of satiric punitive violence, involve recurring flights of invariably brutal and often scatological invention, as moral and social deviants (defined as such anyway by the protagonists) are physically punished.[12] Here is one such moment from *Peregrine Pickle*. I choose it because it caps an intensely political phase in Peregrine's life: he has been sent by the ministry to run for a seat held by "a great family in the opposition," and he spares "no expence in treating the electors." As Smollett puts it, "the market for votes ran so high, that Pickle's ready money was exhausted before the day of election" (614, 615). So with the help of the minister who has urged him to run, he borrows £1,200 from the receiver-general of the county and manages to secure with "this new supply" an "evident majority of votes." But his opponent cuts a deal with the ministry, giving up two members elsewhere in exchange for this seat. "This proposal was greedily embraced; and on the eve of election, Peregrine received an intimation from his patron, desiring him to quit his pretensions, on pain of his and the minister's displeasure; and promising that he should be elected for another place" (615). Peregrine refuses and is instantly arrested for the money advanced him by the receiver-general:

At first, all the faculties of his soul were swallowed up in astonishment and indignation; and some minutes elapsed before his
nerves would obey the impulse of his rage, which manifested
itself in such an application to the temples of the plaintiff, as
laid him sprawling on the floor. This assault, which was
committed in a tavern whither he had been purposely
decoyed, attracted the regard of the bailiff and his followers,
who, to the number of four, rushed in upon him at once, in
order to overpower him; but his wrath inspired him with such
additional strength and agility, that he disengaged himself
from them in a trice, and seizing a poker, which was the first
weapon that presented itself to his hand, exercised it upon
their skulls with incredible dexterity and execution. The officer
himself, who had been the first that presumed to lay violent
hands upon him, felt the first effects of his fury, in a blow upon
the jaws, in consequence of which he lost three of his teeth,
and fell athwart the body of the receiver, with which he form'd
the figure of St. Andrew's cross: one of his myrmidons seeing
the fate of his chief, would not venture to attack the victor in
front, but wheeling to one side, made an attempt upon him in
flank, and was received obliquely by our hero's left hand and
foot, so masterly disposed to the right side of his leg, and the
left side of his neck, that he bolted head foremost into the
chimney, where his chin was encountered by the grate, which,
in a moment, seared him to the bone.

(616)

This cartoon violence derives, no doubt, from Smollett's reading of
continental picaresque novels and from the physical punishments that
satire traditionally metes out to villains, but in the mid-century British
context, literary and political, scenes like this also represent Smollett's
explicit choice of action over commentary, his turn here for example
from the intricacies of electoral corruption to the adolescent pleasures
of violent slapstick (a feature of the book from the opening pages), from
a serious exposure of political malpractice to the inventive distortions of
freewheeling comic action. There is enough of this sort of thing in
Peregrine Pickle to set off a subversive noise, as it were, a disruption of the
moral and political control exemplified in the strict structuring of *Tom
Jones*, where even rowdy fist fights are regulated and drained of their
potentially disturbing energy by the presiding force of literary form and
comic moralizing. Smollett's refusal of commentary and his defiant
neglect of structure constitute a Bakhtinian cancellation or subversion

of Fielding's controlling unitary discourse and its supporting ideology. Smollett may be said to include a richly detailed and specific representation of mid-century society in order to render it of secondary interest next to his energetic deployment of language and action.[13]

Smollett's erosion of the symmetrical decorum of fiction is his version as narrator of the memorable idiolects he devises for some of his characters, for example in *Peregrine Pickle* the nautical lingo of Commodore Hawser Trunnion and his lieutenants, Pipes and Hatchway. Smollett's preference, aggressively chosen, for comic violence and satiric distortion over the representation of a conventionalized social and moral structure may signify his disaffection from the conservative ideology that governs Fielding's narrative practice in the special political context of mid-century Britain. But for all his jealous carping about Fielding's moral and psychological commentary, Smollett gives his heroes analytical self-consciousness of a sort, and his first novel features a narrator–hero who is shocked and amazed by the world's knavery and also regularly disappointed by his own lack of resolve.

Early in *Roderick Random* the hero finds himself thrown out of his apprenticeship to an apothecary and the subject of ridicule when the "particulars of [his] small amours" are published. Enraged to learn that he has been betrayed by his old school fellow, "squire Gawky," he issues the first challenge of what will be a fractious career:

> He accepted the invitation, and I betook myself to the field, though not without feeling considerable repugnance to the combat, which frequently attacked me in cold sweats by the way; – but the desire of revenge, the shame of retracting, and hope of conquest, conspired to repel these unmanly symptoms of fear; and I appeared on the plain with a good grace: there I waited an hour beyond the time appointed, and was not ill pleased to find that he had no mind to meet me; because now I should have an opportunity of exposing his cowardice, displaying my own courage, and of beating him soundly wheresoever I should find him, without any dread of the consequence. – Elevated with these suggestions, which entirely banished all thoughts of my deplorable condition, I went directly to Gawky's lodgings, where I was informed of his precipitate retreat, he having set out for the country in less than an hour after he had received my billet.
>
> (25)

Roderick's analysis of the emotions that overcame his "unmanly symptoms of fear" leaves it unclear whether he expects readers to see his understanding of that complicated psychological network as part of his experience of the moment or as the result of mature narrative retrospection. From one point of view, it is obviously the latter, since the scene as Roderick experiences it in those "cold sweats" is comically spontaneous, rearranged in the telling by a controlling analytic perspective. What authorizes the narration is not only the particular self-knowledge granted by Roderick's accumulated experience; we also hear the generalizing summaries of the moral essayist, which may be said to derive from a perennial wisdom that precedes Roderick's experiences and indeed enables him to write about them. That essayistic perspective produces here a familiar mock-heroic psychomachia whose military metaphor matches the occasion: "the desire of revenge, the shame of retracting, and hope of conquest, conspired to repel these unmanly symptoms of fear."

And yet *Roderick Random* is not *Rasselas*. Smollett clearly does not want his narrator to translate his experiences with any consistency or efficiency into the generalized moral–psychological formulas of essayistic wisdom. In effect, Roderick speaks and acts in the same tense, and the necessarily after-the-fact understanding of motives and circumstances that his narrative requires is obscured to an important extent by the scene's particularity and immediacy. Smollett's rough-house comedy disrupts generalized moral–psychological patterns, or subjects these ossified formulations to interrogation by spontaneous and concrete speech. In *Roderick Random*, the knowledge granted by abstract moral–psychological formulations such as the one I have quoted is consistently blurred by entirely external and insistently physical renditions of scenes where Smollett displays little interest in the motives of participants. Roderick's self-analysis is a rare moment of calm in an uproarious, generally unreflective narrative, whose neglect of the complexities of motive can be attributed to the legalistic, deliberately superficial norms of the satiric tradition that Smollett followed. In that tradition, there is an inevitable and recurrent pattern of human behavior that undermines the integrity of individual moral action. But the comic force of that pattern can be moderated by an essayistic rendition in which the smile of recognition replaces the belly laugh of slapstick comedy. The essayistic mode, with its generalized, essentialist view of human nature, is implicitly apolitical or deeply conservative. Smollett's disruption of that mode by narrative particularity is implicitly political; his imagining of grotesquely individualized speaking cuts across the grain of that essentialism to which he is in some sense committed.

A somewhat longer sequence from the novel will illustrate how that political disruption works. Roderick is now in London, where he has become apprentice to a Huguenot apothecary, Lavement. Having provoked the resentment of Lavement's wife and daughter (now married to his cowardly antagonist, transformed into Captain Gawky) by rejecting the amorous advances of the daughter and exposing the adulterous activities of the mother, Roderick is accused of stealing medicines from the shop:

> As I could only oppose my single asseveration to this suspicion, he told me one day, 'By gar, your vord not be give me de satisfaction – me find necessaire to chercher for my medicine, pardonnez moy – il faut chercher – me demand le clef of your coffre a cette heure' – Then raising his voice to conceal the fright he was in, lest I should make any opposition, he went on, 'Oui, foutre, I charge you render le clef of your coffre – moi – si, moi qui vous parle.' I was fired with so much resentment and disdain at this accusation, that I burst into tears, which he took for a sign of guilt; and pulling out my key, told him he might satisfy himself immediately, though he would not find it so easy to satisfy me for the injury my reputation had suffered from his unjust suspicion.
>
> (112)

To Roderick's "horror and amazement," his chest is found to contain the missing medicines, planted of course by his enemies in the house.

> 'Ah ha! vous etes bien venues – mardie, Mons. Roderique, you be fort innocent!' – I had not power to utter one word in my own vindication, but stood motionless and silent, while every body present made their respective remarks on what appeared against me. – The servants said, they were sorry for my misfortune, and went away repeating, 'Who would have thought it!' My mistress took occasion from this to rail against the practice of employing strangers in general; and Mrs. Gawky, after having observed that she never had a good opinion of my fidelity, proposed to have me carried before the justice and committed to Newgate immediately. Her husband was actually upon the stairs in his way for a constable, when Mr. Lavement, knowing the cost and trouble of a prosecution to which he must bind himself, and at the same time dreading lest some particulars of my confession might affect his practice, called

out, 'Restez mon fils! restez, it be veritablement one grand crime wich dis pauvre diable have committed – bot peutetre de good God give him de penitence, and me vil not have upon mine head de blood of one sinner.' – The captain and his lady used all the christian arguments their zeal could suggest, to prevail on the apothecary to pursue me to destruction, and represented the injustice he did to the community of which he was a member, in letting a villain escape, who would not fail of doing more mischief in the world, when he should reflect on his coming off so easily now.

(112–113)

Smollett tends to reproduce (that is, to invent) direct speech only when it is heavily marked for comic effect; or to put it another way, direct speech is frequently in Smollett a comic deviation from standard utterance. Thus, Lavement's *franglais* is quoted at length but his wife and daughter's remarks are merely paraphrased. Their responses are thus identified as utterly predictable and to that extent uninteresting or irrelevant, part of the universally self-serving inversion of moral discourse that Smollett's satire assumes. Lavement's indignation is equally fake, of course, but his macaronic deformations are authentic and immediately engaging. Roderick is reduced to tears and then stupefied silence as this indignation explodes all around him. He, too, exists for most of this scene through paraphrase, since how can the generalized formulas available to injured innocence rival the comic energy of Lavement's irrepressible idiolect? The scene assumes, in effect, an audience familiar to the point of boredom with the standard speeches of hypocrisy and sincerity but convinced and amused by comically self-expressive and historically specific, individualized variations like Lavement's.

At length, however, Roderick finds his tongue. His own indignation rouses him, as he puts it, from his stupefaction. His speech is too long to quote in full, but a sample will identify it as standard moral discourse, unmarked and unindividualized, indistinguishable except for its context in the narrative from the suppressed speeches of his enemies in this scene:

Sir, appearances, I own, condemn me; but you are imposed upon as much as I am abused – I have fallen a sacrifice to the rancour of that scoundrel (pointing to Gawky) who has found means to convey your goods hither, that the detection of them might blast my reputation, and accomplish my destruction ... he knows moreover, that I am no stranger to his

175

dastardly behaviour in this town, which I have recounted before; – and he is unwilling that such a testimony of his ingratitude and pusilanimity should live upon the earth; for this reason he is guilty of the most infernal malice to bring about my ruin.

(113)

What saves the novel from the boring conventionality of such language is Smollett's accompanying emphasis on action and gesture: Mrs Gawky spits in Roderick's face, Gawky himself "assumes a big look" and swears an oath as he threatens Roderick, who arms himself with a handy bottle as Gawky and Lavement retire "in such a hurry, that the one overturned the other, and rolled together down stairs; while my mistress swooned away with fear; and her daughter asked if I intended to murder her" (113). Roderick's parting response is a revealing mixture of moralizing cliché and a specifically vivid and vicious threat: "I gave her to understand that nothing was farther from my intention; that I would leave her to the stings of her own conscience; but was firmly resolved to slit her husband's nose, whenever fortune should offer a convenient opportunity" (113–114).

Trapped as narrator to some extent in what Bakhtin would call an inert normative language and not allowed the differentiated variations of particularized speech, Roderick is regularly granted license for violent action like this. But part of his energizing action as narrator involves contact with and reproduction of crazy accents like Lavement's, eccentric idiolects that expropriate normative language, turning it from what it pretends to be (a cognitive instrument, an authoritative and objective account of things) to what it always becomes in Smollett's novels (a means of self-expression or self-assertion). Those idiolects can be entertainingly nasty like Lavement's, or colorfully benign expressions of simple virtue like the seaman's lingo of Tom Bowling (Roderick's uncle, who is his salvation in the end). Many more are simple comic impersonations or revealing parodies of various levels of the debased unitary language: ignorant pedants pretending to be scholars, cowardly soldiers posing as heroes, bureaucrats, urban parasites, and courtiers mouthing the platitudes of integrity and disinterested judgment. Taken together, they form what Bakhtin calls "stratification," a process whereby the novel, both authors and represented characters, challenges fixed definitions of language.

Many of these idiolects, of course, belong to familiar comic conventions of bragging soldiers, ignorant pedants and quacks, and lying courtiers; they deserve to be called idiolects only within the historical specificity of *Roderick Random*, what Bakhtin calls "the zone of contact" unique to the novel whereby prose narrative incorporates as part of its outlook what he calls "unresolved contemporaneity." In that zone, Bakhtin adds, words can be "reclaimed for contemporaneity," and Smollett is visibly reclaiming old satiric topics for the mid-eighteenth century.[14] The action that Roderick's parting speech provokes is, by these lights, a reclaiming of the conventionalized formula of unjustly treated innocence by the concrete spontaneity of the present: the violent revenge that a self-styled gentleman like Roderick claims as his right against that bogus or at least discredited member of the minor gentry, Gawky. The spitting and swearing, the falling and tumbling, those threatening gestures and promises of slashing and nose-slitting are not just slapstick. They are a subversive and historically particularized inflection of language by its physical accompaniments and emotional sources – a subversion, to be sure, with no particular political direction or purpose except to express rage.

After all, aside from the specific historical circumstances behind Lavement's *franglais*, there seems little enough here drawn from Bakhtin's "zone of contact." In what sense do comic scenes like these have what might be understood in a broad sense as a political context? *Roderick Random* originated in Smollett's scandalized reporting of the brutality and incompetence that he experienced first-hand as a surgeon's mate in the navy, especially in the disastrous expedition against the Spaniards at Carthagena, Colombia in 1740. In that seamless and suggestive joining in the novel between petty tyrants like Lavement and the tyranny and corruption within the larger society between the domestic and unofficial violence in places like Lavement's house and the public and official violence that Roderick goes on to endure, Smollett finds a sphere, more or less in the middle of the narrative, that is not only a zone of contact but a place where the Bakhtinian process of stratification is overtly what there is to represent. That scene of brutality and carnage, populated with characters who are morally indistinguishable in their debasement of moral language and action from the grotesque self-seekers who inhabit Glasgow and London, has a documentary authority that casts a shadow of authenticity and of political meaning backwards and forwards on Roderick's adventures in those cities that frame his nautical career. What appeared to be satiric grotesqueries are now grounded by this parallelism in historical fact and form part of the same crisis of authority. The striking difference is that, in the naval scenes, individualized and idiosyncratic speech temporarily becomes a means of protest against a corrupt social order rather than a sign of disorder.

As their ship and others begin to batter the fortress of Bocca Chica and to receive the relentless fire of the Spanish defenders, Roderick and his fellow surgeon's mate, the Welshman Morgan, are at their post, caught up in the carnage when one of the sailors arrives, horribly wounded:

> 'Yo ho avast there – scaldings.' – 'Scaldings! (answered Morgan) Got knows 'tis hot enough indeed: – who are you?' – 'Here's one' (replied the voice) and I immediately knew it to be that of my honest friend Jack Rattlin, who coming towards me, told me, with great deliberation, he was come to be dock'd at last, and discovered the remains of one hand which had been shattered to pieces with grape shot.
>
> (182)

Heroic and honest Jack Rattlin takes his horrible maiming in his stride, "observing that every shot had its commission," and that if it had taken him in the head "he should have died bravely fighting for king and country. Death was a debt which every man owed, and must pay now as well as another time" (182). But the word that announces this "sea-philosopher," as Roderick calls him, is mysterious quoted out of context. "Scaldings!" in fact is an echo from an earlier scene on the ship as Roderick sits down to a meatless meal of a dish of peas brought by a mess boy who cries "Scaldings!" – a traditional warning cry in the navy, says the note in Boucé's edition, when hot food, especially soup, is being carried from the galley. The word thus also echoes for readers a vivid earlier scene in London when Roderick and Strap dive into a cellar eating house, "an infernal ordinary" choked with the "steams of boiled beef" where Strap accidentally trips the cook as she carries a porringer of soup. "In her fall, she dashed the whole mess against the legs of a drummer belonging to the foot guards, who happened to be in her way, and scalded him so miserably, that he started up, and danced up and down, uttering a volley of execration that made my hair stand on end" (65).

Roderick paraphrases Rattlin's bravely patriotic sentiments but quotes "Scaldings!". The word in this context defies paraphrase in its compactly subversive humor and distinguishes itself by its wit from the carnage and clamor of battle that is its context, from inarticulate cries of rage and pain, from volleys of execrations such as Roderick heard in the infernal ordinary. The din and destruction of battle are answered in opposing and significantly dialogic fashion in the adaptation of a stock phrase. Honest Jack Rattlin's appropriation of the mess boy's warning, like the opposing loquacious and taciturn idiolects of Morgan and the sailor, is an expressive and oppositional subjectivity that is specifically linguistic and political in its implications. But such idiolects derive from the ethnic solidarity of provincial regions and the guild ties of honest working trades, not from class position or social privilege, and Smollett's sentimental investment in such linguistic tokens as moral signs marks his essentially conservative understanding of social–linguistic dynamics. The virtue, freedom, and integrity that he posits for some of his adventurers and their friends are rooted in their opposition and difference from an adversarial social order that is as fixed as it is comically corrupt. A sequence in *Peregrine Pickle* will illustrate what I mean.

Late in the novel, the impetuous, irascible hero vows that he will seek consolation for his rejection by his first love, the fair and virtuous Emilia, "in the possession of the first willing wench he should meet upon the road" (595). Like a character in a folk tale, he does just that, startled out of a "profound reverie … by a beggar-woman and her daughter." Under "her wretched equipage," Peregrine sees in this 16-year-old "a set of agreeable features, enlivened with the complexion of health and chearfulness." "He therefore entered into a conference with the mother, and for a small sum of money purchased her property in the wench, who did not require much courtship and intreaty, before she consented to accompany him to any place that he should appoint for her habitation" (596). Peregrine dispatches orders to his major-domo, Hatchway, to clean and clothe her "so that she should be touchable upon his arrival, which (on that account) he would defer for the space of one day," and he orders his other nautical servant, Tom Pipes, to ride home with this "hedge-inamorata," laying "strong injunctions upon him to abstain from all attempts upon her chastity" (596–597). The sequence that follows is a rough-house version of the Pygmalion story, with Peregrine performing a Henry Higgins experiment designed to expose the shallowness of class distinctions:

> He had (as I believe the reader will readily allow) made considerable progress in the study of character, from the highest rank to the most humble station of life, and found it diversified in the same manner, thro' every degree of subordination and precedency: nay, he moreover observed, that the conversation of those who are dignified with the appellation of polite company, is neither more edifying nor entertaining than that which is met with among the lower classes of mankind.
>
> (599)

179

Primed with "choice sentences from Shakespear, Otway, and Pope," she passes, in the country, "for a sprightly young lady, of uncommon learning and taste" (600). Emboldened, Peregrine tries her in London. He has his Swiss valet de chambre "instruct her in dancing and the French language," and he himself escorts her to a public assembly, where the "evident air of rusticity and aukwardness in her demeanor" is interpreted as "an agreeable wildness of spirit, superior to the forms of common breeding" (600). One evening at cards, this "infanta" catches a lady cheating and, when she is reproved for reporting this, fires back a great burst of invective,

> which she repeated with great vehemence, in an attitude of manual defiance, to the terror of her antagonist, and the astonishment of all present: nay, to such an unguarded pitch was she provoked, that starting up, she snapt her fingers, in testimony of disdain, and, as she quitted the room, applied her hand to that part which was the last of her that disappeared, inviting the company to kiss it, by one of its coarsest denominations.
>
> (601)

In one sense, Peregrine's social experiment is absolutely unnecessary, since this is a world in which fraud and hypocritical self-seeking are universal and to that extent harmlessly predictable and utterly stable. The experiment proves that the social order is both fraudulent and fixed. The upper levels are shown to be factitious and socially constructed by means of the reliable and invariable authenticity of the lower levels. Both within and without the fiction, Smollett and Peregrine devise this social experiment to give pleasure by rehearsing the inevitable and, like all such rehearsals in Smollett's novels, what matters is not the revelation but the style and distinctively ferocious energy of the enactment.

And yet there is something striking in Smollett's exactness in rendering just those sociohistorical circumstances that make Peregrine's joke possible. Underneath the rags and the desperate squalor, Peregrine catches a glimpse of natural energy: "a set of agreeable features, enlivened with the complexion of health and chearfulness" (596). But at the same time, the metamorphosis of this "Nymph of the Road" is possible partly because she has been to a "day-school ... during the life of her father, who was a day-labourer in the country" (599). Peregrine's joke works by suppressing the girl's linguistic identity in order to homogenize class differences, but in the process actually affirms those differences, treating her dialect and its accompanying carnivalesque gestures of defiance as her irrepressible class signature rooted very precisely in her past circumstances; what cannot be suppressed is her "inveterate habit of swearing, which had been indulged from her infancy, and confirmed by the example of those among whom she had lived" (599). The girl's *ressentiment* is both expressed and denied by Smollett's riotous arrangement; traded like chattel, scrubbed clean for sexual consumption, costumed and made to act out a charade, she exists to provide pleasure for Peregrine and us, but that pleasure depends upon her grounding in a realm of experience and specifically determined social identity that Smollett's cruel fun requires and ratifies. Her dialect, he makes clear, is a gutter eloquence such "as would have intitled her to a considerable share of reputation, even among the nymphs of Billingsgate." That volubility, he goes on, has been "culti- vated among the venerable society of weeders, podders, and hoppers, with whom she had been associated from her tender years" (598). In contrast to that membership in a linguistic community, Smollett's (and Peregrine's) manner claims to be free of social determinants. His style is the jokingly mock-elevated discourse of the satiric novelist, the result of his mixture of narrative modes, grounded in mimicry and parody of moral essay and serious biography. To counter the pervasive inauthen- ticity of the babble of dialects around his hero, those jargons of incompetent and ignorant professionals and petty bourgeois tradesmen and bureaucrats, Smollett offers his stylized sailor's patois of Commodore Trunnion, Hatchway, and Pipes, a literary exaggeration and purification of a professional jargon that identifies its speakers with the otherwise non-existent virtues of loyalty and communal solidarity. The narrator and his small virtuous circle signify by their linguistic deformations a refusal of standard idiom that locates resistance in an expressive verbal realm all their own. Not so with Peregrine's Galatea, whose speech is decidedly not a form of resistance but an ineradicable sign of connection with the actualities of rural labor at its lowliest from which she derives. Peregrine's "hedge-inamorata" belongs to that group of wandering proletarians, dependent upon seasonal rural labor and often drawn in desperate and dangerous swarms, according to some observers, to London. But Smollett's joke glosses over such alarming facts and treats working-class life and language as reliable sources of good material, useful satiric energy that is unfocused and ready for amused exploitation.

Peregrine's social experiment can serve as a prelude to a discussion of Smollett's last novel, his masterpiece, *The Expedition of Humphry Clinker* (1771). Smollett reaches new heights of comic invention in rendering uneducated discourse but also in granting agency and a measure of humanity to a few servants, notably the nominal hero of the book, Humphry.[15] Matthew Bramble, a Welsh squire in his mid-fifties, is the actual protagonist and main correspondent of this journal novel, which is written in long letters from Bramble and his nephew, Jery Melford, and shorter ones from Lydia Melford, his niece, and his sister, Tabitha Bramble, and her maid, Winifred Jenkins, as they make a tour of Britain, moving from Wales to Bristol Hotwells, to Bath, to London, and then northward to Scotland and back. Hoping to escape the spectacle of *nouveau riche* vulgarity and cultural degeneration that he finds in Bath, Bramble goes to a coffeehouse. Instead of encountering rational conversation about politics for which such places were noted, he seems at first to find further confirmation for his misanthropy as he surveys the scene:

> We consisted of thirteen individuals; seven lamed by the gout, rheumatism, or palsy; three maimed by accident; and the rest either deaf or blind. One hobbled, another hopped, a third dragged his legs after him like a wounded snake, a fourth straddled betwixt a pair of long crutches, like the mummy of a felon hanging in chains; a fifth was bent into a horizontal position, like a mounted telescope, shoved in by a couple of chairmen; and a sixth was the bust of a man, set upright in a wheel machine, which the waiter moved from place to place.[16]

Matt is a man of hidden tender feeling, and as he contemplates this group of grotesques he is "struck with some of their faces." These stirrings of memory lead him to consult the coffeehouse subscription book, where he finds the names of several old friends. From satiric distance and its grotesque and rigid encapsulations, Matt moves in for the closer, more intimate, complicated look sanctioned by his memories and discovers first of all among these cripples the companion of his youth, Rear-Admiral Balderick, now "metamorphosed into an old man, with a wooden leg and a weatherbeaten face, which appeared the more ancient from his grey locks, that were truly venerable" (54). Smollett's scene is both sentimental and satiric, predicting in its interweaving of satiric observation with strands of personal discovery and fulfillment the densely complicated texture of later developments in the book. Matt approaches his old friend, the admiral:

> Sitting down at the table, where he was reading a news-paper,
> I gazed at him for some minutes, with a mixture of pleasure

and regret, which made my heart gush with tenderness; then, taking him by the hand, 'Ah, Sam (said I) forty years ago I little thought' – I was too much moved to proceed. 'An old friend, sure enough! (cried he, squeezing my hand, and surveying me eagerly thro' his glasses) I know the looming of the vessel, though she has been hard strained since we parted; but I can't heave up the name' – The moment I told him who I was, he exclaimed, 'Ha! Matt, my old fellow cruizer, still afloat!' And starting up, hugged me in his arms. His transport, however, boded me no good; for, in saluting me, he thrust the spring of his spectacles into my eye, and, at the same time, set his wooden stump upon my gouty toe; an attack that made me shed tears in sad earnest.

(54)

Revived by this return to youthful friendships, Matt comments to Dr Lewis, his correspondent back in Wales, that he cannot express the half of what he feels at this meeting: "It was a renovation of youth; a kind of resuscitation of the dead, that realized those interesting dreams, in which we sometimes retrieve our antient friends from the grave" (55). But this unexpected, intensely personal reunion also provides occasion and indeed impetus for a renewal of Matt's social critique. All of his old chums, he explains, are now malcontents, and several have excellent reasons to complain about their treatment by society. Admiral Balderick and Colonel Cockril, the bust of a man, "have acted honourable and distinguished parts on the great theatre, and are now reduced to lead a weary life in this stew-pan of idleness and insignificance" (55). Matt's satiric observation modulates into novelistic discovery whereby self-implication and emotional involvement succeed polemical distance, as personal histories throughout *Humphry Clinker* tend to redeem the degraded present by re-establishing forgotten connections with a vital past. For Matt in this sequence, there is also a reinforcement of his earlier social criticism, as personal histories and institutional inequities intertwine revealingly. His old friends and others like them, "many decent families, restricted to small fortunes," came to Bath to live comfortably at small expense, "but the madness of the times has made the place too hot for them" (55). In this coherent fashion, then, the coffeehouse at Bath is a site where public issues emerge not just for discussion but in this case for a dramatized and intensely personal encounter, and to that extent this coffeehouse and various other public meeting places in Smollett's novel represent crucially concrete instances of that bourgeois public sphere as Habermas has defined it.

Indeed, this particular scene is especially important because it refines Matt's thundering social satire, memorably rehearsed in earlier pages for Dr Lewis in a broad denunciation of the spectacle that Bath presents:

> the general tide of luxury, which hath overspread the nation, and swept away all, even the very dregs of the people ... Clerks and factors from the East Indies, loaded with the spoil of plundered provinces; planters, negro-drivers, and hucksters, from our American plantations, enriched they know not how; agents, commissaries, and contractors, who have fattened, in two successive wars, on the blood of the nation; usurers, brokers, jobbers of every kind.
>
> (36)

Implicitly, we may say, Matt's Juvenalian diatribes at Bath initiate communication with Dr Lewis and other readers that cannot be seen as dialogue or rational exchange until he enters the coffeehouse and other places of public assembly and participates in reminiscence and discussion. Novelistic specificity provides historical and personal contexts that enrich and complicate Matt's understanding of social problems, and his over-generalized and at times intemperate satiric denunciation becomes particularized and personalized analysis as he encounters those problems in the contexts provided by his own rediscovered past-life experiences and newly established relationships. So the coffeehouse at Bath is for Matt Bramble both a forum for public discussion and a focus for private discovery that provides evidence and lived experience for a monologue until now not only general and abstract but plainly distorted by illness both physical and mental.[17] Through his private history Matt can begin to refine his analysis of public life, just as later events in the novel will certify his full humanity and at length license a more powerful role for him as social and moral activist.

The fruitful intersection in the Bath coffeehouse marks very precisely, I think, the composition of the public sphere in Habermas's sense and also its limitations. The ideological essence of the public sphere, as I understand it, lies in the historically unprecedented equation of the interests of the property-owning bourgeoisie with those of a newly conceived and promoted universalized humanity; or, to put the case more dramatically, the public sphere elides the distinction between human beings as such and those particular human beings who are owners of goods and persons, thereby making *le bourgeois* identical with *l'homme*, as Habermas puts it. Habermas goes on to evoke the unique

public debate in early eighteenth-century England where political questions are out in the open as they were at the time nowhere else in
Europe, in pamphlets and newspapers and periodicals and in coffeehouses where the notions articulated in the press were argued freely. But
Habermas always returns to what underlies and guarantees the public
sphere: the so-called intimate sphere of private and domestic experience whereby those who meet in public acquire their subjective
autonomy that makes them qualified to speak in public. The new or at
least newly conceived privileges of privacy and domestic autonomy
create the conditions that make entrance into the public sphere possible.

Humphry Clinker turns very specifically on movement through a
complex intertwining of public life and issues from private experience
in ways that have no precedent in Smollett's earlier novels. Matt
Bramble has been an MP, and he returns from the rural periphery of
Wales to the public world of coffeehouses, spas, and metropolitan life
only reluctantly, in pursuit of health, family unity, and even diversion;
but once there he is fully engaged in energetic debate on many aspects
of British eighteenth-century social and political life. *Humphry Clinker*
evokes a world of passionately held notions about social and economic
issues, of specific controversies, and even of particular historical persons
engaged in them. As the Bramble party travels through the island of
Great Britain and visits its major political and cultural urban centers,
modern life is examined pretty thoroughly, and society, as Matthew
Bramble observes it, is in a special sort of early modern crisis. As he
observes in London:

> All the people I see, are too much engrossed by schemes of
> interest or ambition, to have any room left for sentiment or
> friendship. ... Every person you deal with endeavours to over-
> reach you in the way of business; you are preyed upon by idle
> mendicants, who beg in the phrase of borrowing, and live
> upon the spoils of the stranger – Your tradesmen are without
> conscience, your friends without affection, and your depen-
> dents without fidelity.
>
> (121)

Smollett's last novel thus represents something like those conversations
and debates that constitute the public sphere as evoked by Habermas,
but it also enacts through richly achieved novelistic form the difficulties
of participating in such a sphere in eighteenth-century Britain. Parallel
to the public sphere's rational examination of social possibilities is the
narrative exposition of individual personalities for whom in the course

of things the articulation of ideas is rendered by novelistic form primarily as a means of self-expression or even of self-promotion and aggrandizement rather than as any sort of meaningful public or shared cognitive transaction. Novelistic enactment of the public sphere in *Humphry Clinker* may be said to set in motion a potentially subversive tendency that transforms ideas, no matter how cogent or reasonable, into expressive instruments for that special modern emphasis on individual differences that we call personality, which even in 1771 can be seen to be separating itself from the Enlightenment notion of natural character, to use Richard Sennett's terms.[18] Even as it articulates and implicitly evaluates the opinions of various characters, Smollett's novel dramatizes their contextual and pragmatic or even their instrumental force and self-expressive function. As Matt himself admits, "I have perceived that my opinion of mankind, like mercury in the thermometer, rises and falls according to the variations of the weather" (74). And of course Matt is not quite what he presents himself to be, for as his nephew Jery observes at the outset (and proves with an anecdote in which Matt gives a poor widow twenty pounds), "He affects misanthropy, in order to conceal the sensibility of a heart which is tender, even to a degree of weakness. This delicacy of feeling, or soreness of the mind, makes him timorous and fearful; but then he is afraid of nothing so much as of dishonour; and although he is exceedingly cautious of giving offence, he will fire at the least hint of insolence or ill-breeding" (29). Both satiric and sentimental spectator, Matt is both delicate and fearless, containing in his personality what G.J. Barker-Benfield describes as the central tension in the mid- and late eighteenth-century novel "between the high evaluation of refinement in men and the wish to square it with manliness" of the traditional hard and unsentimental sort.[19]

As a way of exemplifying the force of this novelistic enactment of a complex character (who embodies a form of cultural contradiction) within and against the grain of the public sphere, we can consider Matt's relationship to another provincial character, Lieutenant Obadiah Lismahago. Comprised of literary and documentary materials that encompass the contradictory areas of Cervantic caricature, the horrors of North American captivity narrative, and the inequities of advancement in the eighteenth-century British army, Lismahago points to his own complicated status as a character simultaneously comic and deeply serious, both grotesque and engagingly pathetic in his pride and considerable intelligence. As Michael Rosenblum observes, he is one of a large number of minor characters in Smollett's fiction "whose prehistory is sketched in a few sentences," in "conventionalized mini-narratives" that render "Smollett's sense of social causation, of all the ways there are of rising and falling in society (mostly the latter)."[20] Lismahago is Matt's most able intellectual opponent, as he cogently rehearses the commonplaces of conservative virtue in its opposition to modern commercial and political life. But many of Lismahago's arguments are comically derived from his distinctive history and circumstances and the particular deformations of his personality, and they are as much contributions to our situating and understanding his character as to a debate about the best society. Thus Matt remarks that in Scotland itself, Lismahago grows "more paradoxical than ever. – The late gulp he had of his native air seems to have blown fresh spirit into all his polemical faculties" (265). And yet in this same dialogue, when Matt observes that, owing to the union of the kingdoms, the "Scots were now in a fair way to wipe off the national reproach of poverty," Lismahago responds with an eloquence all the more telling for matching the theme of Matt's earlier complaints in Bath and London about the effects of affluence and luxury:

> If poverty be a subject for reproach, it follows that wealth is the object of esteem and veneration – In that case there are Jews and others in Amsterdam and London, enriched by usury, peculation, and different species of fraud and extortion, who are more estimable than the most virtuous and illustrious members of the community. An absurdity which no man in his senses will offer to maintain. – Riches are certainly no proof of merit: nay they are often (if not most commonly) acquired by persons of sordid minds and mean talents: nor do they give any intrinsic worth to the possessor; but, on the contrary, tend to pervert his understanding, and render his morals more depraved.
>
> (265)

In an obvious way, Lismahago moves Matt to embrace moderation by exposing extreme dissatisfaction with modern life as an expression, in large part, of a distorted and incomplete personality, in Jery's words, one "so addicted to wrangling, that he will cavil at the clearest truths, and in the pride of argumentation, attempt to reconcile contradictions" (185). In his sour rectitude and with his considerable (and professional) debating skills, which Matt admits are too much for him, Lismahago argues on "different subjects in war, policy, the belles lettres, law, and metaphysics" (186) and in his strict adherence to conservative positions qualifies Bramble's earlier satiric diatribes, which, as the novel progresses and the group moves away from English urban disorder to semi-feudal Scottish society and then to rural improvements and pastoral happiness in the north of England, come to seem as much the result of his own temporary physical imbalance and dislocation as of rational appraisal. In due course, Matt is converted from "illiberal prejudices which had grown up with my constitution" (225) to a revised opinion of Scotland, partially by discussions with Lismahago but mainly by his own observations in the north, where he finds a satisfying social order lacking in England.[21]

Nonetheless, the Bramble/Lismahago debates are genuine intellectual exchanges. Lismahago's generalizations are seriously, coherently articulated, in spite of his broad Scots accent (which Smollett mentions but does not try to render after the Bramble party's initial encounter with him) and eccentric appearance. And his circumstances, as Matt discovers to his dismay, exemplify the scandalous inadequacy of the British army's rewards for those who have served the nation in its overseas wars: "So you have spent the best part of your life, (cried Mr. Bramble) your youth, your blood, and your constitution, amidst the dangers, the difficulties, the horrors and hardships of war for the consideration of three or four shillings a-day" (185). But in Lismahago private and public are intertwined, reciprocally related, with the private dimension lending pathos and urgency to the public statement and the theory about public life transparently derived from those private circumstances of a half-pay officer of eccentric appearance. Partly because of his poverty, Lismahago lacks as a character the full (propertied) humanity that Smollett allows Matt Bramble, for whom the private dimension has an integrity about it that is not independent of his opinions on public matters. That is to say, Lismahago, by virtue of his economic position, is incapable of praxis in Habermas's sense; his theory is purely and comically abstract, or at least pretty remote from his own experiences and circumstances, and his actions are necessarily self-serving and determined by the neediness and desperate honor of a half-pay lieutenant. The public sphere for Bramble, the wealthy Welsh landowner and philanthropist, in contrast, provides an arena where he can develop his best self and serve others without the taint of self-interest. The arguments articulated there (in dialogue with Lismahago and earlier in his epistolary commentary to Dr Lewis) are, in the narrative's subsequent developments, strongly subordinated to the practical needs of establishing and anchoring that self in its emotional expansions and private discoveries.

Humphry Clinker turns out to be Matt's illegitimate son from his college days, and in recovering him Bramble acquires a humanized and flawed past, an involvement with others that is more than sentimental spectatorship and philanthropy. It is worth noting that the Bramble party's initial encounter with Humphry Clinker is a chance intersection with the realities of rural poverty: recruited to replace a postilion who has quarreled with Tabitha Bramble, he is "a shabby country fellow" (78), plucked from a labor pool of unemployed rural plebeians. Humphry offends Tabitha by the sight of his bare posteriors, revealed by his threadbare clothing as he rides in front of her, and she demands that he be sacked. As Jery describes the scene, Matt calls in the landlord of the inn, who has known Humphry since his infancy, and the story he tells is exactly grounded in the scandalous shortcomings of the eighteenth-century welfare system:

> That he had been a love begotten babe, brought up in the work-house, and put out apprentice by the parish to a country black-smith, who died before the boy's time was out: that he had for some time worked under his ostler, as a helper and extra postilion, till he was taken ill of the ague, which disabled him from getting his bread: that, having sold or pawned every thing he had in the world for his cure and subsistence, he became so miserable and shabby, that he disgraced the stable, and was dismissed; but that he never heard any thing to the prejudice of his character in other respects. 'So that the fellow being sick and destitute, (said my uncle) you turned him out to die in the streets.' 'I pay the poors' rate, (replied the other) and I have no right to maintain idle vagrants, either in sickness or health; besides, such a miserable object would have brought a discredit upon my house –'.
>
> (80)

Initially, then, Humphry is yet another occasion for social satire, and the publican's inhumanity provokes Matt's ironic comment: "Heark ye, Clinker, you are a most notorious offender – You stand convicted of sickness, hunger, wretchedness, and want" (80). But then through a coincidence (Matt's old college chum, Mr Dennison, hails him as "Matthew Loyd of Glamorganshire, who was student of Jesus" (304) and Humphry happens to be present), this romance revelation is accompanied by a legal explanation (Matt had taken his mother's name of Loyd to inherit her estate but returned to his father's name to assume his paternal estate). And the revelation this time is the occasion not for satire but for personal confession, the dramatization of past moral weakness and present repentance: "'And so in consequence of my changing my name and going abroad at that very time, thy poor mother and thou have been left to want and misery – I am really shocked at the consequence of my own folly.' – Then, laying his hand on Clinker's head, he added, 'Stand forth, Matthew Loyd – You see, gentlemen, how the sins of my youth rise up in judgment against me'" (305). But Humphry is not magically transformed into the son of a gentleman; he retains most of his subordinate status as servant, marrying another servant, Win Jenkins, and becoming part of the tribal family group that returns to Wales at the end of the novel. Matt's particular praxis is intended to exemplify moral action deepened and redeemed by personal and emotional expansion, and that discovery involves the establishment of patriarchal links and the assuming of a long-neglected authority at the head of a reinvigorated rural network, an extended family that now through the marriages of Humphry/Winifred, Lismahago/Tabitha, and Lydia/Dennison resolves within this private circle most of the social problems and inequities that the novel has encountered. In their debates, Lismahago has something like the last word, but Matt goes on from these debates to act and to exemplify thereby the sustaining relationship between private wholeness and public virtue in the public sphere that Habermas describes.[22]

Near the very end of the book, Matt writes to Dr Lewis to observe that his health has improved thanks to the physical exertions of the northern phase of his travels: "I begin to think I have put myself on the superannuated list too soon, and absurdly sought for health in the retreats of laziness – I am persuaded that all valetudinarians are too sedentary, too regular, and too cautious – We should sometimes increase the motion of the machine, to *unclog the wheels of life*; and now and then take a plunge amidst the waves of excess, in order to case-harden the constitution" (324). In the same letter he describes his most recent exertion, the rehabilitation of his friend Baynard's estate. In these efforts to save his friend's estate, Matt makes a transition from satiric contemplation to purposeful and effective action. A month before, Matt had paid a visit to his old friend, and found him and his estate the victims of his wife's luxurious excesses, an instance of extravagance so great that "in a few years he should be obliged to sell his estate for the payment of his creditors" (281). Matt's evocation of Mrs Baynard's transformation of a productive country estate into a showcase of fashionable and decadent taste marks a temporary return to his earlier satiric fluency. Among her destructive accomplishments is the transformation of a 200-acre farm a mile from the house into a sterile showpiece:

> To shew her taste in laying out ground, she seized into her own hand a farm of two hundred acres ... which she parcelled out into walks and shrubberies, having a great bason in the middle, into which she poured a whole stream that turned two mills, and afforded the best trout in the country. ... the ground which formerly payed him one hundred and fifty pounds a year, now cost him two hundred pounds a year to keep it in tolerable order.
>
> (281)

Mrs Baynard has managed to import the enervating effects of the consumer revolution into the countryside, destroying the very fecundity and rural simplicity and masculine sociality that Matt has experienced in the surrounding area. So when he hears two weeks later that the lady is near death, he springs into action, driving thirty miles to Baynard's estate and in the aftermath of the lady's demise transforming the estate in a whirlwind of focused activity that reforms luxurious excess. Driving out "that legion of supernumerary domestics, who had preyed so long upon the vitals" (326) of Baynard, Matt sells all the superfluous luxuries that his late wife had accumulated, arranges a loan of £10,000 at 4 per cent to rescue the encumbered estate, and begins to restore it to productivity and comfort and Baynard to rural sociability:

> I ordered the gardener to turn the rivulet into its old channel, to refresh the fainting Naiads, who had so long languished among mouldering roots, withered leaves, and dry pebbles, – The shrubbery is condemned to extirpation; and the pleasure-ground will be restored to its original use of corn-field and pasture, – Orders are given for rebuilding the walls of the garden at the back of the house, and for planting clumps of firs, intermingled with beech and chestnut, at the east end, which is now quite exposed to the surly blasts that come from that quarter.
>
> (328)

In such restoration of fertility and efficient husbandry, Matt is recapitulating in rapidly decisive action for Baynard what he has observed in his recent chance meeting (the context for the revelation that he is Humphry's father) with his old college friend and "fellow-rake," Charles Dennison, who has, since Matt last saw him more than twenty years ago, retired into the country after the death of his father and of his wastrel older brother who had ruined the paternal estate.[23] Dennison is a pattern of sensible, hard-working, and decidedly unluxurious rural existence; he has restored a ruined farm that he has inherited on the death of a feckless elder brother, and he exemplifies all the pastoral and plain-living virtues of an idealized minor rural gentry: "In short, I became enamoured of a country life; and my success greatly exceeded my expectation. – I drained bogs, burned heath, grubbed up furze and fern; I planted copse and willows where nothing else would grow; I gradually enclosed all my farms, and made such improvements, that my estate now yields me clear twelve hundred pounds a year" (314). Unlike the complaisant Matt, bedeviled for part of the novel by his ridiculous sister, Tabitha, Dennison has avoided female luxury, forming, as he tells Matt, the center of a small group of like-minded rural gentry, "a few individuals of moderate fortune, who gladly adopted my stile of living." Many others would have joined this group, he adds, "had they not been prevented by the pride, envy, and ambition of their wives and daughters" (313). This Dennison is also, as it turns out, the father of Lydia's hitherto suspect suitor who has called himself Wilson but is revealed to be George Dennison.

Almost twenty years after writing that suggestive preface to *Ferdinand Count Fathom*, Smollett in *Humphry Clinker* manages to achieve the novelistic and social coherence he promised there. He takes his principal personage from provincial outrage over metropolitan excess to productive participation in moral and social renewal, to private experiences that lead to an enlightened and moderate understanding of public life, and to a revived and balanced rural community. Renewing and deepening old relationships, establishing himself as the benevolent patron of those pockets of merit and worth that he finds as he travels around the island of Britain and back to Wales, Matt projects a coherent alternative to the corrupt self-seeking of modern life, and back home he will preside like a benign patriarch over the extended family created by the marriages of his sister, son, and niece. As Michael Rosenblum summarizes matters, Matt's travels in *Humphry Clinker* trace "the essential movements of the culture." By moving through the "vortex" represented by the urban disorder of Bath and London and into rural sociality, the Bramble party can accomplish the crucial counter-movement that Rosenblum calls the "Return to the Estate."[24] It is a romantic and pastoral alternative, to some extent, but Smollett expects his readers to see it as coherent and conceivable, not simply satire or comic fable but the moral and social renewal made possible by real travel through Great Britain.

NOTES

1 John Barrell, *English Literature in History 1730–80: An Equal, Wide Survey* (London, Hutchinson, 1983), p. 19.
2 Barrell, *English Literature in History*, pp. 209, 32–33.
3 Tobias George Smollett, *The Adventures of Ferdinand Count Fathom*, ed. Jerry C. Beasley (Athens, GA, and London, University of Georgia Press, 1988), p. 4. All further page references in brackets in the text are to this edition.
4 Barrell, *English Literature in History*, p. 206.
5 G.S. Rousseau, "Beef and bouillon: Smollett's achievement as a thinker," in *Tobias Smollett: Essays of Two Decades* (Edinburgh, T. and T. Clark, 1982), pp. 90, 107.
6 Modern commentators on Smollett are not always as Romantic and ingenious as Rousseau, but the majority of the most insightful ones such as Philip Stevick and Ronald Paulson are like him in finding a cumulative unity of tone and effect in the novels rather than any meaningful structure. See Stevick's "Stylistic energy in the early Smollett," *Studies in Philology*, 1967, vol. 64, pp. 712–719; and Paulson's "Satire in the early novels of Smollett," *Journal of English and Germanic Philology*, 1960, vol. 59, pp. 381–402. A few, notably Michael Rosenblum, have argued that there is structure of a sort provided by the persistence of romance motifs that lend most of the novels thematic unity and structural coherence: for Rosenblum the "romance sequence of disinheritance, exile, and restoration provides Smollett with an 'extended fiction,' a plot or group of related motifs which serves to unify the total body of an author's work." And finally the romance generates satire as it highlights a past world that contrasts starkly with the modern world. Michael Rosenblum, "Smollett and the old conventions," in *Tobias Smollett: Modern Critical Essays*, ed. Harold Bloom (New York, Chelsea House, 1987), p. 92.
7 J.G.A. Pocock, *Virtue, Commerce, and History* (Cambridge, Cambridge University Press, 1985), p. 51.
8 Tobias George Smollett, *Continuation of the Complete History of England*, 5 vols (London, 1765), Vol. I, p. 128.
9 Rosenblum, "Smollett and the old conventions," p. 91.
10 Tobias George Smollett, *The Adventures of Roderick Random*, ed. Paul-Gabriel Boucé (Oxford, Oxford University Press, 1979), p. xxxiii. All further page references in brackets in the text are to this edition.
11 Tobias George Smollett, *The Adventures of Peregrine Pickle, in which are included Memoirs of a Lady of Quality*, ed. James L. Clifford (London, Oxford University Press, 1964), pp. 682–683. All further page references in brackets in the text are to this edition.
12 Ronald Paulson, "Satire in the early novels of Smollett."
13 In this connection, the interpolated memoirs of Lady Vane and several other *causes célèbres* of the day, like the Annesley case, function by their inert and nerveless quality to contrast, perhaps rather too well, with the energy and invention of the narrative proper. Compare Smollett's inserted case histories with Fielding's exemplary Man of the Hill's tale, and the difference is instructive: the Man of the Hill's tale is, next to the narrative proper, full and realistic, a circumstantial case history of a passage through university and city life.

14 M.M. Bakhtin, *The Dialogic Imagination: Four Essays*, ed. Michael Holquist, trans. Caryl Emerson and Michael Holquist (Austin, TX, University of Texas Press, 1981), pp. 346.

15 On this issue, see my essay "Representing an under class: servants and proletarians in Fielding and Smollett," in Felicity Nussbaum and Laura Brown (eds) *The New Eighteenth Century: Theory, Politics, English Literature* (New York and London, Methuen, 1987).

16 Tobias George Smollett, *The Expedition of Humphry Clinker*, introduction and notes by Thomas R. Preston, text ed. O.M. Brack (Athens, GA, and London, University of Georgia Press, 1990), pp. 52 53. All further page references in brackets in the text are to this edition.

17 Various critics have pointed out that Matt is a flawed observer whose satirical authority is qualified by the novelistic context. As Eric Rothstein notes, contemporary readers could "have judged what the diatribes about London and Bath were worth, and could have balked without impugning the substance of the novel." Rothstein also reminds us that Smollett, unlike Matt, admired the work of the Bath architect, John Wood the Elder, and even praised the efficacy of the waters at Bath. Eric Rothstein, *Systems of Order and Inquiry in Later Eighteenth-century Fiction* (Berkeley and Los Angeles, University of California Press, 1975), p. 114.

18 See Richard Sennett's *The Fall of Public Man* (New York, Knopf, 1974) for a good general discussion of public life in the eighteenth century and of its breakdown in the nineteenth century.

19 G.J. Barker-Benfield, *The Culture of Sensibility: Sex and Society in Eighteenth-century Britain* (Chicago, University of Chicago Press, 1992), p. 141.

20 Michael Rosenblum, "Smollett's *Humphry Clinker*," in *The Cambridge Companion to the Eighteenth-century Novel*, ed. John Richetti (Cambridge, Cambridge University Press, 1996), p. 187.

21 As Aileen Douglas observes, women tend to disappear in the Scottish portion of the novel, and that "The almost exclusively male commentary we are given on things Scottish suggests that the order, harmony, and health that the place symbolically represents are incompatible with female nature and concerns." Aileen Douglas, *Uneasy Sensations: Smollett and the Body* (Chicago, University of Chicago Press, 1995), p. 175.

22 Eric Rothstein offers a powerful analysis of how this process of understanding is furthered in his view by the entire Bramble party, who constitute "an additional normative character." His summary is a valid expansion of my discussion of Matt's individual growth: "From the party emerges the process of Bramble's healing. He moves closer to Jery in tone; as he grows more tolerant, the plot opens to accommodate reasonable versions of the girls' romance and spirituality; and Tabby, his caricature, softens as Chowder goes and Lismahago comes." Rothstein, *Systems of Order and Inquiry*, p. 128.

23 In "*Humphry Clinker* and the Two Kingdoms of George II," Byron Gassman sees Matt's reconstruction of Baynard's estate in overtly political terms as nothing less than "a symbolic destruction of Hanoverian England, the kingdom of George III's inheritance, and a reconstruction of England as the erstwhile hoped-for kingdom of George III." *Criticism*, 1974, vol. 16, p.108. My argument is that Smollett's novel integrates social allegory and

personal self-development, dramatizing the vital interplay of history and the individual.

24 Rosenblum, "Smollett's *Humphry Clinker*," p. 185.

7

WOMEN NOVELISTS AND THE TRANSFORMATION OF FICTION

I

Visiting Smollett's Sunday supper for his "unfortunate brothers of the quill," Jery Melford in *Humphry Clinker* learns that novel writing "is now engrossed by female authors, who publish merely for the propagation of virtue, with so much ease and spirit, and delicacy, and knowledge of the human heart, and in all the serene tranquillity of high life, that the reader is not only inchanted by their genius, but reformed by their morality."[1] In reality, novels, whether by men or women, were written in response to the flourishing marketplace for printed matter. The quantity of fiction written by women peaked around 1740 and maintained its dominance until the mid-1780s.[2] Smollett summarizes qualities that were associated (if only in booksellers' blurbs) with the female novel in the mid-century – "delicacy and knowledge of the human heart." This understanding of female narrative's distinctive qualities emerged as fiction acquired a measure of moral respectability, partly through the pious example in the 1720s and early 1730s of Jane Barker, Penelope Aubin, and Elizabeth Singer Rowe.[3] Eliza Haywood's career traces the shifting image of the woman novelist. The imitator of Delarivière Manley's scandal chronicles in works such as *Memoirs of a Certain Island* (1725) and *The Secret History of the Present Intrigues of the Court of Caramania* (1727) and the producer of amatory novellas through the 1720s, Haywood turned with the market in the 1740s and early 1750s in *The Fortunate Foundlings* (1744), *Life's Progress Through the Passions: Or, The Adventures of Natura* (1747), *The History of Miss Betsy Thoughtless* (1751), and *The History of Jemmy and Jenny Jessamy* (1753) to much longer, more thoughtful and moralistic narratives. Haywood's career serves for Jane Spencer as "a paradigm for that of the eighteenth-century woman novelist generally: at first praised as amorous, then castigated as immoral, and finally accepted on new, and limiting, terms."[4] Spencer sees Haywood's transformation from purveyor of lubricious scandal and erotic fantasy to moral and historical novelist as acquiescence to new and "limiting" standards for female behavior summed up in "nature, morality, [and] modesty." These same qualities of spontaneity, simplicity, and modesty came to be valued, as the century progressed, not just in women but in all writers, so that "the properly 'feminine' and the properly 'literary' were both being re-defined along the same lines."[5]

Historians have argued that the novel represents and promotes a feminizing transformation of British culture. In that process, beginning roughly after 1660, the male-dominated social order in which women were largely excluded from social life and routinely brutalized by law and custom underwent profound revision. As G.J. Barker-Benfield explains, the eighteenth-century consumer revolution that swept Britain more rapidly than any other European country helped to create a domestic sphere and heterosocial order across classes and ranks. A "culture of reform" and of public decency, in Barker-Benfield's words, rejected male prerogatives, embodied at their most aggressive in the aristocratic-libertine ethos tolerated in young, upper-class males but extending in less dramatic ways through other sectors of society.[6] In the new commercial and consumerist order, the "appetitive" definition of the male personality, bent on crude and egocentric sensual pleasures, was softened and refined, partly by widely available "luxury" goods experienced in a domestic context, and partly by the "civilizing" effects of the new financial world in which traditional ideals of masculine aggression and self-assertion were replaced by passions, fantasies, and anxieties regarded as feminine. In J.G.A. Pocock's summary, eighteenth-century economic man "was seen as on the whole a feminized, even an effeminate being, still wrestling with his own passions and hysterias and with interior and exterior forces let loose by his fantasies and appetites, and symbolised by such archetypically female goddesses of disorder as Fortune, Luxury, and most recently Credit herself."[7] Such anxieties reduce men to passively anxious actors in a drama of large financial forces and point, obviously, to a lingering misogynist suspicion in the culture whereby the feminine is scapegoated as an embodiment of frightening social trends. Women in the early years of the century are often associated with the negative effects of the emerging economic order, summed up in that resonant moralistic term, luxury. Laura Brown has argued that the figure of the woman in early eighteenth-century culture is consistently, even obsessively, linked with "trade, commodification, and consumption." In the process, she says, the figure of woman acquires something of the mystified quality of the fetishized commodity, and as representative of exchange value in "her connection with the material products of accumulation, comes to embody the whole complex question of the real human relations that underlie the fantastic ones created by commodification."[8]

The female novel of mid-century, however, depicts women who, in their aspirations to moral purity, precisely reject luxurious consumption and resist masculine efforts to use them as commodities in the marriage market or in the looser circulation of pleasures and services in which women play a central role. As thrilling as this spectacle of virtuous resistance is (especially for late twentieth-century readers), these heroines are acting out roles that inevitably sustain the very ideology that they oppose. With exceptions that underline the virtuous rule, the heroines of the moral novel produced by women in mid-century and after are essentially ethereal and ascetic beings, rarely fleshly or material but rather collections of moral and sentimental attitudes, designed to project the pathos of female suffering. In this regard, the female novels of mid-century are simply an intensification of the idealization of women that stretches back to the Restoration, a period that, as Janet Todd puts it, sees the "sentimental construction of femininity, a state associated with modesty, passivity, chastity, moral elevation and suffering."[9] Despite the scandalous reputations of actresses, of a few notorious courtesans and *demi-mondaines* (some of whom published their best-selling memoirs), and of some still reviled female authors from the past like Behn, Manley, and the earlier Haywood, these years witness the purification of the female archetype, or at least an increased attention to the inequality, oppression, and injustice that routinely surrounds the female condition. Pope's 1735 "Epistle to a Lady" scandalized some readers by asserting paradoxically that "every woman is at heart a rake." But Pope's narrative of female fate complicates simple misogyny:

In men, we various ruling passions find;
In women, two almost divide the kind;
Those, only fixed, they first or last obey,
The love of pleasure, and the love of sway.
That, Nature gives; and where the lesson taught
Is but to please, can pleasure seem a fault?
Experience this; by man's oppression cursed,
They seek the second not to lose the first.
Men some to business, some to pleasure take;
But every woman is at heart a rake;
Men some to quiet, some to public strife;

But every lady would be queen for life.

(206–218)

For Pope, woman's nature is realized only in an essentially cultural process. In the world that the poem explores, female personality is paradoxical, impenetrable, even frightening in its self-expressive disorder. Caught up in luxury and self-indulgent hedonism, Pope's women are not limited to the two intertwined ruling passions of pleasure and power. Instead, what they have in common is a willful, ever ingenious perversity that refuses to conform or contribute to moral, psychological, or social order. Pope's women in this poem create forms of variety ("like variegated tulips") out of the leisured vacuity that encourages or indeed enforces female sameness. Instead of "characters" (impressed or incised features, conformity to a moral or social type that can be read and understood), these women possess personality in an extreme modern sense; their opportunistic energies are their *raison d'être*, and in their self-expressive eccentricity they are radically anti-social and apolitical, such purely private figures that they render public life and moral distinctions nearly meaningless:

> But grant, in public men sometimes are shown,
> A woman's seen in private life alone:
> Our bolder talents in full light displayed;
> Your virtues open fairest in the shade.
> Bred to disguise, in public 'tis you hide;
> There, none distinguish 'twixt your shame or pride,
> Weakness or delicacy; all so nice,
> That each may seem a virtue, or a vice.

(199–206)

The self-expressive energies of personality deviate amusingly from the stability of the moral and public character offered to men by tradition (in reality by the early eighteenth century already an anachronistic and purely nostalgic way to understand things, or nearly so, if we remember Pocock's evocation of feminized commercial man). Pope's summary of women's twin ruling passion affirms female sameness, since the witty extravagance of his portraits more or less cancels both the pathos and the mystery of the female image they exemplify. Deprived of meaningful existence and moral agency in the public world where a man of their class can acquire an identity and become a "character," a woman is an often dangerous enigma whose essence is disguise and whose inner truth is reserved for a domestic space where the instabilities of personality replace moral character and social identity.

Personality is exactly what novels are drawn to, although in the "moral" novel, writers often seek to purify their characters of the dangers of personalized identity and move them toward conformity to an idealized type that makes them, in spite of misogynistic tradition, exemplary "characters." Prominent women novelists from mid-century on (Haywood, Lennox, Sheridan, and Burney) construct their plots around the exclusion or the redirection (in ideologically safe and unthreatening ways) of those transgressive female energies that fascinated Pope. The challenge that women novelists face is to balance plausibly full and entertaining representations of life and manners within the impossible paradoxes of idealized female personality. This chapter examines the main approaches to this problem by three women novelists of the 1750s and 1760s (Eliza Haywood, Charlotte Lennox, and Frances Sheridan). I then turn to Frances Burney's novels from the following two decades to see how she reconciles novelistic representation with female moral delicacy. What is involved, in one way or another, is a rejection of "romance," which insists that the heroine's improbable virtue is both desirable and achievable, a marvel of luck or, better, of strenuous moral agency. The emotional–romantic fullness of heterosexual destiny such as the amatory novella of earlier decades celebrated so intensely is often enough assigned to the sexually aggressive twin of the modest heroine, and the obsessive erotic and frequently mercenary (or fashionably consumerist) personality of misogynist tradition is treated as a singular aberration. To that extent, the sexually yielding and even materially aggressive woman is also part of the rejection of romance, as her personality is derived from the circumstances of a corrupt social order she lacks the moral will to resist. The heroine's resistance and the easy acquiescence in pleasure and profit of her dark twin are complementary fulfillments of expectations about the pattern of intertwined freedom and necessity that marks the new narrative mode. Somehow, the transgressive freedom of the dark lady must be turned into a form of submission, while the saintly patience of her virtuous opposite needs to be exalted as a triumph of the moral will and a resistance to corrupt society.

Eliza Haywood's *The History of Miss Betsy Thoughtless* (1751) offers a technically virtuous heroine narrowly preserved with her honor intact through a series of amorous adventures, some comic and some deeply serious. The narrator's problem is to balance the demands of an ironic "history" in Fielding's manner whereby Betsy is shaped by the social/economic circumstances that the book takes pains to outline and the pleasures of modified and specifically female "romance," wherein emotional excitement and sexual adventure are provided. As Haywood summarizes Betsy's character, she "was far from setting forth to any advantage the real good qualities she was possessed of: on the contrary, the levity of her conduct rather disfigured the native innocence of her mind, and the purity of her intentions."[10]

True to her surname, Betsy "was too volatile for reflection; and as a ship without sufficient ballast is tossed about at the pleasure of every wind that blows, so was she hurried through the ocean of life, just as each predominant passion directed" (8). Orphaned at 14 by the death of her father, Betsy is whisked off to London at the suggestion of the wife of one of the trustees of the paternal estate, Mr Goodman, a wealthy merchant. Mrs Goodman is Lady Mellasin, "relict of a baronet, who having little or no estate, had accepted of a small employment about the court, in which post he died, leaving her ladyship one daughter named Flora, in a very destitute condition" (9). Mr Goodman has married for love ("consulted no other interest than that of his heart" (9)) and Lady Mellasin through his indulgence lives like an aristocrat in fashionable St James's Square, inconveniently far from the City where Mr Goodman earns his excellent living. So at a "nice and delicate time in persons of her sex," when "they are most apt to take the bent of impression, which, according as it is well or ill directed, makes or mars the future prospect of their lives" (11–12), Betsy finds herself shaped by a household governed by fashionable manners supported by wealth drawn from commercial activity:

> The court, the play, the ball, and opera, with giving and receiving visits engrossed all the time that could be spared from the toilette. It cannot, therefore, seem strange that Miss Betsy, to whom all these things were entirely new, should have her head turned with the promiscuous enjoyment, and the very power of reflection lost amidst the giddy whirl; nor that it should be so long before she could recover it enough to see the little true felicity of such a course of life.
>
> (12)

Clear signals are sent through this evocation of wasteful aristocratic habits built on a solid bourgeois base, and eighteenth-century readers can predict two developments in the events to follow: Lady Mellasin and her daughter, Flora, will come to bad ends; Betsy will be corrupted by their influence but will, somehow in the end, achieve happiness. This scene sets the tone for the rendition of the interesting haunts of leisure-class hedonism and sexual adventure, but Haywood's unconvincing claim is that this milieu purely serves the didactic purpose of inserting a young heroine in these circumstances to warn other "young handsome ladies" who are "possessed of [vanity] in that immoderate degree Miss Betsy was" (68). Betsy's improbably innocent "vanity" turns out to be in practice an asexual urge to accumulate lovers, and her lack of emotional–sexual connection to a parade of suitors marks her as "delicate." Betsy is empty of sexual desire, her flirtations a form of innocuous transgression to provoke excitement for her and for us. In order to certify Betsy as essentially innocent, Haywood makes Flora Mellasin, her erstwhile sister at Mr Goodman's and her implacable rival, a monster (a familiar female "character" to readers of Haywood's erotic novellas of the 1720s) of aggressive and overt sexuality and self-serving treachery, so that the alternative to Betsy's thoughtless flirtations is Flora's obsessive and predatory sexuality. Flora seduces Trueworth (who is in love with Betsy, but when rebuffed by her out of vanity eventually marries another) and actually helps him forget his fondness for Betsy. In the fairly crude and schematic disposition of Haywood's characters, Flora's hysterical infatuation and destructive obsession with Trueworth clarifies Betsy's moral failure, rendering it a relatively harmless hedonistic self-absorption.

Necessarily unaware of her own sexual motives and of the complex social situation that helps to form and focus them, Betsy is aware of her feelings for Truelove only in a moment of triangulation that is perhaps unique in Haywood's fiction. Unbeknownst to Betsy, Trueworth and his friend, Sir Bazil Loveit, are planning to marry: Trueworth to Harriot, Sir Bazil to Miss Mabel, Betsy's friend. Betsy has mistakenly thought that Trueworth was to marry one Miss Blanchfield, who has died of unrequited love after learning of his impending marriage and has left half her large estate to Trueworth, plunging him and his friends into a mourning period that delays their double wedding. Trueworth has lately been Betsy's timely rescuer from a rape and forced marriage engineered by a fake baronet, Sir Frederick Fineer, who turns out to be a treacherous serving-man he knew in Paris. These circumstances converge in a remarkably concrete sequence, as Betsy and two female friends walk on the Mall in Hyde Park, first meeting Trueworth and Sir Bazil alone, and then, as Betsy's friends leave her at St James's and she walks toward Spring Garden, the gentlemen reappear with three ladies, including Miss Mabel, Betsy's friend. Mysteriously, Mabel tells Betsy that since she is out alone "it is improper for me to ask you to join us" (434). Flustered, Betsy goes home, where her two brothers ask her to go next morning to view "several bustos, pictures, pieces of old china, and other curiosities belonging to a nobleman, lately deceased, being to be exposed to sale" (434). Betsy resolves to visit Mabel first, where she learns from a servant that his mistress is married that morning to Sir Bazil and Trueworth to Harriot. Dazed and shocked, Betsy orders the chairmen to carry her to the auction in Golden Square, which by an interesting coincidence is where Sir Bazil lives. What follows is perhaps the most subtle scene in all of Haywood's fiction, transferring attention from the heroine's confused emotions to a richly rendered world that nonetheless, in its profusion of upper-class privilege and "spectacle," dramatizes her longings and forces her to experience (if not to admit) desire at its most enviously consumerist, involved, as she watches from the crowd (part of it but hidden in her sedan chair, a privileged but excluded onlooker), with the objects and rituals of privilege. By virtue of such a fully realized scene of the appurtanances of pleasure and privilege (three coaches and six for the wedding party!), desire is located in social and even geographical particularity. Betsy's desire is rationalized, no longer mysterious and unpredictable but embodied and precisely enumerated in the rich urban setting in which she is both participant and excluded spectator:

It seemed as if fate interested itself in a particular manner for the mortification of this young lady; every thing contributed to give her the most poignant shock her soul could possibly sustain. It was not enough that she had heard the cruel tidings of what she looked upon as the greatest of misfortunes, her eyes must also be witness of the stabbing confirmation. The place of sale was within two houses of Sir Bazil's; but as she had never heard where that gentleman lived, could have no apprehensions of the spectacle she was to be presented with. On the chair turning into the square, she saw that side of it, to which she had directed the men to carry her, crouded with coaches, horses, and a great concourse of people; some waiting for the bridal bounty, but more as idle spectators. At first she imagined it was on the account of the sale; but the same instant almost shewed her her mistake. Several footmen, with wedding-favours in their hats, two of whom she knew by their faces, as well as by their liveries, belonged to Mr Trueworth, were just mounting their horses. The crowd was so thick about the door, that it was with some difficulty the chair passed on; and she had an opportunity of seeing much more than she desired. There were three coaches and six: in the first went Sir Bazil and the new-made Lady Loveit, the father of Miss Mabel, and a young lady whom Miss Betsy had sometimes seen in her company; in the second were seated Mr

Trueworth, his bride, Mrs Wellair, and a grave old gentleman; the third was filled by four maid-servants, and the two valet de chambres of the two bridegrooms, with a great deal of luggage before and behind. The ladies and gentlemen were all in extreme rich riding-habits; and the footmen, eleven in number, being all in new liveries, and spruce fellows, the whole cavalcade altogether made a very genteel appearance.

(437)

In a narrative where dialogue and action dominate, where the narrator almost never pauses to survey a scene and enumerate its participants, this is an extraordinary and revealing incident, viewed by Betsy from the interior of her chair and evaluated from what another novelist (Fielding, for example) would have gone to some trouble to label, comically and dismissively, as her vulgar and superficial perspective. But here Haywood grants Betsy a consumerist envy and longing that are beyond such judgmental gestures, and the vulgar evocation of those eleven footmen in new liveries and the cavalcade making "a very genteel appearance" appears without a trace of the moral irony or pious asceticism and female renunciation we expect in eighteenth-century comic and moral fiction. The scene has a solidity and density, a psychosocial meaningfulness that for the moment transcends the novel's fairly silly monitory moralism, dramatizing an emptiness in Betsy that might be filled by all these objects of desire in ways that various suitors have so far failed to provoke.

Betsy marries unhappily to please her brothers, but her unfaithful husband's death through dissipation rescues her. Since Trueworth has become a widower (thanks to smallpox) it is not very long until the happy ending. Like all such endings, Haywood's in *Betsy Thoughtless* is very much worth waiting for, since the preceding hundreds of pages are crowded with entertaining obstacles to marital happiness. *Betsy Thoughtless* is a rollicking romp through high life, with a heroine whose only fault is that consumerist curiosity for new experiences that readers of the novel enjoy sharing. So Haywood's superficial tracing of Betsy's moral development from coquette to grimly faithful wife to blushing widow/bride is entirely adequate. Within its world of genteel privilege, Haywood's novel celebrates individual if delayed moral agency, marking with appropriate condemnation the schemes for power and pleasure of its interesting villains and with satisfied approbation the achievement of moral integrity and happiness by its central couple. The novel is a fantasy of leisure-class independence in which society's moral balance is unthreatened by the various male and female profligates who inhabit it. The painful, deep cultural contradictions that define the intersection of the novel and the woman writer at mid-century are subordinated to Haywood's easy rehearsals of melodramatic and comic tableaux.

Betsy's adventures are a series of hedonistic encounters and excursions in which a woman enjoys her status as a desirable object and postpones her transformation into a financial and biological male asset. Such fantasy is both celebrated (in sanitized and de-eroticized form) and satirized in Charlotte Lennox's *The Female Quixote* (1752), whose heroine is literally convinced that the heroic amatory world of French seventeenth-century romances is identical to her mid-century domestic reality. Arabella is the only daughter of a disillusioned and disgraced courtier, the Marquis of ____, who resolves "to quit all Society whatever, and devote the rest of his Life to Solitude and Privacy."[11] His daughter is born in this rural solitude, and with the death of her mother after giving birth, Arabella is educated at home by her father and allowed to read freely in his library, which contains "great Store of Romances, and, what was still more unfortunate, not in the original *French*, but very bad Translations" (7). Owing in large part, as the narrator makes clear, to her rural isolation and class privilege, with "no other Conversation but that of a grave and melancholy Father, or her own Attendants," Arabella supposes that the romances are "real Pictures of Life" and from them she draws "all her Notions and Expectations" (7). Out of this delusion there springs Lennox's intially amusing rehearsal of the Don Quixote story. In spite of her obsession, Arabella is both beautiful and intelligent, and when her father presents his nephew, Mr Glanville, as her prospective husband, this young man is charmed as well as puzzled, finding in her "so much Wit and Delicacy, that he could not help admiring her, while he foresaw, the Oddity of her Humour would throw innumberable Difficulties in his Way, before he should be able to obtain her" (45). Arabella suffers from actual cognitive dissonance whereby the prosaic world of aristocratic leisure that she enjoys is perceived through the filters of amatory romance at its most extravagant.

On their own crazy terms, her transformations of this ordinary realm make perfect sense. Strictly speaking, they are not like Don Quixote's febrile fantasies that turn poor inns into castles and flocks of sheep into armies. Thus, she observes a new gardener who has lived in London and there acquired a degree of sophistication so that "he appeared a very extraordinary Person among the Rustics who were his Fellow-Servants" (22). Arabella becomes convinced, following a common pattern in the romances, "that he was some Person of Quality, who, disguised in the Habit of a Gardener, had introduced himself into her Father's Service, in order to have an Opportunity of declaring a Passion to her" (22). Arabella's reading simply encourages her to elaborate her private version of what Haywood's Betsy Thoughtless and other coquettes enjoy in public, the pleasures and the power of being desired. Thus when Glanville falls ill, Arabella naturally assumes it is "occasioned by the Violence of his Passion for her" (131), and when he grows seriously worse she reacts in two ways. On the one hand, she is genuinely alarmed, weeping and revealing "a Grief for Mr Glanville's Illness, little different from that she had felt for her father" (134), but on the other, she treats his illness as disobedience of her commands: "I will also permit you to love me, in order to make the Life I have bestowed on you, worthy your Acceptance" (136).

Arabella's madness is an intensified version of the realities of leisure-class life in which young and attractive, wealthy women are thought to fulfill themselves by collecting the erotic attention of men of their class, and her deluded romantic version of that situation is implicitly satiric of the moral deformation of such a prelude to serious life in marriage and reproduction. Arabella's fantasy is rooted in fact, since she is desired for her wealth as well as her beauty by several young men; but her literary transformation of normal courtship can be considered a subversive refusal of the process of courting and a revelation as well of its narcissistic self-indulgence. The impossible demands that she makes on her lovers as well as the solipsistic readiness with which she turns prosaic features of her surroundings into aspects of her erotic centrality are subversively strong gestures of independence, outrageously reactionary choices of an archaic realm of romance and heroism over modern realities of sex and marriage. And yet next to these imperiously ridiculous preferences of literary models to prosaic actualities, Arabella is subject to psychosexual process, as Lennox takes care to inform us from time to time. She is genuinely moved by Glanville's illness, and although he is "far from coming up to Lady Bella's Idea of a Lover, yet by the Pains he apparently seemed to be in at obliging her, made every Day some Progress in her Esteem" (57). Laid over Arabella's static, a-temporal fantasy is the unavoidable emotional result of her own personal history, so that when Glanville is maliciously slandered as the unfaithful lover of another, she discovers that she has been "ignorant till now of the true State of her Heart" and is "surpriz'd to find it assaulted at once by all the Passions which attend disappointed Love" (349). For all her madness, like other Quixote figures in English fiction such as Parson Adams, Arabella is capable of cogent satiric comment on the triviality of life in Bath and London in the last three books of the novel, when

Glanville and his father persuade her to leave her solitude for normal society in the hope of restoring her to sanity. Ronald Paulson sees this widening of the narrative as a failure, since "the intense psychological scrutiny of Arabella made possible by the small circle and the single locale is replaced by a rather clumsy attempt at the rapid satiric survey of society."[12] To the extent that the journey is out of solipsistic solitude and toward social associations and intellectual relationships that will turn Arabella to sanity, this part of the narrative is a failure because it reduces what had been a powerfully expressive delusion to a mere lack of information and purposeful, rational instruction (provided by the wise Countess of __ at Bath and a learned Doctor of Divinity in London). Left to herself, especially after the death of her father, Arabella in her demented but intensely coherent romantic fantasies is not really Paulson's psychological subject, not a case history of delusional megalomania, but a powerful projection of the central contradiction in woman's fate as rendered by women's fiction: deprived of work and meaningful opportunities for self-expression in social or public life, women are forced to define themselves in exclusively psychosexual and private terms, exploiting as long as they can the pleasure and power they derive from manipulating their status as objects of desire, as objectified and materialized entities subject to the male gaze as it calculates sexual enjoyment, biological reproduction, and economic exploitation. Arabella's romance fantasies, as long as they last, are a disturbing insistence in their determined absurdity and precise, demented consistence of a female irrationality that grasps and appropriates this essence of female identity and, in a revival of courtly love and heroic romance, parodies male power by making the woman the source of transforming fantasy. Her refusal of reality, which has at times nearly fatal consequences for her suitors and at last for herself, is frightening not simply in its madness but in its negation of the orderly and rational social world that the realistic novel promotes. In a chapter traditionally thought to have been written by Lennox's friend, Samuel Johnson, the Doctor argues against the disruptions of fiction persuasively:

> It is the Fault of the best Fictions, that they teach young Minds to expect strange Adventures and sudden Vicissitudes, and therefore encourage them often to trust to Chance. A long Life may be passed without a single Occurrence that can cause much Surprize, or produce any unexpected Consequence of great Importance; the Order of the World is so established, that all human Affairs proceed in a regular Method, and very

little Opportunity is left for Sallies or Hazards, for Assault or
Rescue.

(379)

Although she is at last converted by the Doctor's reasoning and
"yields to the Force of Truth" (381), Arabella has already produced just
the sort of exciting sequences that he identifies as impossible, since by
her fantasies she has encountered surprises and provoked assault and
rescue. Her obsessive personality has necessitated the Doctor's interven-
tion, and to that extent she is the meaningful exception to the rule of
passive uniformity he enunciates. The concluding events of the narrative, to whose violence the Doctor is responding, make this clear.
Observing a lady whom he assumes is Arabella receiving amatory
attention from his treacherous rival for her hand, Sir George (the lady is
actually his sister, disguised as Arabella), Glanville wounds him in a
duel. Luckily, the wound is not mortal, and the chastened Sir George
confesses his attempt to supplant Glanville in Arabella's affections by
hiring an actress to impersonate Cynecia, the "Princess of Gaul," and
to recite a romantic story wherein Ariamenes (Glanville) has betrayed
her. After hearing the story, Arabella first believes it and then (encouraged by precedents in the romances), hoping that Cynecia has been
mistaken, she goes in search of her. Seeking her in Twickenham near
the Thames, where she has accompanied four young ladies she has
recently met, Arabella is urged by them to give up her search. As she
reassures them (to their amazement) with stories of rescued maidens,
Arabella's imagination grows warm and "spying three or four
Horsemen riding along the Road towards them, she immediately
concluded they would be all seiz'd and carry'd off" (362). So to escape
she jumps into the Thames, where she is rescued by Glanville's steward,
Roberts, who had been set to follow her. While Sir George lies bleeding
from his wounds, Arabella is brought home in a fever, "given over by
the Physicians" (365). Although all ends happily as both recover and
marry (Sir George and Miss Glanville, Arabella and her long-suffering
Glanville), Arabella's romance fantasies have consequences, provoking
in the main characters a violence and vehemence that testify to the
unpredictable force of passion that affirms the figurative and
metaphoric truth behind Arabella's romances. The Cervantic model
tends to encourage a lingering positive valence in Arabella's nonsense,
and her emotional and intellectual depth is signified by the intensity of
her unswerving commitment to the romance ideal.

Although recent feminist criticism has testified to the subversive truth
behind Arabella's fantasies, we might pause to consider that, in her

ardent appropriations of romance ideals, Arabella is also exemplifying an emerging set of habits that characterizes the modern bourgeois consumer ethic: her emotional self-determinism is what the sociologist Colin Campbell calls "modern self-illusory hedonism," the key, as he sees it, to the puzzle of the new consumerism. Why, asks Campbell, did a huge and insatiable market develop at this time (chiefly among the middle classes) for consumer goods that went far beyond the satisfactions of normal needs or the improvement of everyday life? A large part of the traditional answer to this question is social emulation, the imitation of their social betters by the English middle classes who now, thanks to modern production and distribution, have the opportunity and the means to ape the aristocracy. Campbell offers a more persuasive and logical answer when he suggests that with affluence "regular satisfaction of needs can be guaranteed" so that pleasure becomes "the crucial, sought-after, scarce commodity, with the consequence that for the first time the pursuit of pleasure for its own sake, rather than its mere appreciation as an adjunct of action pursued for other purposes, takes on the character of a clearly defined and distinct goal of action."[13] As Campbell puts it, "Modern autonomous imaginative hedonism" is a new form of creative day-dreaming made possible by the momentous shift whereby emotions, formerly seen as "inherent in aspects of reality, from whence they exert their influence over humans," come to be located within the self-consciousness of individuals as the world is secularized and disenchanted, as agency is seen as originating in human beings rather than in external forces that provoke action and stimulate emotions. With the decline of what Campbell calls the common "symbolic resources of a culture" (and Arabella's fantasy life is resolutely secular, free of the symbolic resources of Christianity), literacy and individualism combine to grant "the individual a form and degree of symbolic manipulation which was previously restricted to groups."[14] Although Arabella is too rich to desire any particular consumer goods, her substitution of romantic ideals for modern reality is essentially like the always deferred fulfillment offered by modern consumer goods, since, as Campbell suggests, what the consumer wants is not the goods themselves but rather "the desire to experience in reality the pleasurable dramas which they have already enjoyed in imagination, and each 'new' product is seen as offering a possibility of realizing this ambition."[15] Arabella articulates in her fantasies the perfection of modern consumption. Her solipsism and self-enclosure are rarefied and elegant versions of the more commonplace longings encouraged by modern consumer goods such as the romantic novel, and indeed Arabella's affluence leaves her nothing concrete to desire except the perfect and always receding world of romantic perfection. To consume and thereby to create a state of pleasure and power as Arabella does is certainly a subversive act, but of course it is precisely what leisure-class, male-dominated culture offers woman in the plots of many novels. Inescapably, though, there is a contradiction in such freedom, since novels are themselves part of the consumer revolution, offering as objects both the experience of and the infinite deferral of fulfillment.

Insulated in the past and certainly in the privileged future that her narrative projects for her, Arabella can well afford to treat the world as a topic for moral discussion and to reserve the option of virtuous spectatorship. More often in novels by women about specifically female problems, there is no such luxury available, since a woman's destiny is precisely comprehended within the circumstances that Arabella's fantasies seek to negate and that her wealth will enable her to avoid. Women in mid-eighteenth-century fiction confront head on their own special psychosexual and social–moral inevitability. Female destiny often includes resistance to that inevitability, both comically fantastic and seriously moralistic, and in that combination of looming necessity and the self-conscious individualities of resistance to it lies the defining shape of the modern novel. Nancy Armstrong has argued that the eighteenth-century novel represents a feminization of experience whereby middle-class individuals are defined in private and domestic terms that gives them power by making them like women: "narratives which seemed to be concerned solely with matters of courtship and marriage in fact seized the authority to say what was female ... they did so in order to contest the reigning notion of kinship relations that attached most power and privilege to certain family lines."[16] One might modify Armstrong's influential thesis to say that women in their moral revision of the amatory tradition in the novel of love, courtship, and marriage (contradictory intertwinings of freedom and necessity) dramatize in domestic and private travail the characteristic shape and the utopian possibilities of modern experience in the larger public and historical sphere. With female existence oriented toward romantic love/marriage, individual freedom and submission to a larger social destiny necessarily converge: marriage is a submission to romantic fate but also a creative and, in the best of newly defined middle-class circumstances, a freely chosen and self-expansive act. Marriage should be a contribution to social coherence, nothing less than the recreation of the primal community, but of course almost invariably in women's fiction of the mid-eighteenth century the depiction of courtship and marriage is instead the occasion for an examination of the cultural impasse created by new expectations surrounding companionate marriage and full affective individualism for women in the face of lingering authoritarian patriarchalism as well as the sexual double standard.

The most harrowing exploration of such female fate (that dramatizes the dangers of middle-class individualism rather than the formation of those bourgeois powers that Armstrong talks about) may be Frances Sheridan's popular *Memoirs of Miss Sidney Bidulph* (1761).[17] "I know not, Madam, that you have a right, upon moral principles, to make your readers suffer so much," remarked Dr Johnson, and it was in part a compliment.[18] Set in Queen Anne's reign, the *Memoirs* tells a pathetic and sordid tale: Sidney's betrayal by her husband when he becomes infatuated with an unscrupulous *femme fatale*, Mrs Gerrarde, and her descent with him into financial ruin and then into impoverished widowhood and massive regret at her hopelessly unlucky love for another man. These troubles stem from Sidney's refusal of her brother's friend, Orlando Faulkland, when her mother discovers that he has fathered an illegitimate child. Lady Bidulph tells Faulkland to marry the young woman (Miss Burchell) he has ruined. The dutiful Sidney breaks off her engagement to him and soon after marries Mr Arnold, a man for whom she feels no particular attraction except esteem and gratitude but whose energetic suit is promoted by her mother and her friends. With their two children, they take up residence at Arnold's small estate in Kent, where among their neighbors and intimates is the young Widow Gerrarde. In short order, not only does Sidney discover that Arnold and Mrs Gerrarde are lovers but, as her husband grows indifferent to her, Sidney is unjustly accused of infidelity with Faulkland, now a visitor in the area, and she is turned out of her house by her brutal husband. After much suffering, including separation from her two daughters, Sidney is rescued by, of all people, her still devoted suitor, Faulkland. He pretends to seduce Mrs Gerrarde, and tricks her into eloping with him to France, where she is manipulated into marriage with his French valet, Pivet. In the meantime, Arnold loses most of his estate in a lawsuit brought by his elder brother's scheming widow, and what Sidney and her now repentant husband have to live on is only her small marriage portion, and even that is reduced to a mere fifty pounds a year as one of Arnold's creditors insists on full payment of a crucial loan.

The final blow seems to come when Arnold dies after a hunting accident. But, no, to widowed poverty Sidney adds (at her mother's urging) the refusal of Faulkland's second marriage proposal and her own successfully self-sacrificing exhortation that he marry the wronged Miss Burchell. But not long after this sacrifice, as she sinks into worse poverty in a small London apartment (her children nearly die of smallpox and she herself almost succumbs to fever), Sidney discovers that Miss Burchell was the initiator of the sexual encounter with Faulkland. In the meantime, in the only fortunate turn of events that the novel allows, her cousin, Ned Warner (who has prospered in Jamaica) rescues her from poverty by giving her an income of £3,000 a year and making her the mistress of his newly acquired London mansion. But then Sidney learns from her brother, Sir George, the whole shocking truth about Miss Burchell, who is in his words "a female libertine, a rake in the worst sense of the word."[19] For proof he reveals that he, too, enjoyed her charms. Sir George predicts that Miss Burchell will betray Faulkland, and in due course Sidney is shocked yet again when Faulkland returns suddenly from Ireland to say that he has caught his wife in adultery and in his rage murdered her and her lover. The distraught Faulkland asks Sidney to marry him, and at the urging of her cousin and her brother she reluctantly agrees to a secret ceremony. Faulkland is persuaded, however, to flee to Holland without Sidney. But after he departs, news arrives that Mrs Faulkland is not dead after all; she had fainted and was covered in her lover's blood. Sidney's memoirs break off at this appalling point, with her closing exclamation: "Adieu, my Cecilia, adieu; nothing but my death should close such a scene as this" (457). Cecilia herself relates the final melancholy coda to these events: learning from Sir George and Mr Warner that his perfidious wife is alive, Faulkland is found dead a few days later, perhaps a suicide. Sidney and her daughters retire to the country, but Cecilia's last paragraph refers to "new and dreadful calamities to her, which, by involving the unhappy daughters of an unhappy mother in scenes of the most exquisite distress, cut off from her even the last resource of hope in this life" (467). Mercifully, at least for Sheridan's readers, the manuscript breaks off here.[20]

These unrelenting sorrows give Sheridan's novel a unity lacking in the ordinary novel of courtship and marriage, which tends like *Betsy Thoughtless* or *The Female Quixote* to stress a personal agency and resourcefulness whereby problems are in due course solved. The gathering force of calamity in *Memoirs of Miss Sidney Bidulph* has an inescapable quality that seems to testify to the order of things, and Sidney plays out a Job story with no happy coda. From the beginning, the hapless Sidney is trapped within an encircling tornado of destructive sexuality while she remains still and suffering, nobly submissive to a narrowly conceived domestic duty. Near the end of her story Sidney wonders, after finally marrying Faulkland, about her life so far: "There is something so amazing in all this, I can scarce credit my senses; but my life has been a series of strange, strange events" (448). Sidney's continual self-effacements are a heroic revision of that emotional determinism that the ordinary novel of courtship still endorses. As she contemplates the marriage between Faulkland and Miss Burchell, Sidney rejects female stereotypes, declaring that "disappointment in a first love" can be overcome by moral will like hers and that only weakly vulnerable hearts allow themselves "to be so entirely immersed in that passion, that all the other duties of life are swallowed up in it, and where an indolent turn of mind, a want of rational avocations, and perhaps of a new object, all contribute to indulge and confirm the disease" (334). In this cruel and ironic disposition, Sidney finds that her "best purposes, by some unseen power, are perverted from their ends" (391). As Margaret Anne Doody has argued, Sheridan's novel is a meditation on the effects of the past on the present. Doody points out that Lady Bidulph's first love revealed on what was to be their wedding day that he had been engaged to another woman whom he had seduced with a promise of marriage. Stricken with remorse, he decided to marry this woman, and Lady Bidulph went on to marry someone else. So Sidney's refusal of Faulkand at her mother's insistence is a fated repetition. In Doody's words, in *Memoirs of Miss Sidney Bidulph* "the past never ceases, a past action is never cleared out of the way; the past never stops having an effect on the present."[21]

What Sheridan renders, however, is not an inscrutable totality but a visible network of obligations, relationships, and reciprocities that can entangle the unwary and the unlucky, catch and destroy the naïf who, like Sidney, is unworldly and innocent. She is directly the victim, for example, of the conspiracy of silence between Miss Burchell and her brother whereby Sir George promises not to reveal their dalliance. As Sir George declares when all is revealed, "I had no conception that Faulkland could ever be brought to think of marrying her, I thought myself bound not to injure her in his opinion" (385–386). But he did not reckon with his sister's powers of moral persuasion, nor with a narrative logic whereby female paragons like her are bound to misunderstand the motives of ordinary mortals. Sheridan's book is both wildly melodramatic and quietly attentive to domestic routine at its most uneventful. Thus, just after refusing Faulkland, Sidney and Lady Bidulph are at Lady Grimston's country estate, where the boredom of upper-class female life as she evokes it for Cecilia is intense and serves as prelude and incitement to another marriage proposal:

> August 10. All our motions here are as regular as the clock.
> The family rise at six; we are summoned to breakfast at eight;
> at ten a venerable congregation are assembled to prayers,
> which an ancient clergyman, who is curate of the parish, and

her ladyship's chaplain, gives us daily. Then the old horses are put to the old coach; and my lady, with her guests, if they chuse it, take an airing; always going and returning by the same road, and driving precisely to the same land-mark, and no farther. At half an hour after twelve, in a hall large enough to entertain a corporation, we sit down to dinner.

(62–63)

Just as Sidney is "beginning to despair of matter to furnish out a quarter of an hour's entertainment," a coach full of visitors arrives, including "a Mr Arnold, a gentleman who is a distant relation of lady Grimston's" (63). Unlike other memorable heroines who qualify for narrative centrality by their deviation in some way from the female norm, Sidney is a heroic self-effacer, and her narrative is a record of deferrals in which she is "actively" and aggressively passive, allowing readers to see through her experiences and sufferings the operations, both trivial and melodramatic, of the upper-class circles in which she moves. Mr Arnold, for example, discusses Sidney with Lady Grimston, who recommends her "strongly to him." Asked by Cecilia to describe him, Sidney remarks that he "is reckoned" handsome and although she says she does not know the color of his eyes, she offers a summary of his social and financial standing: "of a very good family; and has an estate of about fifteen hundred pounds a year" (79). His proposal has not yet been offered, but "we all know that he intends it, from his uncommon assiduity towards me" (79). This romance is a community affair, promoted by the Grimston set, acknowledged and affirmed not simply by the couple but by their friends and relations. As Sidney summarizes the proposed financial arrangements and the comfortable but limited income that Arnold brings to the marriage, she slides into a revealing admission of her essential passivity:

Things are now gone so far, that my mother and lady Grimston talked today of settlements. ... My mother, who you know is integrity itself, thinks that I ought not to have more settled on me than the widow of Mr Arnold's brother had, whose fortune was superior to mine. Mr Arnold makes a much handsomer proposal; lady Grimston is for laying hold of it. The dean was for striking a medium. I do not care how they settle it; but I fancy my mother will have her own way in this.

She purposes going to town next week, that the wedding – (bless me! whose wedding is it that I am talking of so coolly?)

(93–94)

More of a resigned spectator than a participant, Sidney undergoes experiences by which she is of course deeply affected but of which she is not in fact the initiator nor even at times actively involved. A passionless and sexless paragon, Sidney is hopelessly naive in her understanding of the realities of female sexuality as the novel renders them. Both Miss Burchell and the formidable Mrs Gerrarde are sexually aggressive and economically self-serving, and especially in her miscasting of Miss Burchell as a defenseless and seduced maiden Sidney displays a remarkable ignorance of the world, an almost literary falsification of female behavior derived from the amatory pattern. "She is only," Sir George reveals to his shocked sister, "a sly rake in petticoats, of which there are numbers, that you good women would stare at, if you knew their behaviour" (387). Sidney replies that he has given her "an idea of a character, which I thought was not in the female world" (388).

Sheridan's novel is an ambitious exploration of the unresolved eighteenth-century problem of female character, and her long-suffering heroine is a lamb among the she-wolves revealed by novelistic probings. Sidney is exalted but in the process Sheridan destroys her plausibility and even erodes her moral intelligence; Sidney's function as an observer of moral behavior, including her own, may be to recommend by her grim example the simpler gratifications of ordinary desire and healthy submission to emotion. Although according to Cecilia, Sidney is "one of the greatest beauties of her time" (11), she is hardly a physical or sexual presence in the narrative, and a description of her written by one of the other characters as she kneels by her dying husband's bed evokes her memorably in ethereal fashion as an icon of suffering, "an angel interceding for us poor mortal sinners": "Surely nothing ever appeared so graceful; her fine hands and her fine eyes lifted up to heaven. Such a reverential, such an ardent, yet such a mournful supplication in those fine eyes! She looked like something more than human!" (286–287). Sidney's anti-types, Mrs Gerrarde and Miss Burchell, are, of course, the familiar figures of the sexually aggressive woman but unlike, say, Flora in *Betsy Thoughtless*, there is nothing hysterical or obsessive about their pursuit of pleasure and privilege.

The liveliest and most complex part of Sheridan's novel is Faulkland's kidnapping/seduction of Mrs Gerrarde in which he lures her away from Mr Arnold by holding out hope that he will marry her and then bribes her to marry his French valet. Temporarily at least, the numbing pathos of Sidney's noble suffering is exchanged for the reader's immersion in a clash of strong wills and opposing purposes. Faulkland's extra-legal plot is playful and resourceful; he treats the adventure as a difficult game to outwit his adversary by converting her understandable assumption that he is out to seduce her to his own purposes of cutting her off from the Arnolds without compromising himself sexually. He traps her into a strategic profession of remorse for her affair with Arnold so that, hoping to secure a better prize in Faulkland, she agrees to write a letter to Arnold breaking off their relationship, which he knows will "appear, as I intended it should, the contrivance of an artful jilt, who having almost ruined the wretch she had in her power, would afterwards make a *merit* of deserting him" (204).

Faulkland's long letters describing these events are among the various documents that supplement Sidney Bidulph's proper "memoirs," and indeed in the final analysis Orlando Faulkland shares the book almost equally with the heroine, presenting in his comic and tragic relationships with Mrs Gerrarde and Miss Burchell (as well as, of course, with Sidney herself) an alternative scenario of meaningful action in which personality is revealed and moral character developed. Sidney's embodiment of patient female suffering necessarily turns inward, for social relationships are subordinated in her narrative to those events that escalate or vary her sufferings. In sharing the spotlight with a man of action, energy, and passion like Faulkland, *Memoirs of Miss Sidney Bidulph* dramatizes the novelistic limitations of solitary female suffering such as the heroine endures. In its instinctive worldliness, its attraction to personality expressed and developed in particular social relationships, its aversion to moral absolutes, and its delight in dialogical variety of language and self-dramatization, the British novel moves away from the simple if affecting spectacle of female distress and toward much more inclusive social and moral interactions. Frances Burney's *Evelina* (1778) and *Cecilia* (1782) are the two most successful fusions of suffering female virtue and novelistic richness and variety achieved in the late eighteenth century by a woman novelist.

II

Evelina (1778) is a comic revision of the novel of seduction and betrayal. Burney imagines as the melodramatic climax of her book a Lovelace figure, Sir John Belmont, in reformed middle age confronting the innocent offspring of his profligate younger days, Evelina, the guilt-inducing replica of her abandoned mother. *Evelina*'s melodramatic plot is balanced by comedy and by the histories of a tangle of unfortunate marriages across class and national boundaries. As the Rev. Arthur

Villars explains to Lady Howard, he had been tutor to the heroine's grandfather, Mr Evelyn, who married beneath his station to a tavern waiting-girl, and upon his death in France shortly thereafter left his estate to his wife but named Villars as guardian of his daughter, Caroline. The remarried Mrs Evelyn (now Madame Duval) sent for the 18-year-old Caroline. In Paris, says Villars, she grew rebellious under her ill-bred mother's tyranny "and rashly, and without a witness, consented to a private marriage with Sir John Belmont."[22] Deserted and disowned by her rake husband and disinherited by her mother, Caroline died shortly after giving birth to Evelina, who has been brought up by Villars in virtuous rural seclusion.

As the novel opens, Lady Howard writes to Villars that she has heard from Madame Duval, who wishes to see her granddaughter. This alarming possibility arouses his concern that history will repeat itself if his teenaged ward is exposed to her grandmother's influence. Some months later, Lady Howard writes to ask him to release Evelina for a visit to London with her granddaughter, Maria Mirvan. "It is time," argues Lady Howard, "that she should see something of the world. When young people are too rigidly sequestered from it, their lively and romantic imaginations paint it to them as a paradise of which they have been beguiled; but when they are shown it properly, and in due time, they see it such as it really is, equally shared by pain and pleasure, hope and disappointment" (17). Young women of the privileged classes (for young men are not "sequestered") need for their moral education to see the world in order to dispel the romantic illusions provoked by seclusion. Villars concedes that this sequence is educationally apt, that in Evelina's case "the time draws on for experience and observation to take place of instruction" (18), although in his reluctance he offers some balancing aphorisms: "A youthful mind is seldom totally free from ambition; to curb that, is the first step to contentment, since to diminish expectation, is to increase enjoyment" (18). Ominously and in fact accurately, Villars predicts that in the "circle of high life" where she shall be seen, Evelina has "too much beauty to escape notice, has too much sensibility to be indifferent to it; but she has too little wealth to be sought with propriety by men of the fashionable world" (18).

What, we may ask, are the dangerous desires that this world is likely to inspire in a young and beautiful girl from which Villars wishes to protect Evelina? The experience of urban, leisure-class pleasures, which center on that sexual self-display central to a young girl's appearance in the world, will lead, at the best, to a financially and socially advantageous marriage, and to all the privilege and pleasure that wealth can bring, or at the absolute worst, participation in such a world may lead to an illicit sexual connection with an upper-class man, which can certainly bring power and pleasure but also a loss of moral and social status – that spells out crudely what he renders in discreet generalities. Villars' plan collides, naturally, with what readers expect to enjoy in a novel, which may provide a good dose of healthy disillusion for young heroines but offers entertaining involvement in those varieties of transgressive or extravagant behavior. In fact, this little debate at the beginning of *Evelina* rehearses the attractions and the moral strategy of fiction in the eighteenth century: novels are advertised as cautionary tales, but readers are also assured that they will experience vicariously plenty of those exciting dangers that the novel promises they will learn to avoid in their own lives.

Villars' moral verities will remind readers of *The Female Quixote* of the Johnsonian moralizing that converts Arabella. But just as readers of Lennox's novel do not turn to it for these maxims but for the heroine's specifically bizarre personality and adventures, so too Burney's novel in its energetic comic rendition of unruly urban manners is much more than the final stage of a young lady's education in the sobering truths of human nature. To serve her readers' desires, Evelina must go forth eagerly into the world and seek to gather the rich fruits that it has to offer, but the narrative problem for Burney is the classic dilemma of the eighteenth-century moralizing woman novelist: how to preserve her heroine's innocence and moral integrity without lapsing into static didacticism and, more difficult, how to express her heroine's complex desire for all the pleasures that worldly experience can bring to a young beauty (in this case one deprived of her proper social status) without turning her into the sexually active and materially omnivorous woman whose shadow haunts the eighteenth-century imagination. Or to advance the natural sequence of such a master narrative, once a beautiful young woman gets her heart's desire and enters by marriage the privileged circles of the leisured classes, what is to prevent her from becoming, now that she has nowhere else to turn and nothing more to desire or to accomplish, like one of Pope's female grotesques?

Of all the woman novelists of mid-century and after, Burney is in the root sense of the terms the most purely secular and social: without resorting to the quasi-religious emotional authenticity so often granted to embattled heroines in the female tradition and without dwelling excessively on the psychosexual conflicts of the isolated young virgin, she offers in *Evelina* a comprehensive, detailed, and convincing evocation of experience across as wide a range of society as any novelist of the century had provided, in the process transcending the purely domestic limitations of the novel of female suffering. By the late 1770s the 26-year-old Burney seems to have absorbed the lessons of her male predecessors. She told herself in her diary that she had not "pretended to shew the World what it actually *is*, but what it *appears* to a Girl of 17."[23] But she also recorded in her diary the initial general opinion that the novel's author was a man and quotes a tribute from her friend, Mrs Thrale, to the book's powers of comprehensive social observation: "She recommended it to my mother to read! ... & she told her she would be much entertained with it, for there was a great deal of human Life in it, & of the manners of the present Times: & added that it was written 'by somebody who knows the *Top & the Bottom, the highest & the lowest of mankind.*'"[24]

As the novel's principal narrator (*Evelina* is mainly the heroine's journal of her visits to London and the spa town of Bristol Hotwells, with Villars and Lady Howard contributing a few letters in the course of events), Evelina is much more than an impressionable, fanciful senti-mental heroine (although she is also that). Evelina quickly develops the ability to deliver a sharply observed world, full of comic variety and satiric complexity. The dialogue is as witty as the best of, say, Sheridan's plays, and Burney renders with great comic verve the accents of her varied cast. As narrator, Evelina for the most part is able to place herself at the edge of the various social groupings that she observes, deeply involved in events but also shrewdly watching and vividly recording events from her often satirical vantage point. Given her displaced, ambiguous origins as well as her rural solitude until her entrance into the world, Evelina the narrator possesses a revealingly neutral and even objective perspective. Allowed to claim moral superiority to the coarse and brutal behavior and naked pleasure-seeking that she witnesses, she assumes as well an implicit, specifically linguistic superiority to the varied class dialects and correspondingly specific moral distortions that she reproduces, from lower middle-class ignorance and vulgar pretension to aristocratic nonsense and decadent upper-class hedonism and false sophistication. Nominally the naive young girl from the provinces, Evelina as narrator does not miss a thing; she speaks confidently, with satiric exactness and novelistic fullness. Even her frequent silences and deep anxieties as a participant become in this context of her powers as a recorder of the flawed discourse and unruly desires of others an eloquent refusal to speak improperly and to become the victim of her own desires. To that extent her relative reticence as a character (next to, say, the gushing and manipulative innocence of Pamela or Betsy Thoughtless's flirtatious protestations of purity) is a distinctive female self-reservation and strategic modesty that serves her very well and makes *Evelina* an orig-inal variation on the novel of a young woman's coming of age.

Evelina explores a paradoxical balance worked out in late eighteenth-century culture between submission to patriarchal ideology and the acquisitive, aggressive upward social movement of exceptional young women. Kristina Straub articulates what she calls this "strategy of feminine duplicity" when she finds that Evelina is "both conventional and outside of convention, a practitioner in the fashionable rites of town life who is, nonetheless, not morally defined by the role that she plays in them."[25] But to notice that Evelina is at times judiciously critical of some of the pleasures of the town, like shopping and gourmandizing, is not to cancel her aspirations to secure membership in the leisure class nor her deep conformity to the values of that class.[26]

Evelina balances narrative power with the sentimental heroine's weakness and diffidence and thereby expands female possibilities, locating varieties of female speaking and acting in the space between those two extreme positions of strength and weakness. Several scenes late in the novel illustrate how Evelina draws both narrative strength and emotional distress from her marginal location. Having returned to Villars' house in the country, she falls ill (mostly, it would seem, from the disappointment and embarrassment brought on by her month-long sojourn with her vulgar relations) and agrees to go to Bristol Hotwells for her health with one of their country neighbors, "Mrs Selwyn, a lady of large fortune" (260). Mrs Selwyn has in the past offended Villars by her "unmerciful propensity to satire," and her "want of gentleness" (269). This lady, Evelina reports, is "extremely clever; her understanding, indeed, may be called *masculine*; but, unfortunately, her manners deserve the same epithet; for, in studying to acquire the knowledge of the other sex, she has lost all the softness of her own" (268–269). While in Bristol, they visit the home of Mrs Beaumont who, in Mrs Selwyn's satirical description of her, is a caricature of snobbery: "She has some good qualities, but they rather originate from pride than principle, as she piques herself upon being too high born to be capable of an unworthy action, and thinks it incumbent upon her to support the dignity of her ancestry" (284). And in Mrs Beaumont's house Evelina meets Lady Louisa Larpent, Lord Orville's sister, who is a parody of female delicacy: "Your Ladyship's constitution," a friend observes, "is infinitely delicate," to which she responds, "Indeed it is … I am *nerve* all over!" (286).

Some days later, Evelina finds herself especially isolated and therefore silent among these three women: "I took my usual place, and Mrs Beaumont, Lady Louisa, and Mrs Selwyn, entered into their usual conversation. – Not so your Evelina: disregarded, silent, and melancholy, she sat like a cypher, whom, to nobody belonging, by nobody was noticed" (340). Humiliated by her dependence on rich patrons, Evelina is noticed for her beauty and for her vulnerability as a sexual prize, as she is subjected to unwelcome sexual importunities and even on several occasions potential sexual assault. Among her suitors is the insistent rake, Sir Clement Willoughby, who makes his appearance again at this point and agrees to attend the three ladies as they take an airing in Mrs Beaumont's coach. That evening, he summarizes the world's view of the trio who conversed as she sat silent: " 'The world in general,' answered he, 'has the same opinion of them that I have myself: Mrs Beaumont is every where laughed at, Lady Louisa ridiculed, and Mrs Selwyn hated' " (343). Mrs Selwyn has a wit that trivial men of pleasure like Sir Clement must fear: " 'She has wit, I acknowledge, and more understanding than half her sex put together; but she keeps alive a perpetual expectation of satire, that spreads a general uneasiness among all who are in her presence; and she talks so much, that even the best things she says, weary the attention' " (343). Evelina never wearies the attention, and she inspires admiration and erotic excitement. She charms with her striking physical beauty and rarely speaks without being spoken to first. She is what Sir Clement calls a "sweet reproacher," whose physical attractions are perfectly complemented by her strict observance of the decorum of female speaking, even when she refuses the sexual attentions of others. Only in the subversive private world of her correspondence and her journal does she play out the satirist's role that the world assigns to Mrs Selwyn, whose violation of female decorum (and her age, to be sure) makes her in the end a comic figure and secondary player, lumped with the other two sorts of female absurdity represented by Lady Louisa and Mrs Beaumont. Just as social privilege and leisure-class gender stereotypes determine their ludicrous and deformed personalities, Mrs Selwyn's incessant and scornful wit is in its personalized excess a marked form of improper female behavior, a defensive reaction to the mostly male stupidity all around her. Each of these three women defines herself by her comically predictable and specifically female personality. Thanks in part to her declassé status, Evelina evades classification by such socially determined female habits, even though she proves herself as snobbish in practice, if not in theory, as Mrs Beaumont and as delicate (if more genuinely sensitive and discriminating) in her own decorous way as Lady Louisa. In spite of her feminine qualities, Evelina as narrator articulates an intelligence and identity beyond gender roles, deliberating on the signif-icance of complicated social and moral relationships rather than dramatizing her own self-expressive location within them. As a fairly original kind of novelistic participant–narrator, she redefines female volubility. She speaks without speaking, as it were, in reproducing and classifying a wide range of discourse. Assertive without aggression, silent and demure but thereby eloquent and critical, Evelina thus plays a dual role as narrator and participant that enables her to exercise power and gain knowledge without violating her defining female delicacy.

Exceedingly delicate as well as sharply observant (related qualities), Evelina is frightened by ruffians at Vauxhall and at Marybone gardens, reduced to gasping, inarticulate emotion and fainting fits at various distressing moments. But her reserve, her meaningful silence, is a constant feature of her personality, and her distress is most often wordless and strategically inarticulate. For example, after her biological father, Sir John Belmont, rejects her petition for recognition as his daughter, she writes to Mr Villars: "Well, my dear Sir, all is now over! the letter so anxiously expected is at length arrived, and my doom is fixed. The various feelings which oppress me, I have not language to describe; nor need I – you know my heart, you have yourself formed it – and its sensations upon this occasion you may but too readily imagine" (158). To some extent, Evelina in moments like this disposes of turbulent female interiority by conventionalizing it, referring us to an appropriate pattern instilled by education and too familiar to need rehearsal.

As speaker–participant within the scenes that she narrates and as frequent self-analyst and dramatizer, Evelina's narrative is also, necessarily, self-expressive, revealing herself as hesitant and diffident, often reduced to embarrassed silence in the face of self-seeking vulgarity or to blushing deference and even shame when confronted with the tactful self-effacement of good breeding. For example, upon first arrival in London at a private ball she is shocked by the "careless and indolent manner" of the men there, who "looked as if they thought we were quite at their disposal" (28). A fop called Lovel and then another man ask her to dance. In what she learns is a serious breach of public etiquette, Evelina turns Lovel down only to accept a more graceful proposal from another (and much better looking) gentleman, who turns out to be Lord Orville: "His conversation was sensible and spirited; his air and address were open and noble; his manners gentle, attentive, and infinitely engaging; his person is all elegance, and his countenance the most animated and expressive I have ever seen" (30). On only brief acquaintance, it seems, Lord Orville overcomes the insincere conventionality and leering sexuality that Evelina is surprised to find in interactions between upper-class women and the men who pursue them. Lovel's ugliness, his clumsy gestures, foppish clothing, and hyper-affected speech – all these satirically marked features are differences of degree, in fact, from Orville's behavior, or for that matter, from Evelina's own conduct. Sexual ritual and self-display are the purpose of dances and ridottos and other public gatherings of the eligible members of the leisure class. Evelina knows that as well as anybody, and her confused embarrassment signals her virtuous (and ritualized) reluctance to appear as eager for pleasure as her choice of the handsome Orville over the ugly Lovel indicates that she is. In a social sphere like the one that she has entered – saturated with such total and defining privilege, idleness, conspicuous consumption, and self-display that a modern reader is probably hard pressed to imagine such an existence – manners require that such extravagant power be ritualistically denied or deferred. The sign of this privilege is its easy and polite restraint, its refined postponement of gratification, its containment by various public forms of (temporary) refusal of gratification. Evelina is, obviously, new to all this and in refusing the repulsive Lovel (who correctly accuses her in due course of "ill manners") and accepting handsome Orville she violates the code, breaking the rule whereby women do not interfere with the screen of manners that decorates the positioning for pleasure involved in such occasions. She thus reveals (quite nakedly) her desires. Evelina learns "delicacy" in the adventures that follow this introduction to the polite world, for she is confronted by several aggressive suitors whose overt pursuit enables her to perfect her manners, that is, to master the steps of those ritualized public rejections or deferrals of pleasure that signify leisure-class power and self-possessed privilege, both male and female. In place of her giggling refusal of Lovel and her embarrassed (and embarrassing) acceptance of Orville, Evelina fends off in the course of the novel the attentions of two other men: Sir Clement Willoughby and Mr Smith, aristocrat and citizen, who display with comic energy distinct social types of egregious pleasure-seeking and allow Evelina to perfect her skill at the arts of refusal and the deferrals that define female delicacy at its best.

Orville is both powerful patron and disinterested lover–servant for Evelina, and his moral worth in the social–linguistic economy of the novel lies in his exemplary restraint and moderation, his very lack of insistence, his easy refusal to exercise or exploit his power and sexual charm. Orville in his discourse is a muted, polite version of the courtly lover whose only expressed wish is to serve and to please. Sir Clement's amatory bombast is manifestly aggressive and signals his desire to have Evelina as his mistress, and of course his speeches are accompanied by unlicensed physical encroachments like hand-kissing and a near-abduction and rape at one point as he instructs his coachman to drive them to an isolated spot. But even the aggressive Sir Clement appears "modest" in comparison with the bold stare and rude behavior of a nobleman (later identified as Lord Merton, the fiancé, as it turns out, of Orville's sister, Lady Louisa) at the public assembly hall called the Pantheon. When he seizes her unwilling hand to convey her to a coach, Evelina is led to muse on the variety of characters "in all ranks and all stations of life":

> Lord Orville, with a politeness which knows no intermission, and makes no distinction, is as unassuming and modest, as if he had never mixed with the great, and was totally ignorant of every qualification he possesses; this other Lord, though lavish of compliments and fine speeches, seems to me an entire stranger to real good-breeding; whoever strikes his fancy, engrosses his whole attention. He is forward and bold, has an air of haughtiness towards men, and a look of libertinism towards women, and his conscious quality seems to have given him a freedom in his way of speaking to either sex, that is very little short of rudeness.
>
> (113–114)

Politeness and "breeding" are negated for Evelina by unfettered displays of social and sexual power, and yet behavior like Lord Merton's is nothing more nor less than an undisguised appetite for that pleasure and variety that readers bring to the novelistic table. Paragons of restraint like Orville and Evelina are necessary, in practical terms, to provoke in others entertaining overtness and honestly brutal deviance from polite standards. The bland and boring Orville and the blushing and reluctant Evelina will not sustain the narrative, and so Burney balances these abstemious paragons against a cast of voraciously self-seeking personalities who reveal the truth, as we may call it, of desire and appetite that prevail in market society. The commonplace logic of comic narrative balancing cooperates in *Evelina* with its exposure of the enervating and confusing moral ideology of privilege that is the heroine's peculiar and defining problem as a young woman of no fortune and dubious parentage who must somehow reconcile desire and deferral.

The comic high point of the book has always been the heroine's great embarrassment in the presence of her cousins, the lower middle-class, shopkeeping Branghtons. Forced by her grandmother (Madame Duval, who suddenly appears in London) to spend a month with her at lodgings in Holborn (a distinctly unfashionable neighborhood), Evelina responds to the change in her situation with a snobbish mortification that has deeply offended twentieth-century commentators. As she writes to Maria Mirvan, London for her "now seems a desart" in which the realities of weather and social class are oppressive: "the air seems stagnant, the heat is intense, the dust intolerable, the inhabitants illiterate and under-bred. At least, such is the face of things in the part of town where I at present reside" (172). As she sighs to Maria, her recent experiences now seem like "a dream, or some visionary fancy, than a reality." However embarrassing and even sexually dangerous her sojourn in the purlieus of pleasure, Evelina's descent into a region where the urban realities of class, weather, and work are visible dramatizes her longing for the "world" that Villars fears will corrupt her, a leisure-class fantasy land where the day-to-day actualities of life are banished by a constant round of pleasures and diversions. In addition to her coarse and ill-bred grandmother, Evelina is chiefly bedeviled by her cousins, the Branghtons: two daughters, Polly and Biddy (with Polly's beau, Mr Brown, a haberdasher), a son, Tom, and their father, a silversmith in Snow Lane in Holborn. Complicating her distress over being restricted to the company of this vulgar lot are the amorous attentions of the Branghtons' friend and lodger, the citizen-beau, Mr Smith (Dr Johnson's favorite). In all these characters, "ill breeding" consists of undisguised pleasure-seeking, simple consumerist materialism, and unrestrained curiosity about the social ranks above them – precisely the qualities that leisure-class politeness transforms and softens by its code of manners by which the privileged classes enjoy but simultaneously seem to defer and deny all these satisfactions. In their vulgarity, these characters make comically explicit and overt what upper-class characters are supposed to express only indirectly and tactfully. As William Dowling puts it, the Branghtons are an embarrassment because they have been produced by modern market society and derive from "a world governed by the impersonal forces of exchange value and driven by Hobbesian or Mandevillian self-interest." Dowling's perceptive commentary on "the genealogy of literary shame" in *Evelina* links it with an earlier satiric tradition in that Burney dramatizes how in such a modern world there is no real distinction between the Branghtons and noblemen like Sir Clement and Lord Merton, who "are as free as common tradesmen to constitute themselves mere creatures of blind or importunate drives."[27]

But Dowling overstates the moral nostalgia in Burney's novel, which does not exempt Evelina and Orville from the dance of class privilege and pleasure. What separates the leisure classes, both delicate paragons and brutal voluptuaries, from the upstart Branghtons and Mr Smith is only their language and relative sophistication (and, of course, their incomes). The exact source of Evelina's contempt for her relations is, predictably, what she denounces as their social pretensions. Dinner with them, she notes, is chaotic: "ill-served, ill-cooked, and ill-managed," but "Had they been without *pretensions*, all this would have seemed of no consequence; but they aimed at appearing to advantage, and even fancied they succeeded" (174–175). Aiming to appear to advantage means that the Branghtons are self-conscious, betraying their ambition to rise socially. Evelina herself has been guilty of awkwardness at polite forms of behavior, and her contempt for her relations is obviously intertwined with her own guilt and shame as she sees herself and her upwardly mobile aspirations caricatured in them. In their hilarious vulgarity, the Branghtons project the unabashed, expansive materialist–consumerist energy of modern personality that virtuous women (especially) in the female eighteenth-century novel must reject or, perhaps, simply evade or disguise. What they actively and aggressively seek, Evelina hopes will be given to her because she deserves it, because she has mastered (or hopes to master) the forms of leisure-class behavior.

Mr Smith's attempts to ape gentility provoke Evelina's finely tuned scorn, but his awkward self-consciousness is parallel to her own deep unease and anguished self-examinations in unfamiliar upper-class situations. He is ungainly in his insecure class position, and with characteristically sharp attention to social nuance Evelina watches him watching himself: "the inelegant smartness of his air and deportment, his visible struggle, against education, to put on the fine gentleman, added to his frequent conscious glances at a dress to which he was but little accustomed, very effectually destroyed his aim of *figuring*, and rendered all his efforts useless" (219). As they visit Vauxhall, Sir Clement Willoughby makes an unexpected appearance. She watches, again, with great satisfaction, almost laughing as she looks "at Mr. Smith, who no sooner saw me addressed by Sir Clement, than, retreating aloof from the company, he seemed to lose at once all his happy self-sufficiency and conceit; looking now at the baronet, now at himself, surveying, with sorrowful eyes, his dress, struck with his air, his gestures, his easy gaiety; he gazed at him with envious admiration, and seemed himself, with conscious inferiority, to shrink into nothing" (201–202). This scene is typical in that it features a complicated chain of knowing appraisal, of socially and sexually informed glances, as Evelina resents Sir Clement's "unrestrained curiosity" (201) when he finds her in such bourgeois company, and asks her questions with a disrespectful abruptness that sharpens his sense of her sexual vulnerability, her lack of a secure social position. But she watches Mr Smith watching Sir Clement, and her condescending sexual enemy becomes her class ally, since her conversations with this elegant aristocrat separate her from the likes of Mr Smith. Evelina does not see (as readers can) that Mr Smith's embarrassment is a version of her own deep inferiority in similar encounters with her social superiors, that she is in her turn being watched (and watching herself) for tell-tale signs of social awkwardness by others above her in the social order.

Evelina is deeply embarrassed, over and over again, by such bourgeois company and connections, who mirror her own shame at her own aspirations and ambitions and whose egregious social blunders intensify her own mistakes. Eager consumers of London's public pleasures, like Evelina only less discriminating, Tom Branghton and Mr Smith vie with one another to propose exciting spots for her to visit with them: George's at Hampstead, Don Saltero's at Chelsea, Sadler's Well, the Tower of London, the Monument, Vauxhall, Marybone – she has been to none of them, and Tom exclaims, "Why then you might as well not have come to London, for aught I see, for you've been no where" (187). Readers are expected to laugh at this undiscriminating vulgarity, but here and elsewhere in *Evelina* the differences between lower middle-class and upper-class enjoyments are a question of degree, and indeed when the Branghtons and Madame Duval take Evelina to Vauxhall and Marybone there is a promiscuous and, as it turns out, a dangerous mixing of classes at such places, with Sir Clement and even Orville making their appearance there.

In both these popular public spots, Evelina is menaced sexually and reduced to hysteria when she finds herself left alone and threatened by strangers. But she is also an appreciative if discriminating tourist who takes care to describe the particular delights that each place affords. At Vauxhall, for example, she finds the garden pretty but too formal. The effect is nonetheless enrapturing: "The trees, the numerous lights, and the company in the circle around the orchestra make a most brilliant and gay appearance; and, had I been with a party less disagreeable to me, I should have thought it a place formed for animation and pleasure" (193). And at Marybone, Evelina is equally judicious, finding the garden "neither striking for magnificence nor for beauty" but thrilling to the music and then to the fireworks display, which "was really beautiful, and told, with wonderful ingenuity, the story of Orpheus and Eurydice: but at the moment of the fatal look, which separated them for ever, there was such an explosion of fire, and so horrible a noise, that we all, as of one accord, jumpt hastily from the form, and ran away some paces, fearing that we were in danger of mischief, from the innumerable sparks of fire which glittered in the air" (232). *Evelina* dramatizes the intertwining of pleasures and dangers in the public world, where classes mix promiscuously and where the beautiful can turn out to be like the fireworks display, explosive and illusory. In several terrifying moments of distress and danger at public places like Vauxhall and Marybone all the social and moral polish that she has received, presumably, from Villars is threatened by the compulsions of pleasure-seeking in the promiscuous mixing of public places.

Evelina has beauty, brains, and even pluck, but the advancement of a young woman into the upper stratum of the leisure classes by virtue of such qualities is a subversive proposition – in pure terms, such as the moral novel proposes, something of an impossibility and certainly a scandal. In the implications that emerge in various scenes of panic and humiliation and in the case of Madame Duval, of brutal degradation at the hand of the boorish Captain Mirvan, *Evelina* is an astonishingly conservative book. Social ambition is met with ridicule and punishment, and even the heroine must be subjected to these terrors and embarrassments in public places to illustrate the dangers that accompany the pursuit of pleasures implicitly defined as the province of the privileged classes, who at their best know how to surround the infinite leisure which is their defining business with grace, elegance, and reserve.

Like her tragic predecessor, Clarissa, Evelina is only a teenager, at 17 two years younger than Richardson's heroine. Yet it is clearly anachronistic and inadequate to treat her story as solely an adolescent case history; Evelina is mature and sophisticated well beyond her years, and her story explores the intertwining of social and psychological adaptation required for her return to the privileged sphere to which she is partially affiliated by her birth. Patricia Meyer Spacks calls *Evelina* a pessimistic novel of adolescent accommodation in which the heroine's growth "leads her back towards childhood; the 'happy endings' of Burney novels reassert the charm and irresponsibility of the child as the greatest achievement to be hoped for by adolescents."[28] Indictments of the ideological failings (by our standards) of the more or less formulaic plot of *Evelina* fail to do justice to the mature realism of its sexual and social observations, to its tracing through the eyes of this wise 17-year-old how the lines of class power can be penetrated. Evelina is, of course, technically pure and perfectly chaste, but she is hardly immune to the hedonism that rules the world she has entered and in which she scores the greatest triumph imaginable in the securing of an aristocratic husband on the strength of her unsupplemented beauty and wit.

Burney's narrative goes out of its way to stress the singularity of Evelina's triumph. For example, Mrs Selwyn reports a conversation that she has overheard between Orville and Sir Clement, so that Evelina learns that Orville has come to value not only her beauty but her "modest worth, and fearful excellence" that have with "dangerous fascination" (347) stolen his soul. And when Orville asks Sir Clement what his intentions are toward Evelina, he responds that she is indeed "the loveliest of her sex," but wonders that his lordship would think he would ever marry "a girl of obscure birth, whose only dowry is her beauty, and who is evidently in a state of dependency" (347). One way to understand this conquest is to credit Orville for, in Gerard Barker's words, redeeming "his own decadent class" and "raising her above the social position her mother's imprudence had forfeited."[29] But the narrative belongs to Evelina, and the emphasis is upon the transformative effect that she has upon Orville, and he is the one who compromises his class standards in proposing marriage. *Evelina* is, to be sure, an eighteenth-century fairy tale with a Cinderella and a Prince Charming, but it is a fairy tale whose happy resolution is accomplished not by magic or fairy godmothers but by the heroine's special agency, that combination of luck, beauty, brains, and sheer perseverance that novels can grant to their heroines.

Cecilia (1782), Burney's second novel, is no fairy tale but a grim modern fable. Cecilia has inherited a fortune of ten thousand pounds from her parents and an income of three thousand pounds a year from her uncle, although she is not yet of age and has three official guardians. Unlike Evelina, whose problem is that she "earnestly wishes for, the advice and assistance of her friends" (306), Cecilia Beverley is surrounded by too many advisors and entangled in a web of circumstances. And, unlike Evelina, she is from the beginning a fully formed moral actor, not only rich and almost independent but, as the novel opens, self-consciously in search of a *modus vivendi* "to make at once a more spirited and more worthy use of the affluence, freedom, and power which she possessed."[30] Cecilia is led to make this resolution by her disgust at the dissipation that she observes at the London home of one of her three guardians, Mr Harrel, where she has chosen to live for the nine months until she comes into her inheritance. Finding no one at Harrel's to respect, Cecilia turns to her books and "secured to herself, for the future occupation of her leisure hours, the exhaustless fund of entertainment which reading, that richest, highest, and noblest source of intellectual enjoyment, perpetually affords" (27). She determines to adopt "a scheme of happiness at once rational and refined" (51) and to select as her friends "such as by their piety could elevate her mind, by their knowledge improve her understanding, or by their accomplishments and manners delight her affections" (51). And, finally, Cecilia sketches out a philanthropic dream: "A strong sense of DUTY, a fervent desire to ACT RIGHT, were the ruling characteristics of her mind" (52). The narrator's evocation of the satisfactions that Cecilia derives from her resolve shows that such an imaginary scene is really its own reward:

> Many and various, then, soothing to her spirit and grateful to her sensibility, were the scenes which her fancy delineated; now she supported an orphan, now softened the sorrows of a widow, now snatched from iniquity the feeble trembler at poverty, and now rescued from shame the proud struggler with disgrace. The prospect at once exalted her hopes, and enraptured her imagination; she regarded herself as an agent of Charity, and already in idea anticipated the rewards of a good and faithful delegate: so animating are the designs of disinterested benevolence! so pure is the bliss of intellectual philanthropy!
>
> (52)

Cecilia's desires are both rational and sentimental. She imagines using her power to choose good works and thereby to give herself the pleasures of emotional participation in the happiness of others. Like Samuel Johnson's Prince of Abyssinia in his moral tale, *Rasselas* (1759), Cecilia seeks a life of clear-eyed moral choices, and in that regard (like Johnson's characters) she responds to a lingering rationalist resistance in eighteenth-century literary culture to the sentimental ethics of which the novel is a great promoter. "If I had the choice of life," says Johnson's Rasselas as he listens to the poet Imlac's tales of the world beyond the enclosure called the Happy Valley in Abyssinia where they live in an imposed and unhappy paradise, "I should be able to fill every day with pleasure. I would injure no man, and should provoke no resentment: I would relieve every distress, and should enjoy the benedictions of gratitude. I would choose my friends among the wise, and my wife among the virtuous; and therefore should be in no danger from treachery, or unkindness."[31] But when Rasselas, accompanied by his sister, Nekayah, and by his advisor, Imlac, leaves the "tasteless tranquility" of the Happy Valley, the contradictory variety of the outside world defeats his plan to make a simple or definitive choice in life. The controlling irony of Johnson's fable is that the characters' aphorisms have a negative or paralyzing effect, as their experiences discover the balancing contradictions that Imlac warns Rasselas about before they leave the Happy Valley: "Inconsistencies … cannot both be right, but,

imputed to man, they may both be true" (56). As Rasselas and Nekayah
explore the varieties of life, they prove the justice of Imlac's observation
that "Very few … live by choice. Every man is placed in his present
condition by causes which acted without his foresight, and with which
he does not always willingly cooperate" (77). Johnson's tale renders in
general terms human recurrences such as novels dramatize in particular, intensely localized forms.

Cecilia also finds no purely moral and intellectual relationships nor
untainted and disinterested advisors, and her extensive philanthropy
reveals in her efforts later on the limits of local charity in the face of
systemic problems and of her own finite resources. As one might
expect, Cecilia finds difficulty in surrounding herself "with the society
of the wise, good, and intelligent," since "few answered this description,
and those few were with difficulty attained" (776). With the support of
the narrative's obtrusive essayistic decorum, Burney's somewhat frigidly
balanced third-person narration that largely excludes the raucous
chorus of class dialects featured in *Evelina*, Cecilia perseveres in her
choice of life, in spite of many obstacles and a number of horrendous
experiences that might well have taught her that moral independence
and pure agency are illusions supported by the verbal formulations of
the moralizing tradition (if not by Johnson's *Rasselas*). Such persistence
is a sign of Burney's longing for a distinct kind of independent heroine,
but of course at the same time this enormous novel pulls in the opposite
direction, and Cecilia is made to pay dearly for her temporary success
at moral integrity and self-control. Even at her most ambitiously philanthropic, Cecilia is largely contained by the self-seeking schemes of
others. Hemmed in by a network of designs on her and her fortune,
Cecilia cannot cancel her own entangling romantic destiny. The novel
traces instead her ultimate descent into confusion, perplexity, sorrow,
and an anguished suffering that leads her into madness and close to
martyrdom.[32] For all her considerable moral eloquence, that is to say,
Burney's Cecilia is for most of the novel, in spite of her resolute will,
moved toward the passive position of a suffering female icon rather like
Sheridan's Sidney Bidulph.

Cecilia is an interesting precursor of the great novels of the mid-nine-
teenth century: populated by intensely individualized characters who
seek, like the heroine (if not for her altruistic ends), to exercise their free
expressiveness and autonomy, the novel subordinates such striving to
the inherited weight of the past and the circumstantial force of a
complicated present conceived as a socioeconomic process that works
steadily against simple choice and personal agency. Margaret Anne
Doody observes that Cecilia's dreams of independence "have been

shaped by her own situation, including immediate psychological needs, but her entire situation is not just her psychological state, or even her personal background." Cecilia, says Doody, is both a participant in and a product of the society she lives in, and the reality that the book delivers is the ideological vicious circle that the middle-class novel specializes in revealing whereby free individuals are simultaneously produced by their social circumstances.[33]

The most obvious inheritance is Cecilia's legacy, which is hedged by the stipulation in her uncle's will that her husband must take her surname or she forfeits the £3,000 a year income that he leaves her.[34] The weight of her uncle's dead hand is also felt in the three guardians that he appointed for her till she comes of age: Mr Harrel, Mr Briggs, and Mr Delvile, each of whom complicates Cecilia's struggle to achieve maturity and independence, each of whom represents a particular sort of modern moral deformity: Harrel a wastrel and spendthrift, Briggs a rich miser who lives in squalor, Delvile a stupid but insolent and imperious snob. A child of pure privilege but legal dependence on these three guardians, Cecilia is hampered as well by that exaggerated isolation and improbable innocence with which heroines like her are routinely saddled: meditating how to help one of the potential objects of her philanthropy get on in life, Cecilia finds that "she could suggest nothing, for she was ignorant what was eligible to suggest. The stations and employments of men she only knew by occasionally hearing that such were their professions, and such their situations in life; but with the means and gradations by which they arose to them she was wholly unacquainted" (241). The deeply thoughtful Cecilia can only see the world as a *fait accompli*; her vision as an innocent woman precludes precisely that involvement in the socioeconomic world available to men. Cecilia will discover what readers are encouraged to envision: a multi-layered world of classes and occupations, of idiosyncratic personalities and economic interests in which everyone is maneuvering for advantage and in which Cecilia is in truth not so much an independent agent as a desirable object, sought after and manipulated by various men and also by her own inescapable and, in the end, irresistible emotional needs.

Burney focuses on how key characters are indistinguishable from their particular circumstances, so that the emphasis falls strongly on rendering the cancellation of individual initiative by the weight of the past. Such attention to the social construction of individuals, however unsystematic and instinctive, is striking if we look back to *Evelina*, where characters lack this historical and dynamic dimension and live almost purely in the pleasure-seeking present and are contained by the social and moral types that they tend to represent. Indeed, Burney's first novel is resolved happily when the past (the heroine's birthright) is finally attended to, but the narrative's main concern is wholehearted involvement in the pleasures, dangers, and possibilities of the urban here and now. *Cecilia* often enough brings us inside the complex and as yet unresolved histories and evolving personalities of its characters. Reflection is the essence of the action in *Cecilia*, but it is a thoughtfulness framed in terms of dense and particular social and psychological histories rather than in the generalized or universalized aphorisms of Johnson's *Rasselas*.

Mr Monckton, Cecilia's neighbor and unofficial advisor, displays the best grasp of the required social and historical necessity and also exemplifies the unfinished and unfulfilled personality that broods on the future's possibilities and dangers. He has set his spies to investigate Harrel's disgraceful profligacy and knows that Cecilia has been browbeaten into lending him over nine thousand pounds, borrowed at exorbitant interest from a Jewish moneylender. He knows, moreover, and tells the shocked Cecilia that Harrel had gambled these huge sums away and that his house was about to be seized by hordes of creditors – hence Harrel's suicide at Vauxhall, the single most spectacular event in the book. Monckton arrives to pay Cecilia's debt to the moneylender and to provide her with an explanation of Harrel's treachery. To Cecilia, Harrel had seemed "Expensive, indeed, and thoughtless and luxurious he appeared to me immediately," but she is appalled to find him "capable of every pernicious art of treachery and duplicity...his very flightiness and levity seemed incompatible with such hypocrisy" (425). Monckton's reply is worth quoting at length: he reduces the pathetic Harrel to an automaton, his career in dissipation and extravagance merely a response to what the reigning fashion pushed him into:

> "'His flightiness,' said Mr Monckton, "proceeded not from gaiety of heart, it was merely the effect of effort; and his spirits were as mechanical as his taste for diversion. He had not strong parts, nor were his vices the result of his passions; had economy been as much in fashion as extravagance, he would have been equally eager to practise it; he was a mere time-server, he struggled but to be *something*, and having neither talents nor sentiment to know *what*, he looked around him for any pursuit, and seeing distinction was more easily attained in the road to ruin than in any other, he galloped along it, thoughtless of being thrown when he came to the bottom, and sufficiently gratified in showing his horsemanship by the way."
>
> (425)

Cecilia is weighed down by pompous moral generalizing that inhibits action, but Monckton's speech is shrewdly specific. Burney's plot impels her characters, from virtuous and vicious motives, to make the attempt to ignore or contradict the generalizing restrictiveness of the narrator's (and the heroine's) moralizing style. Aphoristic brevity and finality give way to novelistic dilation and uncertain temporality. These issues are raised with special clarity in an exchange between a Mr Belfield and Monckton. The former is a merchant's son who has been educated beyond his station at Eton and the university, gone bankrupt in the business he has inherited from his father, failed at several occupations, and at last become a manual day-laborer in the country. Now resolved to turn Grub Street writer, Belfield has a renewed understanding of his limitations: "We may fight against partial prejudices, and by spirit and fortitude we may overcome them; but it will not do to war with the general tenor of education. We may blame, despise, regret as we please, but customs long established, and habits long indulged, assume an empire despotic, though their power is but prescriptive" (718). Made unfit for simple labor by his education, Belfield turns writer to express his "independence," "to maintain it by those employments for which my education has fitted me" (719). To all this, Monckton responds contemptuously that "independence" is "a mere idle dream of romance and enthusiasm; without existence in nature, without possibility in life" (719). Mockton offers in place of Belfield's idealism a picture of systemic dependence and compulsion, as he asks sarcastically whether anyone "can pretend to assert his thoughts, words, and actions are exempt from control? even where interest, which you so much disdain, interferes not" (719).

In their actions, Belfield and Monckton illustrate the limitations of the positions they occupy in this debate. Belfield's "independence" is a series of failed dependencies; following an unsuccessful stint as a law student and an army officer, he has been bankrupted by a corrupt manager of his business, and he has been fired as tutor to the children of a lord because of his pride. Belfield's string of failures marks him as deluded individualist, distorted by his inappropriate education, brought up to think that he belongs to the leisure class but lacking the wherewithal to sustain his membership in it. Monckton, on the other hand, is the younger son of a noble family, "a man of parts, information and sagacity; to great native strength of mind he added a penetrating knowledge of the world, and to faculties the most skilful of investigating the character of every other, a dissimulation the most profound in concealing his own" (3). Impatient for wealth, he has married a rich dowager, "whose age, though sixty-seven, was but among the smaller species of her evil properties, her disposition being far more repulsive than her wrinkles" (3). Monckton waits in vain for his elderly wife to die, even as he hopes to marry the rich and beautiful Cecilia. In place of Belfield's ingenuous independence, Monckton bows to economic necessity and seeks to serve his own ultimate interests. The narrator warns us that Monckton's "selfish cunning" is short sighted, that in "aiming no further than at the gratification of the present moment, it obscures the evils of the future, while it impedes the perception of integrity and honour" (4).

Like virtually all of the characters in *Cecilia*, Belfield and Monckton help readers understand the heroine. They occupy untenable positions and contribute in their distinct miscalculations to the novel's catalogue of varieties of self-destructive behavior which constitute the web of circumstances that ensnares and nearly destroys the heroine. Acting as a friend, Monckton seeks to manage Cecilia's future for his own ultimate ends. Acting as a friend and potential patron, Cecilia tries to help Belfield's impoverished mother and sister and to advance his prospects after he is wounded in a duel with one of her aspiring suitors, Sir Robert Floyer, a duel provoked by a quarrel over Cecilia at the opera. These intertwined relationships are part of the larger network that this huge novel traces, and its varieties of interaction can be grouped under just two main categories: selfish manipulation for material advantage, and various forms of altruism and service to a larger ideal, including philanthropy and moral self-development becomes Cecilia's chief mission in life.

Cecilia's noble self-sacrifice (mingled with a humanizing resentment and her own class pride) is canceled when she is at last persuaded to a secret marriage with Mortimer Delvile, her guardian's son. With that crucial step, she relinquishes the identity that Burney has fashioned for her in the tight circle of possibilities open for female upper-class self-expression: scornful resistance to marriage as a woman's defining moment and the embrace of activist philanthropy (Clarissa's definition of female independence, we may remember). Supplemented by intellectual and moral seriousness that rejects the trivial pleasure-seeking of the women of her class that she encounters in London, Cecilia's heroic identity as paragon involves rigorous adherence to two kinds of potentially contradictory duty: to her own emotional cum intellectual attraction to Mortimer (Mr Right, as it were, for Burney perpetuates, albeit with some reluctance and delay, the romance myth of one perfect soul mate) and to her own sense of ethical integrity that impels her to reject marriage to Mortimer in the face of his parents' opposition. Cecilia's individuality and the pathos that it generates lies in this uncompromising integrity and her increasing isolation as she resists the deepest currents of her own attraction for Mortimer. Of all the characters in *Cecilia*, only she aspires to act out of a categorical ethical imperative, an essentially unmotivated or disinterested morality. Even Albany, her crazed mentor in philanthropy, has a sinful and tragic sexual history that accounts for his vision of contemporary moral corruption and drives him to seek out objects worthy of charity to expiate his past crimes of seduction and betrayal. In the larger contexts of novelistic narrative where character is defined by its entanglements in social circumstances and of the woman's novel in which innocent passivity in the face of those determinants signifies virtue, Burney's problem is how to render Cecilia's transition from integral virtue and eloquent morality to emotional intensity and pathetic involvement, how to reconcile moral intelligence with emotional vulnerability of an extreme and specifically female sort, how to turn Cecilia from moral agent to helpless victim and to wrench the narrative from resistance to romantic ideology to melodramatic surrender to its imperatives.

When Cecilia finds herself residing for a time with the Delviles at their decaying castle, Mortimer rises in her esteem until within a fortnight she is "conscious her happiness was no longer in her own power" (244). Love for Mortimer brings Cecilia to "a scene entirely new" in which "neither the exertion of the most active benevolence, nor the steady course of the most virtuous conduct, sufficed any longer to wholly engage her thoughts, or constitute her felicity" (245). However involuntary such a "loss of mental freedom" may be, it is still "approved by her principles and confirmed by her judgment" (245). The lingering instability in such an attraction is the main business of the last half of the novel. Long after Monckton has arranged an interruption of their first attempt at a secret marriage (causing Cecilia to change her mind and to reject her rash consent to so irregular a proceeding), when she has at last entered upon her majority and financial independence, young Delvile appears. "A sight so unexpected, so unaccountable, so wonderful, after an absence so long, and to which they were mutually bound, almost wholly over-powered Cecilia from surprise and a thousand other feelings" (780). Delvile has proposed to his parents that he marry Cecilia if she agrees to give up the fortune left her by her uncle and in taking the name of Delvile brings to the marriage only the ten thousand pounds from her parents. Having been treacherously informed by Monckton that she has been stripped of that money by the miserable Harrel, Delvile's father agrees to this. When Mortimer learns the truth from Cecilia, he is outraged: "to consent to a plan which *could* not be accepted! – to make *me* a tool to offer indignity to Miss Beverley!

– He has released me from his power by so erroneous an exertion of it" (792). So Cecilia is offered a cruel choice: marriage to Mortimer and loss of her fortune or the serenity of philanthropic independence: "And thus again was wholly broken the tranquillity of Cecilia; new hopes, however faint, awakened all her affections, and strong fears, but too reasonable, interrupted her repose. Her destiny, once more, was as undecided as ever, and the expectations she had crushed, retook posses-sion of her heart" (793). With Mrs Delvile's reluctant "separate consent" (802), they are finally married, and Cecilia wonders, after all she has been through, if such happiness can be real: "To be actually united with Delvile! to be his with the full consent of his mother, – to have him her's, beyond the power of his father, – she could not recon-cile it with possibility; she fancied it a dream, – but a dream from which she wished not to awake" (814).

In fact, it is the beginning of Cecilia's final nightmare. Events now crowd the narrative, and various plots and purposes collide at the very end: Mortimer discovers that it was Monckton who told his father a distorted version of Cecilia's loss of her fortune to the moneylenders, and after wounding Monckton (perhaps mortally) in a duel, he is forced to flee to the continent; Cecilia has to surrender her estate when her marriage to Delvile is revealed by an unfortunate coincidence and a distant relative, Mr Eggleston, becomes the heir and demands imme-diate possession. Burney draws the scene with a melodramatic antithesis that predicts worse things to come:

> from being an object of envy and admiration, sunk into distress, and threatened with disgrace; from being everywhere caressed, and by every voice praised, she blushed to be seen, and expected to be censured; and, from being generally regarded as an example of happiness, and a model of virtue, she was now in one moment to appear to the world, an outcast from her own house, yet received into no other! a bride, unclaimed by a husband! an HEIRESS dispossessed of all wealth!
>
> (848)

And worse things do come to pass for Cecilia, all of them – like the preceding events here at the disastrous conclusion – the result of a furi-ously accelerated chain of coincidences and external accidents, the transformation of the narrative from a leisurely moral debate into a tale of compulsions and irreversible consequences. Resolved to follow Mortimer to the Continent, Cecilia goes to London and turns to the well-traveled Belfield for advice on how to hire a French-speaking servant. But unexpectedly Delvile returns, finds Cecilia closeted with Belfield and, thanks to insinuations about their intimacy offered by Belfield's vulgar mother, he flies into a jealous rage and orders Cecilia to go to his father's. Fearing that Mortimer means to challenge Belfield to a duel, Cecilia in a hackney coach searches frantically for them. Urban confusion suddenly intrudes, as the drunken coachman demands his fare and a mob gathers. Bursting from the crowd, the frantic Cecilia, still dressed in the riding habit that she wore on her journey from the country, roams the London streets:

> She called aloud upon Delvile as she flew to the end of the street. No Delvile was there! – she turned the corner; yet saw nothing of him; she still went on, though unknowing whither, the distraction of her mind every instant growing greater, from the inflammation of fatigue, heat, and disappointment. She was spoken to repeatedly; she was even caught once or twice by her riding habit; but she forced herself along by her own vehement rapidity, not hearing what was said, not heeding what was thought. Delvile, bleeding by the arm of Belfield, was the image before her eyes, and took such full possession of her senses, that still, as she ran on, she fancied it in view. She scarce touched the ground; she scarce felt her own motion; she seemed as if endued with supernatural speed, gliding from place to place, from street to street, with no consciousness of any plan, and following no other direction than that of darting forward wherever there was most room, and turning back when she met with any obstruction; till, quite spent and exhausted, she abruptly ran into a yet open shop, where, breathless and panting, she sunk upon the floor, and, with a look disconsolate and helpless, sat for some time without speaking.
>
> (875–876)

Supposing that she is a lunatic escaped from a private asylum, the shop-keepers recognize her social class from her clothes, and decide to hold her for the expected reward: "'She's a gentlewoman, sure enough,' said the mistress of the house, 'because she's got such good things on'" (876). Cecilia passes into madness and incoherent raving, languishing for two days, locked in an upstairs room by the shopkeeping couple, rescued at last when Albany, her crazed mentor in philanthropy, turns out to live in the neighborhood. When Delvile arrives with a doctor, Cecilia is raving mad, imagining at her worst that her rescuers intend to bury her alive with Mr Monckton. She falls into a deep stupor, and the doctor fears the worst. But in the end she revives, physically diminished but morally intact. The novel ends, at last, with Cecilia enjoying in Mortimer's love and the affection of Mrs Delvile "all the happiness human life seems capable of receiving: – yet human it was, and as such imperfect," as she contemplates her lost fortune and "grateful with general felicity, bore partial evil with cheerfullest resignation" (919).

The modern reader may well ask at the end of this harrowing *via dolorosa* what eighteenth-century readers saw in such a heroine. For the Marquis de Sade just a few years later, "the misfortunes of virtue" (the subtitle of *Justine; ou les Malheurs de la vertue* (1791)) provided a delicious spectacle of sexually arousing female suffering, and Sade's overt exploitation of the theme is in a sense simply his subversive (and "sadistic") extraction of what was always implicit in the late eighteenth-century British novel of woman's pain. Cecilia is systematically humiliated and stripped of her financial and emotional stability, and the narrative balances its admiration for her resistance to female stereotypes with an extended punishment that relieves her of those defining strengths and transforms her into a suffering physical entity. From a life dominated by exalted moral and emotional self-exploration, Cecilia passes, disastrously, to self-management in a world of limited financial means and difficult living arrangements. From an ethereal and cerebral beauty pondering the decadence of modern life and manners, she becomes an upper-class physical specimen, recognized by the lower classes by her dress. The full weight of novelistic specificity as it locates individuals by class and fortune, which she has to some extent evaded for so long, comes crashing down. Burney's purpose may well have been to dramatize the inherent injustice surrounding the contemporary cultural meaning of the leisure-class woman, who is damned for triviality and conformity to female stereotypes and damned even more conclusively for non-conformity. But the effect in strictly novelistic terms of Cecilia's transformation is to render very powerfully if not quite coherently the force of psychosocial circumstances and to validate the expressive power of the suffering female body at the expense of the luxurious possession of a mind and spirit. In place of the moralizing fluency of both narrator and various characters, the sublime spectacle of female virtue in specifically physical and physiological distress turns out to be the only effective reproach to the corrupt social scene that the novel evokes. As Delvile exclaims over her motionless body: "Oh, my Cecilia! lovely, however altered! sweet even in the arms of death and insanity! and dearer to my tortured heart in this calamitous state, than in all thy pride of health and beauty!" (897).

NOTES

1 Tobias George Smollett, *The Expedition of Humphry Clinker*, introduction and notes by Thomas R. Preston, text ed. O.M. Brack (Athens, GA, and London, University of Georgia Press, 1990), p. 126.

2 Cheryl Turner, *Living by the Pen: Women Writers in the Eighteenth Century* (London and New York, Routledge, 1992), p. 38.

3 See my *Popular Fiction Before Richardson: Narrative Patterns 1700–1739* (Oxford, Clarendon Press, 1969), pp. 210–261 for a discussion of the works of these three novelists.

4 Jane Spencer, *The Rise of the Woman Novelist: From Aphra Behn to Jane Austen* (Oxford, Basil Blackwell, 1986), pp. 76–77.

5 Spencer, *The Rise of the Woman Novelist*, p. 77.

6 G.J. Barker-Benfield, *The Culture of Sensibility: Sex and Society in Eighteenth-century Britain* (Chicago, University of Chicago Press, 1992), p. 49.

7 J.G.A. Pocock, *Virtue, Commerce, and History* (Cambridge, Cambridge University Press, 1985), p. 114.

8 Laura Brown, *Ends of Empire: Woman and Ideology in Early Eighteenth-century English Literature* (Ithaca and London, Cornell University Press, 1993), pp. 119–20.

9 Janet Todd, *The Sign of Angellica: Women, Writing and Fiction, 1660–1800* (New York, Columbia University Press, 1989), p. 4.

10 Eliza Haywood, *The History of Miss Betsy Thoughtless*, introduction by Dale Spender (London and New York, Pandora Press, 1986), p. 195. All further page references in the text are to this edition.

11 Charlotte Lennox, *The Female Quixote*, ed. Margaret Dalziel, with an introduction by Margaret Anne Doody (Oxford and New York, Oxford University Press, 1989), p. 5. All further page references in the text are to this edition.

12 Ronald Paulson, *Satire and the Novel in Eighteenth-century England* (New Haven and London, Yale University Press, 1967), p. 277.

13 Colin Campbell, *The Romantic Ethic and the Spirit of Modern Consumerism* (Oxford, Basil Blackwell, 1987), p. 65.

14 Campbell, *The Romantic Ethic*, p. 72.

15 Campbell, *The Romantic Ethic*, pp. 89–90.

16 Nancy Armstrong, *Desire and Domestic Fiction: A Political History of the Novel* (New York, Oxford University Press, 1987), p. 5.

17 It reached a second edition within three months, and a fifth edition appeared in 1796.

18 *Boswell's Life of Johnson*, ed. George Birkbeck Hill and L.F. Powell, Vol. I, pp. 389–90, n.4. Modern readers may not see Johnson's remark as a compliment, and I can testify that re-reading the novel to write about it was a painful experience. One way to understand Johnson's comment is that the book's tracing of female miseries is an excessive reminder to male readers of the injustice built into patriarchal arrangements. Since the book is still

relatively unknown, in spite of renewed attention lately by some revisionist critics, and since its pathetic effects depend upon its elaborate spiral of complicated suffering, a detailed plot summary seems in order.

19 Frances Sheridan, *Memoirs of Miss Sidney Bidulph*, ed. Patricia Köster and Jean Coates Cleary (Oxford and New York, Oxford University Press, 1995), p. 383. All further page references in the text are to this edition.

20 Sheridan published a sequel, *Conclusion of the Memoirs of Miss Sidney Bidulph*, in 1767, the year of her death, which traces the lives of Sidney's daughters, Dolly and Cecilia, and Faulkland's son by Miss Burchell. Margaret Anne Doody maintains that Sheridan's originality lay in tracing the inexorable effects of the past upon the present. See her "Frances Sheridan: morality and annihilated time," in Mary Anne Schofield and Cecilia Macheski (eds) *Fetter'd or Free: British Women Novelists 1670–1815* (Athens, OH, and London, Ohio University Press, 1986), pp. 346–350.

21 Doody, "Frances Sheridan: morality and annihilated time," p. 345.

22 Frances Burney, *Evelina or The History of a Young Lady's Entrance into the World*, ed. Edward A. Bloom and Lillian D. Bloom (Oxford, Oxford University Press, 1982), p. 15. All further page references in the text are to this edition.

23 *The Early Journals and Letters of Fanny Burney*, Vol. III, ed. Lars E. Troide and Stewart J. Cooke (Oxford, Clarendon Press, 1994), p. 1.

24 *Early Journals and Letters of Fanny Burney*, p. 52. Hester Lynch Thrale was married to the wealthy brewer, Henry Thrale, and in her suburban house in Streatham presided over a salon that included at its center the great critic and moralist Samuel Johnson. Burney was introduced to Johnson at the Thrales', and he became her friend and one of the first champions of *Evelina*.

25 Kristina Straub, *Divided Fictions: Fanny Burney and Feminine Strategy* (Lexington, KY, University Press of Kentucky, 1987), pp. 7, 82.

26 Margaret Anne Doody, to my mind, goes too far in linking Burney to Austen and Dickens as a social critic who "attacks society's principles" and "offers not a reflection but an examination of her society in its structure, functions, and beliefs." What is interesting about *Evelina*, at least, is that the moral critique of society's deeper principles and structures is subordinated to the heroine's triumphant accommodation to them. See *Frances Burney: The Life in the Works* (New Brunswick, NJ, Rutgers University Press, 1988), p. 3.

27 William Dowling, "*Evelina* and the Genealogy of Literary Shame,"*Eighteenth-century Life*, 1992, vol. 16, pp. 212, 213.

28 Patricia Meyer Spacks, *The Female Imagination* (New York, Alfred A. Knopf, 1975), p. 129.

29 Gerard Barker, *Grandison's Heirs: The Paragon's Progress in the Late Eighteenth-century English Novel* (Newark, DE, University of Delaware Press, 1985), p. 83.

30 Frances Burney, *Cecilia or Memoirs of an Heiress*, with an introduction by Judy Simons (New York and Harmondsworth, Viking Penguin, 1986), p. 51. All further page references in the text are to this edition.

31 Samuel Johnson, *The History of Rasselas, Prince of Abyssinia*, ed. D.J. Enright (London, Penguin, 1985), p. 66. All further page references in the text are to this edition.

32 Kristina Straub calls Cecilia's life plan "a *Rasselas*-like search" for the "occupations and employments best suited to genteel female happiness" – a
conventional mix of philosophical narrative and romantic fiction. But to
equate Cecilia's high seriousness with the caution learned by previous heroines like Richardson's Harriet Byron and Haywood's Betsy Thoughtless
seems wrong-headed. Cecilia has an intellectual weight and philanthropic
ambition worthy of Clarissa. See *Divided Fictions*, p. 110.

33 Doody, *Frances Burney*, p. 118.

34 It is worth remembering that this is a substantial sum, the modern equivalent of about $300,000, and a great deal more in terms of
eighteenth-century purchasing power.

8

SENTIMENTAL NARRATIVE

Philanthropy and fiction

Writing on Queen Anne's birthday, an occasion to display jewelry and to wear new clothes, Richard Steele in *The Spectator* is struck by the gulf between the wealthy few and "the Multitudes that pass by them," by the grotesque disparity between the resplendent rich man and the starving beggar:

> When a Man looks about him, and with Regard to Riches and Poverty beholds some drawn in Pomp and Equipage, and they and their very Servants with an Air of Scorn and Triumph overlooking the Multitude that pass by them: and in the same Street a Creature of the same Make crying out in the Name of all that is good and sacred to behold his Misery, and give him some Supply against Hunger and Nakedness, but who would believe these two Beings were of the same Species?[1]

This vivid contrast is a preface to his plea for "Charity-Schools," a project to provide poor children with a rudimentary education, enough literacy to read the Bible and to write their names. In the fourteen years since the movement was launched, Steele complains, it has found only limited support, and he exhorts "any Lady in a Hoop-Petticoat" to give "the Price of one half Yard of the Silk toward cloathing, feeding and instructing" poor girls. Such charity will have a cosmetic effect, he jokes, giving the gorgeous lady's "Features a nobler Life on this illustrious Day, than all the Jewels that can hang in her Hair, or can be clustered in her Bosom." For male readers, Steele offers more serious reasons. Charity schools will produce a better class of servants, purged of their resentments, grateful to their masters, trained in good manners:

> A good Man might have a Knowledge of the whole Life of the Persons he designs to take into his Home for his own Service,

or that of his Family or Children, long before they were admitted. This would create endearing Dependencies; and the Obligation would have a paternal Air in the Master, who would be relieved from much Care and Anxiety from the Gratitude and Diligence of an humble Friend attending him as his Servant.

Steele's outrage at social inequality slides into sentimental paternalism; helping the poor will help to create a reliable and tractable servant class. Steele observes the gaping social wounds whereby beggar and rich man belong to different species, but instead of taking the logical next step into social critique, he exchanges his analytical distance for an idealized scene of female benevolence and male paternalism.

The charity school movement was a philanthropic failure: it offered poor children only token literacy and sought to control and pacify the deprived rather than to enlighten them and give them opportunities for improvement. Steele's complicated response to the street theater of social inequity is compromised by something like the same contradictions; the distance between the intensity of his concern for the poor and his condescending resolution reveals a conceptual gap between the particular experience of injustice and a grasp of its causes and implications. Poverty and misery are apprehended but transformed by sympathy and benevolence, offering Steele in this case a vision of a perfected patriarchal order in which servants become friends and family and naked beggars, somehow, disappear.

The sentimental novel that flourishes from the 1740s onwards reveals a similar confusion in its approach to social problems. By cultivating private sympathy and self-indulgent emotional responses to misery and injustice, fiction offers a controlling evasion or consoling moral gesture that stands in place of analytical understanding or systemic criticism. The sentimentalism that informs the novel, as John Mullan observes, implies in its very form "a contract, by the terms of which a reader was set apart from the anti-social vices or institutions which the novels were able to represent."[2] Mullan contends that eighteenth-century novels, and especially those featuring or promoting scenes of sentiment and sensibility, are a form of cultural wish-fulfillment in the face of early modern conditions in which traditional sociability was painfully experienced by many as fading fast, giving way to reorganized social relationships dominated by the impersonality of the cash nexus and the rapacity of possessive individualism. For Mullan, the British novel and moral philosophy in the middle of the century seek to produce (or model or stage) in writing "society as a scheme of consensus and unanimity" and to warn "against the forces or habits which threaten such a scheme."[3] Mullan points, for example, to Hume's reconceptualizing of the passions in *A Treatise of Human Nature* (1739), a revision of Hobbes' and Mandeville's account of them as essentially selfish and anti-social, whereby "passion is made less dangerous and becomes not appetite but sentiment."[4] In a passage from Book II of the *Treatise* ("Of the Passions"), he ascribes "our esteem for the rich and powerful" and our natural "contempt" for "poverty and meanness" to nothing less than "the principle of sympathy by which we enter into the sentiments of the rich and poor, and partake of their pleasure and uneasiness."[5] A tropism for pleasure, comfort, and riches is for Hume the essence of humanity and the sustaining cause of social order:

> Riches give satisfaction to their possessor; and this satisfaction is convey'd to the beholder by the imagination, which produces an idea resembling the original impression in force and vivacity. This agreeable idea or impression is connected with love, which is an agreeable passion. It proceeds from a thinking conscious being, which is the very object of love. From this relation of impressions, and identity of ideas, the passion arises. ... The best method of reconciling us to this opinion is to take a general survey of the universe, and observe the force of sympathy thro' the whole animal creation, and the easy communication of sentiments from one thinking being to another. In all creatures, that prey not on others, and are not agitated with violent passions, there appears a remarkable desire of company, which associates them together, without any advantages they can ever propose to reap from their union. This is still more conspicuous in man, as being the creature of the universe, who has the most ardent desire of society, and is fitted for it by the most advantages. We can form no wish, which has not a reference to society. A perfect solitude is, perhaps, the greatest punishment we can suffer. Every pleasure languishes when enjoy'd a-part from company, and every pain becomes more cruel and intolerable. Whatever other passion we may be actuated by; pride, ambition, avarice, curiosity, revenge, or lust; the soul or animating principle of them all is sympathy; nor would they have any force, were we to abstract entirely from the thoughts and sentiments of others.

(362–363)

Hume's sympathy is a more neutral term than it is for other writers of the time and, as he describes it, seems not purely or necessarily benevolent in its implications. Humean sympathy is a selfish and sustaining need, an empathy that even the worst humans have with their fellows by which they understand their own desires as they are embodied in others. All self-expression requires an object or a relationship with another, and there is "sympathy" in all human interconnection, even violent and selfish versions of it.

In *The Theory of Moral Sentiments* (1759), Adam Smith proposes that ethical action requires our removal from passionate involvement as we view our own conduct from the perspective of an impartial spectator, "the inhabitant of the breast, the man within, the great judge and arbiter of our conduct" who "calls to us, with a voice capable of astonishing the most presumptuous of our passions, that we are but one of the multitude."[6] Without this internalized spectator, moral chaos would ensue:

> every passion would, upon most occasions, rush headlong, if I may say so, to its own gratification. Anger would follow the suggestions of its own fury; fear those of its own violent agitations. Regard to no time or place would induce vanity to refrain from the loudest and most impertinent ostentation; or voluptuousness from the most open, indecent, and scandalous indulgence. Respect for what are, or for what ought to be, or for what upon a certain condition, would be, the sentiments of other people, is the sole principle which, upon most occasions, overawes all those mutinous and turbulent passions into that tone and temper which the impartial spectator can enter into and sympathize with.
>
> (262–263)

Smith's "impartial spectator" shifts Hume's vision of universal sympathy to a controlled positioning to serve a self-interest (implicitly economic) that will be endangered by the passions. Smith's treatise emphasizes the turbulence of passions that, as he evokes them here, have a strong contemporary reference to controversial modern habits of consumption ("impertinent ostentation") and luxury. Eighteenth-century sentimental fiction examines these distinct moral and psychosocial positions, positing with Hume a sympathetic human essence and a driving instinct for society (and not always for benign purposes) and, simultaneously and paradoxically, depicting with Smith a moral arena of specifically contemporary difficulty in which feeling can be dangerous or destructive and in which social restraints on natural passions are crucial. Novels may be said to specialize in making manifest what philosophers occlude in their theoretical search for universals: a specific historical accounting of the many ways that virtue, vice, sentiment, and passion are playing themselves out here and now as you read. Such fiction is often enough melodramatic and for most modern readers insufferably lachrymose, populated by impossible paragons and cardboard villains, deeply improbable by current standards; but such features of sentimental fiction can be understood as expressive devices, as it were, for responding to modern social conditions of moral breakdown whose urgency is underlined by melodramatic representation.

Hume and Smith, essentially optimistic philosophers, see moral action as inevitable, but the sentimental novel tends to dramatize it as rare, indeed endangered to the point of near extinction. The sentimental novel records a crisis in which such action is increasingly precious, in need of promotion and exaltation through heroic exemplars. And yet the term "sentimental novel" is broadly uninformative. Most eighteenth-century fiction explores moral problems, meditating on the difficulty of regulating the passions and navigating virtuously through a vicious and unjust world. Male and (especially) female paragons in this fiction are meant to provoke intense emotional involvement in readers by their complicated distress or marvelous deliverance into wealth, love, and happiness. Certain novels can usefully be labeled "sentimental" because they quite deliberately extend or intensify such involvement, moving away from various kinds of thematic coherence or moral and intellectual resolution. G.A. Starr identifies the spontaneity and moral simplicity that define the sentimental novel when he notes that in place of other novels' tracing of development through progressive experiences, sentimental fiction tends to ignore process and growth, to prefer moral melodrama to complexity or ambiguity, and to idealize impulse and emotional immediacy over moral or intellectual discrimination. Starr also observes that sentimentalism tends "to leave the existing social hierarchy intact or stronger than ever" and is nothing less than a form of fairly stylized pastoral for a privileged class of readers.[7]

But Starr's generalizations about the sentimental novel miss a crucial feature of three of the most successful of such fictions, Sarah Fielding's *David Simple* (1744), Samuel Richardson's *Sir Charles Grandison* (1754), and Henry Brooke's *The Fool of Quality* (1766–1772). Each of these presents the history of a community as much as the story of an individual: each subordinates the exploration of the titular character's personality as such to a dramatization of how that character's history projects a community or constructs an ethical group within the larger society. That titular individual's improbable simplicity, purity, goodness, or philanthropy serve in their very rigidity and clarity to qualify him as a moral leader and to set off the opposing negative qualities and moral murkiness in the larger social world. In so doing, these novels simplify and intensify a tendency inherent in relatively non-sentimental novels with which they share the stage: eighteenth-century novels of the various kinds that I have surveyed in previous chapters may be said to measure experience as a test for its protagonists and to reward them for refusing to accommodate themselves to its complexities and compromises. Personality or character for this fiction, whether comic or tragic in its circumstances, aspires to stability rather than process, set more or less on vice or virtue, with action affirming or revealing that disposition; discovery of moral potential and its self-expression in sentimental action rather than development in the nineteenth- and twentieth-century sense of the word seems a more accurate description of its understanding of moral psychology and social conditioning. Sentimental novels, in this context, differ in degree rather than in kind from what we now think of as the main tradition of eighteenth-century fiction. In their didactic single-mindedness and their melodramatic intensity, they pose a problem for late twentieth-century readers accustomed to value representations of moral uncertainty and the rigid separation of the ethical and the social realms. These novels by Fielding, Richardson, and Brooke can serve as revealing examples of the problem we face in reading sentimental novels and as opportunities for understanding their appeal.

Sarah Fielding's *David Simple* is bound to strike a modern reader as intolerably maudlin as it traces David's search to meet a "real Friend," that is to say "a human Creature capable of Friendship; by which Word he meant so perfect a Union of Minds, that each should consider himself but as a part of one entire Being; a little Community, as it were, of two, to the Happiness of which all the Actions of both should tend with an absolute disregard of any selfish or separate interest" (26–27).[8] As Sarah's brother labels it in his preface to the 1744 edition which he revised, such desire is a "noble Passion" (7), and Sarah herself calls David "an Enthusiast ... in this point only as mad as Quixotte himself could be with Knight Errantry" (27). *David Simple* marches readers through an escalating series of betrayals and calamities, beginning with his brother's forged version of their father's will which deprives David of his fair share of the family fortune. Restored to affluence by the death of his uncle, David begins his quest for a true friend and thinks he has found one in Mr Orgueil. What he quickly learns about the world literally "amazes" David, as one Mr Spatter reveals the secret springs of behavior in his friend, Mr Orgueil, one of those who "live in a continual war with their Passions, subdue their Appetites, and act up to whatever they think right; they make it their business in all Companies, to exalt the Dignity of human Nature as high as they can; that is, to prove Men are capable, if it was not their own fault, of arriving to a great degree of Perfection, which they heartily consent every one should believe *they themselves* have done" (74). This worldly Spatter conducts David through a satirically observed London scene, and our hero is disgusted not only by what he sees but by the cynical teachings of his guide who, he learns, has been ridiculing him behind his back.

David Simple is conventional satire, but the book's originality lies in the hero's longing for ethical purity by resisting absorption into the complicated world that he experiences. Smith's impartial spectator or man in the breast is for David's antagonists nothing more than a cunning desire to appear virtuous, a degraded form of sociability. From this cynical philosophical survey of human nature and society, Fielding turns her hero and her readers to direct observation and vicarious participation in unmitigated and flagrant misery. In effect, this is her self-conscious refusal of generalized social and moral understanding, a turn or shift in emphasis from the narrative knowledge promised by the allegorical characters that David encounters like Orgueil, Spatter, and Varnish to the affecting immediacy of the tableau of wretchedness and cruelty that introduces David to Camilla and Valentine. Having taken "ordinary Lodging" and dressed in "a mean Habit" as he observes the depressingly "mercenary Views" of the "Lower Sort of People," David hears his landlady scolding above stairs and when he climbs to the garret, this is what he sees:

> There lay on a Bed (or rather on a parcel of Rags patched together, to which the Mistress of the House *chose* to give the *Name* of a Bed) a young Man, looking as pale as Death, with his Eyes sunk in his Head, and hardly able to breathe, covered with half a dirty Rug, which would scarce come round him. On one Side of him sat holding him by the Hand, a young Woman in an old Silk Gown, which looked as if it had been a good one; but so tattered, that it would barely cover her with Decency. Her countenance was become wan with Affliction, and Tears stood in her Eyes, which she seemed unwilling to let fall, lest she should add to the Sorrow of the Man she sat by, and which, however, she was not able to restrain. The Walls were bare, and broke in many places in such a manner, that they were scarce sufficient to keep out the Weather. The

> Landlady stood over them, looking like a Fury, and swearing
> 'she would have her *Money*; that she did not understand what
> People meant by coming to lodge in other Folks Houses,
> without paying them for it'.
>
> (125–126)

"Struck dumb at this Scene," David rescues this brother and sister, his heart overflowing, "his Sensations ... too strong to leave him the free Use of his Reason," and learns their story from Camilla, a tale of a wicked young stepmother, Livia, who has alienated them from their father by accusing them of incest. Eventually, David marries Camilla and Valentine marries Cynthia, a young woman whom David had earlier befriended. In due course the perfidious Livia dies and Valentine, Camilla, and their father are reconciled. In spite of numerous obstacles, this first part of *David Simple* concludes, these characters (and their children) form a "little Society ... in the true Proof of each other's love" (304) and illustrate against the grain of the invariable self-seeking that all have hitherto encountered that "real Happiness" is attainable if everyone "would perform the Part allotted him by *Nature*, or his *Station in Life*, with a sincere Regard to the Interest and Pleasure of the Whole" (304).

Nine years later, Fielding published the sequel to this first part, "Volume the Last," in which all such happiness is dismantled by a series of heart-rending fatal disasters for this "little Family of Love" (372). By the bleak end, his friend, Valentine, his wife, all his children but one, are dead. David becomes on his own deathbed a Christianized Job, who welcomes even the death of his beloved wife, Camilla ("That I have lost my *Camilla* is my Pleasure, – that she has gained by that Loss, softens every Pain" (432)), but these final consolations do not cancel what has been a sentimental indulgence in the spectacle of unmerited poverty, betrayal, and untimely death. There is a balance in *David Simple* (or perhaps a tension) between an outraged rehearsal of nearly universal moral depravity (an intellectual as much as an emotional project) and the purely sentimental representation of suffering virtue and outraged innocence whereby the reader's agility at Christian understanding and joyful acceptance of outrageous suffering is put to a severe test. Or perhaps Fielding's strategy is to use this Christian paradox to neutralize any guilt attaching to the luxuriously self-indulgent rehearsals of ever more intense and morbid pathos that is her novel's main attraction. Even the most pious of Christian readers, I would guess, found it difficult to keep steadily in mind that the last shall be first and that death is a joyful release to heavenly bliss. David's deathbed speeches are eloquent testimony to the ideological dead end of Christian passivity and the utopian rejection of modern economic individualism. Or perhaps these strained Christian consolations are a balance to the genuine outrage with modern life that Fielding's book also expresses.

Although Fielding's novel glances at contemporary social–economic life – the dispossessed *rentier* protagonists have no viable means of supporting themselves, David is ruined by a nine-year lawsuit, Valentine and Cynthia emigrate to Jamaica – the unrelenting calamities that sweep away the virtuous derive from a universal depravity rendered as natural and inevitable. In this regard, *David Simple* is a typical instance of the sentimental novel, which may be said to engage very specifically with the social–economic realm, not by representing it in the manner of nineteenth-century social realism as an oppressive and mysteriously irresistible totality but by imagining in the sentimental hero a heroic and improbable alternative. But in place of Sarah Fielding's Christian bleakness, other sentimental novels choose to generate compensatory fantasies of omnipotent personal goodness and transforming heroic philanthropy such as we find in Richardson's *Sir Charles Grandison* and Henry Brooke's *The Fool of Quality*.

In spite of its amazing popularity (fourteen editions by 1800) and its influence on later novelists like Jane Austen, Richardson's third novel is nowadays unreadable in its massive, priggish didacticism and in its glacial narrative pace. Finding, to his dismay, that many readers of *Clarissa* were more taken with the rakish Lovelace than the saintly heroine, Richardson set out to delineate in Sir Charles a hero powerfully masculine as well as perfectly virtuous, and he also sought, as Jocelyn Harris notes, to address the various moral ambiguities surrounding domestic relationships that *Clarissa* had set in motion.[9] Richardson and his readers found in Sir Charles' perfection a resolution of the troubling opposition between strong and assertive masculinity and sentimental female moral virtue. Margaret Anne Doody explains Sir Charles' character with some complacency as a perfect instance of "rational virtue," as articulating "the moral excellence most admired by his age, a union of intelligence and heart which benefits the whole of society and allows that society to realize what it could and ought to be."[10] But Terry Eagleton reminds us that intelligence and feeling were difficult to reconcile, and he sees Grandison as an ideologically original character. Richardson, says Eagleton, produces "a new kind of male subject ... raiding the resources of the feminine to 'modernize' male dominance."[11] And Tom Keymer insists that there is nothing less than a "profound ethical indeterminacy" in *Grandison* "in which characters are presented not as perfect exemplars of right conduct but rather as anxious analysts of their own vexed situations – situations that can never be reduced to black and white, and consistently fail to yield a set of unequivocal imperatives to be obeyed."[12] Precisely in bridging the ideological gap of which Eagleton speaks and resolving the "ethical indeterminacy" that Keymer discerns, Sir Charles establishes or renews moral clarity and social order, and his individual accomplishments are means to a communal end.

Sir Charles returns from residence abroad upon the death of his dissolute father, Sir Thomas. He quickly sets about restoring order to the entangled relationships left behind by his father, who dies not only intestate but in the midst of negotiating for a new young mistress. Sir Charles treats his father's former live-in mistress, Mrs Oldham, with a kindness and Christian charity that astonishes his sisters and his cousin, Everard Grandison; he shows that he is a prodigy not just of compassion and rectitude but of managerial efficiency and judicious benevolence:

> What I think to do, cousin, said Sir Charles, is, to interr the venerable remains (I must always speak in this dialect, Sir) with those of my mother. This, I know, was his desire. I will have an elegant, but not sumptuous monument erected to the memory of both, with a modest inscription, that shall rather be matter of instruction to the living, than a panegyric on the departed. The funeral shall be decent but not ostentatious. The difference in the expence shall be privately applied to relieve or assist distressed housekeepers, or some of my father's poor tenants, who have large families, and have not been wanting in their honest endeavours to maintain them.
>
> (I, 361–362)

Sir Charles examines their father's house in town and his suburban retreat in Essex; inviting Mrs Oldham to join him and his sisters, he presides over the opening of his father's effects, and he amazes all concerned by his generosity not only to his sisters but to the terrified Mrs Oldham. Harriet Byron recounts these events to her friend, Lucy Selby, as she hears of them from Sir Charles' two sisters: "But, do you wonder, that the sisters, whose minds were thus open'd and enlarged by the example of such a brother, blazing upon them all at once, as I may say, in manly goodness, on his return from abroad, whither he set out a stripling, should, on all occasions, break out into raptures, whenever they mention THEIR brother?" (I, 373).

Sir Charles opens and enlarges moral possibilities from the minute he returns to England: he persuades his uncle, Lord W., to rid himself of his mistress and marry; he protects his young ward, Emily Jervois (daughter of an unhappily married late friend), from her dissipated mother and her unsavory companions (in due course converting them by his noble example and generosity to the cause of virtue); and he negotiates the marriage of his fickle sister, Charlotte, to the estimable Lord G. (after settling with diplomatic tact her entanglement with a Captain Anderson, with whom she had indiscreetly exchanged letters). All these complicated good works are performed with a grave, sententious perfection that readers nowadays can only find ludicrous, but Sir Charles' virtue lies as much in that articulation of principles as in his flawless embodiment of them. Action is for him inseparable from, intertwined with, constantly flowing and fluent moral commentary, and the copious weeping he provokes by his benevolent magnanimity is a response to the moral precision and uncanny aptness of his language as it accompanies and promotes his actions. As Mark Kinkead-Weekes sees more clearly than other critics, feeling in *Sir Charles Grandison* is a "response to morality and not merely a self-rewarding pleasure."[13] Grandison is a poet of moral *sentiment* (a producer of memorable moral maxims) as well as a perfect embodiment of *sensibility* (he feels and causes others to experience powerful moral emotions). He is the Falstaff of sensibility: not only sentimental in himself but the cause of that sentiment in other men (and women).

For all the unrelenting sententiousness of which he is the supreme master, Sir Charles is also a man of passion and pathos: driven by deep emotions, his eyes often fill with the same tears he provokes in others by his goodness and generosity. Richardson's book is so long, perhaps, because it attempts to balance sentiment and sensibility; *Sir Charles Grandison* elaborates with indefatigable repetitions a fantastic aristocratic (and upper bourgeois and ruling gentry) world of refined fellow feeling and philanthropy in which moral emotions and rational ethical understanding are perfectly reciprocal, or at least are depicted as in process (thanks to Sir Charles' magnetic goodness and irresistible moral pedagogy) of achieving balance. The book's twin engines of sentiment and sensibility may be said to spin and to seek equilibrium as Sir Charles articulates and acts, feels and excites feelings in those around him, surprising, delighting, and often astonishing by his capacity for instructive moral enactment that draws those around him into new social–moral formations. As Grandison says to his now reformed uncle, Lord W., men need to project their values to women and thereby to form moral communities:

Were we men, my Lord, to value women (and to let it be known that we do) for those qualities which are principally valuable in the sex; the less estimable, if they would not be reformed, would shrink out of our company, into company more suitable to their taste; and we should never want objects worthy of our knowledge, and even of our admiration, to associate with. There is a kind of magnetism in goodness. Bad people will find out bad people, and confederate with them, in order to keep one another in countenance; but they are bound together by a rope of sand; while trust, confidence, love, sympathy, and a reciprocation of beneficent actions, twist a cord which ties good men to good men, and cannot be easily broken.

(II, 45)

Sir Charles' moral authority and his magnetic ability to organize communities of virtue around himself are, in practice, more than just the theoretical rejection of Mandevillian suspicion and selfishness. In spite of this novel's essentially static rehearsal of sentiments and staging of sensibility, Richardson's plot turns on some violent and heroic actions.

Part of the romantic improbability that accompanies Richardson's minute domestic realism is Sir Charles' aptitude for turning up just in time to thwart villainy. An early instance of this is his rescue while in France of his merchant friend, Mr Danby, from assassins hired by that gentleman's disgruntled brother. That episode is merely a warm-up for more significant adventures. The novel's double courtship plot turns on Sir Charles' dramatic deliverance of two of the main characters from violence: in Italy he rescues Jeronymo della Porretta from assassins, converting that young man to virtue, and in England he providentially encounters Harriet Byron as she is about to be forced into marriage by the dissolute Sir Hargrave Pollexfen. These two romantic episodes, dependent of course upon fortuitous coincidences, are intertwined to produce the book's driving issue – whether Sir Charles shall marry Jeronymo's sister, Clementina, or Harriet Byron. Melodramatic as they surely are, these deliverances also immediately involve Sir Charles in ever-expanding social networks, tangled relationships that stretch from London and nearby rural counties and across France and Italy. Sir Charles' heroic exertions are necessarily brief; they serve as introductions to the spiral of specifically social, moral, and religious complications surrounding love and marriage that are the novel's real subject.

Sir Charles' accounts of Jeronymo's and Harriet's rescues have a rapid concision necessarily absent from the expansive moral ruminations and psychological examinations of the rest of the book. His talent for narrative bespeaks his resourcefulness and managerial alertness and contributes to his heroic profile. Pursuing a "lady less celebrated for virtue than beauty," Jeronymo (Sir Charles tells Harriet) is set upon by "Brescian bravos" hired by a jealous rival:

> The attempt was made in the Cremonese. They had got him into their toils in a little thicket at some distance from the road. I, attended by two servants, happened to be passing, when a frighted horse ran cross the way, his bridle broken, and his saddle bloody: This making me apprehend some mischief to the rider, I drove down the opening he came from, and soon beheld a man struggling on the ground with two ruffians; one of whom was just stopping his mouth, the other stabbing him. I leapt out of the post-chaise, and drew my sword, running towards them as fast as I could; and, calling to my servants to follow me, indeed calling as if I had a number with me, in order to alarm them. On this, they fled; and I heard them say, Let us make off; we have done his business. Incensed at the villainy, I pursued and came up with one of them, who turned upon me. I beat down his *trombone*, a kind of blunderbuss, just as he presented it at me, and had wounded and thrown him on the ground; but seeing the other ruffian turning back to help his fellow, and, on a sudden, two others appearing with their horses, I thought it best to retreat, tho' I would fain have secured one of them. My servants then seeing my danger, hastened, shouting, towards me. The bravoes (perhaps apprehending there were more than two) seemed as glad to get off with their rescued companion, as I was to retire, I hastened then to the unhappy man: But much was I surprised, when I found him to be the Barone della Porretta, who, in disguise, had been actually pursuing his amour!
>
> (II, 120–121)

This romantic swashbuckling occurs in a world lacking modern institutional law enforcement, and even in more centralized and regulated England Sir Charles' exploits are purely private responses to crime. He and his utterly devoted, completely fearless and disciplined servants function as a paramilitary unit, and Sir Charles renders his rescues with exact attention to strategy, protocols of command, and rules of engagement. In both instances, Sir Charles' tactical skill can be regarded as predictions of his behavior in the infinitely more complex moral and social relationships that they set in motion, as Sir Charles will in each case move from heroic savior and man of action to a submissive suitor faced with delicate issues of morality and religion. External action in both cases inserts Sir Charles into situations where simple oppositions dissolve and where action is a matter of diplomatic social maneuvering, moral positioning, and sentimental articulation. As Jeronymo's deliverer, he is absorbed into the bosom of the fabulously wealthy and powerful della Porretta clan of Bologna, the Marchese and Marchessa, with Jeronymo's elder brothers (a bishop and a general), and with his beautiful and pious sister, the Lady Clementina. After he tutors her in English (they read Milton together – "Our Milton has deservedly a name" among Italians – and they are often joined by Jeronymo and their mother and father), Sir Charles is urged by the family to help them convince the lady to marry her suitor, the Count Belvedere. But Clementina resists even Grandison's urgings, grows distracted, and throws out many hints that she is in love instead with the Chevalier Grandison, and her distress is heightened even to madness as she realizes that he will not turn Catholic to marry her.

Such bald summary does no justice to the exfoliating, intertwining complexity of these sequences and their massively slow and stately unfolding to readers and to Harriet Byron, who reads a series of documents (including some of Sir Charles' letters) compiled by Dr Bartlett, the Grandison chaplain, and sends her own reactions to her cousin, Lucy Selby. All this information arrives as Harriet falls in love with Sir Charles and he (urged by the della Porrettas) makes plans to return to Italy to attempt to cure the distracted Clementina (and to bring expert British medical help for the still enfeebled Jeronymo). A second trip to Italy and endless confabulations with the della Porrettas and with a restored Clementina, who finally refuses (after protracted negotiations) Sir Charles' modified proposal (he to remain a Protestant and to raise their male children in his faith, she to bring up their daughters as Catholics and to have her own personal confessor). Of course, all of this activity causes Sir Charles to shine ever more brightly, and even Clementina's last refusal of him is a tribute to his powers:

> My Tutor, my Brother, my Friend! O most beloved and best of men! seek me not in marriage! I am unworthy of Thee. Thy SOUL was ever most dear to Clementina: Whenever I meditated the gracefulness of thy person, I restrained my eye, I checked my fancy: And how? Why, by meditating the superior

graces of thy mind. And is not that SOUL, thought I, to be saved? Dear obstinate, and perverse! And shall I bind my Soul to a Soul allied to perdition? That so dearly loves that Soul, as hardly to wish to be separated from it in its future lot. – O thou most amiable of men! How can I be sure, that, were I thine, thou wouldst not draw me after thee, by Love, by sweetness of Manners, by condescending Goodness? I, who once thought a Heretic the worst of beings, have been already led, by the amiableness of thy piety, by the universality of thy charity to all thy fellow-creatures, to think more favourably of all Heretics, for thy sake?

(II, 564)

Clementina's extraordinary testimonial is that, even for a saint like her, Sir Charles is irresistible. Individuals are drawn to him; they constellate themselves around the magnetic moral force that he radiates. So Richardson designs a plot in which a romantic hero redefines romance, maintaining in Clementina and Harriet "a double Love" (III, 57), forming communities of reciprocal affections and improving, elevating, enlarging subordination to his presence. *Sir Charles Grandison* resembles a giant centripetal field in which the hero, nobility and magnanimity itself, inspires such qualities in those who come within his orbit and feel the force of his overwhelming moral power. Thus, when Sir Charles, after Clementina's refusal, proposes to Harriet as soon as his feet touch English soil, he realizes the potential indelicacy but appeals to her "magnanimity," urging her (and her aunt and grandmother) in effect to imitate him and rise above "common forms":

And if, madam, you can so far get over observances, which perhaps on consideration, will be found to be punctilious only, as to give your heart, with your hand, to a man who himself has been perplexed by what some would call (particular as it sounds) a *double Love* (an embarrassment, however, not of his own seeking, or which he could possibly avoid) you will lay him under obligation to your goodness (to your magnanimity, I will call it) which all the affectionate tenderness of my life to come will never enable me to discharge.

(III, 57)

Note that the proposal is delivered not just to Harriet but to her aunt and grandmother. Sir Charles lives and breathes communal air; all his actions, especially his private and personal moments, are creatively, thickly relational and involve him in ever-expanding social networks and moral affiliations which radiate from his central presence. Clementina and Harriet are, in different ways, the origins of such networks, and Sir Charles' connections with these lovers place him in multiple relationships with a variety of persons in several countries. The intensely private and personal, in other words, is linked through him to a public realm, and he helps to produce or to manifest that public world. Ultimately, Sir Charles is a mid-eighteenth-century culture hero in his ability to link those worlds, transforming in Richardson's fantasy the relations between a morally corrupt aristocracy and the populace, whose deference to the powerful becomes, in his company, genuine devotion. As Lady Grandison (née Harriet Byron) remarks with wonder, one of their servants

> has often observed to me, that if my master either rides or walks in company, tho' of great Lords, people distinguish *him* by their respectful love: To the Lords, they will but seem to lift up their hats, as I may say; or if women, just drop the knee, and look grave, as if they paid respect to their quality only: But to my master, they pull off their hats to the ground, and bow their whole bodies: They look smilingly, and with pleasure and blessings, as I may say, in their faces: The good women courtesy also to the ground, turn about when he has passed them, and look after him – God bless your sweet face; and God bless your dear heart, will they say – And the servants who hear them are *so* delighted!
>
> (III, 287)

For all of his impossible perfection, however, Sir Charles is not some sort of fairy godfather; he is just and fair-minded, his benevolence and philanthropy carefully placed in Richardson's excruciatingly detailed narrative within quite precisely managed socioeconomic circumstances. These good people whose hearts are truly touched by Sir Charles, as they are not by the lords in whose company he shines all the brighter, are moved by a person who redeems and purifies the existing social order. Or, better, he operates in an implied social universe where virtue and goodness can operate at the highest levels and percolate to the lower strata, solidifying and ratifying society as a stable moral order. The ultimate and controlling sentimental moment in *Sir Charles Grandison* is social in this larger sense: Sir Charles creating moral communities by righting wrongs, preventing evil, redeeming libertines, rescuing the innocent, reconciling quarreling relatives, arranging marriages, rewarding service and fidelity, and inspiring devotion and moral imitation. In his shining perfection, Sir Charles brings tears of joy and happiness to all concerned, and those emotions bespeak an awareness of his singularity and of a normal state of affairs in which a paragon like him is an impossible fantasy. As R.S. Brissenden notes in his study of the novel of sentiment, there was in the sentimental era a "deepening realisation ... that individual acts of benevolence could not alter a general social condition which was fundamentally unjust; and also that there was perhaps something suspect in being able to derive pleasure from feeling pity and acting charitably in a situation which was irredeemable."[14]

With its huge cast of characters and its crowd of domestic correspondents, Richardson's novel surrounds with an aura of probability and normality Grandison's function as a fantastic culture hero who works against the grain of such pessimism. To appreciate Richardson's achievement in this regard and to understand the appeal of the sentimental fantasy of heroic philanthropy a brief glance at Henry Brooke's *The Fool of Quality: or, The History of Henry Earl of Moreland* (1766–1770) is illuminating. Reprinted often until the late nineteenth century, Brooke's novel is an amazing fantasy of fabulous mercantile accomplishment and heroic philanthropy. The Earl of Moreland has retired from public life and, when the story opens, has two young sons: Richard the elder, raised in splendor as his heir, and Harry the younger, brought up by a nurse as a simple rustic. When 5-year-old Harry is brought to the manor house, he displays a free, instinctively generous personality at odds with his effete and selfish brother. But Harry is quickly spirited away from his family by a Mr Fenton, a rich old man he meets in the village, and together the two of them set off to practice philanthropy on an epic scale and in the process to educate the young Harry. As we discover in due course, Mr Fenton (Clinton) is really his uncle, the Earl's retired and fabulously wealthy merchant brother. In a series of extravagant episodes we learn his incredible history and watch the growth in piety and benevolence of his nephew. Playfully Sternian, piously and patriotically didactic, sententiously sentimental, packed with financial adventures (Mr Fenton has helped finance King William's wars to the tune of some £200,000!), with sweetly pathetic and pious romance (Mr Clinton's first wife, the daughter of his mentor and partner, dies young, a model of Christian resignation and sanctity), with swashbuckling adventure (in France Mr Clinton has saved the life of a Prince of the Blood and married an aristocrat, winning her hand in a rivalry with a noble French suitor), *The Fool of Quality* is ostensibly a novel of young Harry's education; but he is, to say the least, an apt pupil for whom piety, spontaneous compassion, and heroic philanthropy come naturally. Despite its historical references, the book is actually a modern fairy tale in which the hero's magical or divine assistant (fairy godmother, talking animal, shrewd dwarf) is a pious and wealthy British merchant (who has also, like Sir Charles Grandison, a talent for heroic swashbuckling).[15] The English countryside and London, as it happens, afford constant opportunity for philanthropy, and this ready availability of misery glances at a contemporary situation that is the necessary ground for Brooke's fantasy:

> From this day forward, Harry and Ned [a playmate] by turns were frequently out on the watch; and often single, or in pairs, or by whole families, Harry would take in a poor father and mother, with their helpless infants, driven perhaps from house or home by fire or other misfortune, or oppressive landlord, or ruthless creditor; and having warmed, and fed, and clothed, and treated the old ones as his parents, and the little ones as his brothers and sisters, he would give them additional money for charges on the road, and send them away the happiest of all people except himself.[16]

If you have limitless funds, philanthropy comes naturally, and *The Fool of Quality* dramatizes benevolence (in spite of the author's good intentions) as a class privilege, the moral equivalent for the ruling classes of physical games designed to teach teamwork and to build character. And unlike Sir Charles' carefully managed executorships and moral tutorings of wayward relatives and acquaintances, this philanthropy is random and opportunistic, meant chiefly as part of young Harry's sentimental education, lacking in Richardsonian moral grandeur and Grandisonian community building.

Philanthropy in *The Fool of Quality* feeds on those conditions created by the Mandevillian or Hobbesian struggle for pleasure and power in which its philanthropists redeem a representative selection of society's victims. Young Harry and his rich uncle, in imitating the selfless wisdom of the deity, run up against the paradox revealed even by Brooke's romantic fantasy: the sympathetic and benevolent connection with unfortunate fellows of the sentimental/philanthropic moment is compromised by social/psychological superiority and the rescue and rehabilitation of the deprived is a form of benign exploitation, of selfish appropriation. As Ellis Markman puts it, these scenes in Brooke's novel present a "specular economic voyeurism" and "a significant revalorisation of poverty, arguing that poverty itself is not emotionally interesting, but distress is."[17] The sentimental moment (in fiction) contains within it as well a mixture of pain and pleasure, an untroubled acceptance of things as they are along with a utopian fantasy of amelioration and reconciliation that signals its lack of authenticity in its personalized, emotional luxuriance (and in *The Fool of Quality* its fantastic extravagance).

Such ambiguities and contradictions are most clearly resisted or at least refined in the most influential instance of sentimental fiction from this period, Henry Mackenzie's *The Man of Feeling* (1771). In place of Brooke's fantasy of heroic philanthropy, Mackenzie's Harley is a ghostly presence, memorialized in some scattered textual fragments, some pages of a manuscript written by his friend, left behind in his lodgings, and rescued by the book's "editor" from the local curate, who had been using its pages as wadding for his gun. Not only is Harley a nearly forgotten provincial gentleman of very modest means, the narrative in its extreme sketchiness seems a deliberate rejection of the representational fullness and social comprehensiveness of most of its predecessors. Rather than the articulation of sentiments whose moral fluency is a sign of benevolent greatness, *The Man of Feeling* offers a hero whose most eloquent moments are tearful silences or sobs of sympathy. Heroic moral agency is nowhere in sight in Mackenzie's enormously popular brief narrative, which is an anthology of other people's calamities as attended to by his sympathizing hero (a good listener, if ever there was one), who purifies sentimental spectatorship by his weakness and earnest passivity. Implicitly, Harley's situation as powerless but deeply sympathetic observer of other people's suffering attempts to purge the sentimental relationship of its exploitative self-indulgence and powerful appropriation of other people's miseries. It is not really paradoxical to claim that this most egregiously sentimental hero is in fact a dramatization of sentiment and sympathy as morally irrelevant, merely personal reactions to a pervasive injustice in the world at large. In a real sense, one can argue that in his consolatory, after-the-fact position in the narratives he hears, Harley projects the pathos of his own impotence and marginality and suggests the necessity of moral activism in a consistently harsh and unforgiving world.

Harley's weakness and passivity allow *The Man of Feeling*, even in its brevity, to attend more exactly to the moral scandals of eighteenth-century society than Richardson's or Brooke's philanthropic epics. Indeed, Harley's story proper begins with his attempt (urged on by his friends) to secure a loan on "some crown-lands which lay contiguous to his estate" in order to solidify his precarious financial position.[18] Harley goes to London to sue for the patronage of a

who can influence the first lord of the treasury to grant the
.ventually, the lease is awarded to a gauger (an exciseman, a
e officer who inspects bulk goods to assess their taxable value),
dividual whose history is summed up for Harley by another
applicant for the lease as rising from "a footman; and I, believe, he
had sometimes the honour to be a pimp. At last, some of the great
folks, to whom he had been serviceable in both capacities, had him
made a gauger" (28). This gauger secures the lease by prostituting his
sister to the baronet. So if we add to his own disappointment the
various tales of betrayal and exploitation that Harley hears from
others, we have a picture of a moral world for which his naiveté
makes him totally unfit. For his own failure, Harley is not much
moved; he shrugs it off and returns to the country. But the tale of
seduction and betrayal that he hears from a London prostitute, the
harrowing story told by the old soldier, his former country neighbor,
Edwards – these draw copious tears from Harley, as does the sight of
the girl in Bedlam who mourns her dead lover, sent away by her
greedy father who tried to marry her to a rich miser. These are
familiar stories to any reader of eighteenth-century fiction, and they
serve as the briefest epitomes, as it were, of the recurring plots of the
genre. Harley's response to them may usefully be considered as
Mackenzie's summarizing comment on fiction's moral and emotional
failure as the eighth decade of the century opens. Harley and
Mackenzie's readers, that is to say, are grieving not just for these
particular instances of injustice but for the persistence and recurrence
of the forms of moral and social injustice that fiction has been
recording for many years. Or, more generally, we can say that *The
Man of Feeling*'s real theme is the failure of narrative didacticism, the
irrelevance of conventional cautionary tales in the face of the
corruption that they continually expose but cannot prevent or even
mitigate.

Mackenzie's recessive hero can only record corruption and sympa-
thize with its victims, including himself. In place of sentimental
formulation and heroic philanthropy (for which he lacks the means),
Harley has ready and copious tears, it is true, but he mainly offers
sympathy and understanding which involve a critique of his own security and relative immunity to calamity. When the prostitute whom he
befriends faints and says (sobbing) that she has not eaten in two days, he
responds, "'Two days!' – said he; 'and I have fared sumptuously every
day!'" (50). And after this girl has been restored to her father, who
mourns "the death of her honour," Harley consoles and corrects him
eloquently: "'Let me intreat you, Sir,' said he, 'to hope better things.

The world is ever tyrannical; it warps our sorrows to edge them with keener affliction: let us not be slaves to the names it affixes to motive or to action. I know an ingenuous mind cannot help feeling when they sting: but there are considerations by which it may be overcome; its fantastic ideas vanish as they rise; they teach us – to look beyond it"' (73). Isolated and out of context (textual and historical), such speeches are unremarkable, but the effect of Harley's relative insubstantiality as a character, his existence in a few textual fragments and as a collection of anecdotes from a brief and obscure private existence, give such utterances an odd pertinence and solidity. As Mackenzie arranges matters, Harley's several speeches lack the expressivity that accompanies and tends to undermine novelistic didacticism. Harley's sketchy indistinctness as a literary character, his lack of personality, enforces the objectivity of his moral views, makes him, as it were, disinterested.

Perhaps the best sequence in *The Man of Feeling* to illustrate the function of Harley's recessiveness is his meeting with the old soldier, Edwards. As he first spies the sleeping man, Harley performs the classic (made famous by Sterne) sentimental objectification and appropriation of the pathetic subject:

> An old man, who from his dress seemed to have been a soldier, lay fast asleep on the ground; a knapsack rested on a stone at his right hand, while his staff and brass-hilted sword were crossed at his left.
>
> Harley looked on him with the most earnest attention. He was one of those figures which Salvator would have drawn; nor was the surrounding scenery unlike the wildness of that painter's backgrounds. The banks on each side were covered with fantastic shrub-wood, and at a little distance, on the top of one of them, stood a finger-post. ... A rock, with some dangling wild flowers, jutted out above where the soldier lay; on which grew the stump of a large tree, white with age, and a single twisted branch shaded his face as he slept. His face had the marks of manly comeliness impaired by time; his forehead was not altogether bald, but its hairs might have been numbered; while a few white locks behind crossed the brown of his neck with a contrast the most venerable to a mind like Harley's. 'Thou art old,' said he to himself, 'but age has not brought thee rest for its infirmities; I fear those silver hairs have not found shelter from thy country, though that neck has been bronzed in its service.'

(85)

When the old man awakens, he approaches Harley, "who by this time found the romantic enthusiasm rising within him" (86), and discovers that they have the same destination. As they speak, the stranger recognizes him and declares that he is "old Edwards," a neighbor and friend from Harley's boyhood. As they walk, now together, Harley hears the old man's tale. Forced by his landlord to rent a larger farm than the small one on which his family had toiled for many generations, he goes bankrupt. With his son, Edwards takes on another and smaller farm, but their simple life shatters when his son's quarrel with the squire's game-keeper leads to an unjust action for assault and a crippling fine, followed by a press gang's selection (encouraged by the vengeful squire) of Edwards' son. This pitiless gang interrupts the Edwards' Christmas Eve and the birthday of the older man's grandson. As they drag him away, Edwards pays them a bribe and agrees to go in his son's place. "'Our parting, Mr. Harley, I cannot describe to you; it was the first time we had ever parted: the very press-gang could scarce keep from tears'" (92). Edwards serves in India, where he refuses to grow "rich at the expence of [his] conscience" and is court-martialed and given two hundred lashes for helping in the escape of an Indian held by his officers to extort treasure from him. Befriended by the grateful Indian, Edwards has made his way back to England and is now returning home to his family. Tearfully embracing him as this relation ends, Harley accompanies Edwards home, where they encounter his orphaned grandchildren, his son and his wife, thanks to "bad crops, and bad debts," both dead of "broken hearts" (98).   Narrative.

Maudlin and melodramatic, this sequence is nonetheless striking in its careful grounding in the particulars of institutional injustice and corruption, including the scandal of empire (eliciting from Harley a speech deploring the bloody spoils of the British conquest of the subcontinent). Harley's romantic haze and dreamy self-absorption give way very quickly as he gazes at Edwards to an outraged sense of the corrupt institution that doubtless put this old soldier homeless on the road. The story of Edwards concludes with the narrator (not the "editor") of Harley's own tale moved, as never before, to step back and show us Harley helping Edwards to cultivate the small farm on his estate where he has installed his old friend and his orphaned grandchildren. He has seen Harley

> at work in this little spot, with his coat off, and his dibble in his hand: it was a scene of tranquil virtue to have stopped an angel on his errands of mercy? Harley had contrived to lead a little bubbling brook through a green walk in the middle of the

ground, upon which he had erected a mill in miniature for the diversion of Edwards's infant-grandson, and made shift in its construction to introduce a pliant bit of wood, that answered with its fairy clack to the murmuring of the rill that turned it. I have seen him stand, listening to these mingled sounds, with his eye fixed on the boy, and the smile of conscious satisfaction on his cheek; while the old man, with a look half-turned to Harley, and half to Heaven, breathed an ejaculation of gratitude and piety.

Father of mercies! I also would thank thee! that not only hast thou assigned eternal rewards to virtue, but that, even in this bad world, the lines of our duty, and our happiness, are so frequently woven together.

(101–102)

If we think back to Harley's first view of Edwards, the contrast is instructive. Thanks to the narrator who intervenes at length here, in one of the longest objective renderings of a scene that this brief novel contains, Harley is within the frame of the narrative rather than acting as the compromised sentimental spectator; he is emotionally involved but also active, both farming and playing, indulging himself emotionally but producing pleasure and productivity in those around him. Instead of weeping with outraged impotence, he embodies for his audience an instructive alignment of duty and happiness. And he does so entirely without irony or stylistic distance, without the literary bracketing that surrounds *The Man of Feeling*'s most prominent sentimental predecessors, Sterne's two novels.

Mackenzie's hero justifies Marshall Brown's observation that sensibility "almost seems to entail a kind of inverse solipsism, a belief that everything is real except oneself."[19] In *Tristram Shandy* (1760–1767) and *A Sentimental Journey Through France and Italy* (1768), Laurence Sterne rendered the sentimental personality in all its suspect fluency and luxuriant affective intensity, so that in both of his books solipsism is dramatized as a nervous over-compensation for such self-doubting. Tristram and Parson Yorick accomplish absolutely nothing; their stories are deliberately fragmented, comically incomplete, lacking in symmetry or closure or even plot in the customary sense. And yet Sterne's implicit claim is that their stories are full of meaning, exemplary precisely because they are intensely personal and self-expressive, in some meaningful way typical, standing in their absolute eccentricity and isolation for general humanity.

As *A Sentimental Journey* opens, Parson Yorick is struck by a sudden fancy triggered by a friend's challenge to his assertion that "They order ... this matter better in France." [20] To settle the argument, Yorick hops on the stage to Dover and sits down to dinner in Calais the next afternoon. With comic abruptness, without context or explanation, curiosity and idiosyncrasy replace moral or social necessity as motives for action; purposeful progress through experience yields in the narrative itself (such as it is) to random movement and playful improvisation. Of course, Yorick had by 1768 become a persona for the celebrity author, Laurence Sterne, and the outlines of his personality were familiar to readers from the wildly popular *Tristram Shandy*. which had appeared in installments beginning in 1760. Indeed, Sterne in 1760 had supplemented his triumph by publishing his own sermons to great acclaim under the title *The Sermons of Mr. Yorick*, capitalizing on the success of the first two volumes of *Tristram Shandy*, published earlier that year.[21] In a few of the short vignettes that comprise *A Sentimental Journey*, there are allusions to Yorick's connection to the Shandy family and conversations with his friend and interlocutor, Eugenius, from the earlier book. In spite of the familiarity of the character, *A Sentimental Journey* deliberately shatters narrative fullness and sequence, as Yorick (whose death, after all, had been staged in the first volume of *Tristram Shandy*) offers his journey as some sketches of his impulsive movements and whims, emotions that lead him to comic encounters, embarrassments, flirtations, and sometimes to sentimental scenes and sympathetic effusions.

In *A Sentimental Journey*, the sentimental moment is unabashedly an occasion for pleasurable self-expression and therapeutic emotionality, although the articulation of Yorick's sensibility is compromised by the same whimsicality that encourages it and (at its most extreme) by the constructed, merely associational, deeply (or comically) subjective nature of his apprehension of events and involvement with others. Sterne's ironies are vertiginous, as generations of commentators on his work have observed; he inextricably blends the sentimental and the comic, with sentimentality both endorsed and satirized, articulated as self-expressive discovery or intense sympathy and exposed as constructed, inauthentic, and self-indulgent trifling.[22] In one remarkable sequence in *A Sentimental Journey*, Sterne's hero manages simultaneously to meditate on deeply serious historical and political issues and to reduce them by the force of sentimental imagining to an exercise in narcissistic self-affirmation. Having "left London with so much precipitation," it has somehow not occurred to Yorick that England and France are at war and that without a French passport he is in danger of arrest, perhaps of incarceration in the Bastille.[23] With characteristic insouciance, Yorick makes light of the danger and calls upon the transforming power of mental rearrangements to hold off anxiety:

> Beshrew the *sombre* pencil! said I, vauntingly – for I envy not its powers, which paints the evils of life with so hard and deadly a colouring: the mind sits terrified at the objects she has magnified herself and blackened; reduce them to their proper size and hue, she overlooks them – 'Tis true, said I, correcting the proposition – the Bastile is not an evil to be despised – but strip it of its towers – fill up the fossé – unbarricade the doors – call it simply a confinement, and suppose 'tis some tyrant of a distemper – and not of a man which holds you in it – the evil vanishes, and you bear the other half without complaint.
>
> (95–96)

Yorick's mind, he insists, is its own place and his rearrangements of external calamities, even the political and social weight of the Bastille, the embodiment of French absolutism, are aesthetic re-imaginings that transform massively threatening sociohistorical objectivity into physiological phenomena that the mind can master. Yorick's fantasy of Stoic control is interrupted by what sounds like a child crying "I can't get out," a cry which turns out to come from a caged starling who has been taught to repeat that phrase by an English groom. When Yorick is unable to let the bird out, he declares that he "never had my affections more tenderly awakened" (96). The bird's "mechanical" sounds are for Yorick "so true in tune to nature ... that in one moment they overthrew all my systematic reasonings upon the Bastille" (96). Such feelings and musings upon precious "LIBERTY" pursue Yorick to his room, where he throws himself upon his bed and gives "full scope" to his imagination, as he draws a vivid picture of a prisoner:

> I was going to begin with the millions of my fellow-creatures born to no inheritance but slavery; but finding however affecting the picture was, that I could not bring it near me, and the multitude of sad groups in it did but distract me –
>
> – I took a single captive, and having first shut him up in his dungeon, I then looked through the twilight of his grated door to take his picture.
>
> I beheld his body half wasted away with long expectation and confinement, and felt what kind of sickness of the heart it

was which arises from hope deferred. Upon looking nearer I
saw him pale and feverish: in thirty years the western breeze
had not once fanned his blood – he had seen no sun, no moon
in all that time – nor had the voice of friend or kinsman
breathed through his lattice – his children –
    – But here my heart began to bleed – and I was forced to go
on with another part of the portrait.

(97–98)

Yorick watches his imaginary prisoner marking with a rusty nail on a
small stick the passage of another day of misery, and he moves from
passive imagining to actual manipulation of this vivid figment. "As I
darkened the little light he had, he lifted up a hopeless eye towards the
door, then cast it down, shook his head, and went on with his work of
affliction." As the prisoner gives a deep sigh, Yorick bursts into tears: "I
could not sustain the picture of confinement which my fancy had
drawn" (98).

Unable to contemplate the collective historical reality of slavery (or
unable to project himself into its "multitude of sad groups"), Yorick
dramatizes his need for knowledge as experience, as vivid, controlled
sensations. Knowledge is not the distanced understanding or reasoned
contemplation of the general and objective phenomena of slavery and
absolutism but rather a personalized imaginative projection, an intimate
and vicarious involvement with (and curiously cold-blooded control of)
the particular subject of what is, when Yorick is finished imagining it,
only incidentally institutional oppression within a particular historical
context. Acknowledging (indeed celebrating) the force of accidental
particulars and "mechanical" connection, of the arbitrary circumstances that brought him and the starling to form this intersection of
the personal and the historical – without a passport in the most
powerful absolutist monarchy in the world with whom his nation is at
war, for control, we might add, of the balance of power in Europe and
for imperial domination in the Indian subcontinent and North
America[24] – Yorick reduces the social and momentously historical to
accident and artifice, the latter in effect the defensive, self-enclosing,
and self-ratifying construction of an emotional scenario. As John
Bender observes, the sequel to this fantasy is a trip to Versailles where
Yorick obtains his passport, which will certify him as a "legal
personage" who is now free "to traverse the authoritative grid of the
state." But in a wonderful comic moment of fanciful mis-identification,
the Comte de Bissy (a great admirer of Shakespeare) grants him a passport as Yorick, the king's jester he knows from *Hamlet*. As Bender puts it,

Yorick's prison fantasy leads to "the opposite of incarceration: his new passport grants total liberty because of a mistake about his identity."[25]

The grotesque intensity and political–historical seriousness of this moment stand out among other incidents in Yorick's travels which are deliberately trivial or purely personal (the dead mule and his distraught owner) or pastoral (Maria, the mad peasant girl, who had appeared in *Tristram Shandy*, and the dancing peasants in Savoy). For the "sentimental traveller," such as Yorick labels himself, distinctions among these disparate scenes are meaningless, since what he sees are not "customs, climates, and religion" (which are simply "different disguises") but "NATURE, and those affections which arise out of her, which make us love each other – and the world, better than we do" (108–109). So, too, instead of philanthropy the thrifty Yorick gives others his sympathy (a few sous to beggars, to be sure), and in the case of the imaginary prisoner a sympathy with no actual object but himself. Sterne in his brilliance makes Yorick an allegory of the eighteenth-century sentimental reader, for whom fictional philanthropy is indulgent self-affirmation and moral superiority purchased at no real cost.

Yorick is never really serious. Playful is the best term to describe many of his adventures, and even the sentimental scenes are suffused with the character's self-conscious sense of the ridiculous, of the constructed and self-serving nature of deep feeling. Yorick is a connoisseur of emotion, a detached spectator on the lookout for what he finds, for instance at the very beginning of his travels, in the Flemish lady he meets at Calais, whose face "was interesting; I fancied it wore the character of a widowed look, and in that state of its declension, which had passed the two first paroxysms of sorrow, and was quietly beginning to reconcile itself to its loss" (41). But mixed in with Yorick's narcissism and emotional opportunism, there is a cold-blooded, analytic intellectuality, and the word "interesting" bespeaks an essential boredom looking for experiences that stimulate and amuse rather than instruct.[26]

Boredom is one of the dangerous side effects of social privilege and a life of leisure, and in a sense it is Sterne's subject in *Tristram Shandy*. His narrator is a feckless country gentleman, a learned dilettante and literary practical joker, an easily distracted autobiographer, and a man of feeling without philanthropic focus. The main characters in his memoir are his father and his uncle: Walter Shandy, a retired "Turkey" merchant, and Captain Toby Shandy, a superannuated army officer. As Tristram evokes them, these two former representatives of the twin pillars of British wealth and power are wholly absorbed in private activities and quirky hobbies whose comic interest is their absolute irrelevance to a social or public world. Disabled by a wound in the groin received at the siege of Namur in 1695 (a crucial victory for the English and their allies against the French), Toby with his fellow soldier and servant, Corporal Trim, has retired to a little house near his brother's estate to study military science. He finds occupation in building with Trim toy models on his bowling green of the ongoing wars for European domination being fought by Britain during the early years of the eighteenth century against the French and their allies, his whole existence a recapitulation and re-examination of his past trauma and a miniaturized staging of contemporary military campaigns. Walter Shandy is an amateur scholar and aspiring philosopher, a polymath with ambitiously absurd (and retrograde or archaic) notions about everything, including the crucial relationship between Christian names and personality and between the length of noses and penile size and potency (the Shandys having a tradition of snub noses). Starting by giving his second son what he considers the single most auspicious and powerful name – "Trismegisthus" (after the legendary sage, Hermes Trismegisthus) – he hopes to raise him according to his own eccentric pediatric principles. Looking back on a life full of disasters, which begins with his father's attention being distracted at the very moment of his conception (thereby scattering and dispersing the "animal spirits" that form our hero) and his unlucky christening by the very name deemed the worst possible by Walter, Tristram proposes to reconstruct his past to understand his present state ("a thousand weaknesses both of body and mind") which in his view (an intellectual inheritance from his father) derives exactly from events commencing with his botched conception:[27]

> I wish either my father or my mother, or indeed both of them, as they were in duty both equally bound to it, had minded what they were about when they begot me; had they duly considered how much depended upon what they were then doing; – that not only the production of a rational Being was concerned in it, but that possibly the happy formation and temperature of his body, perhaps his genius and the very cast of his mind; – and, for aught they knew to the contrary, even the fortunes of his whole house might take their turn from the humours and dispositions which were then uppermost: – Had they duly weighed and considered all this, and proceeded accordingly, – I am verily persuaded I should have made a quite different figure in the world, from that, in which the reader is likely to see me.

(I, 1, 35)

Published in a series of two-volume installments from 1760 to 1767 (except for Volume 9, the last), Sterne's book is not a novel in the customary sense of the term, and its representations are filtered through its presiding hybrid comic literary form. Inspired by Sterne's satiric masters, Rabelais and Swift, drawing on other literary models such as Cervantes, Montaigne, and Robert Burton, with Sterne lifting whole passages from these and other sources (especially Ephraim Chambers' *Cyclopedia: or, an Universal Dictionary of Arts and Sciences* (1738), from which he derived most of his learned references), *Tristram Shandy* is almost *sui generis*, Tristram's zany autobiographical monologue (and occasional dialogue with his readers) in which he attempts to reconstruct the events and personalities surrounding his birth and early years, in the process deriving his own comically skewed character (both rationalistic and sentimental but also bawdily irreverent and relentlessly satiric of both reason and sentiment) from the distinct influences of his father and uncle. At once a proleptic parody of the novel of sentimental education and a satire of the possibilities of heroic moral striving and self-understanding of the Grandisonian sort, Sterne's book both ridicules and ratifies the individual eccentricities that it articulates, offering us varieties of solipsism as the inevitable outcome of the efforts of all three of his main male characters to attach themselves to an elusive objective world. In Ronald Paulson's words, Sterne "makes us see his characters and situations first as the old satiric ones and then as the recipients of comic–sympathetic laughter. The thesis is as much a part of the effect as the antithesis, and the transition becomes for Sterne a basic theme."[28] Much modern criticism of *Tristram Shandy* tends to ignore the satiric–sympathetic shift and to take the book's playfulness very seriously indeed, "abstracting Sterne's notions into ethereal linguistic or metaphysical realms," as Melvyn New puts it.[29] For Sternian exegetes, the zany and improvisatory qualities of Tristram's memoirs produce profound meanings. For example, in a quite brilliant reading of *Tristram Shandy*, Jonathan Lamb traces Sterne's enactments of Humean and Hartleyan associationist epistemology, so that "the symptoms of endless reciprocation are evident not only in the casual starts and indeterminate conclusions of Shandean stories, and of the stories within those stories, but also in the incidents, gestures and phrases that compose them." In what Lamb calls the "double principle," *Tristram Shandy* operates rhetorically by pervasive pleonasms "in which originals and copies perpetually circle one another, and parallels accompany each other to infinity."[30]

The philosophical idiom and frame of reference that critics like Lamb employ tend to obscure the self-canceling absurdity of characters to whom readers are invited to condescend, to view, as Paulson says, both satirically and comically. Their positive valence, when it arrives, is a sentimental alliance in which they form a male community of touching affection even as they pursue what Tristram calls their "hobby-horses." They thus break out of absurdity at times and accomplish what Carol Kay labels "remasculinization" in their relationships with one another. Her point is that Sterne's book features male bonding, male couples (Walter and Toby, Corporal Trim and Toby, Tristram and Toby) who in their intimacy and in their hobbyhorsical theories and preoccupations seek to exclude women and to redefine the sentimental personality in masculine terms.[31] As many critics have noted, such male couples are a biological dead end, and *Tristram Shandy*'s central theme is impotence and infertility. The disabling self-enclosure of the three main male characters seems to be related to their social and sexual identities: the three Shandy men are distinct from their vigorous servants and sexually active female adjuncts (Mrs Shandy, the Widow Wadman, Tristram's Jenny), and their hobbies (including Tristram's autobiographical experiment) are replacements for sexual fulfillment, productive work, and meaningful social function. Although it sounds inappropriately portentous when applied to Sterne's comic masterpiece, *Tristram Shandy* can be seen as an exploration of the enervating effects of class privilege divorced from social function and communal purpose; the moral and intellectual comedy of Sterne's book derives from the leisured emptiness enjoyed (or endured) by its main male characters. The Spanish philosopher, José Ortega y Gasset, remarked that characters in novels interest us not for what they do but for what they are.[32] We might adapt that maxim to say that Sterne's characters interest us for what they do *not* do; they exist by virtue of their failures and frustrations. In the larger context of eighteenth-century British fiction, they represent a comic rejection or absurd contraction of moral agency and psychological self-awareness as the individual's defining gestures. If we think back to the moral speculations of Hume and Smith, none of the Shandy males has any real "sympathy" beyond the small domestic circle they inhabit; indifferent to the opinions of others and untroubled by Smith's man in the breast, each is encased in a hobbyhorsical world that shuts out normal social intercourse and interconnection.

Writing and recollection are, for Tristram, forms of therapeutic self-observation rather than a road to knowledge or self-understanding; he records his own reactions right alongside the events themselves. Here is his comment on his disastrous entry into the world, his nose (and his father's hopes with it) crushed by Slop's forceps:

I enter upon this part of my story in the most pensive and melancholy frame of mind, that ever sympathetic breast was touched with. – My nerves relax as I tell it. – Every line I write, I feel an abatement of the quickness of my pulse, and of that careless alacrity with it, which every day of my life prompts me to say and write a thousand things I should not. – And this moment that I last dipped my pen into my ink, I could not help taking notice what a cautious air of sad composure and solemnity there appeared in my manner of doing it. – Lord! how different from the rash jerks and hare-brained squirts thou art wont, Tristram! to transact it with in other humours, – dropping thy pen – spurting thy ink about thy table and thy books, – as if thy pen and thy ink, and thy books and thy furniture cost thee nothing.

(III, 28, 222)

Tristram's self-sympathy has no moral effect and serves no social purpose; it stabilizes his normally erratic and nervous personality as he writes. In this regard as in others, he perpetuates the sentimental style of his narrative's characters. Here is one more example, which at first seems to go beyond such therapeutic solipsism. While Mrs Shandy is in her protracted labor upstairs in the first two volumes, Walter, Toby, and Dr Slop are below in the parlor. When Corporal Trim arrives with a volume on fortifications that Toby has asked for, a sermon drops out of it. Walter asks Toby to order Trim to read it aloud: "I have ever a strong propensity, said my father, to look into things which cross my way, by such strange fatalities as these" (II, 15, 136). As Trim reads, he comes to the sermon's denunciation of "religion without morality," exemplified in "the Romish church" and dramatized in the Inquisition. Trim is deeply moved, reminded of his brother, Tom:

'If the testimony of past centuries in this matter is not sufficient, – consider at this instant, how the votaries of that religion are every day thinking to do service and honour to God, by actions which are a dishonour and scandal to themselves.

'To be convinced of this, go with me for a moment into the prisons of the Inquisition.' – [God help my poor brother Tom] – 'Behold *Religion*, with *Mercy* and *Justice* chained down under her feet, – there sitting ghastly upon a black tribunal, propped up with racks and instruments of torment. Hark! – hark! what a piteous groan!' [Here Trim's face turned as pale as ashes.]

'See the melancholy wretch who uttered it,' – [Here the tears began to trickle down] 'just brought forth to undergo the anguish of a mock trial, and endure the utmost pains that a studied system of cruelty has been able to invent.' – – [D–n them all, quoth Trim, his colour returning into his face as red as blood.] – 'Behold this helpless victim delivered up to his tormentors, – his body so wasted with sorrow and confinement.' – Oh! 'tis my brother, cried poor Trim in a most passionate exclamation, dropping the sermon upon the ground, and clapping his hands together – I fear 'tis poor Tom. My father's and my uncle Toby's heart yearned with sympathy for the poor fellow's distress, – even Slop himself acknowledged pity for him. – Why, Trim, said my father, this is not a history, – 'tis a sermon thou art reading.

(II, 17, 153–154)

Trim artlessly appropriates the generalized picture that the sermon paints to excite his own particular sympathy, which in turn moves Walter and Toby and even the Roman Catholic Dr Slop. And of course this appropriation tends to cancel the moral distinctions that the sermon (one of Sterne's) propounds, shifting its dramatic effect away from general application and social understanding and toward Trim's moving but comically irrelevant particularity. These emotions are produced by rhetorical massaging, and behind Trim's artless subversion of the sermon's moral purpose lies Sterne's sly artistry, which as always renders emotion and sympathy as genuine but self-indulgent, comically inattentive to an objective and consequential world. Trim is in this regard like his betters, and his transposing of the moral–historical content of Yorick's sermon into the matter of his own family history anticipates Walter's appropriation of various classical orations when he hears of the unexpected death of his elder son, Bobby.

My father, I say, had a way, when things went extremely wrong with him, especially upon the first sally of his impatience, – of wondering why he was begot, – wishing himself dead; – sometimes worse; – And when the provocation ran high, and grief touched his lips with more than ordinary powers – Sir, you scarce could have distinguished him from Socrates himself. – Every word would breathe the sentiments of a soul disdaining life, and careless about all its issues; for which reason, though my mother was a woman of no deep reading, yet the abstract of Socrates's oration, which my father was giving my uncle

Toby was not altogether new to her. – She listened to it with composed intelligence, and would have done so to the end of the chapter, had not my father plunged (which he had no occasion to have done) into that part of the pleading where the great philosopher reckons up his connections, his alliances, and children; but renounces a security to be so won by working upon the passions of his judges. – 'I have friends – I have relations, – I have three desolate children,' – says Socrates. –

Then, cried my mother, opening the door, – you have one more, Mr Shandy, than I know of.

By heaven! I have one less, – said my father, getting up and walking out of the room.

(V, 13, 364)

Sterne's subversive parody of eighteenth-century classicism, Walter's speech paraphrases classical texts to establish connections between modernity and antiquity but also to distinguish the two epochs for ironic purposes, as in Pope's Horatian Imitations or Johnson's rendering of Juvenal's satires in "London" and "The Vanity of Human Wishes." Walter Shandy, self-educated auto-didact, appropriates classical Stoicism and Socratic heroism to articulate his own modern self-pity; the effect of his classical borrowings is not connection or continuity with antiquity but ahistorical, opportunistic appropriation, parodic undercutting of ancient dignity for slightly mad and wholly selfish contemporary purposes.

Sterne's mimicry of these swirling discourses in *Tristram Shandy* obeys more efficiently and intensely than any other narrative in the century the principle enunciated by Bakhtin as deriving ultimately from Rabelais whereby in the comic novel "the parodic and objectivized incorporation" of literary language "penetrates the deepest levels of literary and ideological thought itself, resulting in a parody of the logical and expressive structure of any ideological discourse."[33] But there is both more and less than formal parodic distancing at work in Sterne's novel, which does not have the oppositional implications that Bakhtin tended to posit for the comic narrative tradition. All these scenes in *Tristram Shandy* are, obviously, outrageously private and deeply personal (the bed of conception and birth) as well as provincial and insignificant. Walter and Toby exist in modes of knowledge and moral self-conception that are deliberately archaic as well as absurd: Walter aspiring to a ludicrous intellectual totalizing that has little in common with the Baconian and Lockean empiricism of his era and Toby adhering to antiquated notions of military honor, a warrior who would not hurt a fly, a man of blood and of sympathetic tears. Their different kinds of learning overwhelm the subjects they study and turn the texts they study into modes of self-expression, drained of cognitive significance. Even Tristram's personality, in the words of one critic, "develops no possibility that they do not offer" and "the bases for his life and opinions are to be found in them."[34] Eighteenth-century narrative's implicit ambition, richly and crudely visible in the other "sentimental" novels that I have surveyed in this chapter, to evoke actions in the large theater of the moral and public world and to provide knowledge of that wider world has been jettisoned as illusory, and Trim's emotional confusion of the historical and the personal is thoroughly justified and repeated in *Tristram Shandy*. To some extent, however, these are impertinent observations, and most Sterne criticism is concerned to explain the happy (comically profound) results of the enclosure and irrelevance that his novels stage as the modern condition. Readers of this book, however, may want to consider *Tristram Shandy* as an epitome of the cultural and moral meaning of narrative in the eighteenth century as much as it is a comic triumph.

In a discussion of *Sir Charles Grandison* in his *Literary Loneliness in Mid-eighteenth-century England*, John Sitter observes that it marks Richardson's desire "to make a structure of words unburdened by history" and seeks with other novels of the time to move toward pure presence and away from the representation of those complex relationships that are the manifest content of the social and historical world of mid-eighteenth-century Britain. Sitter notes that Richardson's novel "turns from experience to the presentation and analysis of experience."[35] His thesis that fiction at mid-century and after is part of a larger tendency in the literature of the time toward exploration of the personal and away from the representation of meaningful public and historical action finds its *reductio ad absurdum* in Sterne, and at the end of a book on the novel and society we might want to ask why his work is the definitive comic surrender of narrative's representational project. Why does British fiction through the century avoid what, from our perspective, are wonderful subjects for narrative in the public world of politics and commerce? Why not show us a vigorous and adventurous (some might say rapacious) Whig oligarchy (refreshed by recruits from the commercial middle classes) solidifying its dominance and transforming Britain into the world's leading power and richest nation by fair means and foul? Why not dramatize in fiction official peculation and political corruption on a gigantic scale? Or why not render the heroic entrepreneurship and finance capitalism that revolutionized in due course the means of agricultural and industrial production and the

scale of domestic consumption? Why not tell the amazing tale of inter-
national commerce and triumphant imperial adventure that led by
century's end to world domination? Why not render in fiction careers
centered on acquisition and accumulation, on spectacular social and
economic movement? This is the question that modern readers are
likely to ask. Why linger on obscure, eccentric, provincial, and private
individuals? The eighteenth-century novel of domestic relationships
and courtship can well be taken as a timid, extremely oblique allegory
of those world-historical individuals and activities, and picaresque
fictions as a coarser and comic enactment of these modern energies
that treats them as individualized exceptions to social morality. Instead
of triumph and transformative accomplishment in the world, the sentimental novel in its various guises represents failure or rejectionist
private activity; it avoids direct encounters with the political and
economic particulars of the time and registers instead a protest against
the disturbingly amoral and liberal structures of the modern state. The
sentimental novel presents in their place a consoling myth encompassing varieties of extravagant heroism and moral community, private
rather than public achievements. In turning away from the attempt to
know the modern world in its spectacular and transforming historical
dimension and in offering instead a comically private epistemology
(which is in fact a literary joke, a parody of intellectual seriousness) and
a rhetorically produced and totally personalized sentimentality, Sterne's
fiction appears at first glance to be the definitive rejection of the social
and historical world by eighteenth-century British narrative. It offers the
proposition that the eccentrically personal and whimsical, the economically privileged and disengaged individual, devoid of communal
function or membership or occupation, pleasing himself and ignoring
or disparaging conventional knowledge of the external social and political world, possesses generalized significance. And yet such a
representation might be seen as a profound allegory of modern life in
its new material abundance, so that, as Joyce Appleby sums it up, the
"cumulative gains in material culture which became manifest by the
eighteenth century ... made it evident that human beings were the
makers of their world."[36] Sterne's odd genius is to render this claim in a
very complex fashion by dramatizing both the absurdity and the
truthful inevitability of such solipsism in a world of privileged and
materially secure individualism.[37]

NOTES

1 Richard Steele, *The Spectator*, No. 294, February 6, 1712, ed. Donald F. Bond (Oxford, Clarendon Press, 1965), Vol. III, pp. 47–48.

2 John Mullan, *Sentiment and Sociability: The Language of Feeling in the Eighteenth Century* (Oxford, Clarendon Press, 1988), p. 14.

3 Mullan, *Sentiment and Sociability*, p. 25.

4 Mullan, *Sentiment and Sociability*, p. 24.

5 David Hume, *A Treatise of Human Nature*, ed. P.H. Nidditch (Oxford, Clarendon Press, 1978), Part II, Section V, pp. 357, 362.

6 Adam Smith, *The Theory of Moral Sentiments*, ed. D.D. Raphael and A.L. Macfie (Indianapolis, Liberty Fund, 1984), p. 137.

7 G.A. Starr, "Sentimental novels of the later eighteenth century," in *The Columbia History of the British Novel* , ed. John Richetti (New York, Columbia University Press, 1994), pp. 180, 193.

8 Sarah Fielding's 1744 novel in two volumes was revised by her brother, Henry, that same year. In 1747 Sarah published *Familiar Letters Between the Principal Characters in David Simple* (which is not an actual sequel but a gathering of essays and short tales on related themes), and in 1753 a continuation and conclusion of the novel subtitled *Volume the Last*. All references in the text are to Malcolm Kelsall's edition, which includes this sequel and uses the second and revised 1744 edition of the first part (London, Oxford University Press, 1969).

9 Samuel Richardson, *The History of Sir Charles Grandison*, ed. Jocelyn Harris, 3 vols (London, Oxford University Press, 1972), Vol. I, p. vii. All further page references in the text are to this edition. He may also, as Mark Kinkead-Weekes suggests, have been irritated by the success of Fielding's *Tom Jones* and sought "to show a truer picture of what a good man's life should be, and rebuke the corruptions of a society that had found *Tom Jones* admirable." *Samuel Richardson: Dramatic Novelist* (London, Methuen, 1973), pp. 282–283.

10 Margaret Anne Doody, *A Natural Passion: A Study of the Novels of Samuel Richardson* (Oxford, Clarendon Press, 1974), p. 276.

11 Terry Eagleton, *The Rape of Clarissa* (Minneapolis, University of Minnesota Press, 1982), p. 96.

12 Tom Keymer, *Richardson's "Clarissa" and the Eighteenth-century Reader* (Cambridge, Cambridge University Press, 1992), p. 73.

13 Kinkead-Weekes, *Samuel Richardson: Dramatic Novelist*, p. 281.

14 R.S. Brissenden, *Virtue in Distress: Studies in the Novel of Sentiment from Richardson to Sade* (London, Macmillan, 1974), p. 82.

15 Mona Scheuermann calls Brooke's novel a children's book meant to be used "in the teaching of children and the shaping of their moral perceptions." A serious teenager might well enjoy the book, but much of the author's commentary and Sternian playfulness would probably have been lost on younger readers. *Social Protest in the Eighteenth-century Novel* (Columbus, OH, Ohio State University Press, 1985), p. 42.

16 Henry Brooke, *The Fool of Quality: or The History of Henry Earl of Moreland* (London, Macmillan, 1876), pp. 54–55. All further page references in the text are to this edition.

17 Ellis Markman, *The Politics of Sensibility: Race, Gender, and Commerce in the Sentimental Novel* (Cambridge, Cambridge University Press, 1996), p. 135.

18 Henry Mackenzie, *The Man of Feeling*, ed. Brian Vickers (Oxford and New York, Oxford University Press, 1987), p. 13. All further page references in the text are to this edition.

19 Marshall Brown, *Preromanticism* (Stanford, CA, Stanford University Press, 1991), p. 83.

20 Laurence Sterne, *A Sentimental Journey*, ed. Graham Petrie, with an introduction by A. Alvarez (London, Penguin, 1986), p. 27. All page references in the text are to this edition.

21 *The Sermons of Mr. Yorick* appeared in two volumes in May 1760, as the first two volumes of *Tristram Shandy* were making Sterne a literary celebrity. Sterne published another collection of his sermons in 1766, and his widow and daughter oversaw the publication of a posthumous third collection, *Sermons by the Late Rev. Mr. Sterne* in 1769. See Arthur Cash, *Laurence Sterne: The Later Years* (London and New York, Methuen, 1986), pp. 40–41, 227–29, 341–343.

22 As Ann Jessie Van Sant remarks perceptively in her recent study, Sterne's sentimental episodes are parodic because of the delicacy of feeling they insist upon: "The miniaturization that arises from microsensation is not only refining but reductive. Minute perceptual capacities simultaneously heighten and trivialize experience. More importantly, however, sensibility is a source of Sterne's parody because the physiological body necessarily physicalizes experience." *Eighteenth-century Sensibility and the Novel* (Cambridge, Cambridge University Press, 1993), p. 107. Modern criticism of Sterne has for many years emphasized this parodic aspect of his approach to sentimentalism. Ernest N. Dilworth's *The Unsentimental Journey of Laurence Sterne* (New York, Columbia University Press, 1948) concluded that Sterne was totally unsentimental: "to Sterne everything is words, the immaterial substance out of which appear the clothes, the rattle, and the handspring of a jester" (109). A more sophisticated account of Sterne's attitudes is Richard Lanham's *Tristram Shandy: The Games of Pleasure* (Berkeley and Los Angeles, University of California Press, 1973), which sees him as a "game-player," a writer whose seriousness is meaningful in terms of his rhetorical play with ideas rather than for any belief in the ideas themselves. Robert Markley puts the case starkly when he says that *A Sentimental Journey* is "a series of strategies designed to mystify the contradictory impulses of sentimentality, to celebrate and to mock Yorick's faith in human nature, and to attempt to reconcile ideas of innate virtue with demonstrations of moral worth." "Sentimentality as performance," in Felicity Nussbaum and Laura Brown (eds) *The New Eighteenth Century: Theory, Politics, English Literature* (New York and London, Methuen, 1987), p. 223.

23 Sterne himself had decided to go to France for his health in 1761, and he was able to go through the officially closed border only by arranging through friends to travel in the diplomatic party of George Pitt, who had just been appointed Envoy Extraordinary and Minister Plenipotentiary to the Court of Turin. As Cash points out, Pitt's party would have had easy passage because the Kingdom of Sardinia, of which Turin was the capital,

had begun to arrange unofficial peace negotiations. *Laurence Sterne: The Later Years*, pp. 116–118.

24 The Seven Years War (1756–1763) was in fact a world war, fought in Europe, India, and North America between France and its allies (Austria, Russia, Saxony, Sweden, and Spain) and Britain, Hanover, and Prussia. Britain emerged from this struggle as the world's leading colonial power, as France lost most of its overseas possessions.

25 John Bender, *Imagining the Penitentiary: Fiction and the Architecture of Mind in Eighteenth-century England* (Chicago, University of Chicago Press, 1987), p. 235.

26 Arthur Cash notes that, for Sterne, "interesting" meant "affecting, appealing to the tender sentiments," and he observes that the *OED* cites *A Sentimental Journey* for the earliest use of the word in its second meaning – "appealing to or able to arouse emotions." *Laurence Sterne: The Later Years*, p. 27.

27 Laurence Sterne, *The Life and Opinions of Tristram Shandy*, ed. Graham Petrie, with an introduction by Christopher Ricks (London, Penguin, 1967), p. 37 (I, 2). All further page (and volume and chapter) references in the text are to this edition.

28 Ronald Paulson, *Satire and the Novel in Eighteenth-century England* (New Haven and London, Yale University Press, 1967), p. 249.

29 Melvyn New, *Tristram Shandy: A Book for Free Spirits* (New York, Twayne, 1994), p. 94.

30 Jonathan Lamb, *Sterne's Fiction and the Double Principle* (Cambridge, Cambridge University Press, 1989), p. 76.

31 Carol Kay, *Political Constructions: Defoe, Richardson, & Sterne in Relation to Hobbes, Hume, & Burke* (Ithaca, NY, Cornell University Press, 1988), pp. 232–233.

32 José Ortega y Gasset, "Notes on the novel," in *The Dehumanization of Art and Other Writings*, trans. Willard Trask (New York, Doubleday, 1954), pp. 61–62.

33 M.M. Bakhtin, "Discourse in the novel," in *The Dialogic Imagination: Four Essays*, ed. Michael Holquist, trans. Caryl Emerson and Michael Holquist (Austin, TX, University of Texas Press, 1981), p. 308. John Bender has provided the most subtle adaptation of Bakhtin's theories, which he paraphrases this way: the "realist novel … represents discourse as it participates in the formation of consciousness under the conditions prevailing in the early modern era." Dialogue in the novel, for Bakhtin, is "the creation of self-consciousness through the use of reported speech that represents discourse to the public sphere in *writing*." Language and thought itself, says Bender, are freed from the necessity of communication and become pure expressivity. *Imagining the Penitentiary*, p. 212.

34 Eric Rothstein, *Systems of Order and Inquiry in Later Eighteenth-century Fiction* (Berkeley and Los Angeles, University of California Press, 1975), p. 63.

35 John Sitter, *Literary Loneliness in Mid-eighteenth-century England* (Ithaca and London, Cornell University Press, 1982), pp. 217, 210.

36 Joyce Appleby, "Consumption in early modern thought," in John Brewer and Roy Porter (eds) *Consumption and the World of Goods* (London and New York, Routledge, 1994), p. 164.

37 John Mullan, however, finds that sympathy such as Sterne depicts is aberrant and eccentric rather than a universal propensity; it is, he argues, "not

a model for behaviour" but rather "an unusual and momentary privilege." Mullan also observes that in *Tristram Shandy*, attempts at intense feeling are "both ludicrous and admirable," that "the bearers of feeling … are imagined as at once absurd and admirable." *Sentiment and Sociability*, pp. 192, 163, 180.

INDEX

It is not only Evelina who writes letters